International Journal on Advances in Security

2016 vol. 9 nr. 3&4

Printed from e-media with permission by:

Curran Associates, Inc.
57 Morehouse Lane
Red Hook, NY 12571

Some format issues inherent in the e-media version may also appear in this print version.

Printed by Curran Associates, Inc. (2018)

International Academy, Research, and Industry Association (IARIA)
412 Derby Way
Wilmington, DE 19810

Phone: (408) 893-6407
Fax: (408) 527-6351

petre@iaria.org

Additional copies of this publication are available from:

Curran Associates, Inc.
57 Morehouse Lane
Red Hook, NY 12571 USA
Phone: 845-758-0400
Fax: 845-758-2633
Email: curran@proceedings.com
Web: www.proceedings.com

The *International Journal on Advances in Security* is published by IARIA.
ISSN: 1942-2636
journals site: http://www.iariajournals.org
contact: petre@iaria.org

Sponsored by IARIA
www.iaria.org

International Journal on Advances in Security
Volume 9, Number 3 & 4, 2016

International Journal on Advances in Security
Volume 9, Numbers 3 & 4, 2016

CONTENTS

pages: 90 - 100
On the Resilience of a QKD Key Synchronization Protocol for IPsec
Stefan Marksteiner, JOANNEUM RESEARCH, Austria
Benjamin Rainer, University of Klagenfurt, Austria
Oliver Maurhart, AIT Austrian Institute of Technology GmbH, Austria

pages: 101 - 110
Prospects of Software-Defined Networking in Industrial Operations
György Kálmán, Norwegian University of Science and Technology, Norway

pages: 111 - 121
Fuzzbomb: Fully-Autonomous Detection and Repair of Cyber Vulnerabilities
David J. Musliner, Smart Information Flow Technologies (SIFT), USA
Scott E. Friedman, Smart Information Flow Technologies (SIFT), USA
Michael Boldt, Smart Information Flow Technologies (SIFT), USA
J. Benton, Smart Information Flow Technologies (SIFT), USA
Max Schuchard, Smart Information Flow Technologies (SIFT), USA
Peter Keller, Smart Information Flow Technologies (SIFT), USA
Stephen McCamant, University of Minnesota, USA

pages: 122 - 132
A Risk Assessment of Logical Attacks on a CEN/XFS-based ATM Platform
Johannes Braeuer, Dept. of Information Systems, Johannes Kepler University Linz, Austria
Bernadette Gmeiner, KEBA AG, Austria
Johannes Sametinger, Dept. of Information Systems, Johannes Kepler University Linz, Austria

pages: 133 - 145
Stabilizing Breach-Free Sensor Barriers
Jorge Cobb, The University of Texas at Dallas, U.S.A.
Chin-Tser Huang, University of South Carolina at Columbia, U.S.A.

pages: 146 - 157
Data Security Overview for Medical Mobile Apps Assuring the Confidentiality, Integrity and Availability of data in transmission
Ceara Treacy, Dundalk Institute of Technology, Ireland
Fergal McCaffery, Dundalk Institute of Technology, Ireland

pages: 158 - 168
Multi-Platform Performance Evaluation of the TUAK Mobile Authentication Algorithm
Keith Mayes, Information Security Group, Royal Holloway, University of London, UK
Stephen Babbage, Vodafone Group R&D, Vodafone Group Services Ltd., UK
Alexander Maximov, Ericsson Research, Ericsson, Sweden

pages: 169 - 183
Cloud Cyber-Security: Empowering the Audit Trail
Bob Duncan, University of Aberdeen, United Kingdom
Mark Whittington, University of Aberdeen, United Kingdom

pages: 184 - 195
Collaborative and Secure Sharing of Healthcare Records Using Attribute-Based Authenticated Access
Mohamed Abomhara, University of Agder, Norway
Huihui Yang, Norwegian University of Science and Technology, Norway

pages: 196 - 206
Detecting Obfuscated JavaScripts from Known and Unknown Obfuscators using Machine Learning
Bernhard Tellenbach, Zurich University of Applied Sciences, Switzerland
Sergio Paganoni, SecureSafe / DSwiss AG, Switzerland
Marc Rennhard, Zurich University of Applied Sciences, Switzerland

On the Resilience of a QKD Key Synchronization Protocol for IPsec

Stefan Marksteiner
JOANNEUM RESEARCH GmbH
DIGITAL - Institute for Information and Communication Technologies
Graz, Austria
Email: stefan.marksteiner@joanneum.at

Benjamin Rainer
University of Klagenfurt
Institute of Information Technology
Multimedia Communication Group
Klagenfurt, Austria
Email: benjamin.rainer@itec.aau.at

Oliver Maurhart
AIT Austrian Institute of Technology GmbH
Digtal Safety & Security Department
Optical Quantum Technology
Klagenfurt, Austria
Email: oliver.maurhart@ait.ac.at

Abstract—**This paper presents a practical solution to the problem of limited bandwidth in Quantum Key Distribution (QKD)-secured communication through using rapidly rekeyed Internet Protocol security (IPsec) links. QKD is a cutting-edge security technology that provides mathematically proven security by using quantum physical effects and information theoretical axioms to generate a guaranteed non-disclosed stream of encryption keys. Although it has been a field of theoretical research for some time, it has only been producing market-ready solutions for a short period of time. The downside of this technology is that its key generation rate is only around 52,000 key bits per second over a distance of 50 km. As this rate limits the data throughput to the same rate, it is substandard for normal modern communications, especially for securely interconnecting networks. IPsec, on the other hand, is a well-known security protocol that uses classical encryption and is capable of exactly creating site-to-site virtual private networks. This paper presents a solution that combines the performance advantages of IPsec with QKD. The combination sacrifices only a small portion of QKD security by using the generated keys a limited number of times instead of just once. As a part of this, the solution answers the question of how many data bits per key bit make sensible upper and lower boundaries to yield high performance while maintaining high security. While previous approaches complement the Internet Key Exchange protocol (IKE), this approach simplifies the implementation with a new key synchronization concept, proposing a lightweight protocol that uses relatively few, slim control messages and sparse acknowledgement. Furthermore, it provides a Linux-based module for the AIT QKD software using the Netlink XFRM Application Programmers Interface to feed the quantum key to the IPsec cipher. This enables wire-speed, QKD-secured communication links for business applications. This paper, apart from the description of the solution itself, describes the surrounding software environment, including the key exchange, and illustrates the results of thorough test simulations with a variety of different protocol parameter settings.**

Index Terms—**Quantum Key Distribution; QKD; IPsec; Cryptography; Security; Networks.**

I. INTRODUCTION AND MOTIVATION

A recent paper presents an approach to combine quantum key distribution (QKD) with IPsec by using QKD to provide IPsec with the cryptographic keys necessary for its operation [1]. This article extends the work described in the mentioned paper such that it further examines the impact of noise (and other effects that are likely to happen in real-world networks) on the presented solution. Quantum cryptography, in this particular case quantum key distribution, has the purpose to ensure the confidentiality of a communication channel between two parties. The major difference to classical cryptography is that it does not rely on assumptions about the security of the mathematical problem it is based on, nor the computing power of a hypothetical attacker. Instead, QKD presents a secure method of exchanging keys by connecting the two communicating parties with a quantum channel and thereby supplying them with guaranteed secret and true random key material [2, p.743]. When the key is applied through a Vernam cipher (also called one time pad - OTP) on a data channel on any public network, this method provides the channel with information-theoretically (in other words mathematically proven) security [3, p.583]. An *information-theoretically secure*[1] system means, besides a mathematical proof, that this system is still secure if an attacker has infinite resources and time at his disposal to cryptographically analyze it [4, pp.659]. The downside of combining QKD with OTP is the limitation to approximately fifty-two kilobits over fifty kilometers, shown in a practical QKD setup [5, p.1], due to physical and technical factors, since in OTP one key bit is consumed by one data bit [6, S.9]. OTP is so far the only known information-theoretically (also called unconditionally) secure encryption algorithm [7, pp.177 - 178]. The offered data rate, however, does not meet the requirements of modern communications. Another practical approach came to the same conclusion and therefore uses the Advanced Encryption Standard (AES) instead of OTP [8, p.6]. As IPsec is a widespread security protocol suite that provides integrity, authenticity and confidentiality for data connections, this approach uses the combination of IPsec and QKD to overcome this restrictions [9, p.4].

To save valuable key material, this solution uses it for more than one data packet in IPsec, thus increasing the effective data rate, which is thereby not limited to the key

[1] Shannon used the term *secrecy* instead of security. In cryptography, more secrecy means more security [2, p.1]. Thus, the two terms are synonymous in this context.

rate anymore. Furthermore, using this approach, the presented solution benefits from the flexibility of IPsec in terms of cryptographic algorithms and cipher modes. In contrast to most of the previous approaches (see Section II), that supplemented the Internet Key Exchange (IKE) protocol or combine in some way quantum-derived and classical keys, this paper refrains from using IKE (for a key exchange is rather the objective of QKD, as described later) in favor of a specialized, lightweight key synchronization protocol, working with a master/slave architecture. The goal of this protocol is to achieve very high changing rates of purely quantum-derived keys on the communicating peers while maintaining the keys synchronous in a very resilient manner, which means to deal with suboptimal networking conditions including packet losses and late or supplicate packets. In order to fulfill this objective, the following questions need to be clarified:

- What is the minimum acceptable frequency of changing the IPsec key that will ensure sufficient security?
- What is the maximum acceptable frequency of changing the IPsec key to save QKD key material?
- Is the native Linux kernel implementation suitable for this task?
- How can key synchronicity between the communication peers be assured at key periods of 50 milliseconds and less?

As a proof of concept, this paper further presents a software solution, called QKDIPsec, implementing this approach in C++. This software is intended to be used as an IPsec module for the multi platform hardware-independent AIT QKD software, which provides already a market-ready solution for OTP-based QKD. The module achieves over forty key changes per second for the IPsec subsystem within the Linux kernel. At present time, the software uses a static key ring buffer for testing purposes instead of actual QKD keys, for the integration of QKDIPsec into the AIT QKD software is yet to be implemented (although most of the necessary interfaces are already present). The ultimate goal is to deliver a fully operational IPsec module for the AIT QKD software.

The following Section II of this paper describes previous approaches on combining IPsec and QKD. Section III describes considerations regarding necessary and sensible key change rates, exhibiting the reflections that lead to the assumed requirements of a quantum key synchronization solution. Section IV contains the architecture of the presented solution and the subsequent Section V its implementation, while Section VI describes its incorporation into the AIT QKD software. Descriptions of the setups and results of laboratory Experiments, showing the practical capabilities of this proof of concept, form the Sections VII through VIII. Section IX, eventually, contains the conclusions drawn.

II. Related Work

This work is aware of some previously developed methods to combine QKD with IPsec. All of them work in conjunction with the IKE [10, pp.234-235][11, p.177-182][12][13, pp.5-9][14, p.21] or the underlying ISAKMP [15, pp.6-8] protocol. They introduce a supplement for QKD parameters or combine IKE-derived and QKD-derived keys. Opposed to this, the presented work tries to use an approach omitting IKE and following the pivotal idea that there is no need for that protocol to exchange keys, for that is the task of QKD. The key feed from QKD therefore provides the material for manual keying in this solution, all that is left is to keep those keys synchronous. For this task, this paper proposes a more slender approach (see Section IV). Furthermore, some of the previous approaches operate at a substantially lower speed than the key change presented in this thesis or use OTP limiting the data rate to the QKD key rate (currently around 52 kilobits per second) or simply suggest applying QKD keys to IPsec without a mechanism for changing keys rapidly, effectively not lowering the number of data bits per key bit.

III. Key Change Rate Considerations

The strength of every cryptographic system relies on the key strength, the secrecy of the key and the effectiveness of the used algorithms [16, p.5]. As this solution relies on QKD, which generates a secret and true random key [17], this means that more effective algorithms and more key material are able to provide more cryptographic security. In this particular case, the used algorithms are already prescribed by the IPsec standard [18]. Therefore, the security is mainly determined by the used key lengths, more precisely by the relation between the amount of key material and the amount of data, which should be as much in favor of the key material as possible - given the low key rate compared to the data rate, naturally the opposite is the case in practice. This section aims on giving feasible upper and lower boundaries of key change rates (or key periods P_k, respectively) and, thus, how much QKD key material should be used in order to save precious quantum key material while maintaining a very high level of security. The two main factors determining the key period in practice are the used algorithms (via their respective key lengths - the longer the key, the more key bits are used in one key period) and the capabilities of QKD in generating keys. The QKD solution of the Austrain Institute of Technology has proven to provide a quantum key rate Q of up to 12,500 key bits per second at close distances, 3,300 key bits at around 25 kilometers and 550 key bits at around 50 kilometers distance [6, p.9]. As this paper presents a practical implementation (see Section V) in the form of a module for the AIT QKD software, the highest of these values should be the reference key bandwidth for the key length and period considerations made in this section.

In order to fully utilize the possible QKD key rate and given the currently shortest recommended key length, which is 128 bits (see below), an IPsec solution using quantum-derived keys should be able to perform around 100 key changes per second ($\frac{12,500}{128} \approx 97,65$), 50 for every communication direction (for IPsec connection channels are in principle unidirectional and therefore independent from each other even if they belong to the same bidirectional conversation). This corresponds to a key period P_k of around 20 ms, as it is a function of the Quantum key rate Q and the algorithm's key length k. The period for a bidirectional IPsec link is $P_K = (\frac{Q}{2k})^{-1}$. At longer key lengths, this period becomes longer, for a single change cycle uses more key material and, thus, less key changes are necessary to utilize the full incoming key stream, therefore this period $P_{k_{min}} = 20ms$ presents a feasible lower boundary for the key period. As stated above, the security of this system depends also on the data rate. Given a widespread data rate of 100 megabits per second, a key period of 20 ms and 128 key bits means a ratio of 8000 data bits per key bit (or short dpk, for the reader's convenience).

A landmark in this *security ratio* is 1 dpk, as this rate would provide unconditional security when applied with OTP. For the cipher and hash suites included in the IPsec protocol stack, there is no security proof and therefore they are not unconditionally secure. However, applying an IPsec cipher (for instance AES) with an appropriately fast key change and restricted data rate to achieve 1 dpk is the closest match inside standard IPsec, especially when the block size equals the key size.

To define an upper boundary (and therefore a minimum standard for the high security application of the presented solution), a very unfavorable relation between data and key bits through a high-speed connection of 10 gigabits of data is assumed. A recent attack on AES-192/256 uses $2^{69.2}$ computations with 2^{32} *chosen plaintext* [19, p.1]. Because of the AES block size of 128 bits, this corresponds to $2^{32} * 2^7 = 2^{39}$ data bits. Although this attack is currently not feasible in practice, as it works only for seven out of 12/14 rounds and also has unfeasible requirements to data storage on processing power for a cryptanalytic machine, it serves as a theoretical fundament for this upper boundary. A bandwidth of 10 gigabits per second equals approximately 9.3 gibibits per second. This is by the factor of 64 (2^6) smaller than the amount of data for the attack mentioned above, which means that it requires 64 seconds to gather the necessary amount of data to (though only theoretically) conduct the attack. In conclusion (with AES-192/256), the key should be changed at least every minute ($P_{k_{max}} = 60s$), while the maximum allowed key period according to the IPsec standard lies at eight hours or 28,800 seconds [20].

For cryptographic algorithms operating with lower cipher block sizes (ω), the *birthday bound* ($2^{\frac{\omega}{2}}$) is relevant. The birthday bound describes the number of brute force attempts to enforce a collision with a probability of 50 percent, such that different clear text messages render to the same cipher text [21]. With a block size of 64 (*birthday bound* = 2^{32}), the example speed of 10 gigabit per second above would lower the secure key period to under half a second. Because of this factor, using 64-bit ciphers is generally discouraged for the use with modern data rates[22, pp.1-3] (although the present rapid rekeying approach is able to cope with this problem). Regarding key lengths, 128 bits are recommended beyond 2031 [16, p.56] while key sizes of 256 bits provide *good protection* even against the use of Grover's algorithm in hypothetical quantum computers for this period [23, p.32].

IV. Rapid Rekeying Protocol

This section describes the *rapid rekeying protocol*, the purpose of which is to provide to IPsec peers with QKD-derived key material and keep these keys synchronous under the low-key-period conditions (down to $P_{k_{min}} = 20ms$) stated in Section III.

This protocol pursues the approach that with QKD, there is no need for a classical key exchange (for instance with IKE). Relevant connection parameters (like peer addresses) are available a priori (before the establishment of the connection) in point-to-point connections, whereas keying material is provided by QKD, mostly obsoleting IKE. Furthermore, IPsec only dictates an automatic key exchange, not specifically IKE [9, p.48] and a protocol that only synchronizes QKD-derived keys (instead of exchanging keys) is therefore deemed sufficient, yet compliant to the IPsec standard. Consequently, it is an outspoken objective to create a slender and simple key synchronization protocol to increase performance and reduce possible sources of error. Another objective for key synchronization is robustness in terms of resilience against suboptimal network environment conditions. The protocol described in this paper uses two channels for encrypted communication: an Authenticaton Header (AH)-authenticated control channel (amongst other tasks, signaling for key changes) and an Encapsulating Security Payload (ESP)-encrypted data channel to transmit the protected data (see Figure 1). The reason for the use of AH on the control channel is that it only contains non-secret information, while its authenticity is crucial for the security and stability of the protocol. The necessary *security policies (SPs)* for the IPsec channels remain constant during the connection. There are four necessary SPs, one data and one control SP for each direction. The complete software solution will, delivered by the AIT QKD software, contain additionally the quantum channel for key exchange and a *Q3P* channel (see Section VI), whereby the latter is another protocol that provides OTP-encrypted QKD point-to-point links.

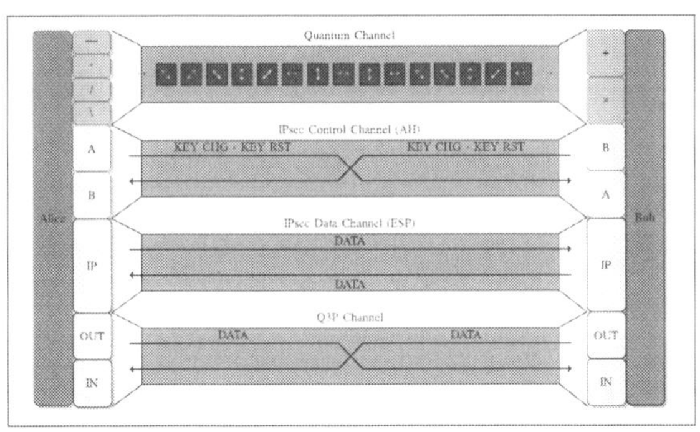

Fig. 1. Rapid Rekeying Channel Architecture

The protocol itself follows, taking account of the unidirectional architecture of IPsec, a *master/slave* paradigm. Every peer assumes the master role for the connection in which the peer represents the sending part. When a key change is due (for instance because of the expiration of the key period), the master sends an according message (key change request) to the slave and the latter changes the key (as does the master). To compensate lost key change signals, every key change message contains the *security parameters index (SPI)* for the next-to-use key. The SPI is simply calculable for the peers through a salted hash whereby the salt and a initial seed value are QKD-derived and each SPI is a hash of its predecessor plus salt, which makes it non-obvious to third parties. This level of security is sufficient, for the SPI is a public value, included non-encrypted in every corresponding IPsec packet, making it a subject rather to non-predictability than to secrecy. Also, using only a seed and salt from QKD, the hashing method safes quantum keying material. As all necessary IPsec parameters are available beforehand, as well as the keys (through QKD), IPsec *security associations (SAs)* may be pre-calculated and established in advance (which are identified by unique SPIs). Permanently changing attributes during a conversation are only the SPI and the key, while all other parameters of an SA (for instance peer addresses, services, protocols) remain constant. The master calculates these two in advance and queues them for future use. Only one SA is actually installed (aplied to the kernel IPsec subsystem), for only one (per default, at least in Linux, the most recent) may be used to encrypt data. The slave, on the other hand, operates differently. For it identifies the right key to use based on the SPI, it may very well have multiple matching SAs installed. This makes key queuing expendable on the receiver side, while the SPI queuing is used as an indexer for lost key change message detection. For reasons of data packets arriving out of synchronization, SAs are not only installed beforehand, but also left in the system for some time on the receiver side, allowing it to process packets encrypted with both an older or newer key than the current one.

On every key change event, the master applies a new SA to the system (using the next following SPI/key from the queues), prepares a new SPI/key pair (SPI generation as mentioned above and acquirement of a new key from the QKD system) and deletes the deprecated data from both its queues and the IPsec subsystem. The slave also acquires a new SPI/key pair (the same the sender acquires) but installs it directly as an SA and only stores the SPI for indexing. It subsequently deletes the oldest SA from the system and SPI from the queue if the number of installed SAs exceeds a configured limit. To sum it up, on every key change event, the two peers conduct the following steps:

- the master acquires a new key and SPI and ads it to its queues
- it sends a key change request to the slave
- it fetches the oldest pair from the queue an installs it as a new SA, *replacing* the current one
- it deletes the deprecated pair from its queue
- the slave receives the key change request and also acquires a new SPI/key pair (the same as the master)
- it installs the pair as a new SA and the SPI into the indexing queue
- it deletes the oldest SA from the system and oldest SPI from the queue
- it sends a key change acknowledgement

This procedure keeps both of the installed SA types up to date. For instance, 50 installed SAs for the slave resulting in 25 queued SPI/key pairs on the master, for the latter does not need to store backward SAs. At the beginning, on every key change, SPI/key pair is acquired, while the already applied remain. When the (configurable) working threshold is met, additionally the oldest SA or SPI/key pair is deleted, keeping the queue sizes and number of installed SAs constant.

Figure 2 illustrates this process for a sender (*Alice*) and a receiver (*Bob*), where the arrows show the changes in case of an induced key change. Naturally, as with SPs, there are four SA types on a peer: one for data and control channels, each for sending (master) and receiving (slave). Each SA corresponds to an SPI and key queue on the master's side and one SPI queue on the slave's side, respectively.

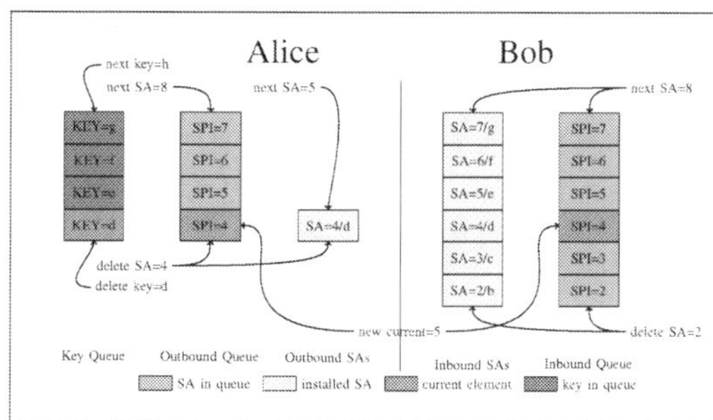

Fig. 2. Key Change Process

As the data stream is independent from control signaling, this calculation in advance prevents the destabilization of the key synchronization in case of lost and too early or too late arriving key change messages. The buffer of previously created SAs compensates desynchronization. For every receiver is able to calculate the according SPIs beforehand, it may, by comparing a received SPI with an expected, detect and correct the discrepancy by calculating the following SAs. Through this compensation process, there is neither need to interfere with the data communication nor to even inform the sender of lost key change messages; the sender may unperturbedly continue with data and control communications. This mechanisms make constant acknowledgements expendable and contribute thereby to a better protocol performance through omission of the round trip times for the majority of the necessary control messages. Because of this, acknowledgement messages (key change acknowledge) are still sent, but serve merely as a keepalive mechanism instead of true acknowledgements (see Figure 3).

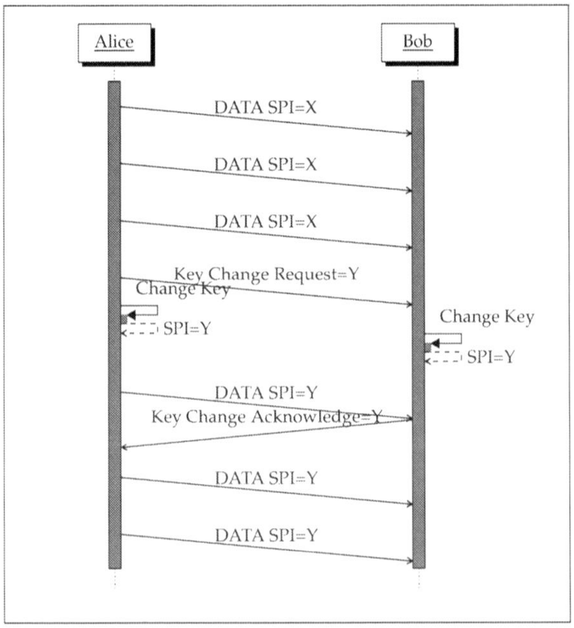

Fig. 3. Key Change Message Flow

In rare occasions, a key change message might be actually received, but the slave might not be able to apply the key for some reason (for instance issues regarding the QKD system or the Kernel). In this case, it reports the failure to the master with an appropriate message (key change fail). In case too many control packets go missing (what the receiver is able to detect by SPI comparisons and the sender by the absence of keepalive packets) or the key application fails, every peer is able to initiate a reset procedure (master or slave reset). The actual threshold of allowed and compensated missing messages is a matter of configuration and corresponds to the queue sizes for the SAs and therefore the ability of the system to compensate these losses. The master does not need to report key change fails, for it is in control of the synchronization process and might just initiate a reset if it is unable to apply its key. An additional occasion for a reset is the beginning of a conversation. At that point, the master starts the key synchronization process with an initial reset. A reset consists of clearing and refilling all of the queues and installed SAs. For the same reason as for the data channel, the authentication key for the control channel changes periodically. Due to the relatively low transmission rates on the control channel the key period is much longer (the software's default is 3 seconds) than on the data channel. As, therefore, control channel key changes are comparatively rare and reset procedures should only occur in extreme situations, both types implement a three way handshake. This is, on the one hand, because of the low impact on the overall performance due to the rare occurrences, on the other hand due to higher impact of faulty packets. The control channel, however, implements the same SA buffering method as the data channel (only with AH SAs, for the reasons stated at the beginning of this section).

V. Implementation

The presented solution, called *QKDIPsec*, consists of three parts (see also Figure 4):

- key acquisition;
- key application;
- key synchronization;

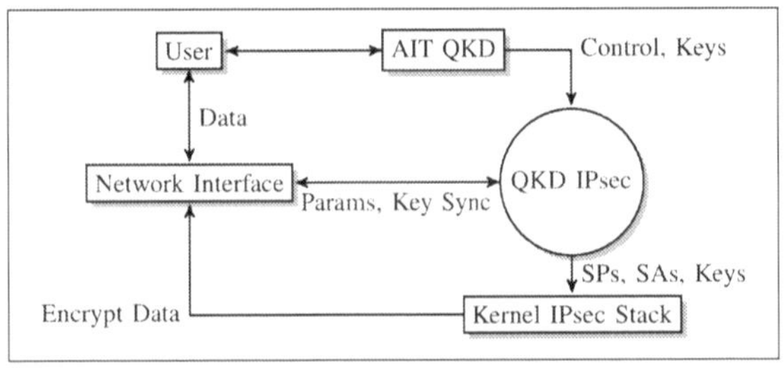

Fig. 4. QKDIPsec Systems Context

Each of this tasks has a corresponding submodule inside QKDIPsec, while the overall control lies within the responsibility of the *ConnectionManager* class, which provides the main outside interface and instantiates the classes of said submodules using corresponding configuration. Also, all of these classes have corresponding configuration classes using a factory method pattern [24, p.134] and according configuration classes, decoupling program data and logic. The first task (key acquisition) is the objective of an interface to the AIT QKD software, the *KeyManager*, which provides the quantum key material. In this proof of concept, this class generates dummy key from a ring buffer, while it already has the according interfaces for the QKD software to serve as a class to acquire quantum key material and provide it in an appropriate way to QKDIPsec. By now, only one function implementation is missing on the QKD software side to fully integrate QKDIPsec into the QKD software.

The second part (*KernelIPsecManager*) enters the acquired key directly into the Linux kernel, which encrypts the data sent to and decrypts the data received from a peer. Responsible for this part are a number of C++ classes, which control the SP and SA databases (SPD and SAD) within the Kernel's IPsec subsystem via the Linux *Netlink* protocol. Therefore, this solution uses the derived class *NetlinkIPsecManager*, but leaves the option to use other methods for kernel access as well. The reason for using Netlink to communicate with the kernel is that it was found the most intuitive of the available methods and that it is also able to handle not only the IPsec subsystem but a broad span of network functions in Linux. Furthermore, using a direct kernel API, as opposed to other IPsec implementations, omits middleware, both enhancing performance as well as eliminating potential source of error. Also using Netlink functions, this part governs the tunnel interfaces and routing table entries necessary for the communication via the classes *KernelNetworkManager* and *NetlinkNetworkManager* as well.

Netlink is a socket-oriented protocol and allows therefore the use of well-known functions from network programming. The difference to the latter is that instead of network peers, communication runs within the system as *inter-process communication (IPC)*, through which also the kernel (via process ID zero) is addressable. Due to its network-oriented nature, a packet structure is used instead of function calls via parameters. This means that commands to the kernel (for instance to add a new SA) needs to be memory-aligned in the according packet structure and subsequently send to the kernel via a Netlink socket. A downside of Netlink during implementation was the complicated nature and weak documentation of its IPsec manipulation part (*NETLINK_XFRM*). While the Netlink protocol itself is present in every message in the form of its uniform header, the *NETLINK_XFRM* parts use a different structure plus individual extra payload attributes for every type of message (add and delete messages for both SAs and SPs), making the according class hierarchy rather inflated. Also, the solution uses the *NETLINK_ROUTE* protocol to add and delete both IP interface addresses and network routes.

To take this into account, the QKDIPsec implementation uses a set of Netlink message classes, deriving from the common base class *NetlinkMessage*. This class contains the common Netlink header. Each message type for IPsec and network function configuration is further a child class, containing the exact data fields necessary for Netlink. Due to the separation of code and data segments in C++, the class functions do not interfere with the netlink data fields and therefore its alignment [25, pp.142-143]. This means that the class hierarchy takes care of the memory alignment necessary for the Netlink protocol. As stated above, the structure for *NETLINK_XFRM* messages is rather heterogenous, basically requiring every message type to be assembled directly in the class, except for the Netlink header. The messages of the *NETLINK_ROUTE* protocol, on the other hand, are more structured, allowing it to introduce intermediate classes for routing table and interface addresses messages.

The key synchronization, eventually, is the main task of the *Rapid Rekeying Protocol*. As this is the very core of the solution, its implementation resides directly inside the connection manager. While it uses the classes mentioned above to acquire and apply the QKD keys in the manner discussed in Section IV, it handles the key synchronization using sender and receiver threads (representing the master and slave parts, respectively), as well as a class for key synchronization messages. Within this class, also the described lost message compensation and reset, as well as initialization and clean-up procedures are implemented. The reset procedure may also include some re-initialization process for the QKD system, triggered via the *KeyManager*. This class also sets the clocking for the key changes, which is dynamically adjustable during runtime.

VI. INTEGRATION

QKDIPsec has been integrated into the current AIT QKD R10 Software Suite V9.9999.7[26]. This Open Source software contains a full featured QKD post processing environment containing BB84 sifting, error correction, privacy amplification and other steps necessary. The final stage of an AIT QKD post processing pipeline is a QKD key store, realized as *Q3P* link.

The central task of *Q3P* is to keep the key material derived from quantum key distribution in synchronization on both ends of a point-to-point link. It does this by managing several buffers as depicted in Figure 5.

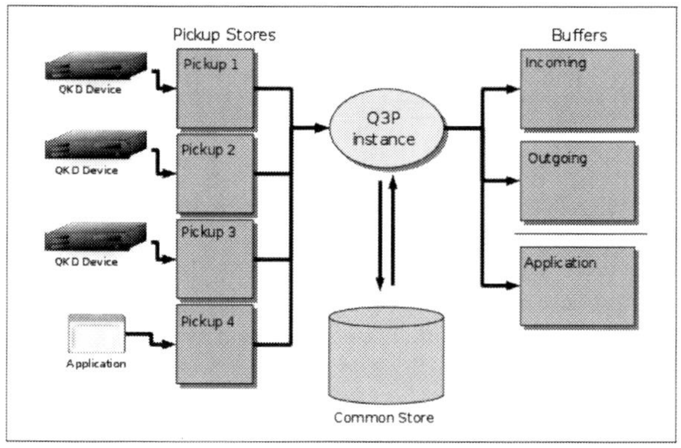

Fig. 5. Q3P Key Store Model

- *A Pickup Store*: Before a key can be used, Q3P has to verify, that a particular key is present on the other side of the connection. Reasons a key may not be present at the same point of time in a peer's key store are found in the highly asynchrony and distributed manner key material is inserted on both machines. Therefore, those key blocks are treated as a collection of potentially usable keys and are stored in a Pickup Store directly related to a certain QKD post processing pipeline. Hence, a single Q3P link can maintain multiple concurrent QKD post processing lines to boost throughput. Also Q3P does not know if a concrete QKD hardware device is pushing keys into the Pickup Store or an application, which might have derived shared secret keys by other means of deployment.
- *A Common Store*: Once the presence of the key material has been verified on both sides the key is transfered to the *Common Store* on disk. This is the only persistent data storage of key material within Q3P. However, keys placed in the Common Store are not bound to any dedicated usage.
- *An Outgoing Buffer*: Once key material is present in the Common Store, Q3P moves chunks of key material to

an *Outgoing Buffer*. Keys residing in this buffer are used to establish an information- theoretically secure channel for encryption and authentication for outgoing messages. Note that, due to the nature of information-theoretically secure ciphers (such as the Vernam cipher), encryption combined with authentication key consumption for single messages is at a minimum as large as the length of the message sent [27, p.15]. Also, keys that are used for messaging are removed from the buffer and destroyed.

- *An Incoming Buffer*: For incoming messages each Q3P endpoint mirrors the Outgoing Buffer of its peer as its local *Incoming Buffer*. The keys for authenticity checks of received messages as well as for decryption are picked from this buffer.
- *An Application Buffer*: On behalf the Incoming and the Outgoing Buffers Q3P established yet a third Buffer: the *Application Buffer*. Key material moved from the Common Store to this buffer in memory is dedicated for use by any application utilizing Q3P.

The rationale for having separate buffers for outgoing messages and one for incoming is based on potential race conditions when doing heavy communication in both directions. Suppose both Q3P nodes do heavy interaction in streaming messages in both directions, then without such separation the situation, in which both key stores utilize the very same key for different messages is most likely. Q3P also introduces a master/slave role model on key dedication: one partner in the communication acts as master, which is responsible for assigning key material from the Common Store to one of the three buffers. The slave on the other side requests such assignments on demand.

The filling of the Outgoing and Incoming Buffers take precedence before the Application Buffer. Only if both buffers used for direct information theoretic communication do share a minimum threshold of key material the Application buffer is filled with keys from the Common Store.

The proposed protocol uses the established information theoretic secured channel provided by Q3P by means of the Outgoing and Incoming Buffer inside Rapid Rekeying. Key material from the Application Buffer is used to create the protocols SPI and SAs. As key material is directed to the Outgoing and Incoming Buffers first, this results in "slow start" of an IPSec enabled connection.

Although the protocol runs inside the process space of a single Q3P instance, from a software engineering point of view the protocol's key withdrawal of the Application Buffer bears no difference to any other application using the same buffer.

VII. THROUGHPUT EXPERIMENTS

The protocol design of the described solution aims on the one hand on speed and flexibility and on the other hand on fault tolerance, hence the architecture is as simple and lightweight as possible (including abandoning the IKE protocol). Due to this, very high IPsec key change rates can be achieved, even under harsh conditions. The solution was implemented in software using C++ and tested on two to five year-old Linux computers (Alice and Bob), both in a gigabit Local Area Network (LAN) and a UMTS-Wide Area Network (WAN) environment (the latter further aggravated by combining it with WLAN and an additional TLS-based VPN tunnel - see Figure 6) by means of data transfer time measurement and ping tests, as well as validation of the actual key changes by a Wireshark network sniffer (Eve).

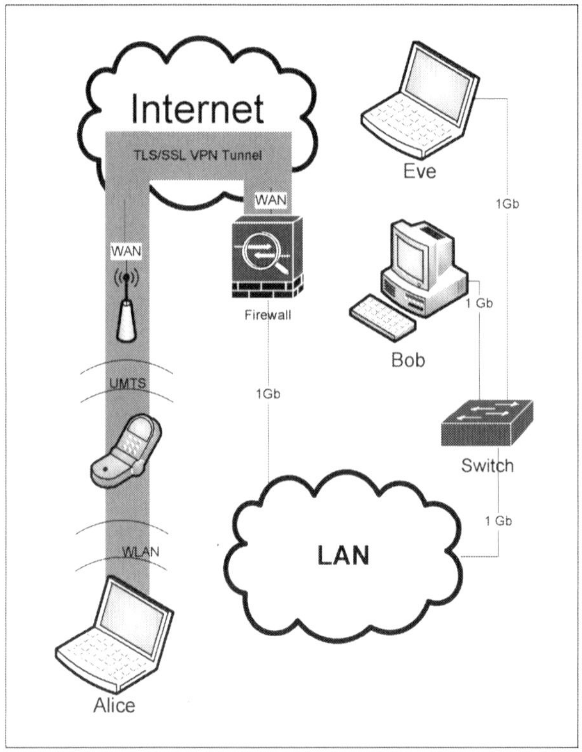

Fig. 6. WAN Test Setup

Table I shows the results in seconds (four trials each, separated by slashes) of data transmission and in percent on ping tests within the mentioned LAN and WAN environments with various configurations: unencrypted, standard IPsec and QKDIPsec with different encryption algorithms, the latter also with different key periods. In these tests, both data transfer and ping were initiated by one peer (*Alice*). While the ping test was continuous, the data transfer consisted each of one data transfer from *Alice* to *Bob* and vice versa. The test file used on the LAN was a video file of 69.533.696 bytes size, while the WAN file was also a video, but only 1.813.904 bytes big. In both cases, key periods of 25 ms and less could be achieved, maintaining a stable data connection. This, using the recommended key length of 256 bit, surpasses the goal of 12,500 key bits per second (the currently maximal quantum key distribution rate under ideal circumstances), even though (deliberately) legacy equipment and a less-than-ideal network environment was used. Comparison of the performance shows a (expectable) higher data transfer period of QKDIPsec and unencrypted traffic, but no significant difference to traditional IPsec. Only the packet losses on a simultaneously running ping test were a few percentage points higher (mainly in the WAN environment).

TABLE I. PERFORMANCE TEST RESULTS

	LAN		
Setting	A→B	B→A	Ping
unencrypted	6/6/7/6	7/9/7/8	100%
AES-256 CCM			
standard IPsec	14/14/16/15	17/18/26/18	100%
50 ms	8/10/8/9	14/16/16/16	100%
25 ms	10/9/8/8	14/15/17/16	100%
20 ms	9/9/9/9	11/16/17/12	100%
AES-256 CBC			
20 ms	9/7/7	11/13/17	100%
Blowfish-448			
20 ms	14/9/7	15/13/14	99%
	WAN		
Setting	A→B	B→A	Ping
unencrypted	10/10/10/10	9/7/6/7	99%
AES-256 CCM			
standard IPsec	11/11/11/11	11/5/6/5	99%
50 ms	14/10/11/13	6/5/5/5	95%
25 ms	10/11/10/10	6/7/6/7	94%
20 ms	12/11/13/10	9/5/6/6	98%
AES-256 CBC			
20 ms	10/11/11	9/7/8	100%

To verify the key changes, a network sniffer, Eve, was keeping track of the actual SPI changes of the packets transmitted between Alice and Bob. Table II shows a random sample of key change periods in milliseconds during the above mentioned LAN 20ms AES-256-CCM test. Within this table, the first column shows the key change times for data (ESP) packets from Alice to Bob while the second shows the opposite direction. As the recorded data contains one file copy from Alice to Bob (in the first half of the record) and one vice versa (in the second half), one randomly chosen sample of five consecutive key changes for each direction and from each half is chosen. This form of sample choosing from different phases and directions of the communication session and averaging them compensates inaccuracies, induced by the pause between key change and respective next following packet, which become greater the less traffic is sent. As the receiver only acknowledges received data and, therefore, sends significantly less packets, the vagueness of the non-averaged results is greater when receiving. The total average of all four of these averaged values is 0.020495 ms, which is approximately 2.5% above 20 ms per key change. This may be explained by the send and receive overhead for processing the key change messages, for the period determines only the sleeping duration of a sender thread.

Because of the lower amount of traffic (due to the lower speed) and higher latency such exact time readings are not possible in the WAN environment. Therefore, the measurement method was changed to averaging a sample set of 20 key change periods, using the same random choosing as above. With approximately 0.2475, the total averaged result lies significantly higher (approximately 19%) than the one of the LAN setting. One possible explanation for this behavior is the latency in this environment.

TABLE II. Network Sniffing Results

	A→B		B→A	
	1st	2nd	1st	2nd
LAN	0.0220	0.0216	0.0208	0.0203
	0.0187	0.0204	0.0197	0.0235
	0.0145	0.0216	0.0203	0.0176
	0.0195	0.0243	0.0204	0.0197
	0.0225	0.0180	0.0207	0.0238
Ø	0.0194	0.0212	0.0204	0.0210
WAN $\sum$ 20	0.5201	0.4899	0.4302	0.5397
Ø	0.0260	0.0245	0.0215	0.0270

Additionally, the recovery behavior was tested by letting the master deliberately omit key change notifications through manipulating the sending routine, while again running ping tests and file copies. Omitting single key change messages (and, thus, testing the recovery mechanism) yield in no measurable impact on the connection (along with 100% of successful pings). Also, by the same method of omitting key change requests, but this time surpassing the recovery queue size, the reset procedure was tested. The queue size was set to 50 and *Alice* was programmed to omit 50 sending key change messages after 200 sent ones. Expectedly, *Bob* initiated a reset procedure during the hiatus, resulting in a cycle of 200 key changes and a subsequent reset. Despite these permanent reset-induced interruptions, bidirectional ping tests only yielded insignificant losses (99.74% from *Alice* to *Bob* and 99.36% vice versa). Furthermore, a file copy in both directions was still possible.

Further, to test the endurance of the solution, one experiment was conducted to show the capability of maintaining the connection over a longer period of time. It was performed with an earlier development version of QKDIPsec and ran in LAN environment over around 16 hours. It consisted of a running ping test on a 50 ms *Blowfish* configuration without control channel key changes. Of 56179 pings returned 56164 resulting in a return rate of approximately 99.97%. This test was also conducted in WAN environment, but (due to both tests ran overnight) an automated network connection reset after around eight hours prevented meaningful results.

The last test was actively severing the network connection. Pulling the plug on one side resulted in a connection loss that was only recoverable by executing the connection setup routine. This normally does not occur automatically in QKDIPsec but can be induced by the calling function (ordinarily the AIT QKD software). The cause for this behavior is that a shut down (or connectionless) interface loses its additional IP addresses and therefore the tunnel address for the data channel. This problem might be circumvented by implementing an own virtual interface in the future. When servering the connection along the path (thus leaving the peer interfaces intact) the solution automatically recovered (loosing only traffic during the servered phase) when reconnected timely or entered the reset procedures (reset trial and function suspension on time) on disruption spanning over more than the timeout period, according to protocol.

VIII. QKDIPSEC IN A SIMULATION

In order to investigate the impact of the time interval between key change notifications on the overall performance and on the underlying data transmission, we implemented the *Rapid Rekeying Protocol* in OMNeT++ [28] using the INET framework. Besides IPSec and the *Rapid Rekeying Protocol* we implemented an UDP application that sends a certain amount of data to its counterpart using IPSec. We built an evaluation setup with two communicating hosts, and introduced delay and packet drops to the setup. The *Rapid Rekeying Protocol* allows to vary the following variables: number of (simultaneous) installed SAs, and the interval between sending a key change request. For now, we assume that the keys can be provided with an infinite rate, thus idealizing the generation of the key material. Table III provides the different parameter settings used for the simulation. For each combination of the parameters (64 in total) we conducted 30 runs. For the simulation we assumed a sufficiently large QKD key rate (such that none of the applications has to wait for new key material). In the following we report the averages of these runs and their 95% confidence interval (CI) for some selecting parameter settings.

TABLE III. Parameter Settings for the Simulation.

Parameter	Values
Installed SAs	5, 15, 40, 70
Key Change Interval (ms)	25, 50, 100, 200
hline UDP Data Traffic (Mbps)	1, 1.5, 1.7, 1.9
Simulation Time (s)	600
Channel Delay (ms)	$X \sim U(5, 25)$
Channel Data Rate (Mbps)	2
Packet Drop Probability	$\min(X \sim U(0, 1)\ , 0.05)$

Figure 7 depicts the average of deciphered packets with 95% CIs for a maximum of 5 installed SAs at the receiving client. With an increase in the re-keying interval the receiver is able to decipher approximately 80% of all data packets. This is valid for the tested data rates. Although, reaching the theoretical channel data rate of 2 Mbps decreases the number of deciphered packets due to the fact that packets are dropped by full queues. Figure 8 depicts the average of out of synchronization packet with 95% CIs relative to the total amount of received packets using the same parameter settings as for Figure 7. It is evident that with a lower re-keying intervals the amount of non-decipherable and out of synchronization packets increases. However, selecting larger re-keying intervals increases the probability that a man in the middle attacks will be successful. Therefore, a tradeoff between data rate and the desired security level has to be found. Although, we have to consider that some packets are dropped because of the chosen packet drop probability (cf. Table III).

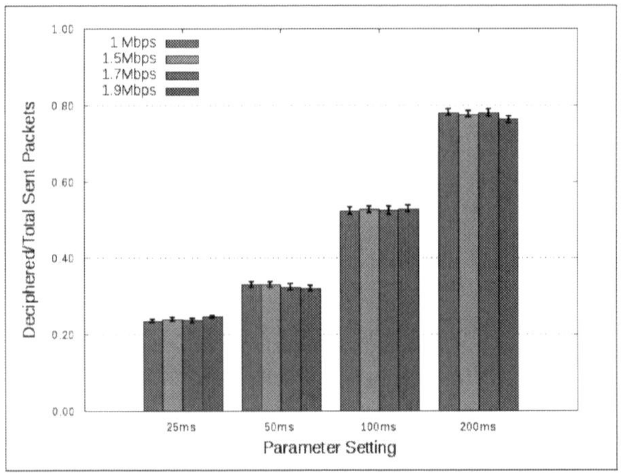

Fig. 7. Packets deciphered relative to the total amount of sent packets for the given data rates with a maximum number of 5 installed SAs for different re-keying intervals, respectively.

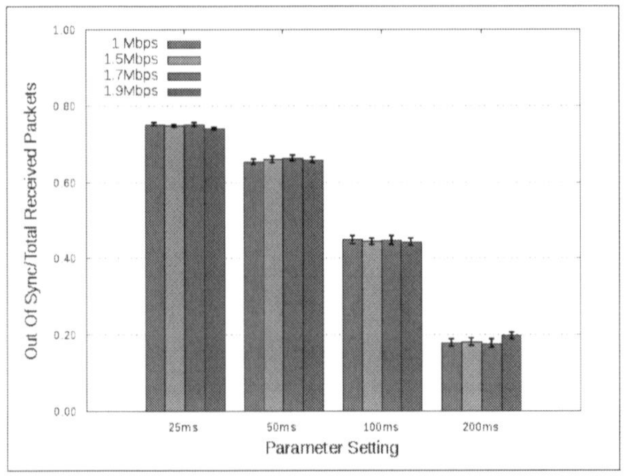

Fig. 8. Packets out of synchronization relative to the total amount of received packets for the given data rates with a maximum number of 5 installed SAs for different re-keying intervals, respectively.

Figures 9 and 10 depict the relative amount of deciphered and out of synchronization packets for a data rate of with 95% CIs for a data rate of 1.5 Mbps. Increasing the the number of simultaneous installed SAs, the probability of encountering out of synchronization packets decreases. Nonetheless, one observes the same behavior as for Figures 7 and 8. Assuming a re-keying interval of 100 ms, a data rate of 1.5 Mbps and a maximum of 15 installed SAs, using QKDIPsec we are able to achieve an effective data rate of approx. 1.1 Mbps on average. If a re-keying interval of 200 ms is acceptable, we are able to achieve an effective data rate of approximately 1.35 Mbps on average. However, it remains the ultimate goal to derive a model by means of ε-security, which provides a trade-off between security and the effective data rate. We devote this to future work.

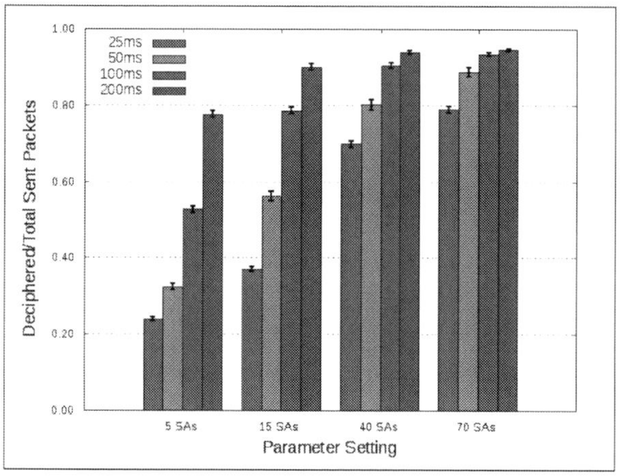

Fig. 9. Packets deciphered relative to the total amount of sent packets for a data rate of 1.5 Mbps.

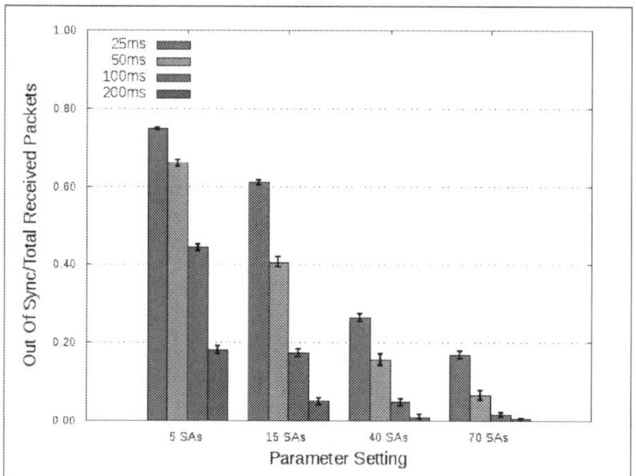

Fig. 10. Packets out of synchronization relative to the total amount of received packets for a data rate of 1.5 Mbps.

IX. CONCLUSION

These proof of concept tests show that using IPsec with appropriate key management is able to overcome the bandwidth restrictions of QKD, even when operating the data channels in less-than-ideal conditions. This, however, comes with the cost of having to reuse the key more than once. Therefore, this paper discussed sensible boundaries of key usage to maintain an acceptable level of security (see Section III). Furthermore, this paper presents an approach to provide QKD-secured links with high speeds meeting the bounds discussed in Section III, including a suitable performant and fault-tolerant key synchronization protocol (the *rapid rekeying protocol*) and a corresponding software solution running under Linux (*QKDIPsec*), integrated into the AIT QKD software. Furthermore, this proof of concept was thouroughly tested both on x86 system architectures and in a simulated machine environments. These tests showed the operability of the principal architecture design as well as possible snares regarding its implementation. During these tests, it became obvious that more installed SAs increase the rate of sucessfully deciphered packets, especially in lower key period settings.

Despite promising test results, there is room for improvement to transform the presented proof of concept module into a fully productive and integrated part of the AIT QKD software. Firstly, there are still obstructions to tackle regarding the integration; the methods for key capturing from the Q3P Application Buffer have to be elaborated and optimized. Secondly, further tests are needed to determine the optimal choice of networking mechanisms. For instance, the implications of switching from TCP to UDP as a transport layer protocol for QKDIPsec have to be examined. Thirdly, some procedures have to be introduced, which automate the reset process in case of hardware connection losses and resets, eliminating the need to restart the system manually. Fourthly, to ease its setup, the solution needs the ability to use virtual interfaces as tunnel endpoints (currently it only supports virtual addresses). Fiftly, while the current version of QKDIPsec already supports on-the-fly adjustments of the key period, the solution should be able to provide interfaces to automatically align this key period to a desired rate of data bits per key bit (dpk). This makes it necessary to provide means to measure the actual data rate running over the data channel and comparing them to the key effective key change rate (consisting of key period and key length). Furthermore, it is desirable to derive a model by means of ε-security, to achieve a trade-off between the data rate and the security of this solution.

REFERENCES

[1] S. Marksteiner and O. Maurhart, "A Protocol for Synchronizing Quantum-Derived Keys in IPsec and its Implementation," in *ICQNM 2015, The Ninth International Conference on Quantum, Nano and Micro Technologies.*, V. Privman and V. Ovchinnikov, Eds. Venice: IARIA, 2015, pp. 35–40.

[2] H. Zbinden, H. Bechmann-Pasquinucci, N. Gisin, and G. Ribordy, "Quantum cryptography," *Applied Physics B*, vol. 67, no. 6, pp. 743–748, 1998.

[3] M. A. Nielsen and I. L. Chuang, *Quantum Computation and Quantum Information*, ser. Lecture Notes in Physics. Cambridge: Cambridge University Press, 2000.

[4] C. E. Shannon, "Communication Theory of Secrecy Systems," *The Bell System Technical Journal*, vol. 28, pp. 656–715, October 1949.

[5] C. Wang, D. Huang, P. Huang, D. Lin, J. Peng, and G. Zeng, "25 MHz clock continuous-variable quantum key distribution system over 50 km fiber channel," *Scientific Reports*, vol. 5, p. 14607, 2015.

[6] A. Treiber, A. Poppe, M. Hentschel, D. Ferrini, T. Lorünser, E. Querasser, T. Matyus, H. Hübel, and A. Zeilinger, "A fully automated entaglement-based quantum cryptography system for telecom fiber networks," *New Journal of Physics*, no. 11, p. 045013, April 2009.

[7] P. Schartner and C. Kollmitzer, "Quantum-Cryptographic Networks from a Prototype to the Citizen," in *Applied Quantum Cryptography*, ser. Lecture Notes in Physics, C. Kollmitzer and M. Pivk, Eds. Berlin, Heidelberg: Springer, 2010, vol. 797, pp. 173–184.

[8] F. Xu, W. Chen, S. Wang, Z. Yin, Y. Zhang, Y. Liu, Z. Zhou, Y. Zhao, H. Li, D. Liu, Z. Han, and G. Guo, "Field experiment on a robust hierarchical metropolitan quantum cryptography network," *Chinese Science Bulletin*, vol. 54, no. 17, pp. 2991–2997, 2009.

[9] S. Kent and K. Seo, "Security Architecture for the Internet Protocol," Internet Requests for Comments, Internet Engineering Task Force, RFC 4301, 2005.

[10] C. Elliott, D. Pearson, and G. Troxel, "Quantum cryptography in practice," in *Proceedings of the 2003 conference on Applications, technologies, architectures, and protocols for computer communications*. ACM, 2003, pp. 227–238.

[11] A. Neppach, C. Pfaffel-Janser, I. Wimberger, T. Lorünser, M. Meyenburg, A. Szekely, and J. Wolkerstorfer, "Key management of quantum generated keys in ipsec." in *Proceedings of SECCRYPT 2008*. INSTICC Press, 2008, pp. 177–183.

[12] MagiQ Technologies, "MAGIQ QPN 8505 Security Gateway," 2007, retrieved at November 11, 2016. [Online]. Available: http://www.magiqtech.com/Products_files/8505_Data_Sheet.pdf

[13] S. Nagayama and R. Van Meter, "Internet-Draft: IKE for IPsec with QKD," 2009, draft-nagayama-ipsecme-ipsec-with-qkd-00, expired work.

[14] D. Stucki, M. Legré, F. Buntschu, B. Clausen, N. Felber, N. Gisin, L. Henzen, P. Junod, G. Litzistorf, P. Monbaron *et al.*, "Long-term performance of the swissquantum quantum key distribution network in a field environment," *New Journal of Physics*, vol. 13, no. 12, p. 123001, 2011.

[15] M. Sfaxi, S. Ghernaouti-Hélie, G. Ribordy, and O. Gay, "Using quantum key distribution within ipsec to secure man communications," in *Proceedings of Metropolitan Area Networks (MAN2005)*, 2005.

[16] E. Barker, "Recommendation for Key Management Part 3: Application-Specific Key Management Guidance(Revision 4 - NIST Special Publication 800-57)," 2016, retrieved at November 11, 2016. [Online]. Available: http://nvlpubs.nist.gov/nistpubs/SpecialPublications/NIST.SP.800-57pt1r4.pdf

[17] A. Poppe, A. Fedrizzi, R. Ursin, H. Böhm, T. Lorünser, O. Maurhardt, M. Peev, M. Suda, C. Kurtsiefer, H. Weinfurter, T. Jennewein, and A. Zeilinger, "Practical quantum key distribution with polarization entangled photons," *Optics Express*, vol. 12, no. 16, pp. 3865–3871, 2004.

[18] Internet Assigned Numbers Authority, "IPSEC ESP Transform Identifiers," 2012, retrieved at November 11, 2016. [Online]. Available: http://www.iana.org/assignments/isakmp-registry/isakmp-registry.xhtml\#isakmp-registry-9

[19] J. Kang, K. Jeong, J. Sung, S. Hong, and K. Lee, "Collision Attacks on AES-192/256, Crypton-192/256, mCrypton-96/128, and Anubis," *Journal of Applied Mathematics*, vol. 2013, p. 713673, 2013.

[20] P. Hoffman, "Cryptographic Suites for IPsec," Internet Requests for Comments, Internet Engineering Task Force, RFC 4308, 2005.

[21] J. H. Kim, R. Montenegro, Y. Peres, and P. Tetali, "A birthday paradox for markov chains, with an optimal bound for collision in the pollard rho algorithm for discrete logarithm," in *International Algorithmic Number Theory Symposium*. Springer, 2008, pp. 402–415.

[22] D. A. McGrew, "Impossible plaintext cryptanalysis and probable-plaintext collision attacks of 64-bit block cipher modes." *IACR Cryptology ePrint Archive*, vol. 2012, p. 623, 2012.

[23] "ECRYPT II Yearly Report on Algorithms and Keysizes (2011-2012)," 2012, retrieved at November 11, 2016. [Online]. Available: http://www.ecrypt.eu.org/ecrypt2/documents/D.SPA.20.pdf

[24] E. Freeman, E. Robson, B. Bates, and K. Sierra, *Head First Design Patterns*. Sebastopol: O'Reilly, 2004.

[25] P. von der Linden, *Expert C Programming: Deep C Secrets*. Upper Saddle River: Prentice Hall, 1994.

[26] O. Maurhart and C. Pacher, "AIT QKD R10 Software," 2015, https://sqt.ait.ac.at/software/projects/qkd, (accessed: Feb.26, 2016).

[27] G. S. Vernam, "Cipher Printing Telegraph Systems For Secret Wire and Radio Telegraphic Communications," *Transactions of the American Institute of Electrical Engineers*, vol. XLV, pp. 295–301, 1926, reprint B-198.

[28] A. Varga *et al.*, "The OMNeT++ discrete event simulation system," in *Proceedings of the European simulation multiconference (ESM'2001)*, vol. 9, no. S 185. sn, 2001, p. 65.

Prospects of Software-Defined Networking in Industrial Operations

György Kálmán

Centre for Cyber and Information Security
Critical Infrastructure Protection Group
Norwegian University of Science and Technology
mnemonic AS
Email: gyorgy.kalman@ntnu.no

***Abstract*—Software-Defined Networking (SDN) is appealing not only for carrier applications, but also in industrial control systems. Network engineering with SDN will result in both lower engineering cost, configuration errors and also enhance the manageability of control systems. This paper analyzes the different aspects of SDN in an industrial scenario, including configuration management, security, and path computation. It also shows the possible enhancements to mitigate the challenges related to network segmentation and shared infrastructure situations. The utilization of SDN in traffic-segregation and security measures is identified as one of the possible solutions for the challenges of an internet-connected automation world.**

***Keywords*—automation; infrastructure; manageability; configuration; life-cycle; DCS; SDN; engineering; path computation.**

I. INTRODUCTION

The following paper is the extended version of [1], Security Implications of Software Defined Networking in Industrial Control Systems. Industrial Ethernet is the dominating technology in distributed control systems and is planned to take over the whole communication network from office to the field level, with sensor networks being the only exception at the moment.

Since its introduction in time critical industrial applications, Ethernet's performance has been questioned, mainly because of the old, coax networks. Current networks are built using full duplex solutions and automation networks follow: these are built with switches, have plenty of bandwidth and the more demanding applications have their specific technologies. These solutions provide intrinsic Quality of Service (QoS), e.g., EtherCAT or try to implement extensions to the Ethernet standards with e.g., efforts to implement resource reservation like the IEEE 802.1 Time-Sensitive Networking Task Group.

Many of the issues the control system engineering is facing, are not new. From the advent of packet switched networks, QoS and resilience was a question. For metropolitan and Wide Area Networks (WAN), different solutions, like Asynchronous Transfer Mode (ATM) or Multiprotocol Label Switching (MPLS) were developed to allow creation of virtual circuits. These virtual circuits can be a natural representation of the control loops.

With the industry moving towards Commercial Off The Shelf (COTS) products in the networking solutions (both hardware and software) opened for direct interconnection of other company networks towards the automation systems [2], [3]. The problems associated with network performance and resilience are similar to the ones, which e.g., MPLS was built to solve.

The possibility to proceed further with adopting technologies developed for WAN or telecommunication use is in large part enabled by the extended use of COTS devices. The common technology enables efficient data exchange, but also opens the possibility to attack the previously island-like automation systems from or through the company network [4].

One of the aspects of such interconnection of systems is that the automation network might be attacked through other systems. For a more structured approach, a possible categorization of attackers is given by [5]:

- Hobbyists break into systems for fun and glory. Difficult to stop, but consequences are low.
- Professional hackers break into systems to steal valuable assets, or on a contract basis. Very difficult to stop, consequences usually financial. May be hired to perform theft, industrial espionage, or sabotage.
- Nation-States and Non-Governmental Organizations (NGOs) break into systems to gather intelligence, disable capabilities of opponents, or to cause societal disruption.
- Malware automated attack software. Intent ranges from building botnets for further attacks, theft, or general disruption. Ranges from easy to stop to moderately difficult to stop.
- Disgruntled employees, including insider threat and unauthorized access after employment.

Engineering efforts have been made to reduce the risks associated with this interconnection, but it only gained momentum after the more recent incidents of e.g., stuxnet and repeated cases of Denial of Service (DoS) incidents coming

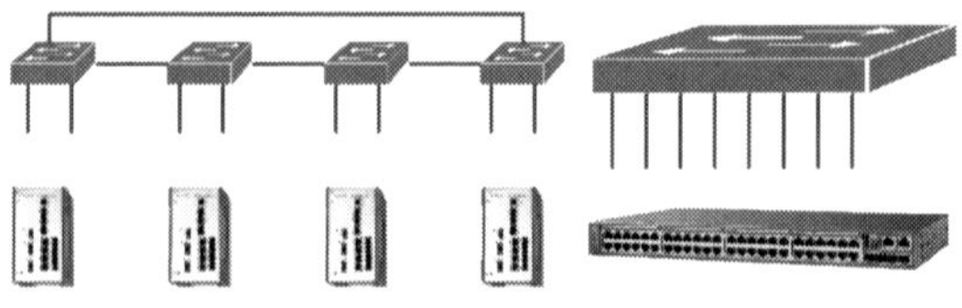

Fig. 1. Low port count switches in automation

from external networks. The first efforts were focused on including well-known solutions from the IT industry: firewalls, Intrusion Detection Systems (IDS), authentication solutions.

The challenge with these solutions is that they were designed to operate in a different network environment [6]. Amongst others, the QoS requirements of an automation system tend to be very different than of an office network. The protocol set used is different and the typical protocol inside an automation system runs on Layer 2 and not on the IP protocol suite [7].

Beside the efforts on adopting IT security solutions to industrial environments, several working groups are involved in introducing security features into automation protocols and protocols used to support an automation system (e.g., IEEE 1588v3 on security functions, IEC 61850 to have integrity protection). The necessity of network management systems are gaining acceptance to support life-cycle management of the communication infrastructure.

In this landscape, SDN is a promising technology [8], [9] to support automation vendors to deploy their distributed control systems (DCS) more effectively, to allow easier brownfield extensions and to have a detailed overview of the traffic under operation [10], [11].

The paper is structured as follows: the second section gives an introduction of Industrial Ethernet and SDN, the third provides an overview of DCS structures, the fourth provides an overview of the security landscape, while the fifth presents an analysis of the impact of SDN on the security controls. The last section draws the conclusion and provides an outlook on future work.

II. State of the Art

Industrial Ethernet is built often as a special mixture of a few high-end switches and a large number of small port count discrete or integrated switches composing several network segments defined by both the DCS architecture and location constraints.

Engineering of networks composed from small switches results in typically a magnitude more devices than a comparable office network (e.g., a bigger refinery can have several hundreds of switches with a typical branching factor of 4-7) as shown on Fig. 1. The engineering cost and the possibility of configuration-related delays has a big impact on competitiveness.

In the majority of cases, the actual configuration of the devices can be described with setting port-Virtual LAN (VLAN) allocations, Rapid Spanning Tree (RSTP) priorities, Simple Network Management Protocol (SNMP) parameters and performance monitoring [12]. These steps currently require manual work.

In a different setting, practically all of these problem scenarios were present previously in the backbone engineering of large networks. The centralized configuration management was present since ATM was launched, offering a control plane for making forwarding decisions and allowing simpler devices inside the network. At that time, the consideration was twofold: one for keeping QoS, but also to reduce complexity of the networking nodes on the transit path. This was at that time forced by the resources available in these nodes. In the current industrial case, the forwarding decision itself is not a resource problem for the local switch or router, but a policy question where resource usage and security considerations play a key role. As a less known alternative, Internet Engineering Task Force (IETF) has defined an entity in RFC 4655 and 5440, called Path Computation Element (PCE).

A. Path Computation Element

PCE is a visibility and control protocol for MPLS networks. The protocol partially moves the control plane of the head-end routers to define network paths. The problem for PCE to solve was that the head-end router is expected to both deal with internal routing and external connections. If a complex path computation algorithm is added, it might exhaust the resources of the device.

Compared to SDN, the PCE protocol presents an evolutionary approach. Although an SDN implementation like OpenFlow offers a wider feature set, PCE only requires a change in the head-end routers and not in all routers and switches.

The approach is noteworthy, because it splits the actual tasks of the central element of an Autonomous System (AS) in a way, which is transparent for the rest of the network and allows a change in algorithm complexity without the exchange of the central component. This can be beneficial in equipment with a long expected life, like most of the automation installations.

The focus on head-end routers however makes it less suitable for use in industrial networks, as the majority of communication is done on Layer 2 (in switches), which is outside the coverage of PCE. From the traffic viewpoint, the possibility of per flow control of switch forwarding makes SDN implementations more suitable.

B. Software-Defined Networking

The main difference from control systems perspective between PCE and a full SDN implementation is the support for Layer 2. Often, solutions developed for other fields of networking fail on this aspect. In a typical network case, where security, manageability and monitoring has key importance is on Layer 3. Although nodes in the industrial networks typically also have a presence on Layer 3, the focus of communication is on a lower layer [13]–[15].

There are also different driving forces in the centralization of the control plane. In a typical non-automation scenario, centralized flow management is driven by reaching higher forwarding efficiency and is applied in carrier networks [16]. Also, the network reaches higher flexibility by centralizing the forwarding decisions as e.g., QoS requirements might lead to different paths for flows with different requirements but the same source and destination.

SDN capabilities for separating traffic and control on carrier networks can be adopted to the control system scenario. The focus, although, in this case is more on management and the implementation of a call admission control-feature is more interesting. The possibility of deploying new services without disturbing the production network and the appealing possibility of having a full overview of network flows from one central controller is presenting a valid business case [17]–[19].

With SDN, a telecom-like network structure is introduced into distributed control systems with splitting the control and the forwarding plane. In such a network, the flows are programmable through a central entity on the control plane [20]. This allows testing and resource reservation for specific flows, not just at commissioning, but also during operation. The ability to isolate new traffic flows can be beneficial from both security and operational viewpoints. These possibilities are appealing for the industrial automation systems, as they are very much in line with the current trends of redundancy, QoS and shared infrastructure.

As defined by the Open Networking Foundation [21], SDN is or offers

- *Directly programmable* Network control is directly programmable because it is decoupled from forwarding functions.
- *Agile* Abstracting control from forwarding lets administrators dynamically adjust network-wide traffic flow to meet changing needs.
- *Centrally managed* Network intelligence is (logically) centralized in software-based SDN controllers that maintain a global view of the network, which appears to applications and policy engines as a single, logical switch.
- *Programmatically configured* SDN lets network managers configure, manage, secure, and optimize network resources very quickly via dynamic, automated SDN programs, which they can write themselves because the programs do not depend on proprietary software.
- *Open standards-based and vendor-neutral* When implemented through open standards, SDN simplifies network design and operation because instructions are provided by SDN controllers instead of multiple, vendor-specific devices and protocols.

SDN architecture is typically represented with three layers, as show compared to a traditional network structure on Fig. 2

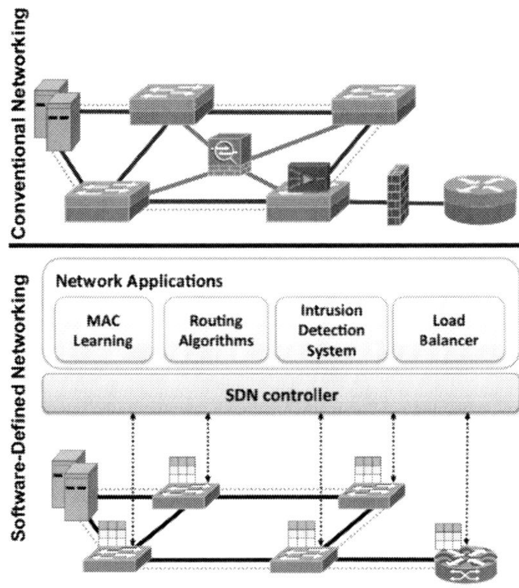

Fig. 2. Traditional network architecture compared to SDN [9]

and on Fig. 3 by OpenFlow. Using several planes in a communication technology is not new, it was present both in ATM, SDH or all the digital cellular networks. What is new, that these management possibilities are now available also in a much smaller scale. It is expected that a network with a centrally managed control plane can better react on changes in traffic patterns and also be more flexible in network resource management [22]. The forwarding performance is expected to be very similar or equivalent to the current switches used. The industrial applications will be run without disturbance in a stable network state [23], [24].

The normal communication traffic is expected to be significantly larger than the control and signalling traffic generated by SDN and therefore not considered as a performance problem. Also the considered communication on an industrial network supports the mitigation of this performance threat, as most of the sessions are periodic machine to machine (M2M), which can be scheduled or event driven, with precisely defined transmission deadlines. The gaps between planned periodic traffic are rarely filled with event-driven communication.

III. DCS ARCHITECTURE

Current DCS networks are a result of an evolution from analog wiring towards digital lines, buses and finally networks. Many challenges related to both engineering and operation of industrial networks originate from this evolution like the problematic expression of QoS parameters and the underestimated importance of the communication infrastructure.

The systems considered by this paper are primarily the current Ethernet-based solutions without special (e.g., EtherCAT, PROFINET IRT) hardware support. These networks

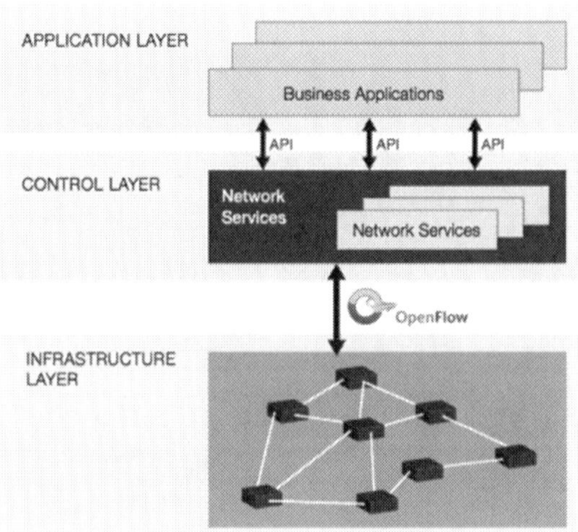

Fig. 3. Three layer SDN architecture [21]

are composed by standard equipment where both the QoS environment, protocols and capabilities used are similar.

The invisibility of the communication infrastructure in the DCS is a constant problem and source of challenges in both engineering and operations. Historically, this was not a seen as problematic, as first there was direct wiring between the components, so failure in the line resulted in immediate errors and typically had no impact on other parts of the system. There was also little change with the bus systems and serial solutions: the communication infrastructure got digitalized, but still it was more the task of an electric technician to create it than one of an IT network specialist.

Current engineering practices still follow manual methods with creating connection lists and per unit configuration. The methods used lead to problems when one has to express situations like shared infrastructure or formalized checking of redundancy.

Traditional Network Management Systems (NMS) are typically not present in industrial deployments, mostly as a result of cost pressure. The existence of the communication infrastructure both in DCS (LAN) or SCADA (WAN) cases is typically hidden from the automation tasks and operations. The separate operation and maintenance of the DCS and the communication infrastructure is inefficient in large scale. With the evolution of control systems, covering more and more processes with integrated solutions, the network complexity is only expected to grow. Thus the current practice of using command line or web interfaces on a per node basis. Even in case of managed equipment (switches, routers), the nodes are configured individually and the efficiency or in more serious cases, the stability of operation is dependent on the communication between the network specialist and the control engineer.

Control systems are traditionally built using a three network levels. The plant, the client-server and the control network. These levels might have different names, but they share the following characteristics:

- *Plant network* is home of the traditional IT systems, like Enterprise Resource Planning (ERP), office services and other support applications. It is typically under the control of the IT department.
- *Client-server network* is the non-time critical part of the automation system, where the process-releated workplaces, servers and other support entities are located. It is firewalled from the plant network and is under the control of Operations.
- *Control network* includes everything close to the actual process: controllers, sensors, actuators and other automation components. Typically follows a strict time synchronization regime and contains the parts of the network with time-critical components. It is accessible through proxies from the client-server network and under the control of Operations.

There are some solutions, where network nodes can communicate status and errors to the DCS, but the possibilities are limited and typically the information conveyed is not enough to fully understand the situation. A possible way to reduce visible network complexity is to use unmanaged switches. These devices melt into the network fabric, but also remove the possibility to analyze the network status or troubleshooting of forwarding. In current engineering regimes, unmanaged devices have their usage areas limited to small installations, where managed equipment is prohibitively expensive or where very high reliability is required, as a typical unmanaged switch has nearly ten times longer Mean Time Between Failure (MTBF) time than its managed counterpart.

In most cases, the use of a programmable network is focusing on flow control. This is a typical efficiency-driven effort to ensure, that the network flows are utilizing the resources in an optimized or optimal way. An Internet Service Provider (ISP) or a carrier network will focus on such use. In case of an industrial deployment, the main motivation is not per flow control, although later a use case related to security will be shown. The main motivation however is the possibility to control the network from one centralized entity. This control functionality is expected to be easily understandable and acceptable by operations, as it can be compared to a Programmable Logic Controller (PLC), the very base of an automation system: an SDN controller operates in a very similar way, telling if the traffic should slow or take a different direction, than a PLC, which can tell a valve to open or close and can regulate the flow of materials or changing the speed of a drive.

SDN concepts have the possibility to streamline the network operations and enable diagnostics with more possible points of entry and a wider tool set [25]. With communication paths controlled through the vertical of the industrial network, it would be possible to create end-to-end QoS links within a system. This would allow more control and continuous monitoring of the network performance. The simplification of configuration and implementation of network architectures with possible use of templates and macro building blocks may both lower engineering costs and lead to higher performance. Also the need of network specialists in operations will be lower as the centralized control is assumed to require less (physical) presence than today's situation with may be hundreds of switches on the plant floor, each of them uniquely configured.

The transition to programmable network on the plant floor is expected to shorten the time needed to identify and locate a problem and to ease tension between operations and IT. With the control plane moved to a central entity, the technician can exchange the identified faulty unit with one having default configuration and, which can be configured by the SDN controller. The automatic configuration also represents a mitigation for some cases of physical misconfiguration of cables.

The centralized management of adding or removing network devices can enable currently unavailable dynamism in an industrial context: it would be possible to reconfigure the network topology to adopt to new situations or tasks.

Real-time Ethernet also represents an area, where SDN can have a positive impact. In the current situation, either an industrial Ethernet technology with intrinsic QoS is used or the network only can give a probabilistic guarantee on delivery. Current engineering practice is, that these network parts are configured once and run without reconfiguration for extended periods, only changed when necessary. This operational regime is acceptable with smaller network segments, but does not scale. Using SDN to control the forwarding of real-time flows can have definitive advantages: continuous evaluation of the Service Level Agreement (SLA), immediate reaction at link failure, prioritization of time sensitive traffic and the possibility to integrate new technologies in a transparent way (e.g., IEEE 802.1AV). To be able to give a deterministic guarantee (upper bound) on forwarding delays, the SDN controller needs to have a connection to real time. This is not a priority in a carrier environment and a feature, which needs to be developed. The main potential of SDN in this case is, that since the forwarding decisions are not being made on a per hop and per frame basis, the traffic situation of a switch has less influence on the jitter and delay of the communication.

The complete view of network paths also allows the controller to choose the optimal route per flow also in a larger environment: time sensitive traffic might be forwarded on an express path and less sensitive on a more economic path, very much implementing the different traffic classes of IntServ.

In case of link failure, the controller can reroute the flow (depending on the SLA) to a precalculated backup path or to a newly calculated alternate route. Precalculated backup paths can also be used as a hot standby with actual forwarding on two independent routes. Following the actual status of the network, an SDN controller can also monitor if the backup routes can still fulfill their tasks. This feature can protect again cascading effects of link failures: the backup routes shall be able to carry all the traffic they carry by default and in addition the traffic of the primary route.

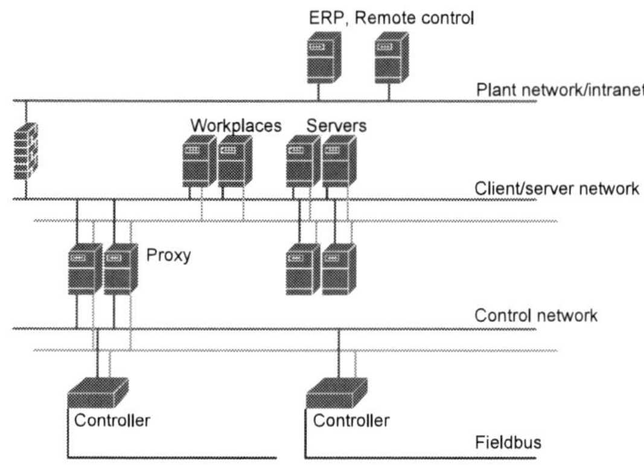

Fig. 4. Traditional DCS network architecture

Since the SDN controller also has a complete view of the network and enough resources, it might precalculate independent backup routes for most of the network flows. Having alternatives ready might considerably reduce the recovery time of the network.

Faster reaction times and status monitoring of the network is also useful in case of node failures. In this case, SDN can again provide better functionality than current solutions. It is not only possible to spot the problematic node, but the system can also show if it is possible to isolate the faulty device with keeping the current SLAs for the involved traffic flows or if now, then, which QoS parameters are achievable.

One of the possible limiting factors of SLA creation and QoS parameter setting is, that traditionally, parameters of a control loop are expressed with different measures.

A. *Control loop parameters*

Requirements definition for the communication network is one of the actual challenges in automation. An example IEC 61850 control loop would be defined as: having a sampling rate of 80 samples per cycle (4800 Hz for 60 Hz networks), with sampling 16 inputs, 16 bit per sample. Event-based traffic is negligible compared to the periodic traffic.

If there is a requirement for synchronous operation, time precision (quality) can also be a QoS metric. Redundancy requirements can lead to topologies, which are unusual in a normal network infrastructure: first, the use of Rapid Spanning Tree Protocol (RSTP) to disable redundant links, second the general use of loops (rings) in the network to ensure that all nodes are dual-homed. With dual-homing, the network can survive the loss of one communication link without degradation in the service level. Path calculation algorithms created for generic network use might not support such constellations.

From the network viewpoint, this control loop will introduce a traffic flow, with a net ingress payload stream of approx. 98Mbps. The sampling will generate 2560 bytes of traffic each second, which can be carried by at least two Ethernet frames, thus the system can expect at least approx. 10000 frames per second. The traffic will be forwarded on a horizontal path to the controller. On the ingress port to the backbone, it will enter with approx. 110 Mbps (header+payload). The traffic flow will be consumed at the egress port to the controller.

For SLA composition, either a definition of the traffic is needed in forehand or the classification at the SDN controller needs to be dynamic: the controller has no information at the first ingress frame, which frequency or payload length will be typical.

The information on the flows is not only beneficial for resource management. Precisely defined traffic flows (which is a possibility in industrial applications) can create an excellent base for configuring and implementing network security functions, like Intrusion Detection Systems or actual firewall configurations.

B. SCADA and grid operations

With interconnection of previously isolated locations, in addition to the traditional Supervisory Control And Data Acquisition (SCADA) operations, industrial wide area networks are being deployed.

Maybe the most important in the current European landscape is the effort to add more intelligence and dynamism into the electric grid control: creation of smart grids. Current grid communication networks are based on standard IP networking, where network parameters and configuration are defined at the design phase, the same process as in DCS. When the network is in operation, and in this sense, the grid control is always expected to be in operation with the possibility to have planned maintenance stops. Dynamic changes outside these planned stops tend to be problematic, both from economic and supply security viewpoint. Such a rigid setup on the other hand can be problematic in the expected dynamic environment of the smart grid: where plants and consumers should communicate about the power generation and usage, bandwidth and path selection parameters might change under operation.

SDN is expected to be able to deliver appropriate QoS, since the network parameters in steady state will not considerably differ from a static network. The more important aspect is how SDN could enhance system resilience. The features are similar of those in case of a DCS and show the scalability of SDN in this perspective. The first one is the possibility of precalculated backup paths, then the possibility to isolate a node if there is a chance, that it got compromised or failed. Then an additional feature might be to reroute the control information over the public internet. This possibility could give a highly independent backup route, where the necessary flows could be rerouted with applying appropriate encryption and integrity protection.

There is also a possibility for coordinated actions between the SDN controller, the security measures (firewall, IDS) and the SCADA control.

IV. Security landscape

Industrial deployments were built traditionally as isolated islands, thus security was more a question of doors and walls then IT [5]. Employees from the operations department had the responsibility to keep the communication network intact.

Security issues connected to computer networks came with, amongst others, the SCADA applications, where remote access to industrial deployments was granted. With the spread of Ethernet and IP-based communication, more and more automation networks could be connected to other networks, to allow easier management and new applications.

Threat analyses showed that industrial systems can be more prone to DoS and related attacks due to the more strict QoS requirements and lack of available processing power in the devices [26]. Typically the deployed network infrastructure can handle a magnitude higher traffic than the end-nodes. This helps in supporting the SDN operation with allowing the traffic, which does not match any of the forwarding rules to be sent to the controller in the normally unused bandwidth. The static traffic picture will also allow the use of sharp heuristics on new traffic, categorizing unknown traffic very early as malicious and drop it early.

DoS attacks require no knowledge of the automation system, only access to the infrastructure, which is a much larger attack surface this case as DCS and especially SCADA systems have a tendency to cover large areas, where enforcing of a security policy (both physical and cyber) is a hard task [27].

This properties have focused the security efforts on protecting the leaves of the network and also on creating policies to ensure the use of hardening practices.

Standard hardening procedures in current industrial deployments include:

- Creation of a *Security Policy* following e.g., the IEC 62443 standard. This allows to have a structured approach for operating the network.
- A standard way to introduce anti-virus solutions in the automation network using central management.
- Specific focus on the configuration of server and workstation machines with e.g., policies and additional software components.
- Access and account management: using Role-Based Access Control (RBAC), OS functions like the Group Policy Object (GPO) or tools like a trusted password manager.
- Backup and restoration as a part of disaster recovery.
- Network topology to support security levels in the IEC 62443, with using firewalls as separator.
- Specific remote access solution and whitelisting of both traffic and nodes.

These tasks show that the there is an understanding of the importance of security in this field and there are efforts on standardization.

The problematic part of the process is, where these guidelines, policies and physical appliances need to be deployed in a new or an existing installation.

Correctness of the implementation is crucial for future reliability of the system. In a typical current workflow, configuration and deployment of devices is a manual task together with the as-built analysis under or before the factory acceptance test (FAT). At the moment there is no merged workflow and software support for all of the steps mentioned earlier.

SDN can be part of the answer: the communication infrastructure, communication security and monitoring under operation can be implemented using SDN, where the whole or part of the tasks could be automated [28], [29].

V. SDN-RELATED CHALLENGES

SDN changes the security model considerably. To enable automatic features, the operation and the way of controlling a SDN system has to be analyzed in the industrial context.

A. The plane structure

After the author's view, the introduction of the separated control and forwarding plane is the biggest enhancement for network security in this relation. In the telecommunication field, separated planes are used since decades to support secure service delivery with minimizing the possibility of a successful attack from the user side towards network management.

In an industrial context, the split planes mean, that the configuration of the devices is not possible from the network areas what clients can see, thus intruders getting access to e.g., the field network through a sensor, will not be able to communicate with the management interfaces.

Attacks at the data plane could be executed with e.g., gaining access to the network through a physical or virtual interface and try to execute a Denial of Service (DoS) attack or a type of fuzzing attack, which might exploit a flaw in the management or automation protocols.

An attacker could also leverage these protocols and attempt to instantiate new flows into the device's forwarding table. The attacker would want to try to spoof new flows to permit specific types of traffic that should be disallowed across the network [30].

B. The SDN controller

The first group of issues are related to the SDN controller. To allow a central entity to control and configure the whole network, it has to gain administrative access over the whole network infrastructure configuration and status. Thus the SDN controller's ability to control an entire network makes it a very high value target.

The SDN controller has predefined interfaces towards other systems:

- Northbound application programming interfaces (APIs) represent the software interfaces between the software modules of the controller platform and the SDN applications. These APIs expose universal network abstraction data models and functionality for use by network applications.
- East-West protocols are implementing the necessary interactions between the various controllers.
- Data plane and southbound protocols: the forwarding hardware in the SDN network architecture.
- Communicate with the network infrastructure, it requires certain protocols to control and manage the interface between various pieces of network equipment.

This can be problematic if the controller has to cross several firewalls to reach all nodes under its control. In the traditional DCS network architecture (Fig. 4) in order to gain control of the whole network, the controller has to pass the firewall between the plant and the client-server network, the proxy towards the control network and the controllers towards the field devices.

In a realistic situation, the controller of the DCS will not be allowed to control also the plant network, but is expected to reside inside the DCS, most probably on the client-server network. Inside the automation network, firewalls and the controllers can be configured so, that they pass the SDN signaling.

Network intelligence is being transferred from the network nodes to the central controller entity. This, if being implemented inside a switched network, might only be a semantic difference in network control, as it extends the possibilities of a NMS, but it does not need to integrate more sophisticated devices in an industrial situation.

It is expected that a network with a centrally managed control plane can better react on changes in traffic patterns and also be more flexible in network resource management.

In addition to the attack surface of the management plane, the controller has another attack surface: the data plane of the switches. When an SDN switch encounters a packet that does not match any forwarding rules, it passes this packet to the controller for advice. As a result, it is possible for an attacker who is simply able to send data through an SDN switch to exploit a vulnerability on the controller [31].

Attacks directed against the controller can for example aim to destruct the topology by taking control over the path calculation. A compromised SDN controller may change the configuration of the communication devices. This can put keeping the SLAs in danger.

The standard SDN controller behavior of getting all the frames forwarded, which were not classified already at ingress, can lead to DoS attacks.

To mitigate the single-point-of-failure what the SDN controller represents, in most installations, it will be required to deploy two of the controllers in a redundant installation.

Also shared infrastructure between different operators can be a problem in this case. Legal issues might arise if the audit and logging of SDN-induced configuration changes is not detailed enough.

C. Service deployment security

In an SDN case, the controller entity can change the configuration and forwarding behavior of the underlying devices. This possibility is a valuable addition to the existing set of features, because an SDN system could deploy a new service without disturbing the current operation, which would reduce costs related to scheduled downtimes.

Also, the fine-grained control of network flows and continuous monitoring of the network status offers a good platform for IDS, Managed Security Services (MSS) or a tight integration with the higher operation layers of the DCS.

D. Central resource management

Currently, SNMP-based NMSs are widely used for monitoring the health and status of large network deployments. Using SDN could also here be beneficial, as the monitoring functionality would be extended with the ability of actively changing configurations and resource allocations if needed.

One of the most significant technological and policy challenges in an SDN deployment is the management of devices from different providers. Keeping the necessary complexity and configuration possibilities is hard to synchronize with entities delivered from different providers.

With SDN's abstraction layer one can hide differences in features but also can introduce problems in logging and audit. Network equipment manufacturers are not supporting by default that their devices are managed by a third party.

Although, the rollout of new services would become safer, as the system could check if the required resources are available and the use of SDN is not expected to have a negative impact on the reliability of the network the problems related to shared infrastructure need to be elaborated further.

E. Security implications of shared infrastructure

As part of the universal use of Ethernet communication, it is now common for vendors to share the network infrastructure to operate different parts of an installation. An example is a subsea oil production platform, which is controlled through a hundreds of kilometers long umbilical, can have a different operator for the power subsystem, an other one for the process control and a third one for well control.

In the current operation regimes, the configuration of the networks is rarely changing and all vendors have a stable view of their part of the network shared with the one being the actual operator. With SDN, the network could be controlled in a more dynamic way.

From the technological viewpoint, the biggest challenge is to find a solution, where both the controller and the devices support encrypted control operations. If they support it, than the logging and audit system has to be prepared for a much more dynamic environment.

From a policy management viewpoint, the possibility of fast per-flow configuration opens for new types of problems: the valid network topology and forwarding situation might change fast and frequently, which is not typical in the industry. Logging has to provide the current and all past network configurations with time stamping to allow recreation of transient setups in case of communication errors.

In such a shared case, the use of SDN could reduce risk in topology or traffic changes, as vendors could deploy new services without an impact on other traffic flows in the network. It is possible to create an overlay network, which follows the logical topology of an application or subsystem. This would improve the control possibilities as the staff could follow the communication paths in a more natural way.

F. Industrial safety

Conversations on Safety Integrated Systems (SIS) mainly include questions on QoS. The cause is that these installations share the communication network between the automation task and the safety function (as they can also share infrastructure with the fire alarm system). In a safety sense, SIS have no QoS requirements. The safety logic is built in a way, that a communication error is interpreted as a dangerous situation and the safety function will trip. So the system avoids dangerous situations at the expense of lower productivity and availability.

Safety as such is an availability question and through availability, it implies QoS requirements on the automation system as any other communication task. Special treatment is not required.

Safety systems are classified into 4 levels, Safety Integrity Level (SIL) 1 to 4. The different levels pose well-defined requirements towards the system. These integrity levels cover all aspects of the system, including hardware, software, communication solution and seen in contrast with the application. A similar approach could be also beneficial for formalizing the relationship between the automation application and the bearer network.

The IEC 61508 standard requires that each risk posed by the components of the safety system is identified and analyzed. The result of the risk analysis should be evaluated against tolerability criteria.

Coverage of safety communication is not only important in itself, but also because many of the processes used in safety can be used effectively in deploying security measures, where the vocabulary and test methods of functional safety help.

G. Wireless integration

Another key field currently is the integration of wireless networks into industrial deployments. SDN could help with integration of wireless technologies by checking if the needs of a new service e.g., can be satisfied with a path having one or more wireless hops or a new rule has to be deployed into the network to steer the traffic of that service on a different path.

H. Integrating Security in the preliminary design

In the bidding phase, the control engineer could leave the planning of the network on a high level with having an SDN rule set to check if the network can be built. The needed security appliances and other entities would be added to the list of required components following rules developed using the relevant standards.

The control engineer could add the control processes and the SDN software will check if the required resources are available on the communication path. In contrast with current methods, the acceptance of a communication session would also give a proof that the required resources are available and the security requirements are met.

I. Network simulation and capacity estimation

The use of SDN and the central management entities will also lead to more detailed information on network traffic and internal states. The data gathered on operational network not only supports the management of the current network, but also can be used to fine-tune the models used in early steps of bidding and planning and can lead to a more lean approach on network resource allocation. SDN could provide better communication security by helping to avoid overloaded network situations.

J. Firewalls

A current limitation on the coverage of SDN is connected to accountability. While automatic changes in the forwarding table on layer 2 is not expected to cause big problems, automatic rule generation for firewalls and other higher layer devices might cause more problems than it solves.

Granting the control rights of network security devices to the SDN controller is necessary to gain full control over all network nodes. The challenge with this setup is, that L2 forwarding can be described with relative few properties, routing tables with some more, but still within a limited size, firewall rules can contain a lot more properties and values to fill. If automatic generation is disabled, then the SDN network split into several security zones can only be partially managed by the controller. If automatic generation is enabled, it can cause security breaches (e.g., the early implementations of Universal Plug and Play (UPnP)). This setup also potentially requires cooperation from several companies, e.g., an MSS provider running the security infrastructure and the operations staff at the location focusing on automation.

From the practical viewpoint, there are several issues. The first is that in most cases, management protocols only offer the implementation of security functions, but they are optional, so having a required encryption (one cannot avoid this when managing firewalls) might result in incompatibility already in the communication. The second is, that one needs much more complex support for firewalls in the management software than for switches or routers.

K. Intrusion Detection Systems

Running IDS in an SDN network is promising. The IDS can notify the SDN controller upon detecting anomalies in the traffic, so that the controller can reconfigure the network accordingly. In addition, the SDN controller can also feed information about legitimate flows to the IDS, enabling the creation of a detailed whitelist.

Current IDS implementations typically use distributed wire-taps or other traffic monitoring sources to watch for malicious traffic and might get aggregated traffic information (e.g., over NetFlow).

SDN can take this functionality into a whole new level. The controller has a complete view of the L2 traffic streams over the whole network, thus not only has a wiretap *everywhere*, but also has the control of the forwarding entities: it can make changes in the forwarding decisions in real time. In extreme cases this can result in, that the malicious packet cannot even travel through the network to its destination, because at the entry the IDS system classifies it as potentially malicious and in transit redirects it into an isolated network.

Industrial deployments are an excellent basis to develop such a fast-reaction IDS: the communication is typically M2M, the network traffic is stationary (whole-new traffic flows are not typical) and the topology is mostly static. The heuristics of the IDS could be as a result, very sensitive on non-planned traffic, thus reacting fast on potential hazards.

If the SDN infrastructure is available because of network management, the extension of providing IDS and firewall management can also lead to cost reduction compared to deploying and operating a separate solution for both.

L. Protecting the SDN controller

As it was mentioned earlier, the SDN controller represents a single-point-of-failure in the network. As most of the industrial deployments are redundant, it is natural to require also a redundant deployment of the SDN controller.

This redundancy is required both from the availability view-point (all crucial components have redundant counterparts in most deployments) and also from network security: protection from e.g., DoS attacks.

Transport security shall be ensured with up to date standard protocols, e.g., TLS for web access or SSH for shell. An effort shall be used to keep the cryptographic suites, which are used by these protocols updated.

VI. Conclusion

SDN is very likely to be the next big step in industrial networks, both on LAN and WAN level. It offers exactly the functionality automation engineers are looking for: hiding the network and allowing the planning and deployment of network infrastructure without deep technical knowledge, based only on definition of network flows and automatic dimensioning rules.

With a complete view over the current network traffic situation, QoS parameters can be checked in a formal way with the help of the central management entity and as such, provide a proof in all stages of the engineering work, that the infrastructure will be able to support the application.

In brown field extensions SDN can reduce risks associated with deploying new equipment and extending the current infrastructure because of the isolation of traffic flows and the complete control over the forwarding decisions.

Network security is the other main area, where, if properly planned and implemented, SDN can provide a big step forward in both security and operational excellence. With the real-time overview on the network infrastructure, an SDN-based IDS could react much faster on attacks.

Technological advancements are clearly moving towards a more automated network infrastructure and in the industrial case, SDN is a promising technology, which has to be taken seriously.

REFERENCES

[1] Gy. Kalman, "Security Implications of Software Defined Networking in Industrial Control Systems," IARIA ICCGI 2015, St. Julians, Malta

[2] N. Barkakati and G. C. Wilshusen, "Deficient ICT Controls Jeopardize Systems Supporting the Electric Grid: A Case Study," Securing Electricity Supply in the Cyber Age, Springer, pages 129-142, e-ISBN 978-90-481-3594-3

[3] Gy. Kalman, "Applicability of Software Defined Networking in Industrial Ethernet," in Proceedings of IEEE Telfor 2014, pages 340-343, Belgrade, Serbia

[4] ABB, "Security for Industrial Automation and Control Systems," White Paper, ABB, Doc. Id. 3BSE032547

[5] M. McKay, "Best practices in automation security," White Paper, Siemens, 2012.

[6] Cisco, "Secure Industrial Networks with Cisco," White Paper, 2015., http://www.cisco.com/c/en/us/products/collateral/se/internet-of-things/white-paper-c11-734453.pdf, Accessed 30.08.2015.

[7] C. Alcaraz, G. Fernandez, and F. Carvajal, "Security Aspects of SCADA and DCS Environments," In Critical Infrastructure Protection: Information Infrastructure Models, Analysis, and Defense, LNCS 7130., Springer, pp. 120-149, September 2012.

[8] M. Jammal,T. Singh, A. Shami,R. Asal, and Y. Li, "Software-Defined Networking: State of the Art and Research Challenges," ArXiv e-prints 1406.0124, May 2014.

[9] D. Kreutz, F. Ramos, P. Verissimo, C. Rothenberg, S. Azodolmolky, and S. Uhlig. "Software-Defined Networking: A Comprehensive Survey," Proceedings of the IEEE, Volume: 103, Issue: 1, January 2015

[10] D. Cronberger, "The Software-Defined Industrial Network," The Industrial Ethernet Book, Issue 84, Pages 8-13, 2014.

[11] D. Cronberger, "Industrial Grade SDN," Cisco, 2013, http://blogs.cisco.com/manufacturing/industrial-grade-sdn, Accessed 28.05.2015.

[12] A. Gopalakrishnan, "Applications of Software-Defined Networks in Industrial Automation," https://www.academia.edu/2472112/Application_of_Software_Defined_Networks_in_Industrial_Automation, Accessed 28.05.2015.

[13] M. Robin, "Early detection of network threats using Software Defined Network (SDN) and virtualization," Master's thesis, Carleton University, Ottawa, 2013

[14] B. Genge and P. Haller, "A Hierarchical Control Plane for Software-Defined Networks-based Industrial Control Systems," IFIP Networking Conference and Workshop, 2016

[15] G. Ferro, "SDN and Security: Start Slow, But Start," Dark Reading Tech Digest, 2014, http://www.darkreading.com/operations/sdn-and-security-start-slow-but-start/d/d-id/1318273, Accessed 28.05.2015.

[16] D. D'souza, L. Perigo, and R. Hagens, "Improving QoS in a Software-Defined Network," University of Colorado, Boulder, Capstone 2016 Interdisciplinary Telecom Program, 2016, http://www.colorado.edu/itp/current-students/capstone-and-thesis/spring-2016-capstone-team-projects/capstone-2016-improving-qos, accessed 08.09.2016

[17] Fujitsu White Paper, "Software-Defined Networking for the Utilities and Energy Sector," 2014

[18] X. Dong, H. Lin, R. Tan, R. Iyer, and Z. Kalbarczyk, "Software-Defined Networking for Smart Grid Resilience: Opportunities and Challenges," Position Paper on CPSS 2015, April 14-17. 2015, Singapore

[19] D. Cronberger, "Software-Defined Networks," Cisco, 2014, http://www.industrial-ip.org/en/industrial-ip/convergence/software-defined-networks, Accessed 28.05.2015.

[20] HP, "Network functions virtualization," White Paper, Hewlett-Packard, 2014

[21] Open Networking Foundation, "Software-Defined Networking: The New Norm for Networks," white paper, https://www.opennetworking.org/images/stories/downloads/sdn-resources/white-papers/wp-sdn-newnorm.pdf, Accessed 28.05.2015.

[22] W. Braun and M. Menth, "Software-Defined Networking Using Open-Flow: Protocols, Applications and Architectural Design Choices," Future Internet, Volume 6, Issue 2, Pages 302-336, 2014

[23] P. Hu, "A System Architecture for Software-Defined Industrial Internet of Things," IEEE International Conference on Ubiquitous Wireless Broadband, ICUWB, 2015

[24] T. Mahmoodi, V. Kulkarni, W. Kellerer, P. Mangan, F. Zeiger, S. Spirou, I. Askoxylakis, X. Vilajosana, H. Einsiedler, and J. Quittek, "VirtuWind: virtual and programmable industrial network prototype deployed in operational wind park," Transactions on Emerging Telecommunications Technologies, Volume 27, Issue 9, Pages 1281-1288, Wiley, 2016

[25] J. Du and M. Herlich, "Sofware-defined Networking for Real-time Ethernet," 13th International Conference on Informatics in Control, Automation and Robotics, July 2016, Lisbon, Portugal

[26] R.C. Parks and E. Rogers, "Best practices in automation security," Security & Privacy, IEEE (Volume:6 , Issue: 6), pages 37-43., 2009.

[27] I. Fernandez, "Cybersecurity for Industrial Automation & Control Environments," White Paper, Frost&Sullivan and Schneider Electric, 2013.

[28] R. Millman, "How to secure the SDN infrastructure," ComputerWeekly, 2015, http://www.computerweekly.com/feature/How-to-secure-the-SDN-infrastructure, Accessed 28.05.2015.

[29] Open Networking Foundation, "Solution Brief: SDN Security Considerations in the Data Center," ONF, 2013, https://www.opennetworking.org/images/stories/downloads/sdn-resources/solution-briefs/sb-security-data-center.pdf, Accessed 28.05.2015.

[30] S. Hogg, "SDN Security Attack Vectors and SDN Hardening," Network World, 2014, http://www.networkworld.com/article/2840273/sdn/sdn-security-attack-vectors-and-sdn-hardening.html, Accessed 28.05.2015.

[31] D. Jorm, "SDN and Security," The ONOS project, 2015, http://onosproject.org/2015/04/03/sdn-and-security-david-jorm/, Accessed 28.05.2015.

FUZZBOMB : Fully-Autonomous Detection and Repair of Cyber Vulnerabilities

David J. Musliner, Scott E. Friedman, Michael Boldt, J. Benton, Max Schuchard, Peter Keller
Smart Information Flow Technologies (SIFT) Minneapolis, USA
{dmusliner,sfriedman,mboldt,jbenton,mschuchard,pkeller}@sift.net

Stephen McCamant
University of Minnesota, Minneapolis, USA
mccamant@cs.umn.edu

Abstract—**SIFT and the University of Minnesota teamed up to create a fully autonomous Cyber Reasoning System to compete in the DARPA Cyber Grand Challenge. Starting from our prior work on autonomous cyber defense and symbolic analysis of binary programs, we developed numerous new components to create FUZZBOMB. In this paper, we outline several of the major advances we developed for FUZZBOMB, including a content-agnostic binary rewriting system called BINSURGEON. We then review FUZZBOMB's performance in the first phase of the Cyber Grand Challenge competition.**

***Keywords*-autonomous cyber defense; symbolic analysis; protocol learning; binary rewriting.**

I. INTRODUCTION

In June 2014, DARPA funded seven teams to build autonomous Cyber Reasoning Systems (CRSs) to compete in the DARPA Cyber Grand Challenge (CGC). SIFT and the University of Minnesota together formed the FUZZBOMB team [1], building on our prior work on the FUZZBUSTER cyber defense system [2], [3], [4] and the FuzzBALL symbolic analysis tool [5], [6], [7].

SIFT's FUZZBUSTER system was built to automatically find flaws in software using symbolic analysis tools and fuzz testing, refine its understanding of the flaws using additional testing, and then synthesize *adaptations* (e.g., input filters or source-code patches) to prevent future exploitation of those flaws, while also preserving functionality. FUZZBUSTER includes an extensible plug-in architecture for adding new analysis and adaptation tools, along with a time-aware, utility-based meta-control system that chooses which tools are used on which applications during a mission [8]. Before the CGC began, FUZZBUSTER had already automatically found and shielded or repaired dozens of flaws in widely-used software including Linux tools, web browsers, and web servers.

In separate research, Prof. Stephen McCamant at the University of Minnesota had been developing the FuzzBALL tool to perform symbolic analysis of binary x86 code. FuzzBALL combines static analysis and symbolic execution to find flaws and proofs of vulnerability through heuristic-directed search and constraint solving. On a standard suite of buffer overflow vulnerabilities, FuzzBALL found inputs triggering all but one, many with less than five seconds of search [5].

Together, FUZZBUSTER and FuzzBALL provided the seeds of a strategic reasoning framework and deep binary analysis methods needed for our FUZZBOMB CRS. However, many challenges still had to be addressed to form a fully functioning and competitive CRS. In this paper, we outline several of the major advances we developed for FUZZBOMB, including a new content-agnostic binary rewriting system called BINSURGEON. We discuss the technical advances that allow BINSURGEON's template-based rewriting of stripped binaries to mitigate vulnerabilities. Finally, we review FUZZBOMB's performance in the qualifying round of the CGC competition, and discuss lessons learned.

II. BACKGROUND

A. DARPA's Cyber Grand Challenge

Briefly, the CGC is designed to be a simplified form of Capture the Flag game, in which DARPA supplies Challenge Binaries (CBs) that nominally perform some server-like function, responding to client connections and engaging in some behavioral protocol as the client and server communicate. The CBs are run on a modified Linux operating system called Decree, which provides a limited set of system calls. In the competition, CBs are provided as binaries only (no source code) and are undocumented, so the CRSs have no idea what function they are supposed to perform. However, in some cases a network packet capture (PCAP) file is provided, giving noisy, incomplete traces of normal non-faulting client/server interactions ("pollers"). Each CB contains one or more vulnerability that can be accessed by the client sending some inputs, leading to a program crash. To win the game, a CRS must find the vulnerability-triggering inputs (called Proofs of Vulnerability (PoVs)) and also repair the binary so that the PoVs no longer cause a crash, and all non-PoV poller behavior is preserved. The complex scoring system rewards finding PoVs, repairing PoVs, and preserving poller behavior, and penalizes increases in CB size and decreases in CB speed.

B. FUZZBUSTER

Since 2010, we have been developing FUZZBUSTER [9] under DARPA's CRASH program to use software analysis and adaptation to defeat a wide variety of cyber-threats. By coordinating the operation of automatic tools for software analysis, test generation, vulnerability refinement, and adaptation generation, FUZZBUSTER provides long-term immunity against both observed attacks and novel (zero-day) cyber-attacks.

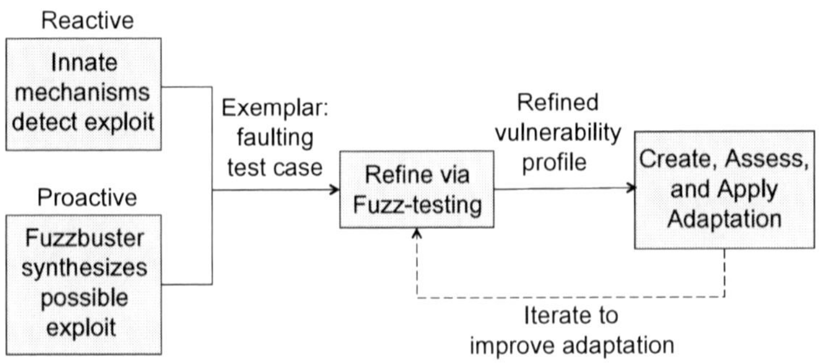

Figure 1. FUZZBUSTER refines both proactive and reactive fault exemplars into vulnerability profiles, then develops and deploys adaptations that remove vulnerabilities.

FUZZBUSTER operates both *reactively* and *proactively*, as illustrated in Figure 1. When an attacker deploys an exploit and triggers a program fault (or other detected misbehavior), FUZZBUSTER captures the operating environment and recent program inputs into a *reactive exemplar*. Similarly, when FUZZBUSTER's own software analysis and fuzz-testing tools proactively create a potential exploit, it is summarized in a *proactive exemplar*. These exemplars are essentially tests that indicate a (possible) vulnerability in the software, which FUZZBUSTER must characterize and then shield from future exploitation. For example, an exemplar could hold a particular long input string that arrived immediately before an observed program fault. Proactive exemplars based on program analysis may be more informative: they can represent not just a single faulting input, but a set of constraints that define vulnerability-triggering inputs. Reactive exemplars pose a greater threat, since they almost certainly indicate that an attacker has already found a software flaw.

Starting from an exemplar, FUZZBUSTER uses its program analysis tools and fuzz-testing tools to refine its understanding of the vulnerability, building a *vulnerability profile* (VP). For example, FUZZBUSTER can use concolic testing to find that the long-string reactive exemplar is triggering a buffer overflow, and the VP would capture this information. Or, FUZZBUSTER can use delta-debugging and other fuzzing tools to determine the minimal portion of the string that triggers the fault. Similarly, constraint relaxation can generalize symbolic analysis exemplars to find additional paths to a vulnerability.

At the same time, FUZZBUSTER tries to create software adaptations that shield or repair the underlying vulnerability. In the simplest case, FUZZBUSTER may choose to create a filter rule that blocks some or all of the exemplar input (i.e., stopping the same or similar attacks from working a second time). This may not shield the full extent of the vulnerability (or may be too broad, compromising normal operation), so FUZZBUSTER will keep working to refine the VP and develop more effective adaptations. Even symbolic analysis may not yield a minimal description of the inputs that can trigger a vulnerability: there may be many vulnerable paths, only some of which are summarized by a constraint description. Over time, as FUZZBUSTER refines the VP and gains a better understanding of the flaw, it may create more sophisticated and effective adaptations, such as filters that block strings based on length not exact content, or actual software patches that repair the buffer overflow flaw. As it creates and applies adaptations, FUZZBUSTER can choose to re-evaluate previous adaptations, keeping those that remain effective and replacing those that have been superceded. FUZZBUSTER already has sophisticated techniques for creating filters that eliminate vulnerability-triggering inputs, which can be used as network-layer filters or application wrappers.

As different adaptations are developed, FUZZBUSTER can assess their performance against the set of tests it has been accumulating for a particular application, determining how effectively each adaptation stops known faulting inputs and preserves the functionality of known non-faulting test cases (either observed in the wild or generated by FUZZBUSTER) [10][1]. For example, Figure 2 illustrates FUZZBUSTER's performance on two applications, showing how it finds vulnerabilities (indicated by faulting test cases, the solid red line) and creates adaptations (patches) that try to fix those faults. The dotted red line indicates the number of faulting test cases that no longer cause a fault in the patched application. We refer to the undesirable area between those red lines, during which known vulnerabilities are still exploitable, as the *exposure*.

The blue lines show the performance of the original application (solid blue) and patched application (dotted) on the non-faulting test cases. In the first example, Figure 2a, FUZZBUSTER's analysis of the detected flaw is perfect: its first patch fixes all the known faulting test cases and does not degrade performance on the reference test cases. In the second example, Figure 2b, FUZZBUSTER creates a series of different patches and filters to shield a large number of different faulting inputs, and in the process, some of those degrade the application's performance on the non-faulting test cases (i.e., a gap appears between the solid and dotted blue lines). However, eventually FUZZBUSTER replaces the lesser adaptations with highly refined adaptations that restore all of

[1] We call this "poor man's regression testing," since it does not require any manually-created regression tests.

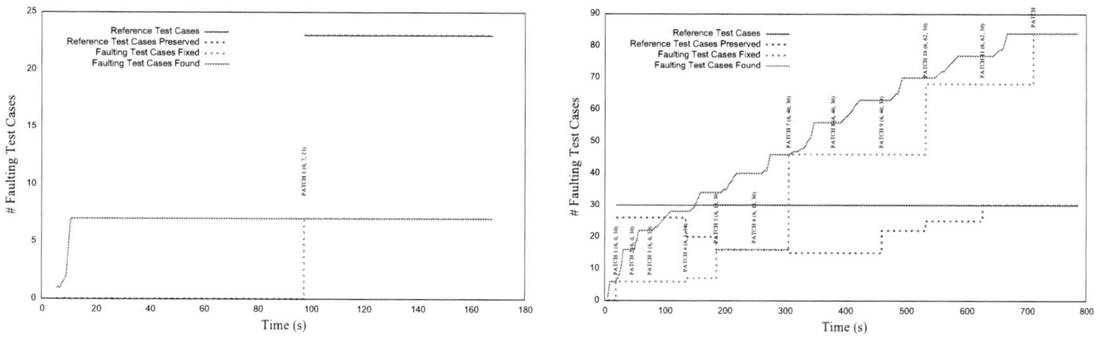

(a) (b)

Figure 2. FUZZBUSTER works continuously to derive better adaptations, improving an application's performance on faulting and non-faulting test cases.

the performance and still prevent exploitation of all the known vulnerabilities.

While FUZZBUSTER already had the coordination infrastructure and representation/reasoning to manage exemplars, VPs, and adaptations, many of the tools we had integrated could not apply to the CGC because they do not operate directly on binaries. To fill these gaps and support the full spectrum of vulnerability detection, exploitation, and repair needed for CGC, we integrated with UMN's FuzzBALL and also developed new components, as described in Section III.

C. FuzzBALL

FuzzBALL is a flexible engine for symbolic execution and automatic program analysis, targeted specifically at binary software. In the following paragraphs we briefly describe the concepts of symbolic execution and explain FuzzBALL's architecture, emphasizing its features aimed at binary code.

The basic principle of symbolic execution is to replace certain *concrete* values in a program's state with *symbolic variables*. Typically, symbolic variables are used to represent the inputs to a program or sub-function, and the symbolic analysis results in an understanding of what inputs can lead to different parts of a program. An interpreter executes the program, accumulating symbolic expressions for the results of computations that involve symbolic variables, and constraints (in terms of those symbols) that describe which conditional branches will occur. These symbolic expressions are valuable because they can summarize the effect of many potential concrete executions (i.e., many possible inputs). When a symbolic expression is used in a control-flow instruction, we call the formula that controls the target a *branch condition*. On a complete program run, the conjunction of the conditions for all the symbolic branches is the *path condition*. We can use an SMT solver [11], [12] (such as STP [13] or Z3 [14]) on a path condition to find a set of concrete input values that would cause the corresponding path to be executed, or to determine what other paths might be feasible.

Many symbolic execution tools operate on program source code (e.g., KLEE, Crest), but FuzzBALL is differentiated by its focus on symbolic execution of binary code. At its core, FuzzBALL is an interpreter for machine (e.g., x86) instructions, but one in which the values in registers and memory can be symbolic expressions rather than just concrete bit patterns. Figure 3 shows a graphical overview of FuzzBALL's architecture. As it explores possible executions of a binary, FuzzBALL builds a *decision tree* data structure. The decision tree is a binary tree in which each node represents the occurrence of a symbolic branch on a particular execution path, and a node has children labeled "false" and "true" representing the next symbolic branch that will occur in either case. FuzzBALL uses the decision tree to ensure that each path it explores is different, and that exploration stops if no further paths are possible.

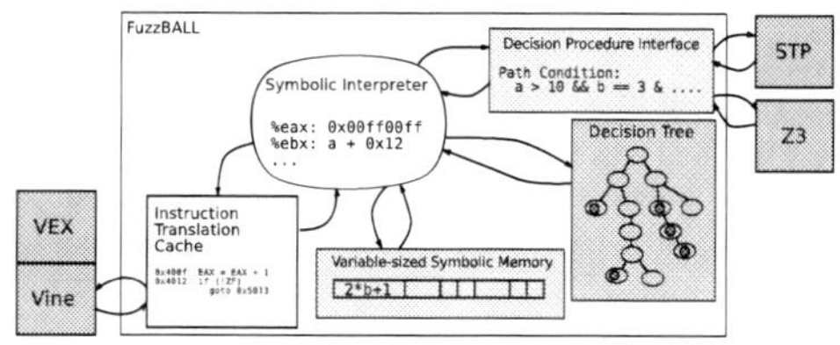

Figure 3. An overview of our FuzzBALL binary symbolic execution engine.

To factor out instruction-set complexity, FuzzBALL builds on the BitBlaze Vine library [15] for binary code analysis, which provides a convenient intermediate language (the "Vine IL") for representing instruction behavior. Another complexity that arises at the binary level is that because memory is untyped, loads may not have the same size and alignment as stores. For example, a location might be written with a 4-byte store and then read back with a sequence of 1-byte loads. FuzzBALL optimizes for the common case by representing symbolic values in memory at the granularity with which they were stored, if they are naturally aligned, using a tree structure. But it will automatically insert bitwise operations to subdivide or assemble values as needed.

We have used FuzzBALL on several CGC-relevant research projects, which typically build on the basic FuzzBALL engine by adding heuristics or other features specialized for a particular problem domain. Babić *et al.* [5] combined dynamic control-flow analysis, static memory access, and FuzzBALL to find test cases for buffer overflow vulnerabilities in binaries, using the results of static analysis to guide FuzzBALL's search toward potential vulnerabilities. Martignoni *et al.* [7] used FuzzBALL to generate high-coverage test cases for CPU emulators, illustrating how exhaustive exploration is feasible for small but critical code sequences. Caselden *et al.* [6] combined dynamic data-structure analysis and FuzzBALL to produce proof-of-concept exploits for vulnerabilities that are reached only after complex transformations of a program's input, using novel pruning and choice heuristics to efficiently find inverse images of transformations such as data compression.

For FuzzBomb and the CGC, we integrated FuzzBALL with the FuzzBuster reasoning framework and significantly extended FuzzBALL's program analysis capabilities.

III. New Developments

A. Hierarchical Architecture

We designed FuzzBomb to operate on our in-house cluster of up to 20 Dell Poweredge C6100 blade chassis, each holding eight Intel XEON Harpertown quad-core CPUs. To allocate this rack of computers, we designed a hierarchical command-and-control scheme in which different FuzzBomb agents play different roles. At the top of the hierarchy, several agents are designated as "Optimus", or leader agents. At any time, one is the primary leader, known as Optimus Prime (OP). All of the other Optimi are "hot backups," in case OP goes down for any reason (hardware failure, software crash, network isolation). All messages sent to OP are also sent to all of the other Optimi, so that their knowledge is kept up to date at all times. We enhanced our existing fault detection and leader election protocol methods to ensure that an OP is active in the cluster with very high reliability. Fault detection methods include monitoring communication channels (sockets) for failure and watchdog processes that send periodic messages to ensure liveness. The Optimi are given unique integer identifiers, and the next-in-order Optimus becomes Prime if the prior OP is determined to have failed; handshake messages ensure that the other Optimi agree on the new OP selection. We usually configure FuzzBomb with three Optimi, each run on a different hardware chassis in the cluster.

Below OP, a set of "FuzzBomb-Master" agents are designated, each to manage the reasoning about a single CB. OP's main job is allocating CBs to those Master agents and giving them each additional resources (other FuzzBombs, DVMs) to use to improve their score on a CB. A FuzzBomb-Master's job is improve its score on its designated CB, using its allocated computing resources in the best way possible (whether that is analysis, rewriting, or testing/scoring). As progress is made on each CB, the responsible FuzzBomb-Master will report that progress and the best-revised-CB-so-far back to OP.

OP's objective is to maximize the system's overall score, keeping in mind deadlines and other considerations. By design, OP should dynamically re-allocate the reasoning assets to the most challenging problems, to maximize the overall system's score. OP is also responsible for uploading FuzzBomb's final best answers to the government-supplied response location.

B. FuzzBALL Improvements

FuzzBomb uses an improved FuzzBALL symbolic execution engine in an approach that combines ideas from symbolic execution and static analysis in order to find vulnerabilities in binary programs. A static-style analysis identifies parts of the program that might contain a vulnerability. Then a symbolic execution search seeks an execution path from the start of the program to the possible vulnerability point that constitutes a proof of vulnerability. Symbolic execution generates a number of input constraint sets, each set representing a family of related program execution paths. The symbolic execution engine uses these constraint sets to determine the inputs to the program that can reach the program vulnerability, offering a proof-of-concept exploit. While exploring this space, the symbolic execution engine will encounter many decision points (such as conditional branches). Each of these decision points branches off a new set of paths, leading to an exponentially growing number of paths. Exploring this search space of paths represents a significant computational effort. Scaling up the search in a way that mitigates this path explosion poses a key challenge. To overcome this problem, we applied parallelization techniques and heuristic search improvements, as well as other algorithmic changes.

1) Heuristic Guidance: Because the space of program executions is vast, even in the constraint-based representations of symbolic reasoning, heuristic guidance is essential. For the CGC, the key objective is to guide the search towards potential vulnerabilities. FuzzBomb identifies potentially vulnerable instruction sequences and uses abstraction heuristics to focus the search towards those targets. Although a wide variety of source-level coding mistakes can leave a program vulnerable, these dangerous constructs are more uniform when viewed in terms of the binary-level capability they give to an attacker. For example, many types of source-code vulnerabilities create binary code in which the destination of an indirect jump instruction can be influenced by an attacker. The source-code and compiler details about why such a controllable jump arises are often irrelevant, and are not our focus. In particular, FuzzBomb does not try to decompile a binary back to a source language, nor will it identify which particular source code flaw describes a vulnerability. FuzzBomb's search guidance strategies target just these end-result capabilities; e.g., searching for an indirect jump that can be controlled to lead to attack code.

FuzzBomb uses ***problem relaxation heuristics*** to reduce the search space of possible executions, drawing on recent advances in heuristic search techniques for directed symbolic execution and Artificial Intelligence (AI) planning. To search through very large spaces, these techniques use rapid solutions to relaxed or approximate versions of their real problems to provide heuristic guidance. Over the last dozen years, research on relaxation heuristics has produced immense improvements in the scalability of AI planning and other techniques (e.g.,

[16], [17]). For example, Edelkamp *et al.* [16] report up to four orders of magnitude reduction in nodes searched in model-checking. Similarly, AI planning systems have gone from producing plans with no more than 15 steps to plans with hundreds of steps (representing many orders of magnitude improvement in space searched). These techniques are only now being applied to directed symbolic execution to help find program paths to vulnerabilities (e.g., Ma *et al.* [18]).

For FUZZBOMB, the problem is to find a symbolic execution path through a program that leads to a vulnerability. One key research challenge is finding the best relaxation method for symbolic execution domains. We developed an approach using causal graph heuristics found in AI planning search [19] to direct symbolic execution, in a manner similar to call-chain backwards symbolic execution [18]. These heuristics use factorization to generate a causal model of subproblems, then "abstract away" interactions between the subproblems to create a relaxed version of the problem that can be solved quickly at each decision point during search. In symbolic execution, solving the relaxed problem determines:

- A reachability analysis to a vulnerability. If the relaxation of the program indicates a vulnerability is unreachable from a particular program decision point, then exploring from that point is fruitless.
- A distance estimate at each decision point, that lets exploration proceed along an estimated shortest path.

To generate the relaxation heuristic, FUZZBOMB uses the causal model present within data-flow and control-flow graph (CFG) structures used in binary program analysis. For instance, in a CFG, nodes represent blocks of code and edges represent execution order. This provides a subproblem structure, allowing for bottom-up solving of each subproblem.

The FuzzBALL approach to hybrid symbolic execution and static analysis needed many other improvements to work on the CGC CBs. Our major developments have included:

- Porting to Decree— We adapted FuzzBALL to handle the unique CB format, including emulating the restricted Decree system calls and handling the specific limitations of the CB binary format.
- Improving over-approximated CFG methods— Prior to symbolic analysis, FuzzBALL requires the control flow graph (CFG) of the target binary. Various existing methods are all imperfect at recovering CFGs, but some can be combined. We developed a new CFG-recovery tool that leverages prior work on recursive disassembly along with an updated over-approximation method that finds all of the bit sequences in a binary representing valid addresses/offsets within the binary and treats those as possible jump targets. While this overapproximation is extreme, FUZZBOMB uses heuristics to reduce the size of the resulting CFGs.
- Detecting input-controllable jumps— As FuzzBALL extends branch conditions forward through the possible program executions, whenever it reaches a jump it formulates an SMT query asking whether the CB inputs could force the jump to 42 (i.e., an arbitrary address). If so, a likely vulnerability has been identified.
- Detecting null pointer dereferences, return address overwrites, etc.— FuzzBALL now uses similar methods to detect various other vulnerable behaviors.
- Making incremental solver calls— We have enhanced FuzzBALL's SMT solver interface so that it can behave incrementally. For example, after querying if a jump target is input-controllable, it can retract that final part of the SMT query and the SMT solver can retain some information it derived during the prior solver call. Microsoft's Z3 SMT solver is state of the art and supports this type of incremental behavior.
- Handling SSE floating point (FP)— The original FuzzBALL implementation used a slow, emulation-based method to handle floating point calculations, and it could not handle the modern SSE FP instructions. We have recently completed major extensions that allow FuzzBALL to handle SSE FP instructions using Z3. We have switched over to using Z3 by default, and are collaborating with both the Z3 and MathSAT5 developers to fix bugs in their solvers and improve their performance.
- Implementing veritesting— David Brumley's group coined this term for a flexible combination of dynamic symbolic execution (DSE) and static symbolic execution (SSE) used to reason in bulk about blocks of code that do not need DSE [20]. We completed our own first version of this capability, along with associated test cases and SMT heuristic improvements. However, as noted in Section VI, this improvement was not used during the actual competition because its testing and validation was not complete.

Symbolic execution can be expensive because it is completely precise; this precision ensures that the approach can always create proofs of vulnerabilities. At the same time, it is valuable to know about potentially dangerous constructs even before we can prove they are exploitable. To that end, we modified FuzzBALL to run as a hybrid of static analysis and symbolic execution techniques.

C. *Proofs of Vulnerability (PoVs)*

We developed two ways of creating PoVs. First, when FuzzBALL identifies a vulnerability that can be triggered by client inputs, it will have solved a set of constraints on the symbolic input variables that describe a class of PoVs for that vulnerability. Depending on the constraints, the PoV description may be more or less abstract (i.e., it may require very concrete inputs or describe a broad space of inputs that will trigger the vulnerability). For the concrete case, FUZZBOMB has a mechanism to translate FuzzBALL's constraints into the XML format required for a PoV.

Second, if a CB is provided with a PCAP file that illustrates how it interacts with one or more pollers, FUZZBOMB uses protocol reverse engineering techniques to derive an abstract description of the acceptable protocols for a CB. FUZZBOMB then feeds this protocol description into one or more fuzzing tools, to try to develop input XML files that trigger an unknown vulnerability.

We initially developed a protocol reverse engineering tool building on Antunes' ideas [21]. However, the techniques did not scale well to the large numbers of pollers present in the CGC example problems, and they are not robust to the packet loss present in the provided packet captures. We then developed a less elaborate protocol analysis tool which, while not providing a full view of the protocol state machine, allows FUZZBOMB to generate protocol sessions which are accepted by the CBs. This tool uses a heuristic approach, based on observations from prior work in the field [22], [23], [24], to identify likely protocol command elements, fields required for data delivery to the CBs (e.g. message lengths and field offsets), and message delimiters. Additionally, the protocol inference tool also attempts to identify session cookies and simple challenge/response exchanges that are required by the protocol. Significant effort was also required to process the DARPA-provided PCAP files because they contain unexpected packet losses and non-TCP-compliant behavior.

IV. BINARY REWRITING

Here we describe background on binary rewriting and related work to clarify the technical contribution of BINSURGEON, FUZZBOMB's binary rewriting subsystem.

A. *Control flow graphs*

BINSURGEON operates on a binary's Control Flow Graph (CFG) to modify the binary. For the purposes of BINSURGEON, a CFG is comprised of assembly instructions grouped into *blocks* with exactly one entry point and one exit point. At the exit point of any block, the program either (a) transitions to the entry point of the adjacent block in memory, (b) transitions the entry point of another block via a *control flow instruction* such as jumps or calls, or (c) terminates. These blocks and the control flows between them comprises the nodes and edges, respectively, of a directed— and often cyclic— graph.

The executable's functions are subgraphs of the CFG, often bounded by called blocks at the source(s) and return blocks at the sink(s), but exceptions exist, e.g., due to uncalled (or indirectly called) functions and functions that conclude with program termination rather than return instructions. To account for these exceptions, BINSURGEON infers function subgraphs by searching forward from called blocks and searching backward from return blocks, merging the intersecting block-sets, and also using common compiler idioms to identify function prologues and epilogues.

CFGs are recovered by disassembling the binary, which is a potentially-unsound process, since it is undecidable whether bytes in a stripped binary correspond to data or code [25], [26]. This means that a smaller rewrite to the CFG is better, all else being equal, since it relies on less of the potentially-incorrect subgraph of the CFG.

Figure 4 shows a small CFG snippet of a single function "Original Fn" rewritten by BINSURGEON to produce "Padded Fn" and then "Cookied Fn," as we describe in more detail

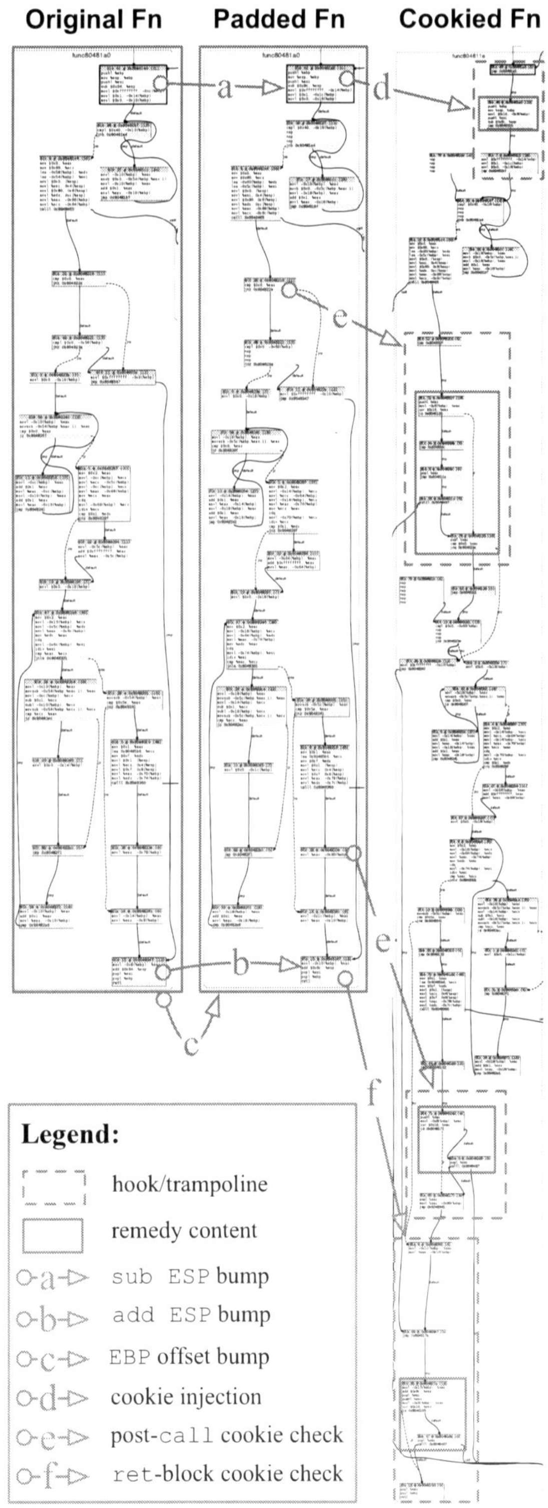

Figure 4. BINSURGEON rewrites a function to (1) add stack padding with space-preserving rewrites and (2) add a stack cookie with non-space-preserving rewrites.

in the next section. Instruction blocks are rendered as lists of instructions, with edges to subsequent blocks in the CFG. The shaded graphs are CFG subgraphs showing different revisions of the same function (original, padded, and cookied). Each directed edge from a version to the next indicates a single rewrite over the outlined blocks. The letter on each edge indicates the type of rewrite. For instance, there is one cookie injection (labeled "d") and two post-call cookie checks (labeled "e") written into the cookied function.

B. Revising CFGs

We distinguish between two types of revisions to a CFG, both of which are supported by BINSURGEON:

1) *Space-conserving* rewrites replace or remove instructions from the CFG without requiring additional space, e.g., by reordering instructions or substituting an instruction for an instruction of equal byte-size.
2) *Space-consuming* rewrites modify the CFG in a way that requires additional space, e.g., by adding instructions to existing functions/blocks or addition new functions altogether.

These rewrites have an important practical difference: space-conserving rewrites will preserve the integrity of the unchanged CFG; but space-consuming rewrites require instructions to be shifted or relocated entirely, which potentially changes the size and byte representation of instructions (including relative control flow instructions). Space-consuming rewrites may thereby cause arbitrarily-large ripples in the CFG, so they require special attention.

One technique for implementing space-consuming rewrites is to write a *trampoline*, where a `jmp` instruction is written over the existing instructions, and the overwritten instructions— and others to be injected— are written to a blank space in the binary, which is targeted by the first `jmp` and terminates in a `jmp` back to the existing control flow.

In Figure 4, solid outlines around rewritten blocks indicate a space-conserving rewrite, and dashed outlines around rewritten blocks indicate space-consuming rewrites that required a trampoline.

C. Related work in binary rewriting

Previous work has explored specialized binary rewriting to harden or diversify binaries. For instance, some rewriters perform targeted rewriting to inject single, specialized defenses such as stack cookies in return blocks [27] or control flow checks in return blocks or before indirect calls [28].

Many recent systems perform binary rewriting to increase diversity. *In-place code randomization* (IPCR) performs space-conserving rewrites to substitute and reorder instructions to help prevent code reuse attacks [29]. Similarly, *chronomorphic* programs perform space-conserving rewrites— including IPCR and block relocation— during their execution [30] to diversify themselves against code reuse attacks and cyber-reconnaissance (e.g., [31]). Other systems perform load-time binary rewriting to diversify binaries with a modified loader [26], [32]. These specialized rewriters locate blocks at randomized locations in memory and then ensure the CFG is intact.

TABLE I
OUTLINE OF BINSURGEON'S BINARY REWRITING PROCEDURE.

GIVEN: Set of insertions/deletions to the CFG.
Compute the scope of the rewrite:
- **SET** affected blocks B = blocks that will change content.
- **SET** frontier blocks $F = B$.
- **WHILE** any block $f \in F$ is too small to hold a `jmp` instruction, add f's source block(s) to F and B; remove f from F.

Label the graph and rewrite it:
- **CLAIM** all space presently occupied by B as freespace.
- **LABEL** every block in B and every internal control flow instruction accordingly.
- **HOOK** control flow at the previous start addresses of all F by writing labeled `jmp` instructions to their new labels.
- **REWRITE** the labled graph in memory with the insertions and deletions.

Inject the rewritten, labeled subgraph back into the binary:
- **ASSEMBLE** instructions to estimate their size in the binary.
- **PACK** instructions into freespaces.
- **TEST** the packing job by assembling a custom linker script.
  - **IF** we overflowed a freespace:
    - ∗ **IF** other freespaces are above `jmp` size, update instruction size(s) accordingly and **GOTO: PACK**.
    - ∗ **ELSE** return *not-enough-space*.

Repair BINSURGEON*'s CFG model in memory:*
- **REMOVE** nodes corresponding to former blocks B and all edges from those nodes.
- **ADD** nodes and incident edges for newly-assembled blocks B^{SIFT}.
- **SPLIT** blocks as necessary if new outward edges from B^{SIFT} fall between a block's entry and exit points.

Other methods exist for translating binaries into an intermediate representation (IR) (e.g., [33], [34]), and then rewriting them back into machine code, e.g., for diversity or safety purposes. In contrast to IR approaches, BINSURGEON rewrites the CFG and assembly instructions directly, which avoids potential IR translation errors and potential performance degradation by making local, targeted changes. As we demonstrate in the next section, the CFG and assembly instructions themselves are expressive enough to write diverse templates for program repair and defense.

Other tools such as DynInst[2] automatically instrument the binary, but they consume substantially higher disk space, memory footprint, or performance overhead. For example, DynInst's instrumentation has been shown to increase runtime overhead by 96% [35]; that performance penalty would have led to zero scores in the CGC.

BINSURGEON's rewrites are far less invasive and costly: BINSURGEON adds no universal function call hooks or virtualization, so the overhead of its modifications is only proportional to the specific installed defenses/repairs.

[2]http://www.dyninst.org/

V. REPAIR AND DEFENSE WITH BINSURGEON

Here we overview BINSURGEON's procedure for rewriting stripped, third-party binaries to add or remove arbitrary content [36]. We then describe some binary rewriting templates that BINSURGEON uses for program defense and repair as part of FUZZBOMB.

FUZZBOMB's binary rewriting algorithm is summarized in Table I. The procedure is given a CFG and a set of insertions and/or deletions to the CFG. The insertions and deletions are specified relative to existing instructions in the CFG (e.g., *insert instructions X before instruction y* or *delete instructions Z*). BINSURGEON does *not* use absolute addresses (e.g., *insert instructions X at address y*) for insertions and deletions, since making space-consuming changes could shift the addresses of subsequent instructions, thereby invalidating other absolute addresses.

BINSURGEON's rewriting procedure first identifies *affected* blocks that must be rewritten and relocated, as well as *frontier* blocks that will connect the affected blocks to the rest of the CFG. The affected blocks will be rewritten, and if BINSURGEON overflows these blocks, it will utilize (or append) remote *freespace* (i.e., available executable memory) within the binary. BINSURGEON identifies frontier blocks iteratively, since not all blocks are large enough to support `jmp` instructions (i.e., for a trampoline, described in Section IV-B). The frontier blocks serve as trampoline `jmp` sites for the affected blocks, which is the trampoline content.

After identifying affected and frontier blocks, BINSURGEON *labels* these blocks from their absolute addresses by injecting assembly labels before each block, and then it rewrites all internal control flow edges (i.e., conditional or unconditional jumps between affected blocks $b_1 \in B$ and $b_2 \in B$) to use these labels. BINSURGEON writes `jmp` instructions at the former entry point of each frontier block to build a compound trampoline into the labled affected blocks. BINSURGEON does not explicitly write `jmp` instructions *back* to the unmodified CFG; rather, it uses the existing control flow instructions of the labled blocks, which will be reassembled later in its procedure. It then rewrites the labeled, labled graph with the given insertions and deletions.

BINSURGEON next injects the rewritten, labled graph back into the binary, using the affected blocks' previous locations— and other claimed/extended executable memory— as freespace. This is a greedy, iterative process of instruction-packing: BINSURGEON finds the next freespace proximal to the last freespace (since near `jmp` instructions require fewer bytes) and writes as many instructions as possible, insofar as it can also write a `jmp` instruction to the next freespace.

After packing its freespaces, BINSURGEON writes out a custom linker script to assemble all of the desired instructions at the desired addresses. This converts every instruction of the labled CFG subgraph into the machine-executable, location-specific opcodes. If the assembling and linking succeeds, BINSURGEON writes the corresponding instruction bytes directly into the binary and reports success.

TABLE II
REMEDIES IMPLEMENTED BY BINSURGEON FOR FUZZBOMB

Support remedies add utilites for defense & repair: • `cleanup`: substitutes instructions in the CFG with instructions guaranteed to re-assemble. • `add-text-section`: appends a new executable section to the binary by extending or adding a program header. • `fn-inject`: adds new function(s) to the binary. • `fn-intercept`: intercepts existing functions by rerouting direct calls to new or existing functions. • `add-data-space`: adds space in the binary for static data storage.
Repair remedies address known PoVs: • `terminate`: injects instruction(s) to terminate the program at the PoV location. • `o/w-terminate`: overwrite existing instructions to terminate the program at the PoV location. • `null-ptr-check`: test a register or memory address, and terminate if zero. • `stack-top-cookie`: write a cookie value to the top of the program stack. Check it at the PoV location; terminate if overwritten. • `heap-cookie`: intercept malloc, write a cookie value after each allocation. Check it at the PoV location; terminate if overwritten. • `bss-cookie`: write cookie value(s) into the binary's static data segment. Check it at the PoV location; terminate if overwritten.
Repair & Defense addresses known/unknown vulns: • `stack-pad`: increase stack frame size; decrement all base pointer offsets below a given threshold. • `stack-cookie`: write a constant to frame pointer between local variables or before the return address. Check the cookie upon return or after function calls; terminate if overwritten. • `range-check`: if a memory address (e.g., pointer or function pointer) is not within a given range (e.g., text section), terminate. • `receive-check`: intercept input functions and terminate if they will write to illegal memory ranges. • `cfi`: range-based control flow integrity on return addresses and indirect `call` and `jmp` addresses.

In some cases, the assembled instructions may overflow a freespace. This occurs when BINSURGEON underestimates instruction sizes and thereby over-packs a freespace. In these cases, BINSURGEON updates its size estimates and attempts to re-pack in the remaining freespaces. Otherwise, if it has no more freespace, BINSURGEON reports that it needs more space.

Finally, BINSURGEON repairs its in-memory model of the program CFG, since the insertions and deletions may well have changed existing functions and blocks connectivity or added new functions and blocks altogether.

BINSURGEON's rewriting procedure is *content agnostic*, which means its rewriting *capability* is decoupled from the rewritten *content*. As a practical consideration, this allowed us to develop BINSURGEON independently of the repair and defense templates it deployed for FUZZBOMB.

A. Repairing & Defending Binaries

BINSURGEON uses rewriting templates— which we call *remedies*— to harden and repair binaries. Figure 5 shows a

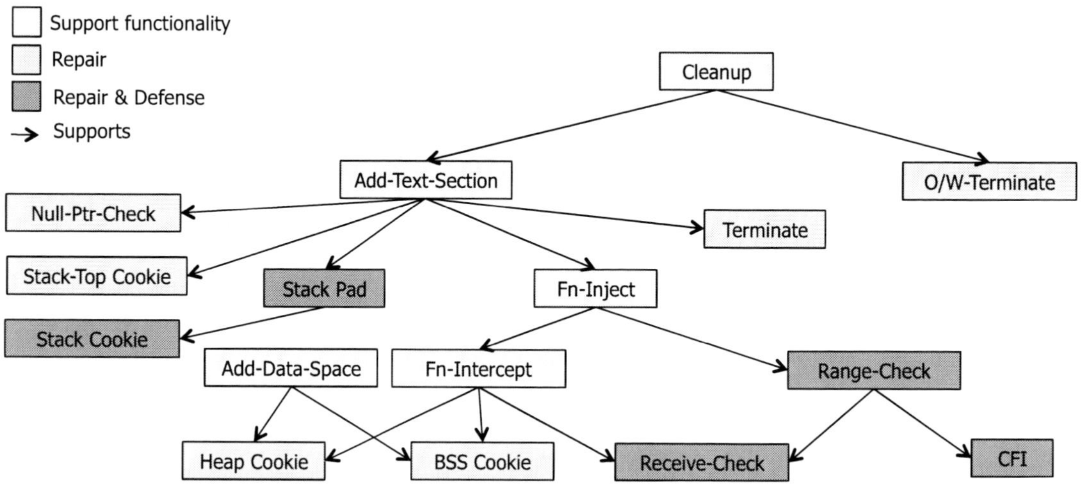

Figure 5. Remedies for templated binary rewriting, including support functionality, targeted repair templates, and defensive templates.

dependence graph of remedies, since some remedies depend on others' functionality, and Table II lists a brief description of each remedy. Each remedy takes one or more parameters (e.g., a vulnerable function or instruction) and produces a set of instruction insertions and deletions to use with BINSURGEON's rewriting procedure.

These specific remedies are designed to avoid compromised states or terminate the program when a compromised state exists. Intuitively, when the program is in a compromised state— or in program states where compromise is imminent and unavoidable— terminating the program safely is preferable to relinquishing control to a cyberattack.

These remedies do not fix the *underlying* problems, such as overflows or off-by-one errors; rather, they mitigate the adverse, exploitable manifestations. Templated repair of the underlying problems are the focus of some source-code repair systems (e.g., [37]), which is evidence that we can also develop BINSURGEON templates to fix underlying problems if they are adequately described. Next, we describe some novel and/or counter-intuitive remedies in additional depth.

The simplest remedies are `terminate` and `o/w-terminate`, which terminate the program at a specified location in the CFG. The `o/w-terminate` (overwrite) remedy does this without first allocating freespace, in case the binary cannot be properly extended.

The `stack-pad` and `stack-cookie` remedies are used in succession to protect a function's stack frame by (1) adding padding to a stack frame before or between the local variables, and (2) writing a *cookie* value within that padding, to flag an overflow if it is overwritten. Figure 4 illustrates the injections and deletions specified by these remedies as performed by BINSURGEON: `stack-pad` (Figure 4, middle) revises the setup and reset of the stack frame (Figure 4 [a] and [b], respectively) and revises all references to the stack via the base pointer (Figure 4[c]); and `stack-cookie` (Figure 4, right) injects a cookie at the head of the function (Figure 4[d]), and adds cookie checks after each function call (Figure 4[e]) and at the return block (Figure 4[f]).

One of the most complex remedies used within FUZZBOMB is the `heap-cookie`. This remedy template is comprised of the following modifications:

1) Injecting functions that intercept memory management functions, e.g., `malloc` and `free`, that allocate and free an extra byte, respectively, and write a specific value to the extra byte, and store the location of the byte within an injected array.
2) Overwriting `call` instructions to `malloc` and `free` to instead invoke the injected functions.
3) Inject a cookie-checking function that iteratively checks the cookie array, and terminates if any have changed value.
4) Inject a call to the cookie-checking function at the location of the PoV.

In conjunction, these modifications to the CFG cause the program to add an extra cookie-byte to each heap allocation and then check these cookie-bytes where specified, terminating if it senses an overwrite.

VI. RESULTS AND CONCLUSIONS

The first year of CGC involved three opportunities to assess FUZZBOMB's performance: two practice Scored Events (SE1 and SE2) and the CGC Qualifying Event (CQE), which determined which competitors would continue to the second year of competition. In SE1, DARPA released fifteen challenge binaries, some of which had multiple vulnerabilities. At the time, FUZZBOMB had only recently become operational on our computing cluster, and it did not solve many of the problems. However, with access to the source of the SE1 examples and many bug fixes, some months later we had improved FUZZBOMB enough that it was able to find vulnerabilities in four of the problems, including at least one undocumented flaw. For each of those vulnerabilities, FUZZBOMB had a repair that was able to stop the vulnerability from being attacked while also preserving all of the functionality tested by up to 1000 provided test cases. FUZZBOMB also create defensive rewrites for all of the other binaries. In SE2, DARPA provided nine new challenge binaries in addition to the prior fifteen, giving a total of twenty-four. Each problem was supplied with either no PCAPs or a PCAP file containing up to 1000 client/server interactions. At the time of SE2, FUZZBOMB was only able to find two of the new vulnerabilities, but that performance was enough to earn fourth place, when the SE1 problems were included in the ranking.

Our progress in improving the system was slowed by major problems with the government-provided testing system: running parallel tests interfered with each other, and running batches of serialized tests could cause false negatives, hiding vulnerabilities. This meant we had to run tests one at a time, incurring major overhead and making test-running a major bottleneck (especially when given 1000 tests from PCAPs, or when FUZZBOMB created many tests itself). We finally resolved these issues by discarding the provided testing tool and writing our own. Our tool supported safe parallel testing and increased testing speeds by at least two orders of magnitude. However, it took many weeks to come to that conclusion. Several key analysis functions were not completed, including handling challenge problems that had multiple communicating binary programs, complete support for SSE floating point instructions, and veritesting. We also were not able to build the ability to have the system re-allocate compute nodes to different CBs or to different functions (DVM vs. running FuzzBALL). By the time of the CQE, in June 2015, FUZZBOMB was only able to fully solve seven of the twenty-four SE2 problems. If given the PoVs for the twenty-four problems, the repair system was able to fix twelve CBs perfectly, and the defense system earned additional points on the remaining CBs.

For CQE, DARPA provided 131 all-new problems to the twenty-eight teams who participated (out of 104 originally registered). Each problem was supplied with either no PCAPs or a single client/server interaction. Unfortunately, this singleton PCAP triggered an unanticipated corner case in FUZZBOMB's logic: the protocol analysis concluded that every element of the single client/server interaction was a constant, so the extracted protocol had no variables to fuzz. And the default fuzz-testing patterns were not used because there *was* a protocol extracted. Thus FUZZBOMB's fuzzing was completely disabled for all of the challenge problems. Also, because the re-allocation functionality was not available, we had to pre-allocate the number of DVMs vs. FuzzBALL symbolic search engines. We chose to use 325 DVMs and only 156 FUZZBOMBS, because testing had been such a bottleneck. However, since there were almost no test cases provided in the PCAP files and fuzzing was disabled, FUZZBOMB had very few tests to run, and the DVMs were largely idle. With most CBs having only a single FuzzBALL search engine, there was little parallel search activity, and FUZZBOMB only found vulnerabilities in 12 CBs (some using prior SE2 PoVs). Of those, with the limited testing available, repair was only able to perfectly fix six (as far as our system could tell). Defense rewrote all of the remaining problems.

When the final CQE scores were revealed, FUZZBOMB came in tenth place and did not qualify to continue in the competition (only the top seven teams qualified). In addition to the singleton PCAP files and other issues, we learned of another "curveball" when the scores were released: among the 131 test cases, there were 590 known vulnerabilities, an average of more than 4.5 flaws per binary. In hindsight, FUZZBOMB's defensive system should have been much more aggressive in adding blind checks, to try to capture some points from all of those flaws. Our conservative rationale had been that retaining performance was more important, but with that many flaws per CB, the balance is changed. Even so, defensive rewriting earned FUZZBOMB more points than its active analysis and repair capability. This result supports our notion that CGC-relevant flaws boil down to a small number of patterns in binary, and can be addressed with a small number of repair/defense strategies.

Fortunately, the story is not over for FUZZBOMB; we have other customers who are interested in the technology, and we are actively pursuing transition opportunities to more real-world cyber defense applications.

ACKNOWLEDGMENTS

This work was supported by DARPA and Air Force Research Laboratory under contract FA8750-14-C-0093. The views expressed are those of the author(s) and do not reflect the official policy or position of the Department of Defense or the U.S. Government.

REFERENCES

[1] D. J. Musliner, S. E. Friedman, M. Boldt, J. Benton, M. Schuchard et al., "Fuzzbomb: Autonomous cyber vulnerability detection and repair," in Proceedings INNOV 2015: The Fourth International Conference on Communications, Computation, Networks and Technologies, 2015.

[2] D. J. Musliner, J. M. Rye, D. Thomsen, D. D. McDonald, M. H. Burstein et al., "Fuzzbuster: Towards adaptive immunity from cyber threats," in Proc. SASO-11 Awareness Workshop, October 2011.

[3] ——, "Fuzzbuster: A system for self-adaptive immunity from cyber threats," in Proc. Eighth Int'l Conf. on Autonomic and Autonomous Systems, March 2012.

[4] D. J. Musliner, J. M. Rye, and T. Marble, "Using concolic testing to refine vulnerability profiles in fuzzbuster," in SASO-12: Adaptive Host and Network Security Workshop at the Sixth IEEE Int'l Conf. on Self-Adaptive and Self-Organizing Systems, September 2012.

[5] D. Babić, L. Martignoni, S. McCamant, and D. Song, "Statically-directed dynamic automated test generation," in Proceedings of the ACM/SIGSOFT International Symposium on Software Testing and Analysis (ISSTA), Toronto, ON, Canada, July 2011.

[6] D. Caselden, A. Bazhanyuk, M. Payer, S. McCamant, and D. Song, "HI-CFG: Construction by binary analysis, and application to attack polymorphism," in ESORICS'13: European Symposium on Research in Computer Security, London, UK, Sep. 2013.

[7] L. Martignoni, S. McCamant, P. Poosankam, D. Song, and P. Maniatis, "Path-exploration lifting: Hi-fi tests for lo-fi emulators," in Proceedings of the 17th International Conference on Architectural Support for Programming Languages and Operating Systems (ASPLOS), London, UK, Mar. 2012.

[8] D. J. Musliner, S. E. Friedman, J. M. Rye, and T. Marble, "Meta-control for adaptive cybersecurity in FUZZBUSTER," in Proc. IEEE Int'l Conf. on Self-Adaptive and Self-Organizing Systems, September 2013.

[9] S. E. Friedman, D. J. Musliner, and J. M. Rye, "Improving automated cybersecurity by generalizing faults and quantifying patch performance," International Journal on Advances in Security, vol. 7, no. 3-4, 2014, pp. 121–130.

[10] D. J. Musliner, S. E. Friedman, T. Marble, J. M. Rye, M. W. Boldt et al., "Self-adaptation metrics for active cybersecurity," in Proc. Adaptive Host and Network Security Workshop at the IEEE Int'l Conf. on Self-Adaptive and Self-Organizing Systems, September 2013.

[11] S. Ranise and C. Tinelli, "The SMT-LIB format: An initial proposal," in Pragmatics of Decision Procedures in Automated Reasoning (PDPAR), Miami, FL, USA, Jun. 2003.

[12] R. Nieuwenhuis, A. Oliveras, and C. Tinelli, "Solving SAT and SAT modulo theories: From an abstract davis–putnam–logemann–loveland procedure to DPLL(t)," J. ACM, vol. 53, no. 6, 2006, pp. 937–977.

[13] V. Ganesh and D. L. Dill, "A decision procedure for bit-vectors and arrays," in Computer Aided Verification (CAV), Berlin, Germany, Jul. 2007.

[14] L. de Moura and N. Bjørner, "Z3: An efficient SMT solver," in Tools and Algorithms for the Construction and Analysis of Systems (TACAS), ser. LNCS, vol. 4963. Springer, Apr. 2008, pp. 337–340.

[15] D. Song, D. Brumley, H. Yin, J. Caballero, I. Jager et al., "BitBlaze: A new approach to computer security via binary analysis," in Proceedings of the 4th International Conference on Information Systems Security. Keynote invited paper., Hyderabad, India, Dec. 2008.

[16] S. Edelkamp, V. Schuppan, D. Bosnacki, A. Wijs, A. Fehnker et al., "Survey on directed model checking," in Model Checking and Artificial Intelligence, 2008, pp. 65–89.

[17] J. Benton, A. J. Coles, and A. Coles, "Temporal planning with preferences and time-dependent continuous costs," in International Conference on Automated Planning and Scheduling, 2012.

[18] K.-K. Ma, K. Y. Phang, J. S. Foster, and M. Hicks, "Directed symbolic execution," in Static Analysis Symposium (SAS), Venice, Italy, Sep. 2011, pp. 95–111.

[19] M. Helmert, "The fast downward planning system," Journal of Artificial Intelligence Research, vol. 26, no. 1, 2006, pp. 191–246.

[20] T. Avgerinos, A. Rebert, S. K. Cha, and D. Brumley, "Enhancing symbolic execution with veritesting," in Proceedings of the 36th International Conference on Software Engineering, 2014, pp. 1083–1094. [Online]. Available: http://doi.acm.org/10.1145/2568225.2568293

[21] J. Antunes, N. Neves, and P. Verssimo, "Reverse engineering of protocols from network traces," in Proc. 18th Working Conf. on Reverse Engineering (WCRE), 2011.

[22] W. Cui, V. Paxson, N. Weaver, and R. H. Katz, "Protocol-independent adaptive replay of application dialog." in NDSS, 2006.

[23] W. Cui, J. Kannan, and H. Wang, "Discoverer: Automatic protocol reverse engineering from network traces," in Proceedings of 16th USENIX Security Symposium on USENIX Security Symposium. USENIX Association, 2007, pp. 1–14.

[24] G. Wondracek, P. Comparetti, C. Kruegel, and E. Kirda, "Automatic network protocol analysis," in 15th Symposium on Network and Distributed System Security (NDSS), 2008.

[25] R. Wartell, Y. Zhou, K. W. Hamlen, M. Kantarcioglu, and B. Thuraisingham, "Differentiating code from data in x86 binaries," in Machine Learning and Knowledge Discovery in Databases. Springer, 2011, pp. 522–536.

[26] R. Wartell, V. Mohan, K. W. Hamlen, and Z. Lin, "Binary stirring: Self-randomizing instruction addresses of legacy x86 binary code," in Proceedings of the 2012 ACM conference on Computer and communications security. ACM, 2012, pp. 157–168.

[27] A. Baratloo, N. Singh, T. K. Tsai et al., "Transparent run-time defense against stack-smashing attacks." in USENIX Annual Technical Conference, General Track, 2000, pp. 251–262.

[28] M. Zhang and R. Sekar, "Control flow integrity for cots binaries." in USENIX Security, 2013, pp. 337–352.

[29] V. Pappas, M. Polychronakis, and A. D. Keromytis, "Smashing the gadgets: Hindering return-oriented programming using in-place code randomization," in Security and Privacy (SP), 2012 IEEE Symposium on. IEEE, 2012, pp. 601–615.

[30] S. E. Friedman, D. J. Musliner, and P. K. Keller, "Chronomorphic programs: Runtime diversity prevents exploits and reconnaissance," International Journal on Advances in Security, vol. 8, no. 3-4, 2015, pp. 120–129.

[31] A. Bittau, A. Belay, A. Mashtizadeh, D. Mazieres, and D. Boneh, "Hacking blind," in Proceedings of the 35th IEEE Symposium on Security and Privacy, 2014.

[32] A. Gupta, S. Kerr, M. S. Kirkpatrick, and E. Bertino, "Marlin: A fine grained randomization approach to defend against rop attacks," in Network and System Security. Springer, 2013, pp. 293–306.

[33] P. Anderson and M. Zarins, "The codesurfer software understanding platform," in Program Comprehension, 2005. IWPC 2005. Proceedings. 13th International Workshop on. IEEE, 2005, pp. 147–148.

[34] D. Brumley, I. Jager, T. Avgerinos, and E. J. Schwartz, "Bap: a binary analysis platform," in Computer aided verification. Springer, 2011, pp. 463–469.

[35] M. A. Laurenzano, M. M. Tikir, L. Carrington, and A. Snavely, "PEBIL: Efficient static binary instrumentation for linux," in Proc. IEEE Int'l Symp. on Performance Analysis of Systems and Software, 2010.

[36] S. E. Friedman and D. J. Musliner, "Automatically repairing stripped executables with CFG microsurgery," in Submitted to Adaptive Host and Network Security Workshop at the IEEE Int'l Conf. on Self-Adaptive and Self-Organizing Systems, 2015.

[37] D. Kim, J. Nam, J. Song, and S. Kim, "Automatic patch generation learned from human-written patches," in Proceedings of the 2013 International Conference on Software Engineering. IEEE Press, 2013, pp. 802–811.

A Risk Assessment of Logical Attacks on a CEN/XFS-based ATM Platform

Johannes Braeuer
Dept. of Information Systems
Johannes Kepler University Linz
Linz, Austria
email: johannes.braeuer@jku.at

Bernadette Gmeiner
Banking Automation
KEBA AG
Linz, Austria
email: b.gmeiner@outlook.com

Johannes Sametinger
Dept. of Information Systems
Johannes Kepler University Linz
Linz, Austria
email: johannes.sametinger@jku.at

Abstract— **Automated Teller Machines (ATMs) contain considerable amounts of cash and process sensitive customer data to perform cash transactions and banking operations. In the past, criminals mainly focused on physical attacks to gain access to cash inside an ATM's safe. For example, they captured customer data on the magnetic strip of an ATM card with skimming devices during insertion of the card. These days, criminals increasingly use logical attacks to manipulate an ATM's software in order to withdraw cash or to capture customer data. To understand the risks that arise from such logical attacks, we have conducted a risk assessment of an ATM platform. This ATM platform is running in a real bank environment and is built on the CEN/XFS specification. The result of this assessment has revealed the main issues that are responsible for vulnerabilities of an ATM platform. The risk assessment has identified effective countermeasures and has additionally provided a prioritization of activities for ATM manufacturers.**

Keywords*— *ATM security; logical ATM attacks; XFS; embedded system security; risk assessment.

I. Introduction

This paper represents an extended version of a previously published article [1]. It provides more details about the risk assessment and discusses the findings in a broader sense.

Automated Teller Machines (ATMs) have their roots back in the late 1930s, but they began to revolutionize the banking environment in the 1960s [2]. With the integration of real-time terminals, ATMs have been developed to data processing units that contained commercially available computers. Today, almost all three million ATMs around the world are running on the operating system (OS) Windows [3]. On top of Windows, an ATM platform controls all peripheral devices and uses the OS to communicate with device drivers. The ATM platform also provides an interface to multi-vendor ATM software, i.e., bank applications that utilize the functionality of the platform. Besides Windows, ATMs use the Internet Protocol (IP) for communication in the banking network [4]. Consequently, the ATM network is part of the banking network, which in turn is part of the Internet. All in all, ATMs have developed from stand-alone equipment with simple cash dispensing capabilities to a network of connected devices for bank transactions.

ATMs contain a remarkable amount of cash for their daily operation. Moreover, they are available around the clock and often located off-premises [5]. They have always been an attractive target for thieves and fraudsters [6]. Fraudulent activities are not only attracted by cash, but also by data that is required to conduct bank transactions. A further type of ATM attacks addresses malicious activities that impair the computer or the network of ATMs. Known as logical attacks, there is the common opinion that they are becoming more sophisticated and based on a well-organized execution. For example, representatives of malware, such as Skimer, Ploutus, or Stuxnet are indicators that these attacks bring up new challenges in securing ATMs and for providing secure banking environments. Furthermore, the XFS specification – see Section V – that represents the main reference for ATM engineers, is out-of-date and missing two-factor authentication for bank applications [7].

We will show an approach for the above mentioned problems and present additional details for implementing a risk assessment at an ATM. This risk assessment aims at providing information to select adequate countermeasures and controls for mitigating the likelihood or impact of risks. We have conducted the risk assessment concentrating on logical risks of an existing ATM platform. While the scope of the assessment is limited to logical risks, the used approach can easily be extended to physical risks and risks resulting from card and currency fraud. Early results of the risk assessment presented in this paper have been published previously at a conference [1]. Here, we provide a more detailed view on the conducted risk assessment including a broader discussion of the identified countermeasures. Besides, we use more recently published information on problems of the specification that is used by ATM manufactures.

In this paper, we will first provide an overview of attacks to ATMs as well as their countermeasures. We will then evaluate the countermeasures for logical attacks by a risk assessment. As a result, we can confirm that suggested countermeasures work for the identified risks. Additionally, we prioritize these countermeasures and provide a guideline for those responsible for ATM security.

The remainder of the paper is structured as follows: Section II provides an overview of criminal activities in context of ATMs and discusses traditional attacks and countermeasures. Section III concentrates on logical ATM security. In Section IV, the used risk assessment approach is presented, which is then applied in Section V to determine the risks of an ATM platform. Findings are discussed in Section VI. Related work and a conclusion follow in Sections VII and VIII, respectively.

II. Automated Teller Machines

An ATM is a cash dispensing machine with the capability to credit or debit a customer account without human intervention [2]. The term ATM has been used synonymously for cash machines, cash dispensers or cash recyclers. However, the designation ATM is inappropriate when a machine cannot perform a complete financial transaction initiated by the customer. In other words, an ATM has to support synchronous or asynchronous electronic data processing operations in an online and real-time manner [2]. With these capabilities in place, ATMs have revolutionized the way of banking. Their widespread dissemination has grown to a worldwide use of around 2.8 million ATMs. This number is expected to reach 3.7 million by 2018 [8].

ATMs have always been an attractive target for thieves. This problem is reinforced by the fact that ATMs are typically available 24/7, often located off-premises, and vulnerable to cash thefts [5]. However, ATM crime, including ATM fraud, goes beyond stealing cash inside the safe. Illegally obtaining personal information of customers, such as bank account data, card number, or PIN is an additional security issue related to ATMs [5][7]. While these digital assets do not provide an immediate profit, they can be sold on illegal credit card data markets [10]. From a general viewpoint, there are three different types of attacks: card and currency fraud, physical attacks and logical attacks [11]. Various Information Technology (IT) security standards have been developed and vendors have recommended security concepts pertaining to ATMs [12]. The goal is to secure an entire ATM and its environment. Similar to ATM crime, ATM security can be divided into the three different core areas: namely, card and currency protection, physical security, and logical security. The former two are briefly addressed in the next subsections. Logical ATM security is more important to the context of our work and follows in Section III.

A. *Card and Currency Fraud*

Card and currency frauds include direct attacks to steal cash or cards as well as indirect attacks to steal sensitive cardholder data that is later used to create fake cards for fraudulent withdrawals [10]. The target of these attacks is a single ATM, which may be physically manipulated for skimming, card fishing and currency trapping. Skimming is the approach to install an additional device, called a card skimmer, to capture the card's information on the magnetic strip. Lower tech card fishing and currency trapping focus on either card or cash capturing, typically using thin plates, thin metallic stripes, transparent plastic film, wires and hooks [5]. There are several security methods that deal with this threat category. Jitters, for example, vary speed and movement of cards or introduce motion. In other words, it distorts the magnetic stripe details and makes it difficult for the skimmer to read data while the card reader pulls the card into the ATM [13]. A further approach of an anti-skimming module is a jammer with the aim to disrupt a skimmer attached to the ATM dashboard. Instead of working on a mechanical level, a jammer uses an electromagnetic field to protect the cards' magnetic strips. Hence, the card reader can generate an error code that can be traced by remote monitoring tools [5].

B. *Physical Attacks*

Attacks that result in the physical damage of the entire ATM or a component thereof primarily focus on stealing cash from the safe [11]. But, some of these attacks are also conducted to prepare a further malicious activity on a single ATM. Vulnerable and easy targets for such attacks are offsite ATMs that are open to the public, less protected and lighter compared to bank-located machines [14]. Physical security guidelines recommend seismic detectors, magnetic contacts, alarm control panels, access control and heat sensors as alarm equipment [15]. Seismic detectors indicate abnormal vibrations and can cry havoc if an ATM is about to be raided. Heat sensors detect any form of unnatural temperature rise. Volumetric detectors on the wall can detect movements in the ATM's surrounding area. Intelligent bank note neutralization or degradation systems use bank note staining. A trigger becomes activated in case an inappropriate movement of the cassettes takes place. As a result, stolen banknotes get marked with a degradation agent or a dye.

III. Logical ATM Security

Logical attacks have become more sophisticated and their execution has typically been well organized [5][7][8]. Recent examples, such as Skimer [16], Ploutus [17], Stuxnet [18] and a logical attack demonstrated at the chaos computing club congress [19] are indicators that these attacks bring up new methods and approaches to ATM crime.

ATM malware is designed to steal cardholder data and PINs or to withdraw cash [13][15]. Typically, malware hides in the system to remain undetected as long as possible. It impairs confidentiality, integrity and authenticity of transaction data for its particular intention [5][10]. ATM networks are based on the Internet protocol and face the same attacks as other IP-related networks, e.g., denial of service (DoS), sniffing, man-in-the-middle attacks, or eavesdropping [3][10]. Communication between ATM and host can be used as entry point to launch remote attacks [5]. Even network devices like routers and switches can be targeted [4]. Logical security focuses on maintaining a secure network, protecting the OS and designing a system so that intruders cannot threaten cardholder's data and software components [5][10]. Subsequent subsections describe such measures.

A. *Cardholder Data Protection*

Sensitive data is the main target of logical attacks [22]. The Payment Card Industry (PCI) Data Security Standard (DSS) is for the protection of sensitive cardholder and authentication data. It proposes a set of twelve requirements divided into six areas [22]. Based on these requirements we have identified four security controls, which are needed to protect cardholder data:

- *Change control* - to guarantee that necessary and wanted changes are made only
- *Data masking* - to disguise cardholder data
- *User access control* - to restrict permsissions
- *Password policy* - to hamper password guessing

B. Host-based Firewall

To operate a secure ATM network, logical ATM security systems must be in place [5]. A firewall and a monitoring system to analyze and authenticate connection attempts are recommended in order to build such a layer of defense [5]. Instead of installing a central firewall, an integrated firewall on the ATM is feasible, controlling network communications on the processes, protocols and ports level [10].

C. Application Control

Traditional security software like antivirus software is used on desktop PCs to prevent unauthorized software execution. But, antivirus software requires processing power that often goes beyond the capabilities of an ATM and relies on a signature database that needs periodic updates. These updates can only provide protection against known malware. Consequently, malware prevention must operate within the limited resources and with a minimal "footprint" to avoid complications with ATM software [10]. Whitelisting restricts software running on an ATM to a known set of applications [10] that are tested and approved for execution. Unapproved software outside the list and malware are prohibited.

D. Full Hard Disk Encryption

Some logical attacks bypass security protection by booting the ATM from an alternative medium, such as a USB stick or CD-ROM. This circumvention provides the possibility to manipulate configurations or to put malware in place [23]. As a countermeasure, the ATM hard disk can be protected with full hard disk encryption [23]. In addition, it is recommended to encrypt data on an ATM's hard disk to make it unreadable in case of theft or unauthorized access [11]. Physically protecting the hard disk is an additional safeguard, because data access becomes more difficult.

E. Patch Management

Logical security includes the handling of software vulnerabilities by patch management to ensure the efficiency and security of ATMs in a timely and efficient manner. Continuous patch management provides protection against viruses, worms and known vulnerabilities within an OS [24]. An example in this context is the Slammer virus, which was responsible for network outages of different systems, such as ATMs with Windows [24]. The incident could have been prevented because Microsoft had provided a patch covering the exploited vulnerability six month before the virus spread out [24]. Needless to say, precautions have to be taken to avoid malicious misuse of update mechanisms.

F. Device-specific Requirements

Depending on the actual installation of ATMs, additional security controls are required for a higher level of defense. Examples of countermeasures include secure test utilities and device controls. Test utilities that are built in an ATM platform must be protected via access control mechanisms. Externally available devices, especially USB ports, must be controlled on BIOS or on OS level.

IV. RISK ASSESSMENT

Risks must be controlled by countermeasures or safeguards [25]. Risk management is an important part of an organization's security program. It provides support in managing information security risks associated with an organization's overall mission [26]. Risk management must repeatedly be conducted in periodical time spans [27]. Each iteration begins with risk assessment, which is initiated at a predefined time, e.g., once a year or after a major IT transformation [28]. It results in the identification, estimation and prioritization of IT risks based on the security goals of confidentiality, integrity and availability [25]. The result represents a temporary view that will be used for further risk management decisions [27].

A. Risk Model

The risk model specifies key terms and assessable risk factors including their relationships [25]. It defines all factors that directly or indirectly determine the severity and level of a particular risk, such as assets, threat source, threat event, likelihood, impact and countermeasure. Assets represent resources of value that need to be protected [29]. A person, physical object, organizational process or implemented technology can represent an asset. A threat is the potential for a malicious or non-malicious event that will damage or compromise an asset [29], e.g., unauthorized modification, disclosure or destruction of system components and information. Depending on the degree of detail and complexity, it is possible to specify a threat as a single event, action or circumstance; or as a set of these entities [25]. A vulnerability is a weakness in the defense mechanism that can be exploited by a threat to cause harm to an asset [27][29]. This weakness can be related to security controls that either are missing or have been put in place but are somehow inefficient [25].

The likelihood of a risk consists of two aspects, i.e., the likelihood of occurrence (initiation of an attack) and the likelihood of success [25]. The likelihood of occurrence demonstrates the probability of a threat to exploit a vulnerability or a set of vulnerabilities [25]. Factors that determine this likelihood value are predisposing conditions, the presence and effectiveness of deployed countermeasures and the consideration of how certain the threat event is to occur. The likelihood of success expresses the chance that an initiated threat event will cause an adverse impact without considering the magnitude of the harm [25].

The impact describes the magnitude of expected harm on an organization [29]. To determine the impact, it is important to understand the value of the asset and the value of an undamaged system. Besides, it is advisable to consider an impact not only as a one-time loss because it can have relationships to other factors that cause consequential damage [25]. A risk is a combination of the likelihood that an identified threat will occur and the impact the threat will have on the assets under review [25]. Risk factors, such as threat, vulnerability, likelihood and impact determine the overall risk. Impact and likelihood are used to define the risk level [28].

B. Risk Assessment Process

Different risk assessment processes, frameworks and methodologies build on the same underlying process structure, which may vary in abstraction level and granularity [26]. These steps, which are listeted below, do not have to be strictly adhered to in sequential order. For example, it is useful to perform threat and vulnerability identification side by side to cover all risk possibilities. Also, some step iterations are necessary to get representative results [25].

1) Definition of Assets

No action can be taken unless it is clarified what the assets are. Asset definition seeks to identify the processes, applications and systems that are highly important and critical to the daily operation of an organization [29].

2) Identification of Threat Sources and Events

Threat sources can be characterized based on their capability, intent and target to perform a malicious activity [25]. Once the list of sources is complete, threat events must be identified that can be initiated by a threat source. Predefined checklists are an easy way to verify whether the listed threat events can occur in the context of the assessment. But, an exclusive use of checklists can negatively influence the outcome because it may impair the free flow of creative thinking and discussing. An important step is the determination of the relevance of each threat event. If considered relevant, an event will be paired with all possible threat sources that can initiate it.

3) Identification of Vulnerabilities and Predisposing Conditions

Next, we have to identify vulnerabilities that can be exploited as well as the conditions that may increase or mitigate susceptibility. Tool support is feasible for this task. For example, vulnerability scanners automatically test internal and external system interfaces in order to find known and obvious weaknesses.

4) Determination of Overall Likelihood

The overall likelihood represents the probability that the threat exploits vulnerabilities against an asset [29]. To get an adequate value and to keep focused on specific aspects, the overall value is divided into likelihood of initiation/occurrence and likelihood of success. These are an assessment of the probability that a non-adversarial threat happens or an adversarial threat source launches an attack [25]. In contrast, the likelihood of success is the probability that an initiated threat event results in an adverse impact [25].

5) Determination of Magnitude of Impact

It is necessary to determine the impact the event will have on the organization [29]. For this task, the values of reviewed assets are an important input because they show the potential *harm* and the severity of the impact in case of a full or partial loss. The harm can be expressed in terms of monetary, technical, operational or human impact criteria [28].

6) Determination of Risk

The risk level is determined by combing impact and overall likelihood [27]. It shows the degree to which an organization is threatened [25]. Formulas, matrices or methods that are used for merging likelihood and impact must be consistent and precisely defined.

V. CASE STUDY

The aim of this case study is a risk assessment to establish a baseline of risks faced by an ATM platform of a specific manufacturer. The applied approach identifies all threats, vulnerabilities and impacts that cause a potential risk to an ATM asset. The focus on the ATM platform limits our investigation to software aspects only. This is why the case study mainly concentrates on logical risks. We have to mention at this point that we refrain from describing attacks in too much detail because this would provide valuable information to potential attackers. However, the given information is sufficient for readers to follow the conclusions.

A. System Characterization

From a general point of view, the logical system structure of an ATM consists of three layers as shown in Figure 1. On the bottom end of the structure is the operating system, which builds the base of all layers above. Hence, the ATM platform uses the functionalities of the operating system in order to communicate with the hardware components. To utilize the features that are implemented in the ATM platform, the ATM platform provides a public interface to multi-vendor ATM software and bank applications.

For providing a standardized interface to the layer above, the platform implements the eXtension for Financial Services (XFS) interface specification defined in CEN [31]. This programming specification has been published by the European Committee for Standardization (CEN) and is designed to control all peripheral devices of an ATM. XFS does not differ between a multi-vendor ATM software and a bank application, but considers both forms of an ATM software as a Windows-based XFS application.

Figure 2 shows the XFS architecture that builds the foundation of the ATM platform. With reference to this illustration, the key element of XFS is the definition of a set of Application Programming Interfaces (APIs) and a

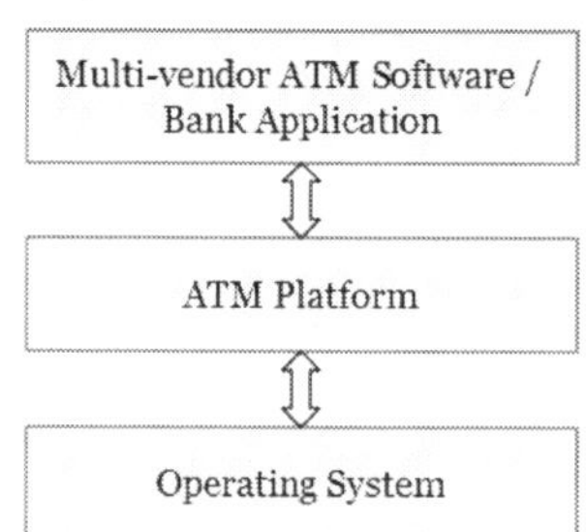

Figure 1. Logical System Structures of an ATM.

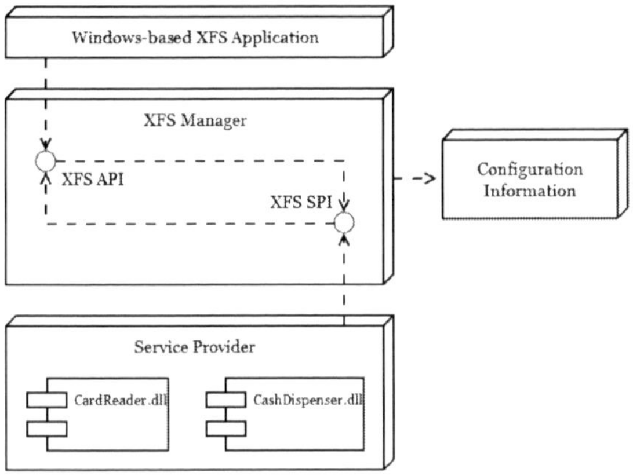

Figure 2. CEN/XFS Architecture.

corresponding set of Service Provider Interfaces (SPIs). The API provides access to financial services for Windows-based XFS applications. The SPI is similar to the API, even though it is utilized for the direct communication of vendor-specific service providers. Each of the service providers represents a peripheral device of the ATM.

1) XFS Manager

The heart of the XFS architecture is the XFS manager that handles the overall management of the XFS subsystem. This component is responsible for establishing and mapping the communication between API and SPI. In addition, the XFS manager is concerned about synchronously or asynchronously calling the appropriate service provider. For this task, a service provider is identified by a logical name parameter, which is unique within each workstation. As support, the XFS manager uses the configuration information component. This component stores the logical name parameter and defines the relationships between the Windows-based XFS application and service providers.

2) Service Providers

Either a vendor of a peripheral device or the ATM manufacturer has to implement the service provider in order to translate the device features into XFS services. Due to the fact that the peripheral devices differ in their capabilities and applications, service providers are grouped according to device classes. For example, the two service providers, Card Reader and Cash Dispenser represented in Figure 2, belong to the device class Identification Card Device (IDC) and Cash Dispenser Module (CDM). Regardless of the device class, a service provider is responsible for the functionality of translating the generic XFS request to commands that are native to the used device.

The main benefit of the XFS architecture is the fact that the XFS manager and the XFS applications are isolated from the communication between service providers and peripheral devices. As a result, vendors can individually develop their service providers, which are tailored to the devices and accessible through the XFS-API. Conversely, the XFS application that is using the ATM platform can be exchanged without changing the underlying implementation. While it would be desirable to not touch the ATM platform when changing the XFS application on the top, customizations are usually required due to some vague definitions in the XFS standard and different interpretations thereof.

B. *Logical Risk Assessment*

The risk assessment conducted in this case study is based on the risk assessment published in [25]. As defined in this document, the frst step focuses on the preparation of the assessment in order to establish the context. This includes the identification and definition of the purpose, scope, assumptions and the risk assessment methodology mentioned below.

1) Purpose

The purpose of this risk assessment is an implementation of an initial assessment to establish a baseline assessment of risks for the ATM platform. At the moment, the ATM manufacturer faces no security issues. This work is considered as preventive measure. In view of ensuring confidentiality, integrity and availability, the risk assessment identifies all logical threats, vulnerabilities and impacts to organizational operations, products and assets. This guarantees that the ATM manufacturer can offer a high level of software security. Additionally, the risk assessment must be reproducible, repeatable and extensible.

2) Scope

The ATM manufacturer sells its banking products in a business area that underlies different regulations designed to protect cash and sensitive data. Equivalent to these regulations, the scope of this risk assessment focuses on the protection of the same assets including the reputation of the company. Latter is part of the risk assessment because security issues are highly correlated to the public image of the ATM manufacturer and its products.

3) Assumptions and Constraints

The risk assessment ignores countermeasures, security solutions and security processes a financial institute or an independent ATM deployer has in place. Moreover, when evaluating risk factors such as threat sources, threat events, likelihood or impact, decisions are based on the worst case scenario.

4) Information Sources

Within the scope of the risk assessment, the ATM manufacturer provides security-related documents. These documents describe the platform architecture, planned and already implemented security mechanisms and possible threat scenarios. We use additional sources like ATM security guidelines [12] and best practice approaches for ATM security [30]. Besides this kind of explicit knowledge, the risk assessment is supported by expert interviews. The experts are employed at the ATM manufacturer and are divided into two groups. The first group contains technical staff with knowledge in developing the ATM platform. The second group has a deep understanding in operating the ATM platform for a financial institute or an independent ATM deployer.

5) Risk Assessment Process

The utilized risk assessment process takes its cue from the process recommended by NIST. A difference to the proposed process is that the definition of assets is in front of the threat source and threat event identification. Although NIST defines asset identification as part of the preparation, this task is added as an additional step in order to point out the assets that are worthy to protect. Consequently, the applied risk assessment process consists of the following six steps:

a) Definition of Assets

The main assets are sensitive data, cash and the company's reputation. Cash can be more precisely defined as real cash represented by bills and coins as well as book money transferred from one bank account to another. The general term of sensitive data summarizes data and information that refers to an individual or is required to secure the system. For instance, card data, personal identification number (PIN), account data or secret keys belong to this category.

b) Identification of Threat Sources and Events

We have derived threat sources by interviewing ATM platform engineers and customer solutions employees. The resulting sources are: attacker (or hacker), thief, cash in transit (CIT) employee, IT specialist (in data center), bank clerk, helpdesk employee, service technician and employee of ATM manufacturer. Threat events were identified in form of brainstorming sessions. Threats were grouped to categories, which were derived from the primary objective of the threat events or an important key passage in an entire scenario:

- *Denial of Service*, making the ATM platform unavailable to a customer by dominating some of its resources.
- *Malicious Software Injection*, injecting malicious software, such as Trojan horses, viruses or worms at the OS level or the ATM platform level.
- *Sensitive Data Disclosure*, gathering unprotected cardholder data.
- *Configuration File Modification*, changing configuration files of the ATM platform.
- *Privilege Settings Modification,* modifying configuration files, focusing on the change of the user access control model to gain more privileges.
- *Software Component Modification,* modifying an executable or an assembly of the ATM platform, assuming the adversary can decompile the target file.
- *Test Utility Exploitation,* exploiting test utilities used by service technicians, IT specialists and ATM platform engineers for maintenance.

Eventually, the events were connected to threat sources and logically ordered to create entire scenarios. As a result, we have designed a directed graph for each threat group. For the graphical representation of the threat events, CORAS, a model-based method for security risk analysis [31], is used. By using this graphical approach, the risk assessment benefits from several advantages.

For instance, CORAS improves the communication and interaction between the involved parties. Therefore, it provides a precise description of the system including its security features in a simple format. Additionally, CORAS provides a tool to support the risk assessment team in documenting, maintaining and reporting the assessment result and assumptions [31]. Figure 3 shows a snippet of the graph regarding the disclosure of sensitive data. With this graphical visualization on the table, the relevance of all threat scenarios was assessed and classified as either confirmed, likely, unlikely or not applicable. This is shown in Figure 3 by a label next to the threat source.

c) Identification of Vulnerabilities

In order to disclose vulnerabilities in the ATM platform, we have analyzed the threat scenarios based on countermeasures recommended in Section III. For instance, as is shown in Figure 3 by the second of the two lock symbols, missing hard disk encryption may allow a thief or service technician to access and read data on an ATM's hard disk.

d) e) Determination of Overall Likelihood and Magnitude of Impact

We have derived the likelihood of occurrence from the characteristics of particular threat sources. These characteristics had been determined in discussions with employees from

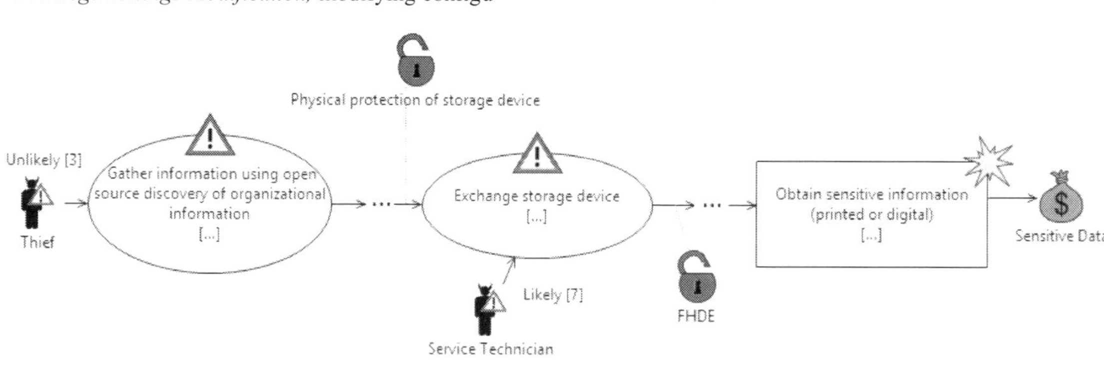

Figure 3. Snippet from Threat Diagram: *Sensitive Data Disclosure.*

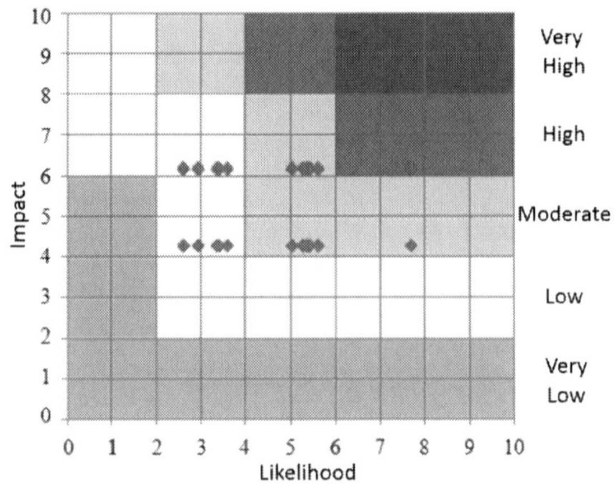

Figure 4. Likelihood Impact Diagram.

the ATM manufacturer and included capabilities of threat sources as well as intent and targeting, see (24). The likelihood of success has been determined by the vulnerabilities of the ATM platform. After the identification of both likelihood aspects (i.e., occurrence and success) they were combined to the overall likelihood of the threat scenario.

The magnitude of impact is expressed by the final result of a threat scenario. Scenarios that were linked to the three assets of the ATM have been assessed as very high (10) or high (8) since they caused an immediate loss when they get stolen or damaged. Harm to the ATM manufacturer is evaluated as high (8) and the impact of indirect harm is considered as moderate (5). The latter is weighted as moderate because a further threat scenario is necessary to actually cause damage.

f) Determination of Risk

Finally, the last step of the risk assessment is the risk determination. The risk determination has the aim to aggregate all assessed aspects of the risk factors to a single value. Therefore, we have used a likelihood impact combination matrix as proposed by NIST; see in [25] on page I-1 of the appendix. According to this matrix the level of impact is heavier weighted than the likelihood. This idea is also applied in this case study because interview partners considered the impact as dominant determinant of the risk level.

Based on the previous assessments of the overall likelihood and magnitude of impact for each threat scenario, both determinants have been combined according to the matrix. As a result, a likelihood impact diagram illustrates the risks of each category, as shown by the example in Figure 4. The coloring of the diagram is based on the likelihood impact combination matrix and represents the five areas in which a risk can fall. For clarification, the ten-step scale on both axes is divided by five with the consequence that two steps count for one qualitative value. In the diagram a risk (caused by a single threat scenario) is indicated through a dot. The position of this dot is horizontally defined by the estimation of its likelihood and vertically by its impact.

The determination of the risk has been conducted for all seven threat groups by simply combining likelihood and impact. As a result, Table I shows the distribution of risks across the seven threat groups. The numbers do not represent individual scenarios, but threat sources of such scenarios. For example, in Figure 3 we have one threat scenario with two different threat sources, i.e., thief and service technician. Table II changes the perspective and shows how countermeasures affect risks of different risk levels. The letters A to F on the left correspond to Sections III.A through III.F as well as to Sections VI.A through VI.F. This table helps in identifying security controls that are useful to mitigate multiple risks at once. Similar to Table I, the numbers do not represent single threat scenarios but threat sources.

TABLE I. DISTRIBUTION OF RISKS.

Threat Group	Risk Level				
	very high	high	mod-erate	low	very low
Denial of Service	-	-	-	2	-
Malicious Software Injection	-	7	40	19	-
Sensitive Data Disclosure	2	8	13	-	-
Configuration File Modification	1	7	13	7	-
Privilege Settings Modification	-	1	15	14	-
Software Component Modification	1	7	37	-	-
Test Utility Exploitation	-	6	12	-	-

TABLE II. DISTRIBUTION OF COUNTERMEASURES.

Countermeasure		Risk Level				
		very high	high	mod-erate	low	very low
A	Change Control	1	7	13	7	-
	Data Masking	-	1	3	-	-
	User Access Control	-	1	15	14	-
	Password Policy	-	1	3	-	-
B	Host-based Firewall	2	6	4	1	-
C	Application Control	1	9	38	-	-
D	Full Hard Disk Encryption	-	9	55	19	-
E	Patch Management	-	2	9	7	-
F	Securing Test Utilities	-	4	8	-	-
	Device Control (for USB Port)	-	2	1	6	-

VI. Discussion

The discussion about countermeasures in the literature reflects the result of the assessment in our case study. The case study additionally highlights security approaches and technologies, which were identified as most appropriate for dealing with logical ATM risks.

A. Cardholder Data Protection

We have identified change control and efficient user access control as most appropriate for protecting cardholder data and also for threat scenarios that focus on settings changes or software components of a running ATM platform. The main purpose is to guarantee that neither unnecessary nor unwanted changes are made. A change control system also supports the documentation of modifications, ensures that resources are used efficiently and services are not unnecessarily disrupted. With reference to ATMs, it can be additionally applied for ensuring PCI compliance because the change control system provides an overview of software that is deployed within the ATM environment. Although data masking is activated by default by the investigated ATM platform, there are threat sources capable to disable this feature. Consequently, the approach of obfuscating data becomes inadequate if user access control is not in place. The most efficient way of implementing a user access control mechanism is by applying the user management that comes with the OS. Not a technical but an organizational countermeasure is the implementation of a password policy, which enforces a periodical change of passwords that are either used for locking user accounts or for switching to the maintenance mode of the ATM platform.

B. Host-based Firewall

Malicious use of the network interface can be mitigated through a host-based firewall. Such a firewall should work on the level of protocols, ports and processes. In other words, the configuration of the firewall must specify the protocol and port that can be used by a particular process for establishing an outgoing connection. The same applies for processes that are receiving incoming traffic. All ports and protocols that are not in use must be blocked by default.

By configuring the firewall for each process and closing all other connections, it is unlikely that an adversary can discover an unauthorized port or protocol. Moreover, it is not possible to open a connection to transmit sensitive data over the network. So, malware that collects data on an ATM platform cannot communicate with a receiving service due to the exclusive utilization of open ports and protocols.

C. Application Control

Other threat events are focused on installing malicious code on the ATM platform. After the infection of the target, this malware hides in the system and can be activated through an adversary. Examples of such malware are discussed in Section III. In order to deal with this type of threat, a countermeasure must be in place that detects and avoids the execution of unauthorized software. In a workstation environment an antivirus solution should be utilized for this purpose. At these endpoints normally an Internet connection is available for regularly updating the signature database or transferring behavior-based malware data to an Internet service for further investigation. However, at an ATM the concept of a blacklist is inappropriate as mentioned in Section III. Consequently, the protection against unauthorized software on an ATM must change the perspective and should focus on whitelisting.

When establishing a whitelisting solution on an ATM, the execution of applications and executables is limited to a known set. This set includes files that are required to run the operating system and ATM platform. All other executable files that are not within the whitelist, even though they are not malicious, cannot be started. As a consequence, threat scenarios that install known or tailored malware on the ATM platform fail in the execution of the malicious software. In more detail, an adversary can apply different approaches to store the malicious file on the system without facing a restriction from the control of a whitelisting solution. However, the security protection raises an alert and stops the execution process when calling the executable.

Additionally, threat scenarios with the attempt to use a modified software component of the ATM platform fail to execute the prepared file. The reason is that almost all whitelisting solutions calculate and store the hash value of a whitelisted executable in order to ensure integrity of the file. Hence, a slight modification can be detected because the difference in one bit results in another hash value. In case the hash values do not match, the executable is considered as untrusted and is prevented from running on the system. As an add-on to hash values, solutions make use of software certificates, trusted publisher or trusted directories. Latter can be a security weakness when a user has write permission on the directory.

D. Full Hard Disk Encryption

Hard disk encryption is a powerful countermeasure against alternatively booting the system for malicious activities. Several threat events require access to an ATM's computer to boot the system from an alternative medium. Although launching an alternative OS would work because the environment is running in the RAM, access to the encrypted hard disk fails. As a result, an adversary is not able to search for sensitive data, to drop malicious files, to collect executables and dynamic link libraries from the ATM platform or to change the privileges of restricted objects.

Furthermore, hard disk encryption tones down threat scenarios that concentrate on stealing or exchanging a hard disk inasmuch as an encrypted hard disk is linked to the computer and cannot be used on another system. A Trusted Platform Module (TPM) chip, which is mounted on the main board of the computer, can be used to establish this connection. Other approaches do not require additional hardware, but can compute the encryption key based on unique characteristics of installed hardware components or network location of the ATM. Consequently, exchanging the hard disk is useless as long as the surrounding environment cannot be made available.

E. Patch Management

A fundamental base for an effective patch management is appropriate hardening of a system. Compared to a firewall that works at the network side, system hardening focuses on the OS level and removes or disables all unnecessary applications, users, logins and services. For instance, non-essential applications, which may offer useful features to a user at a workstation, must be removed because they could provide a backdoor to an ATM environment. Next to hardening, a rule policy with defined user privileges must be in place. The reason is that managing a distributed system like an ATM network still provides a vector for the installation of malware by maintenance staff. Based on that groundwork, a continuous patch management allows a financial institute to provide protection against known viruses, worms and vulnerabilities within an OS.

F. Device-specific Requirements

For dealing with the potential danger arising from test tools used by ATM platform engineers, service technicians and IT specialists, it is important that these tools function only under certain circumstances. Especially, when the ATM is in maintenance mode, the tools should support the activities on the ATM. But, in all other cases they must be disabled. Device control comes into play when the USB ports of an ATM represent possible entry points for a malicious activity. Similar to the concept of application control, device control can be implemented by whitelisting solutions too. Instead of blocking an application, a whitelisting solution can block the USB driver resulting in disabled USB ports.

VII. Related Work

This section highlights related work in the area of ATM security. Financial institutions argue that releasing any technical information about the implementation of an ATM would threaten the security of the devices. Consequently, it is difficult to find work that deals with the risk assessment of ATMs. Notwithstanding, some publications discuss security challenges in operating an ATM.

A. Card and Currency Fraud

In the summary of an ATM risk assessment, DeSomer demonstrates card skimming as the highest ATM risk [32]. In order to detect a card skimming device or the installation of a camera for PIN capturing, the author highlights risk mitigation measures, such as jitter devices, lighting improvements or fraudulent device inhibitors. Furthermore, the article provides recommendations for choosing a nonmanipulated ATM and for using the ATM card in a secure manner.

With focus on installed ATMs in Minna, Nigeria, Adepoju and Alhassan show the result of their empirical research, which analyzes the ATM usage in combination with fraudulent activities in this area [33]. The authors come to the conclusion that most of the fraudulent activities are skimming attacks and PIN thefts by various means. Moreover, they point out that fraudsters are able to keep on track with the further development of ATMs, but banks do not install adequate countermeasures to deal with these types of threats.

By conducting an additional survey about ATM security in Nigeria, Adesuyi et al. derive a similar result like Adepoju and Alhassan [34]. They highlight that some of the security measures of an ATM are obsolete and inadequate. Fraudulent activities on can be easily performed on an ATM. In order to overcome this problem, the work proposes improvements in the authentication process by installing a finger vein technology or a facial recognition system.

B. Logical ATM Attacks

A work that investigates the security of ATMs from a logical viewpoint has been conducted by Bradbury in 2010 [21]. According to this study, logical fraud activities on ATMs are increasing and executed as organized and highly sophisticated attack. Besides, adversaries are capable to manipulate the software inside of ATM to directly withdraw money. The severity of this issue is underlined by the fact that both banks and customers are facing heavy losses.

C. ATM Risk Management

In the article titled ATM Risk Management and Controls, Rasiah discusses the topic of an ATM risk assessment like this paper. But in contrast to our technical perspective, Rasiah adapts a non-technical approach and investigates the risk management and controls by defining general ATM security goals [35]. At the beginning, the work highlights the main points of ATM crime and ATM security as mentioned in Sections II and III, respectively. Without going into details, the work provides a general overview on ATM risk related topics. For instance, it provides recommendations for handling stolen cards and for mailing the PIN to the customer. As a conclusion, the author points out that these issues have become a nationwide problem and banks must meet certain standards to guarantee a secure banking environment.

VIII. Conclusion and Future Work

Automated teller machines have become indispensable in today's banking environment. Although customers primarily use ATMs for withdrawing money, the further development in this area has integrated additional features for other banking activities. This further development is the reason that an ATM is widely accepted and considered secure. However, it is also an attractive target for criminals especially because it processes financial customer transactions and contains real cash. In order to protect the money and customer data inside an ATM, it is essential to understand the threats and their risks.

In this paper, we have discussed various aspects of ATM security, i.e., card and currency fraud, physical attacks as well as logical attacks. Logical risks of a specific ATM have been assessed in a case study to evaluate and prioritize appropriate countermeasures. The risk assessment has provided information about countermeasures in general and their importance in particular. This allows the ATM manufacturer to better plan resources for security and concentrate on the most important countermeasures first. Also, we have found out that countermeasures suggested in the literature are effective for the identified risks. By multiplying risk levels and the number of threat sources of Table II, we have identified application control, full hard disk encryption, and user access control to be most effective, as they provide protection to most identified risks. A host-based firewall is also a must for ATM security, as it protects against very high risks.

Future work should focus on the consideration of additional adversarial threat sources, such as cyber criminals or cyber terrorists. Compared to the threat sources discussed in this work, these groups represent structured organizations with advanced skills for conducting sophisticated attacks. In the subject area of ATM security it is commonly accepted that these groups are gaining power. Another category of threat sources, which we did not consider in this paper, is the group of competitors in the field of ATM development. Threats outgoing from competitors are interesting for investigation because they would primarily focus on disturbing the availability of the targeted ATM in order to damage the manufacturer's reputation. Furthermore, this risk assessment is limited to the operating system and ATM platform. Consequently, future work could consider the entire software stack including multi-vendor ATM software or a bank application on the top of the ATM platform. When a risk assessment contains multi-vendor ATM software, the main attention should concentrate on the interface to the ATM platform. The reason is that the interface can contain an unclosed entry point for malicious software. This vulnerability can be unknowingly exploited, even though both the ATM platform and multi-vendor ATM software are functioning correctly.

ATM frauds not only cause financial loss to financial institutes or independent ATM providers, but they also undermine customers' confidence in the use of ATMs. In order to deal with this issue and to provide a secure environment for the installed ATMs, it is important to understand the associated risks. A contribution to this challenge is made by this work, which emphasizes the consideration of ATM fraud from a logical perspective. This should help to integrate adequate countermeasures in order to make it difficult to conduct and successfully complete an attack.

REFERENCE

[1] J. Braeuer, B. Gmeiner, and J. Sametinger, "ATM Security: A Case Study of a Logical Risk Assessment," ICSEA 2015, Tenth International Conference on Software Engineering Advances, 2015, pp. 355–362.

[2] B. Batiz-Lazo and R. Reid, "The Development of Cash-Dispensing Technology in the UK," *IEEE Ann. Hist. Comput.*, vol. 33, no. 3, pp. 32–45, 2011.

[3] T. Kaltschmid, "95 Prozent aller Geldautomaten laufen mit Windows XP," *heise online*. Available: http://www.heise.de/newsticker/meldung/95-Prozent-aller-Geldautomaten-laufen-mit-Windows-XP-2088583.html. [Accessed: 14-Nov-2016].

[4] C. Benecke and U. Ellermann, "Securing Classical IP over ATM Networks," in *Proceedings of the 7th conference on usenix security symposium (SSYM '98)*, Berkeley, CA, US, 1998, pp. 1–11.

[5] Diebold, "ATM Fraud and Security," *Diebold*, 2012. Available: http://securens.in/pdfs/KnowledgeCenter/5_ATM%20Fraud%20and%20Security.pdf. [Accessed: 14-Nov-2016].

[6] R. T. Guerette and R. V. Clarke, "Product Life Cycles and Crime: Automated Teller Machines and Robbery," *Secur. J.*, vol. 16, no. 1, pp. 7–18, 2003.

[7] Kasperksy Lab, "Jackpot am Geldautomaten: Wie man mit oder ohne Malware zu Bargeld kommen kann - Securelist," *SecureList*, 07-Feb-2016. Available: https://de.securelist.com/analysis/veroffentlichungen/71316/malware-and-non-malware-ways-for-atm-jackpotting-extended-cut/. [Accessed: 14-Nov-2016].

[8] RBR, "Global ATM Market and Forecasts to 2018," *Retail Bank. Res.*, vol. 2013.

[9] ENISA, "ATM Crime: Overview of the European situation and golden rules on how to avoid it," 2009.

[10] GMV, "Protect your automatic teller machines against logical fraud," 2011. Available: http://www.gmv.com/export/sites/gmv/DocumentosPDF/checker/WhitePaper_checker.pdf. [Accessed: 14-Nov-2016].

[11] S. Chafai, "Bank Fraud & ATM Security," *InfoSec Institute*, 2012. Available: http://resources.infosecinstitute.com/bank-fraud-atm-security/. [Accessed: 14-Nov-2016].

[12] PCI, "Information Supplement PCI PTS ATM Security Guidelines," *PCI Security Standards Council*, 2013. Available: https://www.pcisecuritystandards.org/pdfs/PCI_ATM_Security_Guidelines_Info_Supplement.pdf. [Accessed: 14-Nov-2016].

[13] F. Lowe, "ATM community promotes jitter technology to combat ATM skimming," *ATMMarketplace*, 2010. Available: http://www.atmmarketplace.com/article/178496/ATMcommunity-promotes-jitter-technology-to-combat-ATM-skimming. [Accessed: 14-Nov-2016].

[14] T. Kitten, "ATM Attacks Buck the Trend," *BankInfoSecurity*, 2010. Available: http://www.bankinfosecurity.com/atm-attacks-buck-trend-a-2786. [Accessed: 14-Nov-2016].

[15] ATMSWG, "Best Practice For Physical ATM Security," *ATM Security Working Group*, 2009. Available: http://www.link.co.uk/SiteCollectionDocuments/Best_practice_for_physical_ATM_security.pdf. [Accessed: 14-Nov-2016].

[16] DrWeb, "Trojan.Skimer.18 infects ATMs," *Doctor Web*. Available: http://news.drweb.com/?i=4167. [Accessed: 14-Nov-2016].

[17] J. Leyden, "Easily picked CD-ROM drive locks let Mexican banditos nick ATM cash," *BusinessWeek: Technology*. Available: http://www.theregister.co.uk/2013/10/11/mexico_atm_malware_scam/. [Accessed: 14-Nov-2016].

[18] Metro, "Stuxnet worm 'could be used to hit ATMs and power plants,'" *Metro*. Available: http://metro.co.uk/2010/11/25/stuxnet-worm-could-

be-used-to-hit-atms-and-power-plants-591077/. [Accessed: 14-Nov-2016].

[19] 30C3, "Electronic Bank Robberies - Stealing Money from ATMs with Malware," presented at the 30th Chaos Communication Congress (30C3), 2013.

[20] R. Munro, "Malware steals ATM accounts and PIN codes," *theInquirer*, 2009. Available: http://www.theinquirer.net/inquirer/news/1184568/malware-steals-atm-accounts-pin-codes. [Accessed: 14-Nov-2016].

[21] D. Bradbury, "A hole in the security wall: ATM hacking," *Netw. Secur.*, vol. 2010, no. 6, pp. 12–15, 2010.

[22] PCI, "PCI DSS - Requirements and Security Assessment Procedures," *PCI Security Standards Council*, 2013. Available: http://de.pcisecuritystandards.org/_onelink_/pcisecurity/en2de/minisite/en/docs/PCI_DSS_v3.pdf. [Accessed: 14-Nov-2016].

[23] J. J. Leon, "The case of ATM Hard Disk Encryption," *RBR Bank. Autom. Bull.*, vol. 318, pp. 11–11, 2013.

[24] H. Cavusoglu, H. Cavusoglu, and J. Zhang, "Economics Of Security Patch Management," in *Proceedings of the The Fifth Workshop on the Economics of Information Security (WEIS 2006)*, Cambridge, UK, 2006.

[25] "NIST Special Publication 800-30 Revision 1, Guide for Conducting Risk Assessments," *National Institute of Standards and Technology*, 2012. Available: http://nvlpubs.nist.gov/nistpubs/Legacy/SP/nistspecialpublication800-30r1.pdf. [Accessed: 14-Nov-2016].

[26] G. Stoneburner, A. Y. Goguen, and A. Feringa, "SP 800-30. Risk Management Guide for Information Technology Systems," National Institute of Standards & Technology, Gaithersburg, MD, US, 2002.

[27] R. K. Rainer, C. A. Snyder, and H. H. Carr, "Risk Analysis for Information Technology," *J. Manag. Inf. Syst.*, vol. 8, no. 1, pp. 129–147, 1991.

[28] ENISA, "Risk Management: Implementation principles and Inventories for Risk Management/Risk Assessment methods and tools.," 2006. Available: http://www.enisa.europa.eu/activities/risk-management/current-risk/risk-management-inventory/files/deliverables/risk-management-principles-and-inventories-for-risk-management-risk-assessment-methods-and-tools. [Accessed: 14-Nov-2016].

[29] T. R. Peltier, *Information Security Fundamentals, Second Edition*. Boca Raton, FL, US: CRC Press, 2013.

[30] "Best Practices for ATM Security," GRGBanking, May 2011.

[31] F. Braber, I. Hogganvik, M. S. Lund, K. Stølen, and F. Vraalsen, "Model-based Security Analysis in Seven Steps — a Guided Tour to the CORAS Method," *BT Technol. J.*, vol. 25, no. 1, pp. 101–117, Jan. 2007.

[32] F. DeSomer, "ATM Threat and Risk Mitigation," *Thai-American Business*, vol. 2, pp. 28–29, 2008.

[33] A. S. Adepoju and M. E. Alhassan, "Challenges of Automated Teller Machine (ATM) Usage and Fraud Occurrences in Nigeria - A Case Study of Selected Banks in Minna Metropolis," *J. Internet Bank. Commer.*, vol. 15, no. 2, 2010.

[34] F. A. Adesuyi, A. A. Solomon, Y. D. Robert, and O. I. Alabi, "A Survey of ATM Security Implementation within the Nigerian Banking Environment," *J. Internet Bank. Commer.*, vol. 18, no. 1, pp. 1–16.

[35] D. Rasiah, "ATM Risk Management and Controls," *Eur. J. Econ. Finance Adm. Sci.*, vol. 21, pp. 161–171.

Stabilizing Breach-Free Sensor Barriers

Jorge A. Cobb

Department of Computer Science
The University of Texas at Dallas
Richardson, TX 75080-3021
U.S.A.
Email: cobb@utdallas.edu

Chin-Tser Huang

Department of Computer Science and Engineering
University of South Carolina at Columbia
Columbia, SC 29208
U.S.A.
Email: huangct@cse.sc.edu

***Abstract*—Consider an area that is covered by a wireless sensor network whose purpose is to detect any intruder trying to cross through the area. The sensors can be divided into multiple subsets, known as barriers. The area remains protected, or covered, by a sensor barrier if the barrier divides the area into two regions, such that no intruder can move from one region into the other and avoid detection. By having only one barrier active at any time, the duration of the coverage is maximized. However, sensor barriers may suffer from *breaches*, which may allow an intruder to cross the area while one barrier is being replaced by another. Breaches are not dependent on the structure of an individual sensor barrier. Instead, they are dependent on the relative shape of two consecutive sensor barriers. In this paper, the best-performing centralized heuristic for breach-free barriers is transformed into a distributed protocol. Furthermore, the protocol is stabilizing, i.e., starting from any state, a subsequent state is reached and maintained where the sensors are organized into breach-free barriers. A detailed proof of the stabilization of the protocol is also given. Finally, it is shown how the barriers can organize themselves into a sleep-wakeup schedule without centralized support.**

Keywords–Stabilization; Sensor networks; Sensor barriers.

I. INTRODUCTION

Earlier work [1] outlined a distributed protocol for obtaining a set of breach-free sensor barriers in a fault-tolerant manner. In particular, the protocol in [1] is stabilizing. In this paper, the protocol is presented in greater depth, and a detailed proof that the protocol is stabilizing is also given. In addition, a final component of the heuristic that was left in [1] for future work is developed. Before presenting the protocol, the concepts of sensor barriers, breach-free sensor barriers, and stabilizing protocols are overviewed below.

A wireless sensor network consists of a large number of sensor nodes distributed over a geographical area. Each sensor has a limited battery lifetime, and is capable of sensing its surroundings up to a certain distance. Data that is collected by the sensors is often sent over wireless communication to a base station [2].

The type of coverage provided by the sensors is either full or partial. In full-coverage, the entire area is covered at all times by the sensor nodes, and thus, any event within the area is immediately detected [3] [4] [5] [6]. Partial coverage, on the other hand, has regions within the area of interest that are not covered by the sensors [7] [8] [9].

One form of partial coverage that received significant attention due to its application to intrusion detection is barrier coverage [10] [11] [12] [13] [14] [15] [16] [17]. A barrier is a subset of sensors that divide the area of interest into two regions, such that it is impossible to move from one of the regions to the other without being detected by at least one of the sensors. Fig. 1(a) highlights a subset of sensors that provide barrier coverage to a rectangular area such as a corridor in a building. The users are located at one end of the corridor (called the *bottom* of the area) and possible intruders may arrive via the opposite end (called the *top* of the area).

In the specific case of intrusion detection, providing full coverage is not an efficient use of the sensor resources, and leads to a reduced network lifetime. Instead, multiple sensor barriers can be constructed, as illustrated in Fig. 1(b). Only one barrier needs to be active at any moment in time; the remaining barriers can remain asleep in order to conserve energy. When a barrier is close to depleting all of its power, another barrier is placed in service. Given a set of sensors deployed in an area of interest, finding the largest number of sensor barriers is solvable in polynomial-time [12].

Sensor barriers are susceptible to a problem, known as a *barrier-breach*, in which it is possible for an intruder to cross an area during the time that one barrier is being replaced by another [18] [19]. The existence of a barrier-breach is dependent not on the structure of an individual sensor barrier, but on the relative shape of two consecutive sensor barriers. The complexity of obtaining the largest number of breach-free sensor barriers is an open problem. Thus, heuristics have been presented in [18] [19].

An additional heuristic that outperforms those of [18] [19] was presented in [20]. This heuristic, as well as those in [18] [19], are centralized.

In [1], the centralized heuristic from [20] is transformed into a distributed protocol, where the sensor nodes organize themselves into breach-free barriers. In addition to being distributed, the solution is *self-stabilizing* [21] [22] [23] [24], i.e., starting from any arbitrary state, a subsequent state is reached and maintained where the sensors are organized into breach-free barriers. A system that is self-stabilizing is resilient against transient faults, because the variables of the system can be corrupted in any way (that is, the system can be moved into an arbitrary configuration by a fault) and the system will naturally recover and progress towards a normal operating state.

In this paper, the distributed solution of [1] is presented in greater detail and in a manner that is easier to follow. In

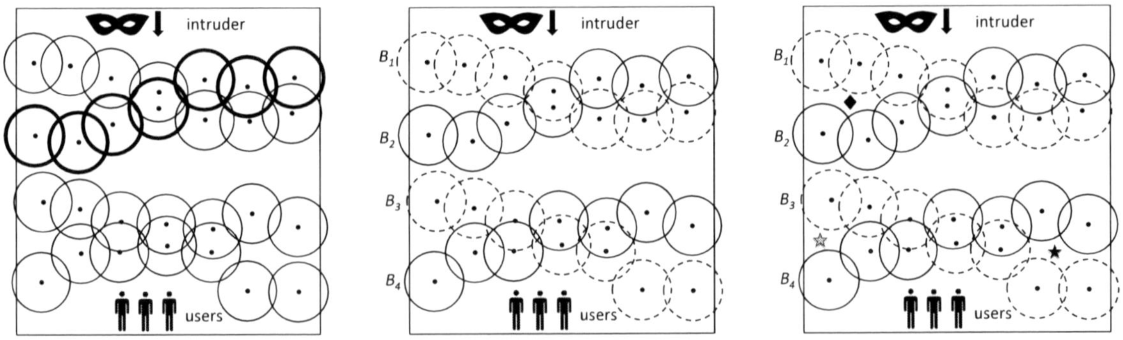

(a) Sensor Barrier (b) Multiple Sensor Barriers (c) Barrier Breaches

Figure 1. Sensor barriers.

addition, a detailed proof is given that the solution is indeed stabilizing. Finally, a feature of the protocol that in [1] was left for future work is explored and developed. Namely, the barriers organize themselves into a sleep-wakeup schedule without centralized support.

The paper is organized as follows. Section II reviews the concept of a barrier breach, and the centralized heuristic for breach-free barriers. In Section III, the basic mechanisms necessary to obtain a distributed version of the heuristic are discussed. Notation for the specification is given in Section IV, followed by the specification itself in Section V. A quick overview of the proof is given in Section VI. The detailed proof is given in the appendix. The specification of the component that allows the barriers to organize themselves into a sleep-wakeup schedule is given in Section VII, followed by the conclusion and future work in Section VIII.

II. Related Work and Background on Barrier Breaches

A. Motivation

The problem of barrier breaches can be seen through the example in Fig. 1(b). The figure shows four different sensor barriers, with each barrier displayed with different line types.

Let us assume that the lifetime of each sensor is one time unit. Furthermore, assume all sensor nodes are operating simultaneously. In this case, the lifetime of the network is simply one time unit, after which an intruder is able to penetrate the area and reach the users.

An alternative approach is to divide the sensors into multiple barriers. In the example above, the sensors are divided into four barriers, B_1 through B_4. Each of these barriers divides the area into two horizontal sections. If the barriers are used in a sequential wakeup-sleep cycle (B_1, B_2, B_3, and finally B_4), the users are protected for a total of four time units. Obviously, while transitioning from barrier B_i to barrier B_{i+1}, there has to be a small amount of time during which both barriers are active. Otherwise, an intruder can reach the users at the moment barrier B_i is deactivated.

Although advantageous in terms of network lifetime, there is a potential drawback to this approach. Consider Fig. 1(c), where specific points in the plane have been highlighted.

(a) The order in which the barriers are scheduled makes a significant difference, in particular, for barriers B_1 and B_2. If B_2 is scheduled first, followed by B_1, then an intruder could move to the point highlighted by a diamond, and after B_2 is turned off, the intruder is free to cross the entire area.

(b) Only one of B_3 and B_4 is of use. To see this, suppose that B_3 is activated first. In this case, the intruder can move to the location of marked by the black star. Then, when B_4 is activated and B_3 deactivated, the intruder can reach the users undetected. The situation is similar if B_4 is activated first, and the intruder moves to the location of the grey star.

B. Definitions

The original definition of a barrier breach was given in [18], as follows.

Definition 1: **(Barrier-Breach)**. An ordered pair (B_1, B_2) of sensor barriers have a *barrier breach* if there exists a point p in the plane such that:

(a) p is outside the sensing range of B_1 and B_2,

(b) B_1 cannot detect an intruder moving from the top of the area to p, and

(c) B_2 cannot detect an intruder moving from p to the bottom of the area.

■

Before presenting our heuristic from [20], some background definitions given in [20] are reviewed.

Definition 2: **(Ceilings and Floors)** Given that a sensor barrier B divides the area of interest into an *upper region* and a *lower region*,

- The *ceiling* of B consists of all points p along the border of the sensing radius of each sensor in B such that one can travel from p to any point in the upper region without crossing the sensing area of any sensor.
- The *floor* of B consists of all points p along the border of the sensing radius of each sensor in B such that one can travel from p to any point in the lower region without crossing the sensing area of any sensor. ■

As an example, consider the sensor barrier depicted in Fig. 2(a). The ceiling and floor of this barrier are depicted in Fig. 2(b), where the ceiling is depicted with a solid line and the floor with a dashed line.

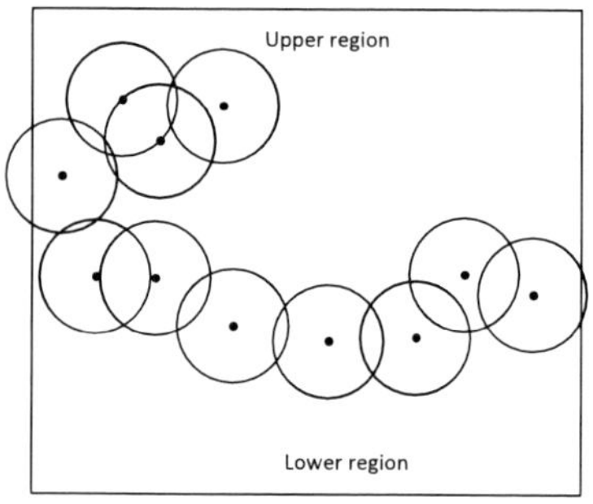

(a) Sensor set.

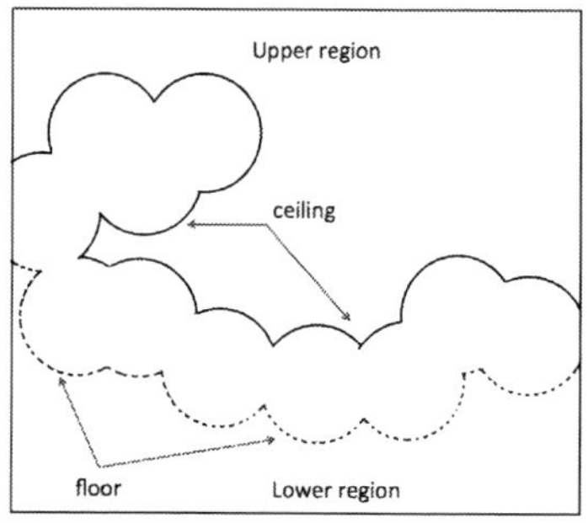

(b) Ceiling and floor.

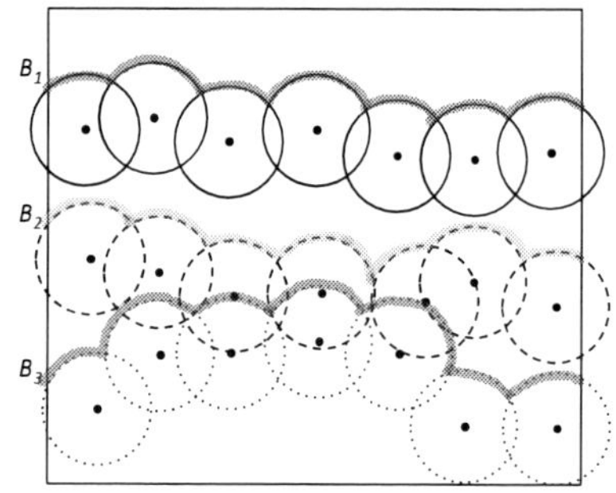

(c) Barriers obtained.

Figure 2. Ordered-ceilings method.

Using these definitions, a condition can be obtained that guarantees that a breach is not present [20].

Lemma 1: **(Breach-Freedom)** An ordered pair (B_1, B_2) is breach-free iff the floor of B_2 is below the ceiling of B_1. ∎

This can then be used to ensure that an intruder does not reach the users, as follows. A schedule, i.e., a sequence, of barriers $(B_1, , B_2, \ldots, B_n)$ is said to be *non-penetrable* if there is no sequence of moves that an intruder can make to reach the users without being detected by any of the barriers during the lifetime of the schedule.

Theorem 1: **(Non-Penetrable)** A schedule $(B_1, B_2, \ldots, B_n)$ of sensor barriers is non-penetrable iff, for each i, $1 \leq i < n$, the ordered pair (B_i, B_{i+1}) is breach-free [20]. ∎

Consider for example Fig. 1(c). The pair (B_1, B_2) does *not* have a barrier breach because the floor of B_2 never crosses over the ceiling of B_1. The pair (B_2, B_1) does have a breach.

Note also that both (B_3, B_4) and (B_4, B_3) have a breach. Thus, they cannot be scheduled one after the other. This, however, does not preclude them from being in a schedule together (although not in the network in Fig. 1). For example, assume that more sensor nodes are added to form a new barrier (that is, from the left border of the area to its right border) and the sensors run along the middle of B_3 and B_4, closing the gaps between these barriers. If this new barrier is B', then the schedule (B_3, B', B_4) is a non-penetrable schedule.

C. Disjoint Paths Heuristics

As mentioned above, several heuristics have been developed to obtain breach-free barriers. The heuristics presented in [18] [19] [25] are based on using a variant of maximum network flow to find the largest number of node-disjoint (i.e., sensor-disjoint) paths (i.e., barriers) that begin on the left side of the area and terminate on the right side of the area.

In [20], a heuristic known as the *ordered ceilings heuristic* is proposed, and it is shown to outperform the heuristics in [18] [19] [25]. The only exception is when the number of sensors per unit area is unreasonably high, in which case the heuristic of [25] outperforms the ordered ceilings heuristic.

D. Ordered Ceilings Heuristic

The ordered ceilings heuristic, which is the focus of this paper, is a centralized method that is based on the following observation that follows from the above theorem.

Observation 1: If a set of m sensor barriers does not have a pair of barriers whose ceilings intersect, then a non-penetrable schedule exists of duration m by scheduling the sensor barriers in order from top to bottom. ∎

The heuristic simply finds each barrier iteratively as follows. Consider the set of all sensor nodes as a barrier, and obtain its ceiling. The first barrier consists of all sensor nodes that take part of this ceiling. These nodes are then removed from the network, and a new ceiling is obtained, which yields a new barrier, etc.. Fig. 2(c) shows a sample sensor network and the three barriers resulting from the heuristic.

III. Distributed Implementation

In this section, the method used to transform the centralized heuristic into a distributed protocol is presented. Assumptions about the network model are presented first, followed by the steps to perform this transformation.

A. Model

Each sensor node is assumed to be equipped with a global positioning system (GPS) or other means by which it can infer its location. The sensing area of each node is assumed to form a circle, or can be approximated by the largest circle within its sensing area. The area of interest is assumed to be rectangular, as shown in Fig. 1, and each sensor is able to determine if its sensing area overlaps either the left or right border of the area of interest. Finally, it is assumed that nodes whose sensing range overlap are able to communicate wirelessly with each other, i.e., the transmission range is greater than twice the sensing range.

The batteries used by the sensors are assumed to be rechargeable, by means such as solar cells or by a station transmitting microwaves, and thus the network can run continuously. However, being actively sensing depletes the battery of the sensor. Sensors must therefore have a period of rest to recharge. However, self-stabilizing systems are assumed to run continuously, otherwise, they would not have time to recover from a transient fault.

Thus, by the above reasons, it is assumed that the network operates as follows. If there are n barriers constructed, then each barrier, from top to bottom, is activated sequentially. By the end of the lifetime of barrier n, the first barrier has had enough time to recharge to the level to be reactivated, and the schedule continues.

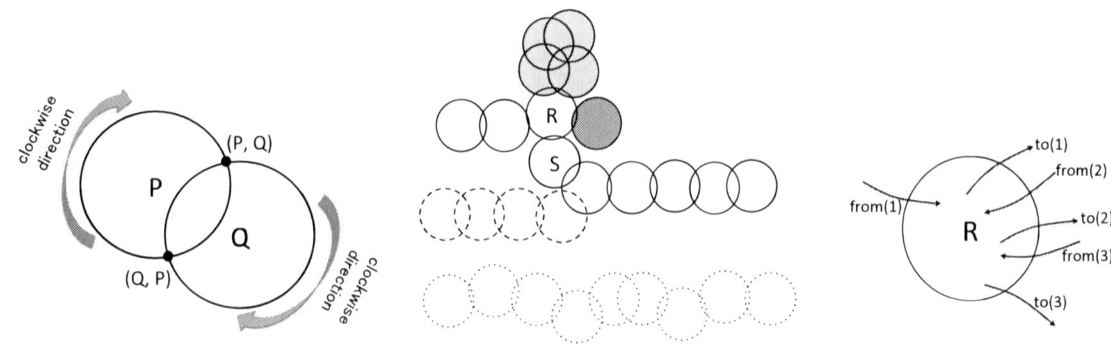

(a) Sensing intersection. (b) Detours (c) Pointers to neighbors.

Figure 3. Neighbor relationships.

There is of course a period of vulnerability when switching from barrier n to barrier 1, since an intruder that moved closer to barrier n could reach the users once the barrier switch is performed. It is expected that the users are aware of the time at which this vulnerability occurs, and they will take additional protection measures during this time.

Finally, sensor nodes, whether actively sensing or not, must wake up at specified intervals and exchange messages with their neighbors to maintain or correct their state.

B. Method

Consider Fig. 3(a). Any two sensor areas that overlap each other will intersect at only two points. These points are viewed as "edges" (P, Q) and (Q, P). These edges are directed according to clockwise order, as indicated in the figure. Hence, the top intersection point corresponds to edge (P, Q) (from P to Q), while the bottom intersection point corresponds to edge (Q, P) (from Q to P).

To form a barrier, a node whose sensing range overlaps the left border finds the outgoing edge clockwise that is closest to its point on the left border. This edge points to the next node on the barrier. This is process is then repeated. That is, the second sensor node chooses the edge that is closest clockwise the the incoming edge of the previous node, and so on. The process continues until the right border is found.

As an example, consider again Fig. 2(a). The node overlapping the border begins by choosing as the next barrier node its neighbor higher up as opposed to its neighbor below. This is because the edge to the higher up neighbor occurs first clockwise, with respect to the point on the border, than the edge to the neighbor below. The process repeats, with the node higher up choosing the first clockwise outgoing edge (relative to the incoming edge of the previous node). The border obtained is given in Fig. 2(b), which corresponds to the ceiling of the nodes.

An interesting observation is that the ceiling may come back to the original node. This is the case in Fig. 2(a), but not in Fig. 2(c). This is illustrated more clearly in Fig. 3(b). Consider the barrier drawn with solid lines. When the barrier construction reaches sensor R, the next sensor in the barrier is directly above it. As the barrier continues to be built, the barrier returns back to R. These nodes constitute a *detour*, and are drawn filled with gray. The next node is to the right of R, which immediately returns back to R. This is another detour, but it consists of a single node. The barrier then proceeds along sensor S. Thus, there are two "detours" at R before continuing on with the barrier. These detours have to be taken into consideration when designing the distributed algorithm for barrier construction below.

Another observation from Fig. 3(b) is that some sensors at the left border are unable to find a path to the right border. This is the case with the barrier attempt with dashed lines. However, it is still possible for a node further below to reach the right border, such as in the case of the barrier drawn with dotted lines. In particular, assume that in a network there exists a set of m barriers with no overlapping sensor regions. For example, Fig. 3(b) has two barriers that do not overlap: the one drawn with solid lines and the one drawn with dotted lines. Then, the ordered ceilings heuristic is guaranteed to find at least m breach-free barriers.

C. Variables and Neighbor Relationships

To implement the above scheme, the main variables (pointers) of a sensor node R are shown in Fig. 3(c). Both variables *from* and *to* are parallel sequences of neighbors. If the node has no detours, then $from(1)$ is the previous neighbor in its barrier, and $to(1)$ is the next node in the barrier. However, assume that node R has two detours, which is the case in Fig. 3(c). In this case, $to(1)$ is the next node after R in the first detour, and $from(2)$ is the neighbor from which the first detour returns. Similarly, $to(2)$ and $from(3)$ are the next node and the returning node for the second detour. Finally, $to(3)$ is the neighbor that follows R in the barrier, and this neighbor is not involved in a detour at R. Hence, in a stable state where all barriers are fixed, $|from| = |to|$, and the last element of to corresponds to the next node in the barrier.

Assume a node R must choose between two neighbors, P and Q, to become its *from(1)* neighbor. That is, P and Q are both pointing towards R, and R must be able to distinguish which one is "best". If P's barrier originated at a higher point on the border than Q's barrier, then R will choose P. However, if both have the same origin point (especially during a stabilization phase), more information is needed to break the tie. Also, R must be able to determine if P and Q are pointing

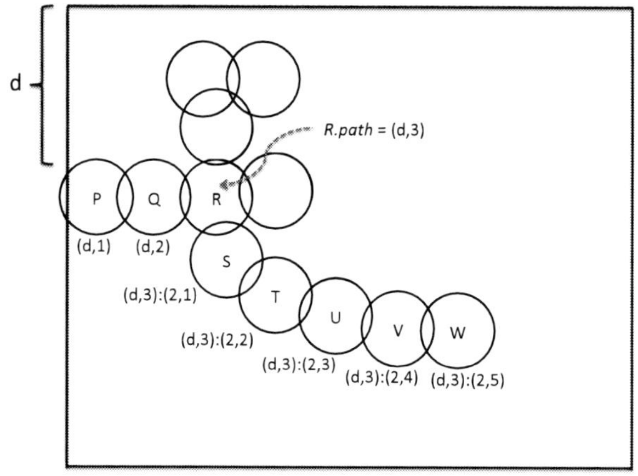

Figure 4. Path example.

at it because they occur before R in the barrier or because they are returning to R from a detour of several hops.

One approach could be for neighbors to exchange the entire path from the border node to themselves when communicating with each other. This is sufficient but somewhat excessive, especially since detours are likely to be either short or non-existent in a barrier, and communication should be minimized in a wireless system. For efficiency, each node instead maintains an abbreviated version of its path as follows.

For a node on the left border of the area, its path is simply the pair $(d, 1)$, where d is the distance from the top of the area to the point on the border where the barrier begins. The second number in the pair is a hop count. Thus, assuming the barrier has no detours, then a node h hops from the left border will have a path equal to (d, h). Also, notice that if there are no detours, then variable $to(1)$ always points to the next node on the barrier.

Assume now that detours do exist. Let $R.to(3) = S$, i.e., S is the beginning of the third detour of R. Then

$$S.path = R.path : (2, 1)$$

where colon denotes concatenation. The first number denotes the number of complete detours in its predecessor, R, and the second number denotes the hop count from the point of the detour. Hence, the number of pairs in a path correspond to the number of nodes encountered that had at least one complete detour. In consequence, if there are no detours after S, then the nodes after S have the same path as S, except that the hop count in the last pair increases with each hop.

Consider as an example Fig. 4, where a barrier is being constructed from left to right (only part of the barrier is drawn). The sensor node on the left border is P, and it intersects the left border at a distance d from the top. Hence, its path is $(d, 1)$. Because P has no detours, node Q has a path equal to $(d, 2)$, i.e., two hops from the left border. Similarly, because node Q has no detours, node R has a path equal to $(d, 3)$. However, R does have two detours, and thus the path of S is $(d, 3) : (2, 1)$. The pair $(2, 1)$ indicates that two detours were skipped at the previous node, i.e., at R, and that S is one hop away from the node where the detours were skipped.

Because neither S nor any remaining node have detours, the paths of the remaining nodes simply consist of increasing the hop count of the last term in the path. E.g., the path of W is $(d, 3) : (2, 5)$, because W is five hops away from the node where the last detour occurred, i.e., from R.

The hop count of a path is denoted by $HC(path)$. It is simply the sum of the hop counts of each term in the path. For example, node $HC(W.path) = 3+5 = 8$ and $HC(T.path) = 3 + 2 = 5$. Note that HC corresponds to the number of hops along the barrier if the nodes involved in a detour are not counted.

Given the paths of two nodes, R and S, $R \prec S$ denotes that R occurs first in the barriers before S. That is, either R occurs in a barrier above the barrier of S, or they occur in the same barrier and R occurs first in the barrier. This is straightforward to determine from the paths as follows.

- If $R.path$ and $S.path$ are equal except in the hop count of the last pair, then $R \prec S$ if the hop count of R is smaller.
- Let (d, h) and (d', h') be the first pair in $R.path$ and $S.path$ where $d \neq d'$. Then, $R \prec S$ if $d < d'$.

IV. Protocol Notation

The notation used to specify the protocol originates from [23] [24], and is typical for specifying stabilizing systems. The behavior of each node is specified by a set of inputs, a set of variables, a set of parameters, and a set of actions.

The inputs declared in a process can be read, but not written, by the actions of that process. The variables declared in a process can be read and written by the actions of that process. For simplicity, a shared memory model is used, i.e., each node is able to read the variables of its neighbors. This can be relaxed to a message-passing model, which is discussed in the conclusion and future work section. Parameters are discussed further below.

Every action in a process is of the form:

<guard> → <statement>.

The <guard> is a boolean expression over the inputs, variables, and parameters declared in the process, and also over the variables declared in the neighboring processes of that process. The <statement> is a sequence of assignment statements that change some of the variables of the node.

The parameters declared in a process are used to write a set of actions as one action, with one action for each possible value of the parameters. For example, if the following parameter definition is given,

par g : 1 .. 2

then the following action

$$x = g \quad \rightarrow \quad x := x + g$$

is a shorthand notation for the following two actions.

$$x = 1 \quad \rightarrow \quad x := x + 1$$

$$\Box$$

$$x = 2 \quad \rightarrow \quad x := x + 2$$

An execution step of a protocol consists in evaluating the guards of all the actions of all processes, choosing an action whose guard evaluates to true, and executing the statement of this action. An execution of a protocol consists of a sequence of execution steps, which either never ends, or ends in a state where the guards of all the actions evaluate to false. All executions of a protocol are assumed to be weakly fair, that is, an action whose guard is continuously true must be eventually executed.

A network *stabilizes* to a predicate P iff, for every execution (regardless of the initial state) there is a suffix in the execution where P is true at every state in the suffix [23] [24].

To distinguish between variables of different nodes, the variable name is prefixed with the node name. For example, variable $x.v$ corresponds to variable v in node x. If no prefix is given, then the variable corresponds to the node whose code is being presented.

V. PROTOCOL SPECIFICATION

The specification of a stabilizing protocol that organizes sensors into breach-free barriers is given below. The sensor barrier of a node can be obtained by following its pointer variables, i.e., the left node is indicated by variable *from(1)* and its right node is indicated by the last entry in its variable *to*.

The code below does not organize the barriers, i.e., assign to each a natural number to indicate its position on the schedule of barriers. This is a simple addition that will be presented in Section VII.

To simplify the presentation of the code, the actions for sensor nodes whose sensing region overlaps the borders, i.e., when nodes are a potential endpoint of a barrier, are not presented. Instead, it is assumed that there are two virtual nodes S and T, where S is beyond the left border and T is beyond the right border. Any sensor node P overlapping the left border is assumed to have an incoming edge (S, P) whose intersection point with P is the point where P intersects the left border. Furthermore, the path that S advertises to P is of the form $(d, 0)$, where d is the depth of the point of (S, P). That is, the distance from the top of the region to this point. In this way, no two sensors on the border will have the same path. In the case when sensors are located right next to each other, ties can be broken by node id's.

The complete specification of an arbitrary sensor node u is given in Fig. 5. The specification is broken down into smaller segments below, and the intuition behind each of them is presented.

The inputs and variables of a sensor node u are as follows. The actions are described further below.

node u
inp G : **set of node id's** {sensing neighbors}
L : **natural number** {max. barrier length}
var $from$: **sequence of element of** G;
to : **sequence of element of** G;
$path$: **sequence of** $(N^+, 1 \ldots L)$;
par g : **element of** G {any neighbor of u}
i : $1 \ldots |G|$

node u
inp G : **set of node id's** {sensing neighbors}
L : **natural number** {max. barrier length}
var $from$: **sequence of element of** G;
to : **sequence of element of** G;
$path$: **sequence of** $(N^+, 1 \ldots L)$;
par g : **element of** G {any neighbor of u}
i : $1 \ldots |G|$
begin
{action 1: new or improved $from(1)$}
$from(1) \neq g \wedge u = g.to(i) \wedge HC(g.path) < L \wedge$
$extend\text{-}one\text{-}hop(g.path, i) \prec path \wedge \quad \rightarrow$
$from := \{g\}; \quad to := \emptyset;$
$path := extend\text{-}one\text{-}hop(g.path, i);$

▯ {action 2: new or improved $to(i)$}
$|from| \geq i \wedge HC(path) < L \wedge g \neq to(i) \wedge$
$clockwise(from(1, i), to(1, i-1): g) \wedge$
$|to| \geq i \Rightarrow between(from(i), g, to(i)) \wedge$
$(extend\text{-}one\text{-}hop(path, i) \prec g.path \vee$
$path \in extend\text{-}multiple\text{-}hop(g.path)) \quad \rightarrow$
$to := to(1, i-1);$
$from := from(1, i);$
if $u \notin g.from$ **then**
$to := to: g;$

▯ {action 3: new or improved $from(i+1)$}
$|to| \geq i \wedge u \in g.to \wedge g \neq from(i+1) \wedge$
$from\text{-}consistent(g, u, i) \wedge$
$clockwise(from(1, i): g, to(1, i)) \wedge$
$|from| > i \Rightarrow between(to(i), g, from(i+1)) \quad \rightarrow$
$from := from(1, i): g;$
$to := to(1, i);$

▯ {action 4: sanity of to, $from$, and $path$}
$\neg(|to| \leq |from| \leq |to| + 1) \vee HC(path) > L \vee$
$(|from| = 0 \wedge path \neq \emptyset) \vee \neg clockwise(from, to)$
$\rightarrow \quad from := \emptyset; \; to := \emptyset; \; path = \emptyset;$

▯ {action 5: sanity of $from(i)$}
$|from| \geq i \; \wedge \neg(u \in from(i).to \wedge$
$from\text{-}consistent(from(i), u, i)) \quad \rightarrow$
$from := from(1, i-1);$
$to := to(1, i-1);$

▯ {action 6: sanity of $to(i)$ and neighbor's path}
$|to| \geq i \wedge g = to(i) \wedge \neg(path \prec g.path \wedge$
$(|from| > i \Rightarrow to(i).from(1) = u)) \quad \rightarrow$
$from := from(1, i);$
$to := to(1, i-1);$
end

Figure 5. Specification of an arbitrary sensor node u.

The node has two inputs. Input G is the set of neighboring sensor nodes. It is assumed that a sensor can determine its neighbor set via a simple hello protocol. The second input, L, is the maximum number of hops that is allowed in a barrier. I.e., the sum of the hop counts of all elements of a path should be at most L. This bound is not necessary to break loops, but it may be used to speed up convergence.

The variables $from$ and to of each process are as described earlier. Variable *path* is the abbreviated path of the node. Also, $from(i, j)$, where $i < j$, denotes the subsequence of $from$ starting at $from(i)$ and ending at $from(j)$. The subsequence $to(i, j)$ is defined in the same way.

Each node has six actions. Due to the semantics, the order in which they are written is irrelevant for their execution. Thus, actions are presented below in the order that is the easiest to describe.

The first action obtains a value for $from(1)$, or replaces it by a better value.

$$\begin{array}{l} from(1) \neq g \wedge u = g.to(i) \wedge HC(g.path) < L \wedge \\ extend\text{-}one\text{-}hop(g.path, i) \prec path \wedge \quad \rightarrow \\ \qquad from := \{g\}; \quad to := \emptyset; \\ \qquad path := extend\text{-}one\text{-}hop(g.path, i); \end{array}$$

The above action checks that if a neighbor g is pointing at u (i.e., $g.to(i) = u$ for some i), and the path of g being offered to u is better than u's current path, then u chooses g as its predecessor. Note that by changing the value of $from(1)$ all other values of $from$ and to may be invalid, since in effect the node is changing from one barrier to another. Hence, to is set to empty, and the path of u is obtained form that of g. This is obtained from function

$$extend\text{-}one\text{-}hop(path, i)$$

that returns the same path with an increased hop count of 1 when $i = 1$, or returns $path : (i - 1, 1)$ when $i > 1$.

If $to(i)$ has a value, then the following action attempts to improve it, i.e., find a neighbor that is closer clockwise than $to(i)$. If $to(i)$ does not have a value, then the action attempts to find a neighbor to point to with $to(i)$.

$$\begin{array}{l} |from| \geq i \wedge HC(path) < L \wedge g \neq to(i) \wedge \\ clockwise(from(1, i), to(1, i - 1) : g) \wedge \\ |to| \geq i \Rightarrow between(from(i), g, to(i)) \wedge \\ (extend\text{-}one\text{-}hop(path, i) \prec g.path \vee \\ \quad path \in extend\text{-}multiple\text{-}hop(g.path)) \quad \rightarrow \\ \qquad to := to(1, i - 1); \\ \qquad from := from(1, i); \\ \qquad \textbf{if } u \notin g.from \textbf{ then} \\ \qquad\qquad to := to : g; \end{array}$$

Although the guard of the above action seems complex, it is just a series of simple tests, one per line.

The first one ensures that $from(i)$ is defined, since otherwise $to(i)$ cannot exist, and it ensures that the hop count of the path of u can be extended (i.e., it is less than L).

Also, $from$ and to should remain in clockwise order after replacing $to(i)$ by g.

Furthermore, if $to(i)$ is already defined (i.e., if $|to| \geq i$), then the new value g has to be closer in clockwise order than the current value of $to(i)$, i.e., g has to be in between $from(i)$ and $to(i)$.

Finally, u points to g under two conditions: either u's path will improve the current path of g (and thus g will choose u as its predecessor in the barrier) or u is part of a detour that started at g and u is the last node in this detour. This is expressed using the functions $extend\text{-}one\text{-}hop$, defined earlier, and $extend\text{-}multiple\text{-}hops(path)$, which is defined below.

Intuitively, $extend\text{-}multiple\text{-}hops(path)$ is the set of all possible path values that can be obtained by extending the given $path$ by any number of hops. More formally, let

$$path = (x_1, y_1) : (x_2, y_2) : \ldots : (x_{n-1}, y_{n-1}) : (x_n, y_n)$$

Also, let $path' \in extend\text{-}multiple\text{-}hops(path)$. Thus, $path'$ must have one of two forms. The first case is when

$$path' = (x_1, y_1) : (x_2, y_2) : \ldots : (x_{n-1}, y_{n-1}) : (x_n, z)$$

where $z > y_n$. This indicates that $path'$ extends $path$ by $z - y_n$ hops and there are no detours along these hops. The second case is when

$$\begin{aligned} path' \quad = \quad & (x_1, y_1) : (x_2, y_2) : \ldots : (x_{n-1}, y_{n-1}) : (x_n, z) : \\ & (a_1, b_1) : (a_2, b_2) : \ldots : (a_m, b_m) \end{aligned}$$

where $z \geq y_n$ and $m \geq 1$. This indicates that $path'$ encounters m nodes with detours after u.

Function $extend\text{-}multiple\text{-}hops(path, i)$ denotes the more specific case where the first hop is extended via $to(i)$. Above, it corresponds to $z = y_n \wedge m \geq 1 \wedge a_1 = i$.

Note that if the value of $to(i)$ changes, then all subsequent values of to and $from$ are no longer valid, and they are thus removed by the command of the action. Also, if g is chosen to become $to(i)$, then g cannot already be pointing at u with $g.from$. This is necessary for the safety properties presented in the detailed proof.

The following action obtains a new value of $from(i+1)$, or attempts to improve if it already exists. Note that this does not apply to $from(1)$. Thus, $from(i+1)$ is the neighbor that completes the return of detour i.

$$\begin{array}{l} |to| \geq i \wedge u \in g.to \wedge g \neq from(i + 1) \wedge \\ from\text{-}consistent(g, u, i) \wedge \\ clockwise(from(1, i) : g, to(1, i)) \wedge \\ |from| > i \Rightarrow between(to(i), g, from(i + 1)) \quad \rightarrow \\ \qquad from := from(1, i) : g; \\ \qquad to := to(1, i); \end{array}$$

The above action checks that if g is the neighbor to become $from(i + 1)$, then the values of u and g are consistent. This is done with function $from\text{-}consistent(g, u, i)$ explained further below. It also checks that the correct clockwise order is maintained. Finally, if $from(i + 1)$ is already defined, i.e., if $|from| > i$, then g is between $to(i)$ and the current $from(i+1)$, i.e., it occurs earlier in the clockwise order than the current $from(i + 1)$.

Similar to above, all values of to and $from$ after $from(i+1)$ are no longer valid, and they are thus removed by the command of the action.

Function $from\text{-}consistent(g, u, i)$, where g is u's neighbor, and $g = from(i)$, is defined as follows. If $i = 1$, then g is the node previous to u in the barrier, and thus it must be that

$$u.path = extend\text{-}one\text{-}hop(g.path, 1).$$

On the other hand, if $i > 1$, then the path of g is actually an extension of that of u, and thus

$$g.path = extend\text{-}multiple\text{-}hops(u.path, i).$$

Thus,

$$\begin{aligned}&from\text{-}consistent(g, u, i) = \\ &\quad (i = 1 \wedge (u.path = extend\text{-}one\text{-}hop(g.path, 1))) \\ &\quad \vee \\ &\quad (i > 1 \wedge (g.path = extend\text{-}multiple\text{-}hops(u.path, i))).\end{aligned}$$

The last three actions are *sanity* actions. That is, they check that the local state of the node is correct and also consistent with respect to that of its neighbors. Otherwise, the state of the node is reset to an appropriate value.

The first of the three sanity actions is as follows.

$$\begin{aligned}&\neg(|to| \leq |from| \leq |to| + 1) \vee HC(path) > L \vee \\ &(|from| = 0 \wedge path \neq \emptyset) \vee \neg clockwise(from, to) \\ &\rightarrow \qquad from := \emptyset;\ to := \emptyset;\ path = \emptyset;\end{aligned}$$

The above action ensures that the lengths of the $from$ and to variables are consistent, and also that they correspond to points that are clockwise around the sensing circle of the node. Also, it ensures that the path has a length of at most L, and there cannot be a path if there is no $from(1)$ node. If any of these is not true, the local variables are reset to an empty value.

The next action ensures that if $from(i)$ has a value, then the local information is consistent with that of neighbor $from(i)$.

$$\begin{aligned}&|from| \geq i\ \wedge \neg(u \in from(i).to\ \wedge \\ &from\text{-}consistent(from(i), u, i)) \ \rightarrow \\ &\qquad from := from(1, i-1); \\ &\qquad to := to(1, i-1);\end{aligned}$$

The above action first checks that $from(i)$ is defined, and if so, it checks if node $from(i)$ is pointing towards u with, and if so, that the path at node u is consistent with that of its neighbor $from(i)$.

In the last action, the value of $to(i)$ and the path of the neighbor it points to are coordinated. The neighbor must have a path that is worse than that of u. In addition, if a detour has completed, then the first node of the detour must point back at u.

$$\begin{aligned}&|to| \geq i \wedge g = to(i) \wedge \neg(path \prec g.path\ \wedge \\ &(|from| > i \Rightarrow to(i).from(1) = u)) \ \rightarrow \\ &\qquad from := from(1, i); \\ &\qquad to := to(1, i-1);\end{aligned}$$

VI. Correctness Overview

For terseness, the detailed proof of correctness of the protocol is deferred to the appendix.

The fairness in the execution model allows the actions of nodes to not be executed for an arbitrary (but finite) amount of time. In practice, all nodes operate at about the same speed, and thus, the proofs are based in the commonly used notion of an execution round.

An *execution round* starting at a state s_0 in an execution sequence $s_0, s_1, \ldots,$ is the minimum prefix of this execution sequence such that every action in every node either is disabled at each state in the round, or is enabled at some state in the round and is either executed or disabled at a later state in the round.

The proof follows the following overall steps. First, due to the sanity actions, from any arbitrary initial state, within $O(1)$ rounds the following will hold and continue to hold at every node.

$$\begin{aligned}&(|to| + 1 \geq |from| \geq |to| \geq 0)\ \wedge \\ &clockwise(from, to) \wedge HC(path) \leq L\end{aligned}$$

I.e., variables satisfy what is depicted in Fig. 3(c).

Because the initial state is arbitrary, the path stored at each node may not be consistent with that of its neighbors. The next step is to show that it will. To this end, an ordered pair of neighboring nodes (g, u) is said to be *i-joined,* $i \geq 1$, if

$$u \in g.to \wedge g = u.from(i).$$

It must be shown that within $O(1)$ rounds, for all i and for all i-joined pairs (g, u), $from\text{-}consistent(g, u, i)$ will hold and continue to hold.

Next, although the upper bound L on the hop count is enforced, the bound L is not necessary to break loops. A loop exists if by following the $from(1)$ variables there is a node that can be reached twice. Loops are broken quickly, because the hop counts must be consistent (differ by exactly one) between nodes, or otherwise all variables are reset to nil and empty values. The total order $\preceq$ on paths prevent new loops to be formed.

Within $O(1)$ rounds, it can be shown that there is no sequence of nodes $(u_0, u_1, \ldots, u_n)$ such that $u_0 = u_n$ and $i\text{-}joined(u_j, u_{j+1}, 1)$, for each j, $0 \leq j < n$. That is, following the $from(1)$ values from one node to another does not lead to a loop.

The following step is to show that all nodes only contain abbreviated paths that have as their first entry a non-fictitious entry point along the left border. The path with a fictitious first entry and with the smallest hop count will not match the path of its $from$ neighbor, and thus will reset its values. Thus, within $O(L)$ rounds all path values with fictitious first entries disappear.

Next, due to the total order of $\preceq$, the nodes along the top barrier will overcome any other path value in the system, thus completing the top barrier in $O(L)$ rounds. The remaining barriers will be constructed similarly in top-down order. If the total number of barriers is B, then within $O(BL)$ rounds all the barriers will be constructed, and the values of the variables of each node will cease to change.

VII. Completing the Protocol

The protocol presented in Section V organizes the sensors into disjoint breach-free barriers, but it does not organize them into a schedule. However, each sensor node must know the number of its barrier (counting from top to bottom) to be able to turn its sensing feature at the right time.

To accomplish the above, the nodes at the right barrier can organize themselves in a simple sequence from top-to-bottom. The steps required to do so are overviewed in this section. The simple proofs of correctness are left to the reader.

First, each node needs to know if the construction of its barrier has completed. To do so, a boolean variable, $built$, is added to indicate if this is the case. The following two actions need to be added to each node u.

$$right\text{-}border \rightarrow built := (|from| \geq 1)$$

$$\neg right\text{-}border \rightarrow built := (|to| \geq 1 \wedge to(|to|).built)$$

Above, *right-border* is true if node u overlaps the right border of the area. The fact that the barrier has been built propagates from the node on the right border back to the node on the left border. If u is on the right border, then its barrier is complete provided it is part of a barrier, i.e., if $from(1)$ is defined. If it is not on the right border, then the last element of array to points to the next node along the barrier (other elements of to point to detour nodes). Thus, if this last element thinks the barrier is complete then node u also will consider the barrier complete.

Next, if its barrier is built, each node must determine the order of its barrier in the schedule. The topmost border is first in the schedule, followed by the next border down. For this purpose, four additional variables are added to each node u:

order : an positive integer, indicating the order of u's barrier in the schedule.
depth : the depth of the barrier of u (i.e., distance from the top of the area.
prev : the depth of the barrier that is previous (right above) the barrier of u.
src : the source of the information for the previous barrier. This is the neighbor of u from whom u learned about the previous barrier. This could be either a neighbor on the same barrier as u that intersects the previous barrier, or u has a neighbor that directly intersects the previous barrier. If there is no previous barrier, $src = u$.

The depth of the barrier of u is determined by the location of the left-most node of the barrier, i.e., the node whose sensor range overlaps the left border. Recall that this information is present in the first item of the path variable. Hence, *depth* is simply defined as the first value in *path*.

There are two tasks. The first task is to improve the choice for the previous barrier. That is, there could be a barrier that is in between node u's barrier and what u believes should be the previous barrier. The second task is to ensure that the values of the four variables are consistent.

For the first task, the following action is added to each node u.

$$(depth > g.depth > prev) \wedge built \wedge g.built \rightarrow$$
$$order := g.order + 1;$$
$$prev := g.depth;$$
$$src := g$$

This action chooses g as the source of the information if its depth is between the depth of the former previous barrier and the depth of the barrier of u.

Next, the values of the four variables must be consistent. If they are inconsistent, then they are reset using the following commands.

$$src := u;$$
$$prev := 0;$$
$$order := 1;$$

With these commands, u assumes that it is the first barrier. It will remain this way until it improves. Let us refer to those three commands as *reset-src*;

There are three different cases when *reset-src* should be executed, depending on the value of the source.

- The first is when the source is u itself, but its values are inconsistent. Let us refer to this case as *bad-u*, and is defined as follows.

  $$src = u \wedge \neg(built \wedge prev = 0 \wedge order = 1)$$

- The second is when the source is either the left or right node on the same barrier. Let us refer to this case as *bad-from-to*, and is defined as follows.
  $src \in \{from(1), to(|to|)\} \wedge$
  $\neg(src.src \neq u \wedge src.built \wedge built \wedge$
  $src.order = order \wedge$
  $(src.prev = prev < depth))$
- The last one is when the source is not on the same barrier as u, denoted by *bad-other*, and is defined as follows.
  $src.depth \neq depth \wedge$
  $\neg(src.built \wedge built \wedge src.src \neq u \wedge$
  $(src.depth = prev < depth) \wedge$
  $src.order + 1 = order)$

Thus, to each node u, the following action is added.

$$bad\text{-}u \vee bad\text{-}from\text{-}to \vee bad\text{-}other \rightarrow reset\text{-}src$$

VIII. Conclusion and Future Work

In this paper, a distributed and stabilizing version of the best-performing centralized heuristic for breach-free barriers is presented. Also, an additional feature is developed that allows the barriers to organize themselves into a sleep-wakeup schedule without centralized support.

The execution model used is based on shared memory. However, a message passing implementation is straightforward using the techniques described in [23] due to the low level atomicity of the actions, that is, each action refers to variables of only a single neighbor at a time.

The stabilization time of $O(B \cdot L)$ rounds is an upper bound on the worst-case behavior of the system when all variables have an arbitrary initial value. A more detailed analysis may reveal an even lower upper bound, such as $O(L)$. This investigation is left for future work. Also, on average, it is expected that the system will recover much faster than this from a few random faults. This could be analyzed via simulations, which are also deferred to future work.

Appendix

Some basic stabilization properties are presented first. For a property P to hold within $O(1)$ rounds, it must be shown that if P holds before each action, then it will continue to hold after the action is executed. In addition, there must be an action that once executed it makes P true. Hence, once P becomes true, it continues to be true.

Theorem 2: Let $S1$ be the following safety predicate.

$$(|to| + 1 \geq |from| \geq |to| \geq 0) \wedge$$
$$clockwise(from, to) \wedge$$
$$HC(path) \leq L$$

Predicate $S1$ will hold and continue to hold after $O(1)$ rounds.

Proof:

Step 1:

Assuming that $S1$ holds before each action, it is shown next that it will continue to hold after the action is executed.

First action: If the action executes, $from = \{g\}$ and $to = \emptyset$, which trivially satisfies the last two conjuncts of $S1$. From the action's guard, $HC(g.path) < L$, and thus, after extending it by one hop, $HC(path) \leq L$ holds. Thus, $S1$ continues to hold.

Second action: If the action executes, then after the action $|to| + 1 \geq |from| \geq |to|$. The path is not affected, so $HC(path) \leq L$ continues to hold. Also, the guard of the action ensures that the new values of $from$ and to will be clockwise. Hence, $S1$ continues to hold.

Third action: If the action executes, then $|from| = i + 1 \wedge |to| = i$, which satisfies $S1$. Also, the guard of the action ensures that the values are clockwise. The path variable is not affected. Hence, $S1$ continues to hold.

Fourth action: The empty values assigned by the action trivially satisfy $S1$.

Fifth action: The fifth action only shortens $from$ and to, with $|from| = |to|$, and hence, all three conjuncts of $S1$ continue to hold after the action.

Sixth action: Similar to above, the action only shortens $from$ and to, and hence, $S1$ continues to hold.

Step 2:

There must be an action that forces $S1$ to become true if it does not hold before the action. This action is the fourth action. If any of the conjuncts of $S1$ does not hold, then the action is able to execute. Due to fairness, it will execute in one round, and thus force $S1$ to become true. ■

Theorem 3: Within $O(1)$ rounds,

$$(\forall i, v, w : i\text{-joined}(v, w) \Rightarrow from\text{-}consistent(v, w, i))$$

holds and continues to hold.

Proof: Let $S2$ be the above predicate. The same two steps as above will be used but now for $S2$. Note that if i-joined(v, w, i) is false for some specific values of i, v, and w, then it is not required to be proven that $from\text{-}persistent(v, w, i)$ holds. The only case where the implication can be falsified is in the case where the left-hand side is true and the right-hand-side is false. Thus, let us focus on when an action turns the left-hand side true (in which case it must also set the right hand side true), or when an action makes the right-hand-side false (in which case the left-hand side must also be set to false).

Step 1:

Assuming that $S2$ holds before each action, it will be shown that it will continue to show after the action is executed.

First action: This action eliminates all the join relations in which node u is included. However, it does establish a new one, 1-joined(g, u). In this case, the new value of $path$, i.e., extending by one hop the path of g, is what $S2$ demands. Thus, $S2$ holds after this action.

Second action: This action also removes join relations since it shortens to and $from$. It has the potential to add a new one due to giving a new value to $to(i)$. However, this is only done if g is not pointing back at u with $g.from$. Hence, no new join relation can be created, and thus $S2$ is preserved.

Third action: Similar to the second action, this action also removes join relations since it shortens to and $from$. It has the potential to add a new one due to giving a new value to $from(i+1)$, thus creating an i-joined(g, u) link. This new link satisfies $from\text{-}consistent(g, u, i)$ due to the guard. Hence, $S2$ holds.

Fourth, fifth, and sixth actions: Executing these actions can only eliminate join relations, and hence $S2$ continues to hold.

Step 2:

There must be an action that forces $S2$ to become true if it does not hold before the action. Consider any triple (v, w, i) such that $S2$ does not hold. This implies that the left-hand-side, i-joined(v, w) is true, while the right hand side, $from\text{-}persistent(v, w, i)$ is false. If within $O(1)$ rounds the left-hand-side becomes false, then there is no proof obligation. Assume otherwise. Then, the guard of action 5 is true with $w = u$ and $v = u.from(i)$. In this case, when the action executes, the pair (v, w) is no longer i-joined, and $S2$ holds and continues to hold for the triple (v, w, i). ■

Observation 2: Within $O(1)$ rounds, there is no sequence of nodes $(u_0, u_1, \ldots, u_n)$ such that $u_0 = u_n$ and $joined(u_j, u_{j+1}, 1)$, for each j, $0 \leq j < n$. That is, following the $from(1)$ values from one node to another does not lead to a loop. Furthermore, this continues to hold.

The above observation follows from the value of $path$ decreasing, with respect to $\prec$, at every hop when the $from(1)$ values are followed (as indicated by Theorem 3), and from the antisymmetry of $\prec$.

Observation 3: Within $O(1)$ rounds, any execution will reach a state where $S1 \wedge S2$ holds, and this continues to hold for all remaining states of the execution.

Recall that all variables can have an arbitrary value in the initial state. Throughout the rest of this section, let us assume a state as indicated in Observation 3 has already been reached. Next, it must be shown that all nodes will have a path variable whose initial position on the left border corresponds to that of a real node on the border, i.e., no fictitious initial nodes will exist in the path variables.

Lemma 2: After $O(L)$ rounds, for any node u, if the first value in its path variable is x, then there exists a node on the left border with depth x.

Proof: Consider any value y such that there is no sensor node on the left border with this depth, and there is at least one node whose path contains (y, h) for some h. It must be shown that all paths with a value of y must disappear.

First note that no new fictitious y can be introduced into the system, since any new path of a node is derived from that of its neighbors.

Let us denote a path value as a y-path if it begins with a depth of y. The first pair in a y-path is of the form (y, h), where h is the hop count. Let h_{min} be the smallest value of h in a y-path. It is argued next that h_{min} must increase.

Let u have (y, h_{min}) in its path. Because of Theorem 3, $from\text{-}consistent(u.from(1), u, 1)$ must be false and continue to be false. This is because this requires the path of

$u.from(1)$ to be (y, h') where $h' < h_{min}$. Thus, either u changes $from(1)$ using the first action, or action 5 will set $from$ to empty (note that by definition $from(1,0)$ is the empty sequence). In the former, the neighbor of u must have a path that does not start with y, or has y and a hop count greater than or equal to h_{min}. Thus, u loses the y value or increases its hop count. In the latter, $|from| = 0$, in which case eventually u chooses a new $from(1)$ and the same argument applies for a higher hop count. It is also possible that action 4 sets the path to empty, in which case node u also loses its y value.

Thus, (y, h_{min}) will disappear. Since the hop count in (y, h) has a maximum value of L, then within $O(L)$ rounds all paths values starting with y will disappear. ■

The main result is presented next, i.e., that the barriers are actually constructed. The first step is showing that the top-most barrier gets constructed, and all the values of its nodes remain stable. The building of the remaining barriers follow simply by induction on the barriers.

Theorem 4: Within $O(L)$ rounds, the $from$ and to variables of the nodes in the top most barrier correctly follow the sequence of nodes in the barrier until the rightmost node is reached.

Proof: The proof is by induction over the nodes in the barrier. Let the barrier nodes be $u_0, u_1, \ldots, u_n$.

Base case: Consider node u_0, which intersects the left border. Let its depth be x. If any node has a path starting with $(x, 0)$, when action 5 executes in the node, the new path will not have $(x, 0)$.

The only node that can advertise $(x, 0)$ is the virtual node S. Thus, consider any node whose path begins with $(x, 1)$. If the node is not on the left border, then the path cannot be consistent with its $from(1)$ node (and if $from(1)$ is not defined then action 4 will set $path$ to nil). Thus, action 5 will set the path to nil. Thus, no node other than the left node can have $(x, 1)$ in its path.

Finally, consider the left-most node. It receives an advertised path of $(x, 0)$ from the virtual node S.

There are four cases to consider.

1) $u_0.from(1) \neq S$ and $u_0.path = (x, 1)$.
   As long as this is the case, the path is not consistent since no node other than S can advertise $(x, 0)$. Thus, action 5 remains enabled until the above case changes.
2) $u_0.from(1) = S$ and $u_0.path$ is worse than $(x, 1)$.
   This is not possible since it is not $from\text{-}consistent$, and violates Theorem 3.
3) $u_0.from(1) \neq S$ and $u_0.path$ is worse than $(x, 1)$.
   Action 1 remains enabled unless the case changes. Since no node can advertise $(x, 0)$ other than S, the only way this case may change is by executing the first action, which establishes the fourth case.
4) $u_0.from(1) = S$ and $u_0.path = (x, 1)$.
   In this case, no node can offer a better path than S, u_0 is consistent with S, and from Theorems 2 and 3 the sanity actions will not fire. Hence, this case remains true forever.

Thus, these three cases must eventually end up in case 4, which remains true forever, as desired. Note that this will be done in $O(1)$ rounds.

Inductive Step: Assume the Theorem holds for $u_0, u_1, \ldots, u_h$, show that it will hold for $u_0, u_1, \ldots, u_{h+1}$.

Let $to(i)$ be the pointer at u_h that is meant to point at u_{h+1} (all pointers less than i at u_h are fixed by the induction hypothesis). It must be shown that eventually $u_h.to(i) = u_{h+1}$, $u_{h+1}.from(i) = u_h$ for the appropriate i, and $u_{h+1}.path = extend\text{-}one\text{-}hop(u_h, i)$.

Note that because u_{h+1} follows u_h in the barrier, there cannot be any node, whether in the barrier or not, that is clockwise in between the last $from$ value at u_h and node u_{h+1}.

There are two cases to consider.

Case 1:

Node u_{h+1} *does not* appear earlier in the barrier. Hence, it should eventually be the case that $u_{h+1}.from(1)$ should point to u_h.

There are two subcases.

Sub-case (a): $u_h.to(i) = u_{h+1}$ already.

In this case $to(i)$ cannot change value. This is because, from Theorems 2 and 3, the sanity actions will not fire. Also, no other neighbor can be clockwise in between u_h and u_{h+1}, as mentioned above. Hence, action 2 cannot change $to(i)$.

Sub-case (b): $u_h.to(i) \neq u_{h+1}$.

From the induction hypothesis, the path at u_{h+1} is worse than that of u_h. Furthermore, as argued before there are no nodes clockwise in between these two nodes. Hence, the second action fires, which clears all the pointers equal or greater than i.

If $u_h \notin u_{h+1}.from$, then $u_h.to(i)$ is set to u_{h+1}, as desired. Note that this continues to hold because there cannot be a node clockwise in between these two nodes.

If $u_h \in u_{h+1}.from$, this prevents $to(i)$ to be set. However, from this point forward, no value $to(j)$, $j > i$, can point to u_{h+1}. This is because if $to(i)$, $to(i+1)$, etc., are set by action 2, then the nodes chosen appear clockwise after u_{h+1}. Hence, u_{h+1} cannot be set to any $to(j)$, $j > i$. Thus, eventually action 5 in u_{h+1} executes and removes the $from$ value pointing back at u_h. Then, nothing can stop action 2 at u_h to set $u_h.to(i) = u_{h+1}$, which is subcase (a).

Hence, since u_h continuously points at u_{h+1}, the first action of u_{h+1} will set $u_{h+1}.from(1) = u_h$, as desired.

Case 2:

Node u_{h+1} *does* appear earlier in the barrier. Hence, it must be shown that $u_h = u_{h+1}.from(i)$, where i is the next index at u_{h+1} that has not been used for earlier parts of the barrier. Note that $from(j)$ and $to(j)$, where $j < i$, are fixed at u_{h+1} due to the induction hypothesis. Similarly, to and $from$ up to $i - 1$ are fixed in u_h from the induction hypothesis.

The first step is to show that eventually $u_h.to(i) = u_{h+1}$ holds and continues to hold. The proof up to this point is the same as in Case 1, except that in Case 1 $extend\text{-}one\text{-}hop$ was used in action 2, while in Case 2 $extend\text{-}multiple\text{-}hop$ is used. Thus, it is assumed below that $u_{h+1}.from(i) = u_h$ holds and continues to hold.

Note that since both u_h and u_{h+1} are both already in the barrier (i.e. $u_{h+1} = u_j$ for some $j < h + 1$). Hence, from the induction hypothesis, their paths are fixed, and the path of u_h is an extension of the path of u_{h+1}.

Also, as argued above there is no neighbor that is clockwise in between u_h and u_{h+1}.

Hence, if $u_{h+1}.from(i) = u_h$, then this will continue to hold (sanity actions no longer fire, and from above, action 3 cannot choose a node better than u_h).

If on the other hand, $u_{h+1}.from(i) \neq u_h$, then also from the above, the guard of action 3 is enabled and continues to be enabled until it fires, setting $u_{h+1}.from(i) = u_h$.

End of inductive step.

Thus, within $O(L)$ rounds, the barrier up to the node at the right border will be constructed. Although discussed earlier, it is assumed that nodes at the right border are aware that they are located on the border. Thus, these nodes have only the first and fifth actions, they restrict $from$ to only one value, and they have no to variable. Thus, their path will be maintained consistent with its $from(1)$ neighbor, and they always choose the best possible neighbor for $from(1)$.

Thus, by induction, the theorem holds. ■

After the top barrier is constructed above, there might be some $from$ and to values that are dangling, i.e., that point to nodes not on the barrier. These have to disappear to ensure that the next barrier is constructed without interference from the first barrier.

Theorem 5: Let x be the depth of the top-most barrier. Within $O(L)$ rounds, there are no nodes that are not in the top barrier that contain a depth of x in their path. Also, the $from$ and to variables of nodes in the top barrier point exclusively to the appropriate nodes in the barrier.

Proof: Consider any node u that is on the barrier. Assume that some of its $from$ or to variables, other than those used for the barrier, have values. Let $to(i)$ be the last value in to pointing at a barrier node. Thus, $from(i+1)$ points to a non-barrier node, let us say, w.

If the path of w is consistent with u, then the value of $w.path$ should be a possible extension of u via detour i, i.e., $w.path \in extend\text{-}multiple\text{-}hop(u, i)$. If it is not, then the fifth action of u will remove all $from$ and to values after $to(i)$. If it is, then u cannot remove $from(i+1)$.

In this case, consider following the $from(1)$ variables (i.e., backwards), starting at w, and continuing as long as the next node's path is the extension by one hop of the previous node. Eventually, a node is reached whose path is not in $extend\text{-}multiple\text{-}hop(u, i)$, and thus is not a one-hop extension of the previous node. Thus, action 5 in this node will execute at the node and remove its pointers. This will also activate action 5 in the previous node, continuing in a cascade of nodes until w is reached. Then, in node u, action 5 will reset all pointers after $to(i)$.

Thus, at all nodes, eventually only those pointers used for the barrier have a value. ■

Since the nodes not in the top barrier cannot receive a path value corresponding to nodes in the top barrier, at this moment the next barrier can be built independently of the previous one, and thus, from induction, all barriers will be built.

Corollary 1: Within $O(B \cdot L)$ rounds, where B is the number of barriers in the ceilings heuristic, the $from$, to, and $path$ variables of all nodes are aligned to these barriers, and continue to be aligned unless a fault occurs in the system.

References

[1] J. A. Cobb and C. T. Huang, "Fault-tolerant breach-free sensor barriers," in Proc. of the International Conference on Systems and Networks Communications (ICSNC), Nov. 2015, pp. 63–69.

[2] J. Yick, B. Mukherjee, and D. Ghosal, "Wireless sensor network survey," Computer Networks, vol. 52, no. 12, Aug. 2008, pp. 2292–2330.

[3] C. Huang and Y. Tseng, "The coverage problem in a wireless sensor network," in Proc. of the ACM Int'l Workshop on Wireless Sensor Networks and Applications (WSNA), Sep. 2003, pp. 115–121.

[4] H. Zhang and J. Hou, "On deriving the upper bound of α-lifetime for large sensor networks," in Proc. of The 5th ACM Int'l Symposium on Mobile Ad-hoc Networking and Computing (MobiHoc), Jun. 2004, pp. 121–132.

[5] M. Cardei, M. T. Thai, Y. Li, and W. Wu, "Energy-efficient target coverage in wireless sensor networks," in Proc. of the IEEE INFOCOM Conference, vol. 3, Mar. 2005, pp. 1976–1984.

[6] M. T. Thai, Y. Li, and F. Wang, "O(log n)-localized algorithms on the coverage problem in heterogeneous sensor networks," in Proc. of the IEEE Int'l Performance, Computing, and Communications Conference, (IPCCC), Apr. 2007, pp. 85–92.

[7] S. Gao, X. Wang, and Y. Li, "p-percent coverage schedule in wireless sensor networks," in Proc. of the Int'l Conference on Computer Communications and Networks (ICCCN), Aug. 2008, pp. 1–6.

[8] C. Vu, G. Chen, Y. Zhao, and Y. Li, "A universal framework for partial coverage in wireless sensor networks," in Proc. of the Int'l Performance Computing and Communications Conference (IPCCC), Dec. 2009, pp. 1–8.

[9] Y. Li, C. Vu, C. Ai, G. Chen, and Y. Zhao, "Transforming complete coverage algorithms to partial coverage algorithms for wireless sensor networks," IEEE Transactions on Parallel and Distributed Systems, vol. 22, no. 4, Apr. 2011, pp. 695–703.

[10] S. Kumar, T. H. Lai, and A. Arora, "Barrier coverage with wireless sensors," in Proc. of the Int'l Conference on Mobile Computing and Networking (MobiCom), Aug. 2005, pp. 284–298.

[11] A. Saipulla, C. Westphal, B. Liu, and J. Wang, "Barrier coverage of line-based deployed wireless sensor networks," in Proc. of the IEEE INFOCOM Conference, Apr. 2009, pp. 127–135.

[12] S. Kumar, T. H. Lai, M. E. Posner, and P. Sinha, "Maximizing the lifetime of a barrier of wireless sensors," IEEE Transactions on Mobile Computing, vol. 9, no. 8, Aug. 2010, pp. 1161–1172.

[13] H. Yang, D. Li, Q. Zhu, W. Chen, and Y. Hong, "Minimum energy cost k-barrier coverage in wireless sensor networks," in Proc. of the 5th Int'l Conf. on Wireless Algorithms, Systems, and Applications (WASA), Aug. 2010, pp. 80–89.

[14] H. Luo, H. Du, D. Kim, Q. Ye, R. Zhu, and J. Zhang, "Imperfection better than perfection: Beyond optimal lifetime barrier coverage in wireless sensor networks," in Proc. of the IEEE 10th Int'l Conference on Mobile Ad-hoc and Sensor Networks (MSN), Dec. 2014, pp. 24–29.

[15] B. Xu, Y. Zhu, D. Li, D. Kim, and W. Wu, "Minimum (k,w)-angle barrier coverage in wireless camera sensor networks," Int'l Journal of Sensor Networks (IJSNET), vol. 19, no. 2, 2015, pp. 179–188.

[16] L. Guo, D. Kim, D. Li, W. Chen, and A. Tokuta, "Constructing belt-barrier providing quality of monitoring with minimum camera sensors," in Proc. of the Int'l Conference on Computer Communication and Networks (ICCCN), Aug. 2014, pp. 1–8.

[17] B. Xu, D. Kim, D. Li, J. Lee, H. Jiang, and A. Tokuta, "Fortifying barrier-coverage of wireless sensor network with mobile sensor nodes," in Proc. of the Int'l Conference on Wireless Algorithms, Systems, and Applications (WASA), Jun. 2014, pp. 368–377.

[18] D. Kim, J. Kim, D. Li, S. S. Kwon, and A. O. Tokuta, "On sleep-wakeup scheduling of non-penetrable barrier-coverage of wireless sensors," in Proc. of the IEEE Global Communications Conference (GLOBECOM 2012), Dec. 2012, pp. 321–327.

[19] H. B. Kim, "Optimizing algorithms in wireless sensor networks," Ph.D. dissertation, The U. of Texas at Dallas, Advisor: J. Cobb, May 2013.

[20] J. A. Cobb, "Improving the lifetime of non-penetrable barrier coverage in sensor networks," in Proc. of the International Workshop on Assurance in Distributed Systems and Networks (ADSN), Jul. 2015, pp. 1–10.

[21] M. Schneider, "Self-stabilization," ACM Computing Surveys, vol. 25, no. 1, Mar. 1993, pp. 45–67.

[22] E. W. Dijkstra, "Self-stabilizing systems in spite of distributed control," Commun. ACM, vol. 17, no. 11, 1974, pp. 643–644.

[23] S. Dolev., Self-Stabilization. Cambridge, MA: MIT Press, 2000.

[24] M. G. Gouda, "The triumph and tribulation of system stabilization," in Proc. of the 9th International Workshop on Distributed Algorithms (WDAG). London, UK: Springer-Verlag, 1995, pp. 1–18.

[25] J. A. Cobb, "In defense of stint for dense breach-free sensor barriers," in Proc. of the International Conference on Systems and Networks Communications (ICSNC), Aug. 2016, pp. 12–19.

Data Security Overview for Medical Mobile Apps

Assuring the Confidentiality, Integrity and Availability of data in transmission

Ceara Treacy, Fergal McCaffery
Regulated Research Centre & Lero
Dundalk Institute of Technology,
Dundalk, Ireland
e-mail: {ceara.treacy, fergal.mccaffery }@dkit.ie

Abstract— **Mobile medical apps are a growing mechanism for healthcare delivery through an increasingly complex network of information technology systems connecting patients, doctors, nurses, pharmacists and medical devices. Characteristically, these apps are designed to gather measure and transmit sensitive personal health data, which is required to be kept secure through regulations and legislation. With the integration of mobile medical apps into the healthcare industry, the multitude of sensitive personal health data transmitted across various applications, technologies and networks is increasing. This raises questions about compromised patient privacy and the security of the data associated with the mobile apps. The detections of increased app hacking by security companies and researchers are especially significant amidst today's rapid growth in healthcare mobile apps. Consequently, security and integrity of the data associated with these apps is a growing concern for the app industry, particularly in the highly regulated medical domain. Until recently, data integrity and security in transmission has not been given serious consideration in the development of mobile medical apps. This paper provides an overview of existing mobile medical apps data security issues and security practices. We discuss current regulations concerning data security for mobile medical apps. The paper introduces our current research in data security for mobile medical apps. There are currently no procedures or standard practices for developers of mobile medical apps to assure data integrity and security. The paper introduces the concept of a process model to assist mobile medical app developers to implement data security requirements to assure the Confidentiality, Integrity and Availability of data in transmission. The research is grounded on the only published medical device security standard IEC/TR 80001-2-2:2012.**

Keywords- Mobile Medical Apps; data security; Mobile Medical Apps data regulations.

I. Introduction

In mHealth, mobile apps are in general classified into mobile health/wellbeing apps (MHAs) and mobile medical apps (MMAs) [1]. This classification is predominantly driven by the Food and Drug Administration (FDA) Mobile Medical Applications Guidance [2] and is outlined in Table I. Medical professionals and the general public use mobile apps to perform many tasks, such as: sharing medical videos, photos and x-rays; health and fitness tracking; blogs to post medical cases and images; share personal health information; and keep track of alerts on specific medical conditions and interests [3].

MMAs are evolving quickly coinciding with the processing capabilities of mobile devices and are currently one of the most dynamic fields in medicine [4]. The use of mobile apps enables dynamic access to personal identifiable information and the collection of greater amounts of sensitive data relating to personal health information (PHI). The use of mobile apps implicates changes in the way health data will be managed, as the data moves away from central systems located in the services of healthcare providers, to apps on mobile devices [5]. MMAs by design collect process and transmit large quantities of information and data. Increasing reliance on mobile apps raises questions about compromised patient privacy [6] and the security of the data accompanying the apps [5]. There is continued mistrust in mobile apps in healthcare handling personal identifiable information and PHI in a secure and private manner. The 2015 PwC's Health Research Institute's survey, claims 78% of surveyed consumers were worried about medical data security, while 68% were concerned about the security of their data in mobile apps [7].

The impact of data breaches in the medical industry is far-reaching in terms of costs, losses in reputation [8] and potential risk to patient safety. Reasons for obtaining access to PHI can be for monetary gain, to inflict harm and for personal intention [9]. An example of the importance of cybersecurity can be seen with the health insurer Anthem in the US. A reported breach involved hackers obtaining personal identifiable information and PHI for about 80 million of its customers and employees [10]. The information stolen falls under the Health Insurance Portability and Accountability Act (HIPAA), which is the federal law governing the security of medical data and could result in fines of up to $1.5million. A data breach that maliciously makes changes to a medical diagnosis or prescribed medication has serious consequences in terms of physical harm and patient safety. With PHI breaches, either through physician diagnosis or a treatment plan, the possibility of personal harm or loss is pronounced. In 2014 the SANS Institute, a leading organization in computer security training, indicates health care security strategies and practices are poorly protected and ill-equipped to

TABLE I. FDA CATEGORIZATION FOR REGULATORY PURPOSES [2]

Medical Mobile Apps - Focus of FDA Regulatory Oversight	Mobile Apps which FDA Intends to Exercise Enforcement Discretion	Mobile Apps that are NOT Medical Devices
Mobile apps that: • Are extensions of one or more medical devices • Provide patient-specific analysis and providing patient-specific diagnosis, or treatment recommendations • Transform the mobile platform into a regulated medical device • Become a regulated medical device (software)	Mobile apps that: • Provide or facilitate supplemental clinical care • Provide patients with tools or access to information • Specifically marketed to help patients document, show, or communicate to providers potential medical conditions • Perform simple calculation. • Interact with PHR systems or EHR systems	Mobile apps that: • Provide access to electronic records, textbooks or other reference materials or educational tools • Are for medical training, general patient education and access, automate general office operations, are generic aids or are general purpose products

handle new cyber threats exposing patient medical records, billing and payment organizations, and intellectual property [11].

It is largely assumed MMAs are not typically deployed in "hacker rich" mobile environments [12]. The detection of increased app hacking by security companies and researchers is significant amidst today's rapid growth in healthcare mobile app usage [7], [11]–[13]. An Arxan report states that many sensitive medical and healthcare apps have been hacked with 22% of these being FDA approved apps [12]. In the MMA domain, developers do not have extensive experience with the types of threats other consumer app industries (e.g., banking) are familiar with. Consequently, privacy has not been given serious consideration until recently, while the importance of security is getting recognized little is yet being done [14]. The FDA regulates medical devices in the U.S and are alert to the cybersecurity of medical devices. In July 2015, the FDA issued a cybersecurity alert to users of a Hospira Symbiq Infusion System pump, where it strongly recommended discontinued use, as it could be hacked and dosage changed [15]. In September 2015, the FBI issued a cybersecurity alert, outlining how Internet of Things (IoT) devices may be a target for cybercrimes and may put users at risk [16]. If a cyber-thief changes patient medical information or a physician diagnosis, serious medical harm or even death can result. An article that references the DarkNet, describes how it is now possible to purchase a medical identity that mirrors individual ailments, size, age and gender, to seek "free" medical services that would not be suspicious to a clinician [17]. According to CISCO the estimated cost associated with medical identity theft in the US, to the healthcare industry in 2015 is $12 billion [18].

Development of MMAs is picking up momentum as many companies are lured into the domain by the explosion of the market and the potential financial gains. However, issues arise such as: many of these developers do not have a background in the highly regulated domain of medical devices and are not aware of the data protection and privacy requirements of electronic PHI (ePHI). Developers coming from the medical device domain are discovering the technical complications of entering the mobile domain. The job of securing mobile apps in health care is primarily up to those building them, which also has its challenges because the developers tend not to be security experts [19]. The European Commission's 'Green Paper on mHealth' findings are that this market is dominated by individuals or small companies, with 30% being individuals and 34.3% are small companies (defined as having 2-9 employees) [20]. This would advocate a lack of experience, knowledge and financial means to address the issues outlined above. The survey conducted by research2guidance [21] highlights that MHA developers regard the main market barrier for the next five years to be the lack of data security. The health industry is reaching out for help in designing security into mobile apps in healthcare that go beyond simple encryption to meet the potential sophistication of future threats [16]. This research aims to assist developers address privacy and security of data for MMAs, drawing from the standards and best practice perspectives.

The rest of this paper is organized as follows. Section II covers background on MMAs, data transmission and MMA data security. Section III, outlines the privacy and security laws for health data. In Section IV, we introduce our research on the development of a process model to assure the Confidentiality, Integrity and Availability (CIA) of data in transmission for developers of MMAs. The concept of a corresponding testing suite is also introduced in this section. Finally, we conclude the paper and present the future work in Section V.

II. MOBILE MEDICAL APP DATA

A. MMAs and Data Transmission

In July 2011, the FDA issued draft guidance for MMAs and defined a "mobile medical app" as a software application run on a mobile platform (mobile phones, tablets, notebooks and other mobile devices) that is either used as an accessory to a regulated medical device or transforms a mobile platform into a regulated medical device and can be used in the diagnosis, treatment, or prevention of disease [2]. Thus, a MMA is an app that qualifies as a medical device and is therefore required to follow the applicable medical device regulatory requirements. Mobile devices, on which MMAs run, now provide many of the capabilities of traditional PCs with the additional benefit of a large selection of connectivity options [22]. Data is transmitted to and from the MMA through various approaches depending on the goal of the application. There are numerous MMA deployment scenarios that require consideration to ensure data is secure. As a result, MMAs use a variety of channels, wired or wireless, for transmission in a point-to-point, point-to-multipoint and multipoint-to-multipoint setting, to communicate information. Transmission of data may occur between the MMA and for example: remote Health/Service Centers; Medical Professionals; or Health Record Networks. In some cases, the information sent to the MMA is processed on the app and retransmitted to the specified device or center. Through MMAs the collection of significant medical, physiological, lifestyle and daily activity data [20] is greatly amplified and transmitted via varied and numerous networks. Data in transit has a higher level of vulnerability to both losses through oversight and to misappropriation. Misappropriation in the context of this research is the unauthorized use of another's name, likeness, or identity without that person's permission, resulting in harm to that person. Consequently, particular attention is necessary to protect information made accessible in transmission, particularly when it is personal data and ePHI.

Common technologies used for data transmission in MMAs include: Wireless Sensor Networks (WSNs) [23]; Body sensor networks (BSN) [24]; Wireless Body Area Network (WBANs) [25]; Bluetooth/ Bluetooth Low Energy (BLE) [24]; ZigBee [26]; UWB [27]; Wireless Medical Telemetry Service (WMTS) [28]; communication networks such as Wi-Fi [22]; wired communication (internet access, broadband and fiber-optic communication) [14]; and mobile networks 3G/4G and as it becomes more widely available 5G [26]. MMAs are predominantly executed from mobile devices and connect to wireless sensor networks. Consequently the data transmission to and from the MMAs will be predominantly via wireless technologies [24].

B. Mobile Medical Application Data Security

Security and privacy related to patient data are two essential components for MMAs. The fundamental concepts when considering data security are confidentiality, integrity and availability (CIA). Confidentiality is protection of the information from disclosure to unauthorized parties. Integrity refers to protecting information from being modified by unauthorized parties. Availability is ensuring that authorized parties are able to access the information when needed. The intention of health data security and protection is to assure patient privacy through confidentiality, within the development of functional devices, while sustaining the data integrity and availability necessary for use [29].

When considering data security risks for MMAs it is necessary to specify what types of security threats they should be protected against. Deployment of MMAs involves security threats from multiple threat sources which include: attacks; the user; other mobile apps; network carriers; operating systems and mobile platforms. These security risks are further extended when consideration is given to the unauthorized access to the functionality of supporting devices and unauthorized access to the data stored on supporting devices [30]. Given the context in which MMAs are deployed and used, the information going to and from the MMA travels across potentially many different and varying networks in diverse operation settings [31]. In addition, consideration that wireless networks and channels are accessible to everyone [32] and have shared features, means information and network security is equally important in this domain [33]. The potential for breaches of CIA of data in transmission is consequently greatly amplified by these circumstances. The 2015 Ponemon report on mobile app security, emphasized that not enough is spent on mobile app security [34].

1) Attacks: Attacks are techniques that attackers use to exploit vulnerabilities in applications. There are numerous tools available for hacking into MMAs and wireless networks. Hackers target mobile apps to gain entry into servers or databases in the form of malware attacks. A recent list of these tools can be found in the Appendix of the Araxan Report [12]. This report examined 20 sensitive medical and healthcare apps and discovered 90% of Android apps and no iOS apps have been subject to hacking [12]. When data travels across a network, they are susceptible to being read, altered, or "hijacked". Potential for breaches of confidentiality of data occurs during collection and transmission of data. Data in transmission to and from the MMAs must be protected from hacking. Some of the most common issues (but not inclusive) are Easvesdropping, Malware, Node Compromise, Packet Injection, Secure Localization, Secure Management, Sniffing Attacks, Denial of Service (DoS), SQL injection attacks, Code Injection and Man-in-the Middle attacks. The consideration of WBANs for MMAs must satisfy rigorous security and privacy requirements [35]. Wireless channels are open to everyone. Monitoring and participation in the communication in a wireless channel can be achieved with a radio interface configured at the same frequency band [36]. This may cause severe damage to the patient since the cybercriminal can use the attained data [35] for many of the illegal purposes mentioned above. The ISO/IEEE 11073 standard deals only with mutual communication protocols and frameworks exchanged between and has never considered security elements until recently, irrespective of all sorts of security breaches [37]. Security issues must be resolved while designing medical and healthcare apps for sensor networks to avoid data security issues [24].

2) Users: Many of the mobile devices will be personal and bypass the majority of inbound filters normally associated with corporate devices which leaves them vulnerable to malware. It is important that the user has good knowledge of the security safeguards, what measures to follow and what precautions to take [38]. A key challenge with MMA data is the lack of security software installed on mobile devices [39]. Many mobile device users do not avail of or are unacquainted with basic technical security measures, such as firewalls, antivirus and security software measures. Mobile device operating systems are very complex and therefore demand additional security controls for the prevention and detection of attacks against them [40]. The accessibility of social media and email make it easy to post or share information in violation of HIPAA regulations. An example being, a New York nurse was fired because she posted a photo to Instagram of a trauma room after treating a patient [41]. Mixed with the availability to mobile phone cameras and social media apps, the risk of employees divulging PHI and violating HIPAA requirements has increased [42]. One of the greatest threats to MMA data security lies with the fact that most are on mobile devices which are portable, making them much more likely to be lost or stolen [43]. Potentially any data on the device is accessible to the thief, including access to any data and hospital networks. Due to the regulatory protection of PHI, it is important that even when the app is on a stolen device the security of the data remains protected and is regularly backed-up [40]. Measures should be available to remotely lock the MMA, disable service, completely wipe out the data [40] and restrict access to supporting devices.

Not all users' password-protect their devices. Even when passwords are used because of the lack of physical keyboards with mobile devices, users tend to not use complex passwords to secure their information. The use of more than one type of authentication technique suggested by Alqahtani, would afford better data security for MMAs [40]. The difficulty is requesting lengthened authentication requirements from a busy medical professional. Inputting numerous passwords, or waiting for an authentication code in a pressurized situation is not desirable.

3) Other mobile apps: Unfortunately, many users download mobile apps often without considering the security implications. Unintentionally, a user can download malware in the form of another application, an update or by downloading from an unauthorised source. The difficulty in detecting the attack was due to the fact that there currently is no mobile device management application programming interface (API) to obtain the certificate information for each app [44]. An attacker can use Masque Attacks to bypass the normal app sandbox and get root privileges by attacking known iOS vulnerabilities [44]. Cloned apps are a concern, over 50% of cloned apps are malicious and therefore pose serious risks. A recently discovered iOS banking app malware, Masque Attacks, replace an authentic app with malware that has an identical UI. The Masque Attacks access the original app's local data, which was not removed when the original app was replaced and steal the sensitive data [44]. The mobile device management interface did not distinguish the malware from the original as it had used the same bundle identifier.

4) Operating systems & development: Consideration with handling data on mobile devices includes unintended data leakage. It is essential that the MMA is not susceptible to analytic providers that will sell the data to marketing companies. The app stores are attempting to address this, e.g., Apple is banning app developers from selling HealthKit data or storing it on iCloud. Google insists that the user is in control of health data as apps cannot be accessed without the user providing permission. Developers could include analytics that report how often a section of the MMA was viewed, similar to the analytics credit card provider's use to flag unwanted access to data. It is equally important to consider the intentional or unintentional sharing of personal information. Leakage of personal data from the device to the MMA and the leakage of MMA data onto personal devices are key considerations. The bypass of outbound filters elevate the risk of non-compliance with data privacy laws and requirements, e.g., the use of personal Dropbox.

A basic requirement such as encryption is not used in many MMAs. Data is encrypted so that it is not disclosed whilst in transit. Data encryption service provides confidentiality against attacks. The requirement of encryption is stressed, not only for the data, but for the code in development to assure data security [24][40]. Data encryption of passwords and usernames if they are to be stored on the MMA is essential; many apps store this information in unencrypted text. This means that anyone with access to the mobile device the MMA resides on can see passwords and usernames by connecting the device to a PC. If the MMA is hacked, the information encrypted will be useless to the cybercriminals. Many apps send data over an HTTPS connection without checking for revoked certificates [45]. MMA developers should ensure that back-end APIs within mobile platforms are strengthened against attacks using state of the art encryption. As discussed above a MMA could expose healthcare systems that had not previously been accessible from outside their own networks. In MMA data security consideration developers should always use modern encryption algorithms that are accepted as strong by the security community.

Hackers are aware that just because a patch was released does not means it was applied, which, in turn make the app vulnerable for attacks [46]. Some recommend the installation of "Prevention and Detection" software for defending and protecting against malware as essential [40]. Consequently, software that tracks detection and anticipates attacks would require consideration in MMA development.

It is essential that developers research the mobile platforms they are developing for. Each mobile OS offers different security-related features, uses different APIs and handles data permissions its own way. Developers should adapt the code accordingly for each platform the MMA will be run on. There are no standards that straddle development or security testing across the different platforms. Developers design security for each individual OS.

III. Regulations for Health Data

This section of the paper highlights some of the difficulties MMA manufacturers encounter understanding PHI data security and privacy requirements. It describes the key regulations on data security and privacy, MMA developers are required to observe in Europe and the United States.

Increasingly, MMA developers must deal with a range of international regulations if they want to perform business in more than one country. The absence of privacy laws in some countries, in addition to inconsistency or even conflicting laws means PHI is often misused and treated superficially. In the rush to market the aspects of privacy and security are not properly considered [47]. Some MMA providers find they are in breach of regulation only when they are warned or fined, blindsided by regulatory issues, due to the complexity [48]. Due to the surge in value of PHI on the black-market, owing to the lack of security controls within healthcare and the increase in the security of credit card data [17], privacy and security policy issues relating to data with MMAs are now of primary importance. The Thomas Reuters Foundation and mHealth Alliance published a global landscape analysis of the privacy and security policies to protect health data [48]. The report states, that most jurisdictions agree, data security is essential. The report proposes the world of privacy law is divided into three major groups: Omnibus data protection regulation in the style of the European laws that regulate all personal information equally; U.S.-style sectorial privacy laws that address specific privacy issues arising in certain industries and business sectors, so that only certain types of personal information are regulated; The constitutional approach, whereby certain types of personal information are considered private and compelled from a basic human rights perspective but no specific privacy regulation is in place otherwise [48].

A. European Union

Data protection and privacy has always been a strong concern for European law makers. Within the EU, the EU Data Protection Directive (Directive 95/46/EC) [49] is the key piece of regulation that will affect how you manage health data. This Directive is currently implemented in laws of Member States and requires establishment of supervisory authorities to monitor its application. However, at the beginning of 2012, the EU approved the draft of the European Data Protection Regulation (EDPR) [50], and will be enforced by 2018. This means the law will apply generally over all states in the EU, it will not require individual Member States implementation. With this progression in regulation, all Member States will be at the same stage of security and data protection [47].

The Directive enables ease in definition of terms. Health data is regarded in the Directive under the 'special category of data' known as sensitive data [49]. The Directive has specific sections in relation to sensitive data which include: Rules on lawful processing of sensitive data, Article 8 (1- 7); Rules on secure processing, Article 17, Article 4 (2), and Article 16. The sections stipulate specific rules about sensitive data, the processing, protection and the requirement that this data is not transferred to an end point that does not have acceptable levels of protection. The Directive is now the international data protection metric against which data protection adequacy and sufficiency is measured [51], [52].

Directive 2002/58/EC of the European Parliament and Council of 12 July 2002 [53], known as the ePrivacy Directive, is concerned with the processing of personal data and the protection of privacy in the digital age. It is now law in all EU countries and covers all non-essential cookies, and tracking devices. This Directive principally concerns the processing of personal data relating to the delivery of communications services. It provides rules on how providers of electronic communication services, should manage their subscribers' data. It also guarantees rights for subscribers when they use these services. The key parts that MMA developers are concerned with in the directive are: processing security; confidentiality of communication; processing traffic and location data; cookies and controls.

B. United States

The key law that applies to health data in the US is HIPAA. HIPAA was established to classify security policies and privacy rights across the healthcare spectrum [29]. As a result, new federal standards were implemented to assure patient's medical information privacy, in addition to security procedures for the protection of privacy [54]. HIPAA is organized into separate Titles and the security and privacy of health data is addressed in Title II, referred to as the 'Privacy Rule' and the 'Security Rule' [55]. The HIPAA Privacy Rule covers all PHI in any medium while the HIPAA Security Rule covers ePHI. The Security Rule necessitates security controls for the physical and ePHI to ensure the CIA of the data. The US does not have any centralized legislation at the federal level regarding data protection and follows a fragmented approach, which requires looking at a number of laws and regulations to form the definition of terms [55]. The basic HIPAA requirements for MMA developers include: Secure access to personal health information via unique user authentication; Encryption of data that will be stored; Regular safety updates to protect from any breaches; A system to audit the data and ensure that it hasn't been accessed or modified in any unauthorized way; A mobile wipe option that allows personal health information to be wiped if the device is lost; Data backup in case of a device loss, failure, or other disaster [56].

HIPAA was updated in the HIPAA Omnibus Rule required by The Health Information Technology for Economic and Clinical Health Act of 2010, (HITECH Act). The HITECH Act established new information security breach notification requirements that apply to businesses that handle personal health information and other health data [57]. The FDA released guidance "Content of Premarket Submissions for Management of Cybersecurity in Medical Devices" [58]. This provides a list of recognized consensus standards dealing with Information Technology and medical device security [58].

The circumstances in which MMAs may transmit information wirelessly places them in the domain of Federal Communications Commission (FCC) regulation, to ensure consumer and public safety [59]. Recognizing the need for regulatory clarity, the FCC, FDA, Office of the National Coordinator (ONC) and the Department of Health and Human Services (HHS) came together in a grouping called the Food and Drug Administration Safety and Innovation Act (FDASIA) Working Group. The group, through the FDA, released a report that contains a proposed strategy and recommendations on an appropriate, risk-based regulatory framework pertaining to health information technology including MMAs [60].

IV. Current Research

A. Research Perspective

As the MMA domain grows and becomes a standard established mechanism for healthcare delivery, both the security and privacy of health data will be essential. The reference [12] report, which included investigation of MHAs and MMAs, highlighted that hacks are on the rise in mobile apps. Mobile apps in healthcare are being developed persistently without proper data security functionality. This is largely due to the lack of understanding of current standards and regulation requirements pertaining to data security and partly due to the fact that many of these apps are developed by businesses not familiar with the medical device industry. Consequently, a gap exists as there is no standardized way to assist mobile app developers in the healthcare domain and particularly the highly regulated MMA domain, to observe security related requirements of regulation or assure data security in operation. A study analyzing security vulnerabilities explicitly in mobile health apps, highlighted the lack of a global security standard for mobile devices [13]. There are no specific MMA standards for cybersecurity, which are visible in other industries where standards and guidance are available, e.g. the NIST Special Publication 800-82 Guide to Industrial Control Systems Security [61]. For mobile apps in healthcare, existing regulation and standards must be applied in a patchwork method to address security.

The aim of this research is to investigate this gap further and provide a solution to assist clarity in relation to data security and regulation for MHA and MMA app developers. The intention of this research is to develop a Process for identifying the most applicable objective evidence to assist MMA developers to assure data security for MMAs during development, with specific focus upon data transmission. Due to the nature of MMAs and their use of public and open networks for data transmission, data is particularly exposed at this stage.

B. Research Setting

1) International standards, technical reports and best practice: This section briefly outlines the international standards, technical reports and best practice literature, in which the research is to be grounded. The research leverages on two medical device standards, IEC/TR 80001-2-2:2012 [62] and IEC/TR 80001-2-8 [63]. The overall objective of the research is to develop a process in order to establish security controls pertinent to MMAs for all 19 security capabilities outlined in the IEC 80001-2-2:2012 standard. IEC/TR 80001-2-2:2012 is the only published medical device security standard and presents 19 high-level security-related capabilities in understanding the type of security controls to be considered and the risks that lead to the controls [64]. It is the only guidance available that specifically addresses security requirements for networked medical devices [65]. IEC/TR 80001-2-8 (currently at a committee draft stage) is a catalogue of security controls developed relating to the security capabilities defined in IEC/TR 80001-2-2. The security controls support the maintenance of confidentiality and protection from malicious intrusion [66]. The report provides guidance to healthcare organizations and MD manufacturers for the selection of security controls to protect the CIA and accountability of data and systems during development, operation and disposal [66].

This research proposes using the applicable security controls in IEC/TR 80001-2-8 relating to two of the capabilities directly associated with data transmission from IEC/TR 80001-2-2, as an exemplar. The intent is to use the measured applicable security controls outlined in IEC/TR 80001-2-8, with further research completed to assemble security controls pertinent to the mobile aspect, with comparative expert validation, by means of analysis of applicable standards and best practices. In addition, the research aims to establish a corresponding testing suite to assure data CIA in data transmission for MMAs against the developed security controls.

The two specific capabilities from IEC/TR 80001-2-2 that relate to data transmission are, TXCF – Transmission Confidentiality and TXIG – Transmission Integrity. Each capability comes with recommended reference material and a common standard to consider when developing and establishing security controls. The security controls established in IEC 80001-2-8 associated to the TXCF and TXIG capabilities will be mapped through the common standard and reference materials to establish security control objectives and technical strategies for MMA developers. Additionally, the security controls will be mapped to wireless network and healthcare standards to determine if further controls are required for MMAs. The standards currently being mapped to the IEC 80001-2-8 established security controls are: ISO/IEC 27033-2:2012; ISO/IEEE 11073; NIST SP 800-153.

2) Threat Modeling Analysis (TMA): The research revealed Threat Modeling Analysis (TMA) assists in understanding and assessing the security risks an asset can be exposed to. A key part of TMA is threat modeling. The research revealed that threat modelling analysis and threat modelling are established methods considered in National Institute of Standards and Technology (NIST) standards and best practice (OWASP) in relation to mobile app security risk assessment. Threat modeling is an important basis for defining security requirements of information systems [67] and information protection. Threat modeling is widely acknowledged in NIST standards [68] and recognised as being best practice [69] in risk assessment for network and mobile app security. Threat modeling is widely recognized as an effective means to establish a solid basis for the specification of security requirements in app development and is considered as a significant step in the security requirement model [70].One of the objectives of this research is to develop an operational threat model from the developed security controls for MMA data transmission. Therefore, an understanding of best practices in threat modeling is essential for this research. The aim of the research is to create a threat modelling analysis framework that incorporates a threat model which is aligned with the developed security controls from the process model. Primary research has established the recommended TMA and threat modeling methods. This will be the foundation for the development of a threat modelling analysis framework, developed through focus groups and validation in two MMA development companies and the standards community.

3) Threats and attacks: The introduction of risk assessment requires an understanding of the threats and how they exploit vulnerabilities to alter or attack an asset from the position of MMA data security. To establish this understanding, additional investigation was conducted in the area of threats and attacks on mobile apps. The research on the classification and some of the most common threats and corresponding attacks in the mobile app field for data in transmission can be seen in Table II, [22], [31], [34], [71]–[73], [74]. This section of the research is currently being written into a conference paper. By understanding the threats and corresponding attacks in this domain, this research will leverage on the existing understandings in app security to the MMA field.

4) Testing suite: The dynamic nature of mobile app development creates difficulties for inexperienced developers and small organizations, particularly in the medical device domain. This is partially due to the budgetary resources or motivation to conduct extensive testing and this in turn can leave an app, the user's device, and the user's network vulnerable to exploitation by attackers [75]. Security testing of mobile apps is largely a manual, expensive and difficult process[76] and security testing is seen as primarily a manual process, with little hybrid or automation testing available for use or used by developers and a significant challenge [77]. Complexity of testing the application security itself and consideration relating to the security requirements of open platforms in which apps transmit data is an additional emphasized difficulty [78]. Investigation has commenced in the area of transmission security testing methodologies and testing methods and mobile apps, to fully review the landscape of transmission security testing. This research was undertaken with the collaboration of data security experts within a specialist testing company. The company and experts have vast experience in working in both network and app data security. In collaboration with the testing company, their experts and academic experts the expectation is to develop a testing suite against the considered security controls. The testing suite will be developed to follow the information discovery process, which includes the threat modeling analysis that was developed to address the MMA security controls. A diagrammatic summary of the adapted OWASP Testing Guide 4.0 [79] and researched considerations required when completing mobile app security testing, concerning this research, can be seen in Figure 1.

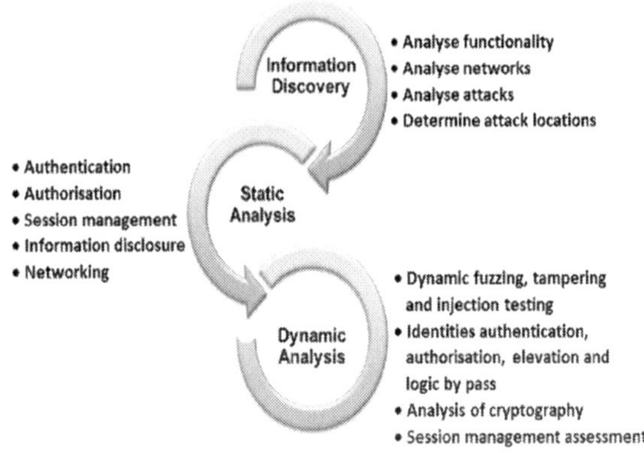

Figure 1. Diagrammatic summary of requirements for mobile app security testing.

OWASP highlight the need to have a clear understanding of the testing objectives and, therefore, the security requirements to have a successful testing program. The information discovery step would be accomplished with the completion of the first step in TMA, the collection of background information, and the first two steps of threat modeling. Both static analysis and dynamic analysis are standard requirements in any software testing process, neither analysis approaches are sufficient alone to address all testing limitations [79]. In recent years much research and development has been completed in the field of static source review tools, called code scanners. These scanners automatically look for coding errors that can determine some security issues. Many organizations are using static source code scanners, however this approach is not effective when used alone [79]. The limitations of dynamic analysis are, it only monitors the behavior of the app during runtime and lacks the ability to identify potential vulnerabilities [80]. The dynamic approach is therefore generally used in the second step of the testing process [75], [80].

5) Validation and trailing: Validation will combine expert opinion from the standards community, recognized experts in mobile data security, testers and developers from within the MMA industry. The trailing will be completed in two identified MMA companies, which are currently collaborating with the research to assure data security of their MMAs. Action Design Research (ADR) was considered the most appropriate approach for this research. ADR methodology was developed to facilitate a useful approach to benefit the interests of both IS research and organisational research [81] and the evaluation of an IT artifact. It was chosen in order to accommodate the development of IT artifacts, in collaboration with industry and stimulate organisational change when addressing transmission security in the development of MMAs. This research involves collaborative development of artifacts through theory- ingrained research and practice inspired research. ADR can account for both technological and organisational contexts, shaping of the artifact via design and use and influences of designers and users [82]. Additionally, consideration of the dynamic setting and development environment in which this research will be conducted, ADR was considered appropriate methodology to facilitate these challenges.

TABLE II. DIFFERENT TYPES OF ATTACKS IN THE MOBILE APP FIELD

Grouping of Attack Vectors	Description	Examples	Security Concern			Classification	
			Confidentiality	*Integrity*	*Availability*	*Passive*	*Active*
Reconnaissance Attacks	Referred to as information gathering, an activity that does not noticeably interfere with the regular operation of the device. They often serve as preparation for further attacks.	Eavesdropping Sniffing Port Scans Distributed Network Services Queries	x	x	x	x	x
Access Attacks	Gaining unauthorized access to a device and its resources.	Spoofing Man-in–the-Middle SSL-stripping SQL Injection Session hijacking/replaying Re-ordering/rerouting Port redirection Backdoor Tampering Cross-site scripting Security Misconfiguration Privilege Escalation Attack	x	x			x
Denial of Service Attacks	Based on the layers Attacks on networks, in order to bring them to a stop or interrupt the system by saturating communication links or by flooding hosts with requests to deny access to the user.	Distributed Denial of Service Attack Physical Layer Jamming/ De-synchronization Tampering Data Link Collision Exhaustion Neglect and greed Homing Misdirection Black holes Transport		x	x		x

Grouping of Attack Vectors	Description	Examples	Security Concern			Classification	
			Confidentiality	*Integrity*	*Availability*	*Passive*	*Active*
		Flooding					
Malware Attacks	A program covertly inserted into another program with the intent to destroy data, run destructive or intrusive programs.	Worms (Mass Mailing) Bot/Botnet /Malicious Mobile Code Viruses (Compiled, Interpreted) Trojan Rootkits		x	x	x	x
Network Attacks	MANET	Re-ordering/Rerouting Path Traversal Byzantine Wormhole Attack Byzantine Attacks Black Hole Attack Worms (Network Services) Flood Rushing Attack Floor Rushing Attack	x	x			x
	WSN	Bluesnarfing Port Scan	x	x		x	x

V. Conclusion and Future Work

This paper examined existing data security issues and practices in relation to MMAs. A summary of regulations relating to data privacy and security MMA providers are mandated by law to adhere to, were outlined. Compliance and improved understanding of data security regulations and best practices will assist developers to meet the security requirements for data in transmission. The security gaps in MMAs are exploited due to lack of knowledge, understanding or amalgamated regulation for data security with MMAs.

The mobile app industry claim innovation is stifled, due to the lack of clarity in regulations and security concerns. Developers will need to find the optimal balance between data security and privacy as MMAs expand and PHI enters into new aspects. The lack of consistent data security to assure privacy, to allow interoperability, and to maximize the full capabilities [83], presents a significant barrier to the industry. The primary focus for the continued research in this area will be two fold. The development of a framework to establish security controls for transmission of PHI to assist MMA developers assure CIA. The security controls will be completed in examining and mapping the referenced standards and best practices currently recognized in the medical, applications and data security domains. The intention is to fill the gap in knowledge and understanding for MMA developers, through ease of accessibility to the most appropriate information. The second objective of the future research is the establishment of a practical testing suite for the MMA developers in the data transmission domain. The testing suite will be developed against the validated mobile transmission security controls for PHI. The aim is to test the implemented transmission security controls during development, use and security patch updates to assure data CIA. The implementation of the transmission security controls would be encouraged from the preliminary development stage with the future research providing a checklist for developers with MMAs in the market.

Validation of the research will be completed in collaboration with two identified MMA development companies. The MMAs being developed will have different transmission requirements and capabilities to assure diversity.

Acknowledgment

This research is supported by the Science Foundation Ireland Research Centres Programme, through Lero - the Irish Software Research Centre (http://www.lero.ie) grants 10/CE/I1855 & 13/RC/2094.

References

[1] C. Treacy and F. McCaffery, "Medical Mobile Apps Data Security Overview," in *SOFTENG : The Second International Conference on Advances and Trends in Software Engineering*, 2016, pp. 123–128.

[2] FDA, "Mobile Medical Applications Guidance for Industry and Food and Drug Administration Staff," *U.S. Deapartment of Health and Human Services Food and Drug Administration*. U.S. Department of Health and Human Services, USA, p. 44, 2015.

[3] B. M. Silva, J. J. P. C. Rodrigues, F. Canelo, I. C. Lopes, and L. Zhou, "A data encryption solution for mobile health

apps in cooperation environments," J. Med. Internet Res., vol. 15, no. 4, p. e66, Jan. 2013.

[4] A. W. G. Buijink, B. J. Visser, and L. Marshall, "Medical apps for smartphones: lack of evidence undermines quality and safety," *Evid. Based. Med.*, vol. 18, no. 3, pp. 90–2, Jun. 2013.

[5] D. He, M. Naveed, C. A. Gunter, and K. Nahrstedt, "Security Concerns in Android mHealth Apps," in *AMIA Annual Symposium Proceedings*, 2014, no. November, pp. 645–654.

[6] Y. Yang and R. . Sliverman, "Mobile health applications: the patchwork of legal and liability issues suggests strategies to improve oversight," *Health Aff.*, vol. 33, no. 2, pp. 222–7, 2014.

[7] Price Waterhouse Cooper - Health Research Institute, "Top Health Industry Issues of 2015 - A new health economy takes shape," 2015.

[8] "Data breach results in $4.8 million HIPAA settlements," *U.S. Department of Health and Human Services*, 2014. [Online]. Available: http://www.hhs.gov/about/news/2014/05/07/data-breach-results-48-million-hipaa-settlements.html. [Accessed: 01-Dec-2016].

[9] N. H. Ab Rahman, "Privacy disclosure risk: smartphone user guide," *Int. J. Mob. Netw. Des. Innov.*, vol. 5, no. 1, pp. 2–8, 2013.

[10] G. S. McNeal, "Health Insurer Anthem Struck By Massive Data Breach - Forbes," *Forbes*, 2015. [Online]. Available: http://www.forbes.com/sites/gregorymcneal/2015/02/04/massive-data-breach-at-health-insurer-anthem-reveals-social-security-numbers-and-more/. [Accessed: 30-Nov-2016].

[11] B. Filkins, "Health Care Cyberthreat Report: Widespread Compromises Detected, Compliance Nightmare on Horizon," SANS Institute, 2014.

[12] Araxan, "State of Mobile App Security: Apps Under Attack - Special Focus on Fincial, Retail/Merchannt and Healthcare/Medical Apps," 2014.

[13] Y. Cifuentes, L. Beltrán, and L. Ramírez, "Analysis of Security Vulnerabilities for Mobile Health Applications," *Int. J. Electr. Comput. Energ. Electron. Commun. Eng.*, vol. 9, no. 9, pp. 999–1004, 2015.

[14] J. Kabachinski, "Mobile medical apps changing healthcare technology," *Biomed. Instrum. Technol.*, vol. 45, no. 6, pp. 482–6, 2011.

[15] FDA, "Safety Communications - Cybersecurity Vulnerabilities of Hospira Symbiq Infusion System: FDA Safety Communication," *WebSite*, 2015. [Online]. Available: http://www.fda.gov/MedicalDevices/Safety/AlertsandNotices/ucm456815.htm?source=govdelivery&utm_medium=email&utm_source=govdelivery. [Accessed: 30-Nov-2016].

[16] G. M. Snow, "FBI — Cybersecurity: Responding to the Threat of Cyber Crime and Terrorism," *FBI Website*, 2011. [Online]. Available: https://archives.fbi.gov/archives/news/testimony/cybersecurity-responding-to-the-threat-of-cyber-crime-and-terrorism. [Accessed: 19-Nov-2016].

[17] J. Williams, "Don't Mug Me For My Password! - InformationWeek," *Information Week Healthcare*, 2014. [Online]. Available: http://www.informationweek.com/healthcare/security-and-privacy/dont-mug-me-for-my-password!/a/d-id/1318316. [Accessed: 29-Nov-2016].

[18] Cisco, "Combating cybercrime in the healthcare industry." pp. 1–7, 2015. [Online]. Available: https://www.google.ie/search?q=Cisco,+%E2%80%9CCombating+cybercrime+in+the+healthcare+industry.%E2%80%9D&ie=utf-8&oe=utf-8&gws_rd=cr&ei=Su0-WJXTNKGBgAaM1rKoCg. [Accessed: 29-Nov-2016].

[19] FDA, "Cybersecurity for Medical Devices and Hospital Networks: FDA Safety Communication," *FDA Website*, 2013. [Online]. Available: http://www.fda.gov/MedicalDevices/Safety/AlertsandNotices/ucm356423.htm. [Accessed: 25-Nov-2016].

[20] European Commission, "Green Paper on mobile Health ('mHealth')," Brussels, 2014.

[21] "mHealth App Developer Economics 2014 The State of the Art mHealth Publishing." research2guidance, Continua Health Alliance, mHealth Summit Europe, Berlin, pp. 1–43, 2014.

[22] M. La Polla, F. Martinelli, and D. Sgandurra, "A Survey on Security for Mobile Devices," *IEEE Commun. Surv. Tutorials*, vol. 15, no. 1, pp. 446–471, 2013.

[23] J. N. Al-Karaki and a E. Kamal, "Routing Techniques in Wireless Sensor Networks: A Survey," *IEEE Wirel. Commun.*, vol. 11, no. December, pp. 6–28, 2004.

[24] M. Al Ameen, J. Liu, and K. Kwak, "Security and privacy issues in wireless sensor networks for healthcare applications," *J. Med. Syst.*, vol. 36, no. 1, pp. 93–101, Feb. 2012.

[25] J. Y. Khan and M. R. Yuce, "Wireless Body Area Network (WBAN) for Medical Applications," in *New Development in Biomedical Engeneering*, D. Campolo, Ed. InTech, 2010, pp. 591–623.

[26] T. V. Ngoc, "Medical Applications of Wireless Networks," Washington University, St. Louis, Student Reports on Recent Advances in Wireless and Mobile Networking (2008). [Online]. Available: http://www.cse.wustl.edu/~jain/cse574-08/ftp/medical/. [Accessed: 18-Nov-2016].

[27] Y. Gao *et al.*, "Low-power ultrawideband wireless telemetry transceiver for medical sensor applications," *IEEE Trans. Biomed. Eng.*, vol. 58, no. 3 PART 2, pp. 768–772, 2011.

[28] J. Ahmad and F. Zafar, "Review of body area network technology & wireless medical monitoring," *Int. J. Inf.*, vol. 2, no. 2, pp. 186–188, 2012.

[29] S. Avancha, A. Baxi, and D. Kotz, "Privacy in mobile technology for personal healthcare," *ACM Comput. Surv.*, vol. 45, no. 1, pp. 1–54, 2012.

[30] J. L. Hall and D. McGraw, "For Telehealth to Succeed, Privacy and Security Risks Must be Identified and Addressed," *Health Aff.*, vol. 33, no. 2, pp. 216–221, 2014.

[31] D. Fischer, B. Markscheffel, S. Frosch, and D. Buettner, "A Survey of Threats and Security Measures for Data Transmission over GSM/UMTS Networks," *7th Int. Conf. Internet Technol. Secur. Trans.*, pp. 477–482, 2012.

[32] S. Singh, M. Singh, and D. Singhtise, "A survey on network security and attack defense mechanism for wireless sensor networks," *Int. J. Comput. Trends Tech*, no. May to June, pp. 1–9, 2011.

[33] M. Li, W. Lou, and K. Ren, "Data Secutiry and Privacy in Wireless Body Area Networks," *IEEE Wirel. Commun.*, vol. 17, no. 1, pp. 51–58, 2010.

[34] Ponemon Institute, "The State of Mobile Application Insecurity," 2015.

[35] S. Saleem, S. Ullah, and K. S. Kwak, "A study of IEEE 802.15.4 security framework for wireless body area networks," *Sensors (Basel).*, vol. 11, no. 2, pp. 1383–95, 2011.

[36] V. Mainanwal, M. Gupta, and S. Kumar Upadhayay, "A Survey on Wireless Body Area Network: Security Technology and its Design Methodology issue," in *2nd International Conference on Innovations in*

Information,Embedded and Communication systems (ICIIECS)2015, 2015, no. I, pp. 1–5.

[37] S. S. Kim, Y. H. Lee, J. M. Kim, D. S. Seo, G. H. Kim, and Y. S. Shin, "Privacy Protection for Personal Health Device Communication and Healthcare Building Applications," *J. Appl. Math.*, vol. 2014, pp. 1–5, 2014.

[38] M. Souppaya and K. Scarfone, *NIST Special Publication 800-124 Guidelines for Managing the Security of Mobile Devices in the Enterprise*. Gaithersburg, USA: National Institute of Standards and Technology, 2013, pp. 1–29.

[39] D. Nyambo, Z. O. Yonah, and C. Tarimo, "Review of Security Frameworks in the Converged Web and Mobile Applications," *Int. J. Comput. Inf. Technol.*, vol. 3, no. 4, pp. 724–730, 2014.

[40] A. S. Alqahtani, "Security of Mobile Phones and their Usage in Business," *Int. J. Adv. Comput. Sci. Appl.*, vol. 4, no. 11, pp. 17–32, 2013.

[41] C. Wiltz, "Mobile App Developers to Congress: HIPPA is Stifling Innovation | MDDI Medical Device and Diagnostic Industry News Products and Suppliers," *Mobile Health*, 2014. [Online]. Available: http://www.mddionline.com/article/mobile-app-developers-congress-hippa-stifling-innovation-140918. [Accessed: 19-Sep-2016].

[42] FierceHealthIT, "Mobile & HIPAA Securing personal health data in an increasingly portable workplace," FierceHealthIT, pp. 1–4, 2014.

[43] P. Ruggiero and J. Foote, "Cyber Threats to Mobile Phones," United States Computer Emergency Readiness Team, 2011.

[44] H. Xue, T. Wei, and Y. Zhang, "Masque Attcak: All Your iOS Apps Belong to US," *FireEye*, 2014. [Online]. Available: https://www.fireeye.com/blog/threat-research/2014/11/masque-attack-all-your-ios-apps-belong-to-us.html. [Accessed: 18-Nov-2016].

[45] M. B. Barcena, C. Wueest, and H. Lau, "How safe is your quantified self?," Mountain View, 2014. [Online]. Available: https://www.google.ie/search?q=%E2%80%9CHow+safe+is+your+quantified+self%E2%80%AF%3F,%E2%80%9D&ie=utf-8&oe=utf-8&gws_rd=cr&ei=KO4-WO6vEcrGgAbpranwBg. [Accessed: 30-Nov-2016].

[46] Y. S. Baker, R. Agrawal, and S. Bhattacharya, "Analyzing Security Threats as Reported by the United States Computer Emergency Readiness Team," in *2013 IEEE International Conference on Intelligence and Security Informatics (ISI 2013)*, 2013, pp. 10–12.

[47] B. Martinez-Perez, I. Torre-Diez de la, and M. Lopez-Coronado, "Privacy and Security in Mobile Health Apps: A Review and Recommendations," *J. Med. Syst.*, vol. 39, no. 1, p. 181, 2015.

[48] Thomas Reuters Foundation and mHealth Alliance, "Patient Privacy in a Mobile World a Framework to Address Privacy Law Issues in Mobile Health," Thomas Reuters Foundation, London, 2013. [Online]. Available: https://www.google.ie/search?q=%E2%80%9CPatient+Privacy+in+a+Mobile+World+a+Framework+to+Address+Privacy+LawIssues+in+Mobile+Health,%E2%80%9D&ie=utf-8&oe=utf-8&gws_rd=cr&ei=Dvw-WNvHB4XmgAb18r7IDg. [Accessed: 30-Nov-2016].

[49] European Union, Directive 95/46/EC of the European Parliament and of the Council of 24 October 1995 on the protection of individuals with regard to the processing of personal data and on the free movement of such data. EU, 1995.

[50] European Commission, Proposal for a regulation of the European Parliament and of the council on the protection of individuals with regard to the processing of personal data and on the free movement of such data (General Data Protection Regulation), vol. 11. 2012, p. 118.

[51] European Commission., "Communication fom the Commission to the European Parliament the Council on the Transfer of Personal Data from the EU to the United States of America under Directive 95/46/EC following the Judgment by the Court of Justice in Case C-362/14 (Schrems)," 2015.

[52] P. De Hert and V. Papakonstantinou, "The proposed data protection Regulation replacing Directive 95/46/EC: A sound system for the protection of individuals," *Comput. Law Secur. Rev.*, vol. 28, no. 2, pp. 130–142, 2012.

[53] European Commission, Directive 2002/58/EC of the European Parliament and of the Council of 12 July 2002 concerning the processing of personal data and the protection of privacy in the electronic communications sector (Directive on privacy and electronic communications). EU, 2002.

[54] J. Li and M. J. Shaw, "Electronic medical records and patient privacy," *Int. J. Inf. Secur. Priv.*, vol. 2, no. 3, pp. 45–54, 2008.

[55] B. Malin, "A De-identification Strategy Used for Sharing One Data Provider's Oncology Trials Data through the Project Data Sphere® Repository," Nashville, 2013.

[56] A. Wang, N. An, X. Lu, H. Chen, C. Li, and S. Levkoff, "A Classification Scheme for Analyzing Mobile Apps Used to Prevent and Manage Disease in Late Life," *JMIR mhealth uhealth*, vol. 2, no. 1, pp. 1–11, Feb. 2014.

[57] L. J. Sotto, B. C. Treacy, and M. L. Mclellan, "Privacy and Data Security Risks in Cloud Computing," *Electron. Commer. Law Rep.*, vol. 186, pp. 1–6, 2010.

[58] FDA, "Content of Premarket Submissions for Management of Cybersecurity in Medical Devices - Guidance for Industry and Food and Drug Administration Staff," 2014.

[59] A. Atienza and K. Patrick, "Mobile Health: The Killer App for Cyberinfrastructure and Consumer Health," *Am. J. Prev. Med.*, vol. 40, no. 5S2, pp. 151–153, 2011.

[60] Food and Drug Administration and Safety and Innovation Act, "FDASIA Health IT Report Proposed Strategy and Recommendations for a Risk-Based Framework," 2014.

[61] K. Stouffer and J. Falco, "Guide to Industrial Control Systems (ICS) Security," 2015.

[62] IEC, "TR 80001-2-2 Application of risk management for IT-networks incorporating medical devices Part 2-2: Guidance for the disclosure," European Commission, pp. 1–54, 2012.

[63] IEC/DTR, "80001-2-8 Health informatics, Application of risk management for IT-networks incorporating medical devices: Application guidance – Guidance on standards for establishing the security capabilities identified in IEC/TR 80001-2-2," no. June 2014. 2015.

[64] IEC, TR 80001-2-2:2012 Application of risk management for IT-networks incorporating medical devices Part 2-2: Guidance for the disclosure and communication of medical device security needs, risks and controls. BSI Standards Publication, 2012.

[65] A. Finnegan and F. McCaffery, "A Security Argument Pattern for Medical Device Assurance Cases," in *2014 IEEE International Symposium on Software Reliability Engineering Workshops*, 2014, pp. 220–225.

[66] A. Finnegan and F. McCaffery, "A Security Argument for Medical Device Assurance Cases," in *Software Reliability Engineering Workshops (ISSREW), 2014 IEEE International Symposium on*, 2014, pp. 220–225.

[67] S. Myagmar, A. J. Lee, and W. Yurcik, "Threat Modeling as a Basis for Security Requirements," in *Proceedings of*

the 2005 ACM workshop on Storage security and survivability, 2005, pp. 94–102.

[68] NIST, "Special Publication 800-30 Guide for Conducting Risk Assessments," 2012.

[69] OWASP, "Threat Risk Modeling," *The Open Web Application Security Project (OWASP) webpage*. [Online]. Available: https://www.owasp.org/index.php/Threat_Risk_Modeling#STRIDE. [Accessed: 07-Mar-2016].

[70] E. A. Oladimeji, S. Supakkul, and L. Chung, "Security threat modeling and analysis: A goal-oriented approach," *Proc 10th IASTED Int. Conf. Softw. Eng. Appl. SEA 2006*, pp. 13–15, 2006.

[71] G. Delac, M. Silic, and J. Krolo, "Emerging security threats for mobile platforms," in *2011 Proceedings of the 34th International Convention MIPRO*, 2011, pp. 1468–1473.

[72] W. Kim, O.-R. Jeong, C. Kim, and J. So, "The dark side of the Internet: Attacks, costs and responses," *Inf. Syst.*, vol. 36, no. 3, pp. 675–705, May 2011.

[73] J. Agbogun and F. A. Ejiga, "Network Security Management," *Netw. Secur.*, vol. 2, no. 4, pp. 617–625, 2013.

[74] K. Scarfone, "SP 800-153 Guidelines for Managing and Securing Mobile Devices in the Enterprise (Draft)." NIST, p. 24, 2012.

[75] S. Quirolgico, J. Voas, T. Karygiannis, C. Michael, and K. Scarfone, "NIST Special Publication 800-163 Vetting the Security of Mobile Applications," U.S. Department of Commerce NIST, U.S., pp. 1–44, 2015.

[76] R. Mahmood, N. Esfahani, T. Kacem, N. Mirzaei, S. Malek, and A. Stavrou, "A whitebox approach for automated security testing of Android applications on the cloud," in *7th International Workshop on Automation of Software Test (AST)*, 2012, pp. 22–28.

[77] M. E. Joorabchi, A. Mesbah, and P. Kruchten, "Real challenges in mobile app development," in *International Symposium on Empirical Software Engineering and Measurement*, 2013, pp. 15–24.

[78] A. I. Wasserman, "Software Engineering Issues for Mobile Application Development," *ACM Trans. Inf. Syst.*, pp. 1–4, 2010.

[79] M. Meucci *et al.*, OWASP Testing Guide 4.0. The OWASP Foundation, 2014. [Online]. Available: https://www.owasp.org/index.php/OWASP_Testing_Project. [Accessed: 30-Nov-2016].

[80] S.-H. Seo, A. Gupta, A. Mohamed Sallam, E. Bertino, and K. Yim, "Detecting mobile malware threats to homeland security through static analysis," *J. Netw. Comput. Appl.*, vol. 38, pp. 43–53, Feb. 2014.

[81] R. Cole, S. Purao, M. Rossi, and M. K. Sein, "Being Proactive: Where Action Research meets Design Research," in *ICIS 2005 Proceedings*, 2005, pp. 1–21.

[82] J. Iivari and J. Venable, "Action Research and Design Science Research," in *17th European Conference on Information Systems*, 2009, pp. 1–13.

[83] European Commission, "Commission Staff Working Document: on the existing EU legal framework applicable to lifestyle and wellbeing apps Accompanying the document Green Paper on mobile Health ('mHealth')," Brussels, SWD(2014) 135 Final Commission, 2014.

Multi-Platform Performance Evaluation of the TUAK Mobile Authentication Algorithm

Keith Mayes
Information Security Group
Royal Holloway, University of London
Egham, UK
keith.mayes@rhul.ac.uk

Steve Babbage
Vodafone Group R&D
Vodafone Group Services Ltd.
Newbury, UK
steve.babbage@vodafone.com

Alexander Maximov
Ericsson Research
Ericsson
Lund, SE
alexander.maximov@ericsson.com

***Abstract*—Support for secure mobile authentication in long-term Machine-to-Machine (M2M) deployments, in which the network operator may change, requires the use of common authentication algorithms. The existing 3G MILENAGE algorithm is suitable for this, however there is need for a back-up/alternative in case vulnerabilities are discovered. TUAK is a new mutual authentication and key generation algorithm proposed by the Security Algorithm Group of Experts (SAGE) of the European Telecommunications Standards Institute (ETSI) and published by the Third Generation Partnership Project (3GPP). TUAK is based on the Keccak sponge function, which has very different design principles to MILENAGE. However, the practicality of implementing TUAK on currently deployed and/or future Subscriber Identity Module (SIM) cards was not well known. This paper extends on work first published in ICONS16/EMBEDDED2016; describing the implementation and performance of TUAK on three smart card platforms and a server.**

***Keywords*-3GPP; GSM; Keccak; SAGE; TUAK.**

I. Introduction

This text describes an extended version of an ICONS 2016 conference paper [1] that considered the performance of new mobile authentication algorithm on two modern smart card platforms. In this paper we also consider the implementation on a third and older/legacy smart card as well as a server representing an Authentication Centre (AuC). We start by considering the history of standards evolution in this area.

The European Telecommunications Standards Institute (ETSI) [2] and later the Third Generation Partnership Project (3GPP) [3] standardised mobile networks so that Mobile Network Operators (MNO) were able to choose/design their own cryptographic algorithms for subscriber authentication and session key generation. In GSM, [4] there is a proliferation of algorithms, however for 3G most MNOs use the well-studied and openly published MILENAGE algorithm [5]. MILENAGE (AES [6] based) was designed and published by the ETSI Security Algorithms Group of Experts (SAGE), and more recently SAGE designed a second algorithm, called TUAK [7] based on the Keccak [8] sponge function. This was done for two main reasons. Firstly, although MILENAGE is currently considered strong, industry should have a proven alternative in case an advance in cryptanalysis exposes vulnerability. Secondly, machine-to-machine (M2M) devices will use "embedded SIMs", whereby a Subscriber Identity Module (SIM) chip is fitted into a device, and the assignment (or re-assignment) to a MNO and the provisioning of security credentials is done later, over the air. Some devices may be deployed for at least twenty years, which is a considerable time in the life of a technical security solution. Having two strong algorithms (MILENAGE and TUAK) built into the hardware, and available for selection, should give good assurance that effective security can be maintained throughout the SIM lifetime.

TUAK inherits most of its security characteristics from Keccak, which is the winning SHA-3 design and has of course been extensively studied. See [9][10] for a closer analysis of TUAK security. TUAK is fundamentally different from MILENAGE in its design, so that an advance in cryptanalysis affecting one algorithm is unlikely to affect the other. There are very few academic publications around TUAK as the standards are quite new, although a comprehensive security assessment [11] of the TUAK Algorithm Set was carried out by the University of Waterloo, Canada. It considered a wide range of cryptanalysis techniques, and finally concluded that TUAK can be used with confidence as message authentication functions and key derivation functions. However, industry acceptance and adoption of TUAK requires not just a secure design, but also confidence that it can be implemented on limited resource SIMs with sufficient performance.

- Is it possible to load the algorithm onto an existing deployed or stocked smart card platform?
- If so, will the algorithm run with acceptable performance?
- Will a new SIM require a crypto-coprocessor for adequate performance?
- Will a new SIM need to have a high performance processor (e.g., 32/64-bit type)?
- Will a new SIM require specialist low-level software for the algorithm?
- Will the algorithm benefit from hardware security protection?

There have been previous performance evaluation and comparisons [8][12][13], around the Keccak core for the SHA-3 competition [14], however these were aimed primarily at specialist hardware, or far more powerful and less memory limited processors than are typically found in SIMs. Therefore, at the request of SAGE, the evaluation described in this paper was undertaken, in which the entire TUAK algorithm performance was determined by experiment with the SAGE specified settings for Keccak, using their published source code as a starting point. The latter is important, as SIM vendors tend to base their implementations on the published security standards examples. In addressing the performance questions it was necessary to define a method of experimentation that would give relevant results yet would not be tied to a particular processor, platform or optimised for particular chip features. The work began with the PC example implementations, before forking to a parallel development suited for smart card evaluation. For the latter, simulation was originally considered, however it is difficult to map results to real card performance. The use of a multi-application card platform was included as a positive means of abstraction from any particular chip, and could be representative of loading the algorithm onto existing/stock SIMs. However, the performance of such platforms (e.g., MULTOS [15]/Java Card [16]) is usually inferior to a native card implementation and so two native mode implementations were initially included (and later a third) as the principal benchmarks. To complete the picture, experimentation was carried out on a server to represent and compare the loading demands of MILENAGE and TUAK on the network Authentication Centre (AuC).

In Section II an overview of MILENAGE and TUAK is provided before describing the experimental setup and software development in Section III and Section IV. Results are presented in Section V and analysed in Section VI. Some comments on security defences and performance are discussed in Section VII and finally, conclusions and future work are presented in Section VIII.

II. TUAK AND MILENAGE OVERVIEW

In each of GSM/GPRS (2G), UMTS [17] (3G) and the Long Term Evolution (LTE 4G), a fundamental part of the security architecture is a set of authentication and key agreement functions [18][19]. The set of functions varies between generations, with 3G providing more security than 2G, and 4G adding some further refinements. These functions exist in the subscriber's SIM card (which is provided by their MNO), and in a network node called the Authentication Centre (AuC) that is run by the MNO. The 3G authentication and key agreement architecture requires seven cryptographic functions. MILENAGE [5] is a complete set of algorithms to fulfil these functions, built from a common cryptographic core (the AES block cipher) using a consistent construction.

A. MILENAGE

The development and publication of MILENAGE was a major step forward in mobile security standardisation. It provided a 3G solution that overcame known security weaknesses in GSM, but it was also developed in an open and peer reviewed manner, unlike the many proprietary approaches used for GSM. MILENAGE and indeed any 3G authentication algorithm is required to support, mutual authentication, replay protection and cipher and integrity key generation; in accordance with best practice for information security. A comparison of 3G and GSM authentication security parameters is presented for information in Table I.

In GSM the AuC generates a random challenge (RAND) that gets sent to the SIM card. The SIM uses the RAND, its secret key (Ki) and algorithms A3/8 to compute the expected result (XRES) and the cipher key (Kc). If the XRES value is the same as the AuC calculation then the SIM is authenticated and thereafter the network and mobile phone use Kc for ciphering.

TABLE I. GSM and 3G Authentication Comparison

GSM			3G		
Desc.	Bits	Alg	Desc.	Bits	Alg
Ki	128		K	128	
RAND	128		RAND	128	
XRES	32	A3	XRES	32-128	f2
Kc	64max	A8	CK	128	f3
			IK	128	f4
			AK	48	f5
			SQN	48	
			AMF	16	
			MAC	64	f1

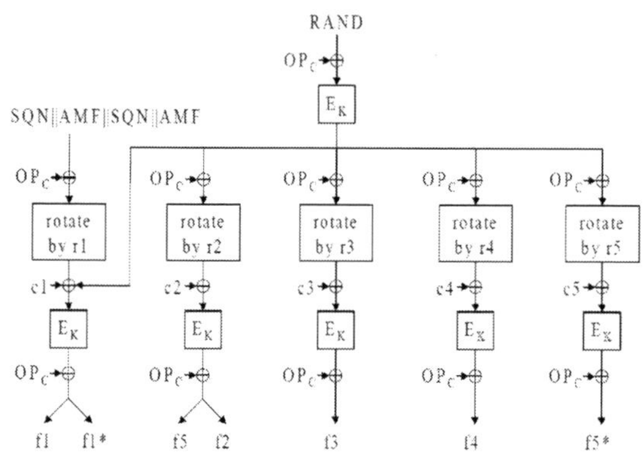

Figure 1. MILENAGE

The 3G solution follows a similar pattern, but is a little more complex and is best described with respect to Figure 1. The challenge is now referred to as an authentication token and includes the RAND as well as a sequence number (SQN) a management field (AMF) and a Message Authentication Code (MAC). If the SQN is correct (not a replayed message) and the suplied MAC value can be recomputed then the SIM considers the challenge genuine and calculates the requested outputs. The CK is similar to Kc, but longer, and the IK is a new Integrity Key. The AK is an anonymity key that can be used to conceal the true value of the sequence number. OPc in the figure is a network operator customisation field that is pre-computed (from a common OP field) to be unique for the SIM and pre-stored on the card. How the various outputs are computed from the input challenge is specific to the chosen algorithm and we can see that in MILENAGE this is implemented as multiple calls to a block cipher with additional rotations (by values r1-5) and XOR with constants (c1-5) and the OPc field. TUAK [7] is an alternative design approach that also offers a complete set of cryptographic functions for 3G authentication and key agreement. Note that LTE security reuses the same set of functions, so both MILENAGE and TUAK can also be used for LTE. There is also a standardised method for using the 3G authentication and key agreement functions in GSM/GPRS. A lot of the strength and credibility for MILENAGE arises from the block cipher being AES based, whereas we will see that TUAK's strength arises from the Keccak hash function.

B. TUAK Algorithm Inputs and Outputs

Whereas MILENAGE was designed with 3G in mind, TUAK was from the outset also designed for LTE and so

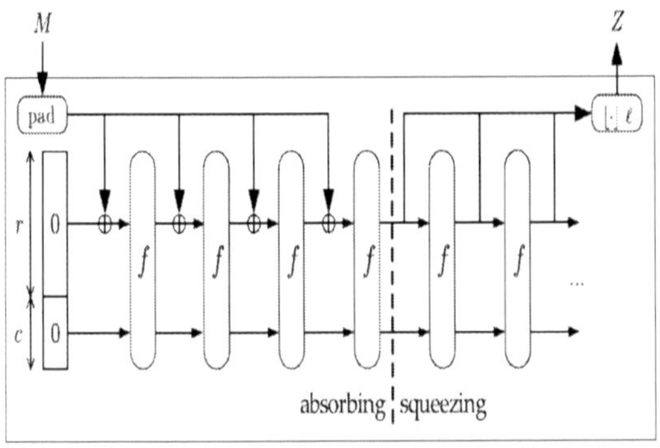

Figure 2. A Cryptographic Sponge Function

supports a 256 bit subscriber-unique secret key as well as the 128 bit key size used in 3G. Moreover, TUAK also allows for the possibility that certain other input or output parameters might increase in length in the future. The input and outputs of TUAK's seven cryptographic functions *f1, f1*, f2, f3, f4, f5 and f5** are defined in [7] and like MILENAGE, the TUAK algorithm-set expects one additional input parameter, an "Operator Variant Algorithm Configuration Field". In the case of TUAK, this field is called TOP (rather than OP) and is 256 bits long; each mobile operator is expected to choose its own value for this, typically the same value for many SIMs. The 3GPP security architecture did not require this extra parameter, but it was included for two main purposes:

- SIMs for different MNOs are not interchangeable, either through trivial modification of inputs and outputs or by reprogramming of a blank SIM.
- By keeping some algorithm details secret, some attacks (such as side channel attacks like power analysis) become a *little* harder to carry out.

TUAK includes an algorithm to derive value TOP_c from TOP and the secret key K, and it is sufficient for the SIM card to be programmed with TOP_c (like OPc in MILENAGE)) rather than with TOP itself. This means that an attacker who is able to extract TOP_c from one card does not learn TOP or TOP_c for other cards.

C. *TUAK Algorithm Building Blocks*

The main building block from which all of the TUAK algorithms are constructed is Keccak [8], the "cryptographic sponge function", which was selected by NIST as the winner of the SHA-3 hash function competition [14]. Sponge functions work by repeated application of a fixed length transformation or permutation *f*, as shown in Figure 2, which is copied from [20]. First the input bits are "absorbed", and then the output bits are "squeezed out".

TUAK uses the Keccak algorithm with permutation size $n = 1600$, capacity $c = 512$ and rate $r = 1088$. This rate value is big enough that each of the algorithms in the TUAK set needs only a single instance of the permutation *f* - repeated iteration of the permutation is not necessary.

Details of the TUAK algorithm can be found in [7], with test data in [21][22]. Keccak is a general purpose cryptographic hash function, so in use, all the input fields are simply written sequentially into a buffer, Keccak is run on the buffer contents, and then the outputs are read from the buffer, as fields in the hash output. This is equivalent, but very different to running the individual *f1-f5* functions used in MILENAGE. If all the inputs were the same, we could just run Keccak once, but the TUAK standards define three algorithm functions as illustrated in Figure 3; although TOP_c is usually pre-calculated. In this diagram:

- The top picture shows how TOP_c is derived from TOP.
- The middle picture shows how MAC-A or MAC-S is computed (*f1* and *f1**)
- The bottom picture shows how RES, CK, IK and AK are computed (functions *f2, f3, f4, f5* and *f5**) - note that these functions all take exactly the same set of input parameters, so can be computed together
- INSTANCE is an 8-bit value that takes different values for different functions, for different input and output parameter sizes, and to distinguish between *f1* and *f1** and between *f5* and *f5**, providing cryptographic separation
- ALGONAME is a 56-bit ASCII representation of the string "TUAK1.0"
- The block labelled "Keccak" is the 1600-bit permutation, with the shaded part corresponding to the 512-bit "capacity" input; see Figure 3.

Although, TUAK is standardised and its security design properties have been investigated [11], it was not until the work in [1] that the feasibility of implementation on real, secured SIM chips, was considered. This paper extend the work, by investigation of an additional legacy SIM chip, and also by providing some experimental insight into side-channel leakage and security of implementation.

III. The Experimental Setup

Based on the arguments presented in the introduction, the goal was to use a combination of PC software, native smart card chip implementations and a secure platform for development and comparative testing. For the initial phase of native implementation, we required two chips of comparable CPU power, yet different security protection to determine if the inherent protective measures impacted performance. Furthermore, to make useful comparisons with the secure platform implementations, we prefered platforms based on similar chips. A solution presented itself based around native implementations on the Infineon SLE77 [23] and SLE78 [24]. The MULTOS platform was selected as the secure platform primarily because test cards (types M3 and M4) were available based on the same Infineon chips. The initial smart card experiments were preceded by measurements on a PC platform that used similar example C code. The code could in future also be ported to Java Card platforms, although the Java coding language would make comparisons less clear.

The extended phase of implementation and experimentation added the code to an additional and older style smart card chip (S3CC9E4/8) and also to a server representative of an AuC to compare the comparative network loading of MILENAGE and TUAK.

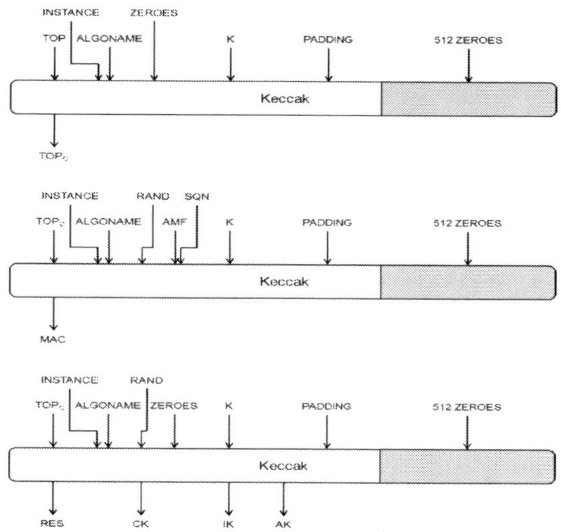

Figure 3. The TUAK Algorithm Functions

TABLE II. PC EXAMPLE CODE IMPLEMENTATION VERSIONS

Version	SupportedBits	ShortDescription
0	8/16/32/64	Size optimized, generic, use of % and more tables
1	8/16/32/64	Speed optimized, generic
2	64	Use of CPU 64-bit rotate instruction
3	8/32/64	Original from the specification
4	64	Similar to v2 but trying to combine more operations
5	32	Totally unrolled version, only C code
6	8/16/32	With bit-interleaving, generic, not optimized
7	32	Optimized bit-interleaving, part unrolled, 32-bit

A. The PC Test Platforms

The initial PC tests used an Intel Core i5-2540M CPU @ 2.60GHz, max turbo frequency 3.30GHz, 2 cores, 4 threads, Intel Smart Cache 3Mb, Instruction set 64-bit + AVX, 4Gb RAM, with a Windows 7 32-bit OS. The Keccak example implementations were written in 'C' and compiled to optimise speed. Although the processor and the compiler supported 64-bit integers, the resulting assembly code was limited by the OS to 32-bit. Execution time was measured in CPU clock cycles, although multiple runs were necessary due to the multi-tasking OS interrupting execution. Various versions of the example code became available during development as shown in Table II. The smart card source code was originally modelled on version 1 and then developed in parallel.

In Keccak, f is a permutation. Keccak is a family of algorithms, from which a particular algorithm is selected by setting three security parameters:

- The permutation size n, which can be 25, 50, 100, 200, 400, 800 or 1600 bits.
- The "capacity" c, which is a security parameter (essentially, for a given capacity c; Keccak is claimed to stand any attack up to complexity $2^{c/2}$).
- The "rate" $r = n - c$, which determines how many input and output bits can be handled by each iteration of the permutation.

For the extended phase work that simulated an AuC, the execution platform was an Intel Core i5-4300 CPU @ 1.9GHz, running Windows 7 x64-bit OS. The evaluation used a single core, so speeds would be scaled up for multiple cores and/or CPUs.

B. The Smart Card Chips

The smart card chips for all experimentation had 16-bit CPUs, which is a size representative of the majority of deployed SIMs (although there are still 8-bit CPUs around, as well as newer 32-bit CPUs). Whilst they are of similar family, horsepower and vintage they are quite different in security aspects.

1) SLE77: The SLE77 is a traditional style security controller intended for mid-range payment applications, and evaluated to Common Criteria [25] EAL5+. Its crypto-coprocessor does not support TUAK/Keccak so was not used in our tests. Details of the chip protection measures against physical, side-channel leakage and faults are not publicised, however in a traditional security chip one might expect protective shields, plus power smoothing and noise insertion to counter power analysis, and sensors/detectors to counter fault attacks. Some protection may arise from the application and OS software e.g., randomised/repeated operation and dummy cycles, although this may be optimised for the included algorithms. For a new algorithm running on this chip, we should expect some protection from the hardware, although the final algorithm code will need to improve this, which would likely degrade the performance measured in our experiments.

2) SLE78: The SLE78 is an innovative security controller intended for high security applications. Instead of relying mainly on shields and sensors it uses "Integrity Guard" [26], which exploits dual CPUs working in tandem. The claimed features include:

- Dual CPU implementation for fault detection
- Full CPU, memory, Bus and Cache encryption
- Error detection codes on all memories
- Error codes for cache protection
- Address and data scrambling of memories
- Side-channel leakage suppression
- Active Shield

Running the algorithm on the SLE78 offers a good deal of hardware protection with less reliance on added software countermeasures; so we would anticipate less performance degradation when compared with the SLE77.

Note that during the course of the initial experiments it was thought beneficial to extend the investigation to an older, but still relevant security controller, as not all networks are deploying modern or higher-end smart card chips. The S3CC9E4/8 was selected for this purpose, in part due to its age and capabilities, but also because a hardware emulator was available.

3) S3CC9E4/8: The target processors supported by the emulation equipment are the Samsung S3CC9E4 and S3CC9E8. The only differ in that the former has 4k + 256 bytes of EEPROM whereas the latter has 8kbytes. The general features are summarised in the Table III.

TABLE III. S3CC9E8 Characteristics

Feature	S3CC9E8
Harvard	Y
RISC	Y
16-bit CPU	Y
Frequency (external clock)	1MHz-5MHz
ROM	96k
EEPROM	8k
RAM	2k
Internal RC Oscillator	Y
DES/T-DES	Y
16 -bit RNG seed generator	Y
Serial port T=0 and 1	Y
Hardware EEPROM write inhibit	Y
Abnormal Voltage/frequency sensor	Y
Voltage range	2.7-5.5v
16 bit timer with 8bit pre-scaler and 20bitwatchdog timer	Y
4 interrupt sources and vectors including FIQ, IRQ, SWI	Y
General purpose 16-bit registers	16
6-bit extension registers	6
Program counter	22 bits
Status register	16 bit
Program Address Space	4M
Data Address Space	4M

The S3CC9E4/8 chips have what might be described as "traditional" hardware security defences. To defend against tampering and side-channel attack, the chip has the typical range of environmental security detectors and a randomising clock option that makes leakage trace averaging more difficult. There are also bus scrambling options and ways to disguise the core crypto operations within dummy operations. The clock frequency can also be manually controlled, but this is intended for performance and power efficiency rather than security.

IV. Software Development

The starting point for the smart card software development was the example code published in 3GPP TS 35.231 [7]. This went through several versions during the project, based on results/feedback and on-going optimisation work. The final versions should be regarded as optimised to the extent that was possible with a generic implementation avoiding chip specific enhancements. Referring to Table II the primary template for the smart card experiments was the generic speed optimised version 1 that could be built for 8, 16, 32 and 64 bits, and made use of generic loops and macros. The 64 bit option was discounted as being unrepresentative of current smart cards and because legacy C compilers cannot easily cope with integer variables beyond 32 bits. Some minor modifications were made to the initial smart card code, but largely it remained true to the original generic code. Later, in order to understand performance issues relating to the algorithm running on the MULTOS platform, a 32-bit version of the code was part-optimised, which involved expanding the Macros and unrolling the inner loops within the main Keccak functions. The final MULTOS version also used fixed pointers for buffer manipulation. Note that in all versions of the code, the calculation of TOP_c was removed from each function. Within a smart card, this value would be pre-calculated and loaded into protected memory and so there is no need to recalculate it; and doing so could halve a TUAK function's speed.

For the S3CC9E4/8 implementation the same non-optimised version was used, as in the Infineon test-cards; so a fair comparison could be made. For this native mode development a notable amount of code/development was needed simply to handle resets, memory management/access, serial I/O and the APDU Command interface, so parts of this were ported from another legacy/dummy project. The S3CC9E4/8 required additional functionality to manually control the internal CPU clock speed as this appears to be automatically handled in the Infineon devices. The default starting pointing for all operation on the new card was the standard (medium) clock speed, which is safe for all memory accesses, whereas the fast speed could not be used with the EEPROM.

TABLE IV. PC VERSION PERFORMANCE COMPARISON

Versions	Minimum Cycles (average cycles)		
	8-bit	16-bit	32-bit
0 (size opt)	168652(380066)	85988(215250)	
1 (speed opt)	49688(116200)	22496(55343)	7152(9024)
2 (N/A)			
3 (original)	202140(221564)		87350(193371)
4 (N/A)			
5 (unrolled)			6368(10391)
6 (bit-interl)	73120(185217)	59307(131112)	
7 (bit-interl opt)			10216(25570)

A. *Software Functional Testing*

To test TUAK functionality, we used the six test data sets published in 3GPP TS 35.232 V12.0.1 [21]. The data sets were designed to vary all inputs and internal values, and assure correctness of an implementation; they thus also serve well for performance tests. To simplify testing the test data sets were included within the card application. This added an extra static data requirement, but meant that tests could be run by simply specifying the test set within the card test command, or by supplementing the test set with command data. Each command had an execution count so the targeted function could be run from 0 to 255 times (on the same input data). Typically the count would be '1', although '0' was useful for estimating round trip delays and higher counts improved measurement precision.

V. Results

In this section, we present the experimental results, based on the 3GPP test data. The smart card results were obtained via a scripting tool that would send a command message to the card in the form of an Application Protocol Data Unit (APDU) and then time the response. Although card processing time should be consistent and repeatable, scripting tools have tolerances. To compensate, the test commands instruct the card to execute a function multiple times before returning a result. A calibration was also carried out using a protocol analyser.

A. *Initial PC Results*

The initial performance experiments used to refine the public example code were PC based, with results (in clock cycles) from the various versions (see Table II) summarised in Table IV. Note that the cycle number includes pre, post data processing and overheads for a single run of Keccak-1600 (24 rounds).

Variation between minimum and average results arises from the OS. The minimum values are representative of the CPU capability. Generally, speed increased with the target build size.

TABLE V. NATIVE MODE PERFORMANCE (ms)

Test	Mode/Chip	SLE77			SLE78		
Data		f1f1s	f2345	f5s	f1f1s	f2345	f5s
	8-bit	18.11	18.17	18.11			
1	16-bit	15.17	15.23	15.17			
	32-bit	19.58	19.64	19.51	19.58	19.70	19.51
	8-bit	18.17	18.17	18.17			
2	16-bit	15.23	15.23	15.17			
	32-bit	19.64	19.76	19.58	19.64	19.82	19.58
	8-bit	18.23	18.17	18.17			
3	16-bit	15.23	15.29	15.17			
	32-bit	19.70	19.82	19.58	19.70	19.88	19.58
	8-bit	18.17	18.23	18.17			
4	16-bit	15.17	15.23	15.17			
	32-bit	19.58	19.76	19.45	19.58	19.76	19.51
	8-bit	18.17	18.23	18.17			
5	16-bit	15.17	15.36	15.17			
	32-bit	19.58	20.01	19.58	19.58	20.00	19.58
	8-bit	36.22	36.27	36.19			
6	16-bit	30.16	30.28	30.10			
	32-bit	38.85	39.15	38.67	38.79	39.15	38.60

TABLE VI. MULTOS PERFORMANCE (ms)

Test	Mode/Chip	ML4 = SLE77			ML3 = SLE78		
Data		f1f1s	f2345	f5s	f1f1s	f2345	f5s
	8-bit	19882	19952	19796	23837	23947	23962
	16-bit	10749	10826	10702	12824	12917	12838
1	32-bit	6396	6505	6350	7239	7348	7192
	32x	3104	3214	3073	3432	3557	3400
	32p	1529	1575	1529	1623	1654	1622
	32-bit	6474	6568	6396	7332	7441	7254
2	32x	3198	3276	3120	3526	3619	3463
	32p	1544	1576	1529	1638	1669	1623
	32-bit	6537	6615	6396	7379	7504	7254
3	32x	3245	3339	3120	3603	3681	3463
	32p	1560	1592	1529	1654	1670	1623
	32-bit	6427	6552	6349	7269	7410	7191
4	32x	3151	3261	3089	3478	3603	3401
	32p	1544	1591	1529	1623	1669	1622
	32-bit	6443	6708	6412	7301	7597	7254
5	32x	3166	3432	3120	3494	3791	3463
	32p	1544	1622	1529	1638	1700	1622
	32-bit	12543	12808	12402	14211	14492	14071
6	32x	5990	6224	5866	6614	6879	6474
	32p	2980	3057	2949	3135	3198	3105

B. *Initial Smart Card Performance*

The initial native card performance tests were mainly carried out on on the SLE77; only the 32-bit algorithm was run on the SEL78. The MULTOS results used both chip types for all tests. The results are shown in Tables V and VI.

Normally, when the MULTOS organisation specifies a new function for the Virtual Machine (VM) it would be coded in low-level software and invoked from an Application Programming Interface (API). The API performance should be closer to that of Table V; however as this is currently not the case, the Table VI figures apply. All versions of the application benefit from a typical memory optimisation i.e., the Keccak main buffer (INOUT) was forced into a reserved section of RAM. Using non-volatile memory (NVM) instead made the 8-bit and 16-bit versions three times slower and the 32-bit version five times slower. The "32x" rows represent the "unrolled" version of Keccak, which is a removal of inner loops and macros in the C code, and the "32p" version also uses fixed pointers rather than array index calculations. These initial smart card test results are further described and analysed in Section VI, but as there was interest in results from an older style smart card, additional results were obtained from some extended experiments.

TABLE VII. S3CC9E4/8 NATIVE MODE PERFORMANCE (ms)

Test	Mode/Chip	Standard Clock (5MHz)			Fast Clock (10MHz)		
Data		f1f1s	f2345	f5s	f1f1s	f2345	f5s
	8-bit	172.76	173.01	172.70	86.44	86.69	86.44
1	16-bit	155.51	156.00	155.39	77.88	78.18	77.82
	32-bit	189.04	189.95	188.79	94.58	95.13	94.45
	8-bit	172.89	173.07	172.76	86.56	86.69	86.50
2	16-bit	155.88	156.24	155.57	78.06	78.31	77.88
	32-bit	189.77	190.51	189.22	95.01	95.44	94.70
	8-bit	173.01	173.19	172.76	86.63	86.81	86.50
3	16-bit	156.06	156.49	155.57	78.24	78.49	77.94
	32-bit	190.32	191.05	189.22	95.31	95.74	94.70
	8-bit	172.82	173.07	172.70	86.50	86.69	86.44
4	16-bit	155.69	156.18	155.39	78.00	78.31	77.82
	32-bit	189.34	190.32	188.73	94.82	95.38	94.45
	8-bit	172.82	173.38	172.76	86.56	86.93	86.51
5	16-bit	155.76	156.86	155.63	78.00	78.67	77.94
	32-bit	189.59	191.79	189.22	94.89	96.23	94.70
	8-bit	344.91	345.46	344.73	172.70	173.13	172.58
6	16-bit	310.11	311.02	309.62	155.33	155.88	154.96
	32-bit	376.24	378.32	375.25	188.36	189.53	187.81

TABLE VIII. AuC PERFORMANCE COMPARISON

Version	Computation Time (ns)							
	8-bit		16-bit		32-bit		64 bit	
	f1f1s	f2345	f1f1s	f2345	f1f1s	f2345	f1f1s	f2345
0	71093	71944	39190	40633	20172	20203	19254	18841
1	35663	35924	15650	15257	12101	11245	7469	7540
2							7463	7400
3	171042	176158			21699	21827	16055	15941
4							6979	7289
5					8012	8090		
6	58631	57406	37963	37396	8158	8513		
7					7672	7867		
MILENAGE					1928	4840		

C. *Extended Smart Card Performance*

In this section we present the results from the S3CC9E4/8 experiments. The native card performance of the Samsung chip was measured on the emulator (for the various bit-size compile targets in the source code) and the results are shown in Table VII. The Fast Clock column is the most realistic in terms of performance, with the Standard Clock column representing a naive implementation.

D. *AuC Comparative Performance*

The focus of the algorithm performance testing was mainly on the resource limited smart card devices, however, it should not be forgotten that the same algorithm is run in the network operator's AuC. Although much more processing power will be available from the AuC server, it will have to deal with (directly or via Visiting Location Registers) large numbers of authentication requests. Absolute performance will be very much dependent on the chosen server, but a comparative measurement is of interest, comparing the performance of TUAK to the currently used MILENAGE algorithm. This was determined experimentally, with the results presented in VIII.

VI. ANALYSIS OF RESULTS

To consider the experimental results, it is necessary to be aware of the parameter sizes (bits) inherent in the standardised test-sets, which are summarised in Table IX. The test data parameters are designed to exercise TUAK in representative modes of use. Note that for the first five test sets (single

TABLE IX. TEST DATA PARAMETER SIZES

Test Data	K	MAC	RES	CK	IK	Keccak Iterations
1	128	64	32	128	128	1
2	256	128	64	128	128	1
3	256	256	64	128	256	1
4	128	128	128	128	128	1
5	256	64	256	256	128	1
6	256	256	256	256	256	2

iteration) the Keccak core has very similar execution time, with TUAK variations arising from the differing amounts of data to absorb or squeeze out of the sponge (working buffer).

Note that the common/fixed parameters sizes (bits) for the TUAK algorithm are: RAND = 128, SQN = 48, AK = 48, AMF = 16.

A. *Performance Target*

We need to define an appropriate performance target, so we can start by recalling the target used for the MILENAGE design [5].

> ..."The functions *f1-f5* and *f1** shall be designed so that they can be implemented on an IC card equipped with an 8-bit microprocessor running at 3.25 MHz with 8 kbyte ROM and 300byte RAM and produce AK, XMAC-A, RES, CK and IK in less than 500 ms execution time."...

Technology has advanced since this target was created and it might be difficult to find a SIM chip with these minimal capabilities, and indeed many do not have ROM. Furthermore, the target is ambiguous and could be interpreted that if you ran the functions in sequence each could take 500ms. It is also unclear how much of the ROM and RAM can be used. A more appropriate and modern target was defined during the study.

> ..."The functions *f1-f5* and *f1** shall be designed so that they can be implemented on a mid-range microprocessor IC card (typically 16-bit CPU), occupying no more than 8kbytes non-volatile-memory (NVM), reserving no more than 300bytes of RAM and producing AK, XMAC-A, RES, CK and IK in less than 500 ms total execution time."...

This revised target definition has been proposed to 3GPP for inclusion in future versions of the standard documents.

B. *Initial Native Mode Results SLE77/78*

If we consider the results from the native implementation on the SLE77, the function execution times for the various test data sets are quite similar with the exception of test set 6. The latter uses a double iteration of Keccak, which roughly doubles the execution time. As can be seen from Figure 4, compiling the generic code for the different target bit widths affects the execution time, but not by an enormous margin. The most efficient version is the 16-bit target, which provides the best fit for the underlying processor.

Due to practical constraints we only have SLE78 measurements for the 32-bit target, which show similar speed to the SLE77 (native). The extra security features of the SLE78 seem not to penalise performance although there may be added financial cost. The striking observation is that native mode

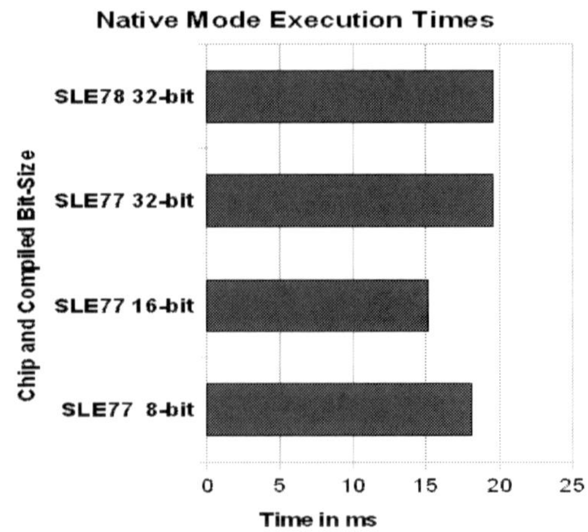

Figure 4. Comparison of Native Mode Execution Times

performance satisfies our target by a very comfortable margin. It is therefore reasonable to suggest that provided the algorithm is custom-coded on a typical SIM chip there is no need for a crypto-coprocessor. Extended experiments on the S3CC9E4/8 (see later) were carried out to confirm this conclusion.

This study focussed more on performance than code-size minimisation, however, all native implementations fitted within our memory targets.

C. *Platform Mode*

Within the study we only considered the MULTOS platform; although a Java Card would make an interesting comparison. The results here were disappointing, although a significant overhead had been expected due to the operation of the secure Virtual Machine and the MULTOS Execution Language (MEL) [27] abstraction. In practice, the best results were around two orders of magnitude slower than native; see Figure 5. Furthermore, the performance improved with increasing compiled bit-size, which suggests that the compilation and MEL interpretation does not map closely to the underlying CPU size for the processing in TUAK.

On inspection of the generic Keccak function one saw extensive use of macros and loops. To determine if they were causing problems for MULTOS, an "unrolled" 32-bit version of Keccak was created, removing macros and inner loops. The results are in the Table VI rows marked "32x" and in Figure 5, showing a doubling of speed. A further improvement was to adapt the algorithm to use fixed location buffer pointers rather than indexed arrays; and the corresponding "32p" version shows a further speed doubling. However, a single function still takes around 1.5s.

If we consider the unrolled Keccak there are many shifts on array contents, however MEL does not have a core shift instruction, but uses shift primitives. The unrolled Keccak is twice as fast as the generic version, partly due to the way that MULTOS handles shifts. The amount of shift on a buffer m can be known at compile time or run time, as shown below.

```
m = m << 3    or    m = m << n
```

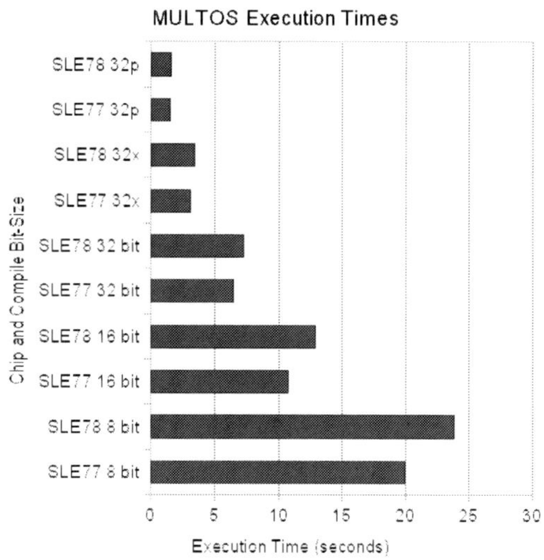

Figure 5. MULTOS f1() Execution Times

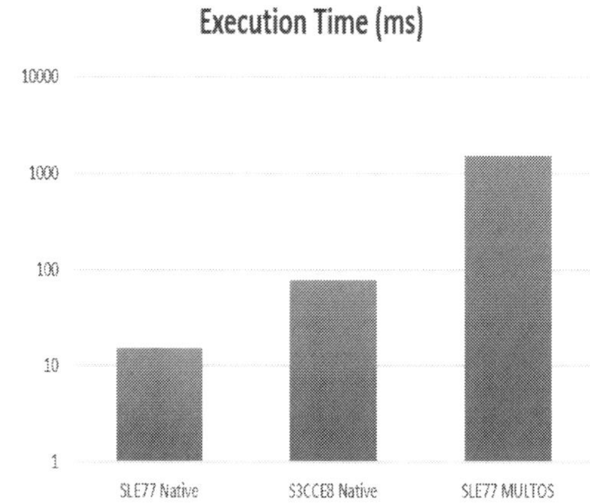

Figure 6. MULTOS f1() Comparative Execution Times

The first example is handled as a single use of the shift primitive, whereas the second will loop n times shifting 1 bit at a time. This still leaves a big question mark over the efficiency of the primitive itself (and other bitwise operations).

If we consider the x2 speed-up from pre-computing TOP_c, the x2 from removing loops/macros and the x2 from using pointers, the application is x8 faster than the generic version. However the conclusion is still that the algorithm cannot meet the target performance if loaded as an application on a card platform (MULTOS at least). This suggets it is not practical to add the algorithm to deployed or existing stock cards. To use a card platform, an API would need to be added so that an efficient native implementation could be called.

D. Extended Native Mode Results S3CC9E4/8

If we consider the results from the native implementation on the S3CC9E4/8, shown in Table VII, we can see that performance is (as expected) optimised for 16-bit builds; matching the CPU size. The use of the fast clock option is essential for algorithm execution, as it is twice as fast as the standard mode. For the single iterations of Keccak (test data 1-5) the functions complete in less than 80ms. Referring to Figure 6 we can see that TUAK is roughly 20x faster than MULTOS and 5x slower than the native SLE77/78.

Ignoring the 's' versions of functions, which are used in resynchronisation, an authentication requires execution of f1() and f2345(), so less than 160ms in total. This is still comfortably within the 3GPP specification, however, when compared to the SLE77/78 there is a smaller margin for performance degradation due to added defensive coding.

E. Extended AuC Results

The results in Table VIII show function execution (ns) for the various TUAK PC software versions and build-sizes (8/16/32/64-bits), plus a reference result representing MILENAGE execution. A first observation is that for MILENAGE, f2345() takes significantly longer than f1(). This is because the performance is dominated by calls to the block cipher and more are used in f2345() than f1(). In TUAK the two functions take about the same time as they both include one Keccak call. The second observation is that TUAK is slower than MILENAGE. Keeping to the 32-bit target the best authentication time for TUAK (time to execute both functions) is 15539ns compared to 6768ns for MILENAGE; so about 2.3x slower. The performance difference is not huge, but should be considered when planning load capacity.

VII. Security Defences and Performance

Modern SIM cards are normally based on tamper-resistant secure microcontrollers, which inherently have a range of defences against physical, side-channel and fault attacks. Therefore, a TUAK implementation on a SIM platform should be much better protected than an implementation on a general purpose microcontroller, with the latter incurring significant performance overhead to achieve modest attack resistance. If we consider the chips used in our tests then the SLE78 would be expected to offer significant protection against physical, side channel and fault attacks [25] due to the innovative underlying hardware; requiring less software countermeasures (and performance degradation) than a conventional secure microcontroller. The SLE77 would also offer hardware based protection, particularly against physical and fault attacks, but adequately preventing side-channel leakage will require additional measures in software. Fortunately, the SLE77 is quite fast and even if the performance was degraded by an order of magnitude, we could still run *f1*, *f2345* and *f5s* and meet the overall performance target. MULTOS platforms are known and marketed for their high security and had they been fast enough they would have been expected to offer added OS security to compliment the underlying chip hardware. However, the current view is that a new MULTOS primitive will be needed for the algorithm and so the issues are similar to the SLE77/78.

A. Fault Attack Defences and Performance Impact

The faults used in attacks are normally achieved by voltage glitches, radiation pulses and operating the target device beyond tolerance. The hardware sensors in tamper-resistant smart cards are intended to detect the likely means of fault insertion and prevent a response useful to the attacker; so there is no significant added overhead for the software. A very sophisticated and skillful attack might bypass the sensors, however by adopting TUAK as an openly published algorithm, with diversified card keys, we are avoiding proprietary secret algorithms that might motivate such effort. An added countermeasure could be to run the algorithm twice and only output a response if the results agree; this would counter attacks that analyse correct and faulty results from algorithms. The added countermeasure is perhaps unnecessary for the chips considered in this work, although halving the speed of operation would still keep it well within specification. Note that an attacker will seek to insert a fault at the most opportune moment, which may be determined from side-channel leakage. For example, disrupting the round counter could mean that TUAK runs a single round instead of 24.

B. Side-Channel Attack Defences and Performance Impact

Timing leakage attacks [28] can be possible when there are observable data dependent delays in the application; in which case added redundancy is needed in the implementation. Timing variations can be sufficiently large that they can be detected despite low level measures to disguise side-channel leakage that might be subject to power analysis. The leakage generation principle is quite simple, e.g., if a variable is true do something time-consuming else do something quick. The variable could represent a value that is tested at the application layer, or just a low-level bit test. A brief inspection of Keccak does not show obvious high-level timing leakage, as there are no conditional branches in the code. However, there could be lower level leakage if bit rotates are used. For example a processor may effect a rotate by shifting the contents of a register up one place and then testing the value that falls out of the register. If the value is '1' then this has to be added back in as the LSB, so unless the designer adds dummy operations, processing a '1' is going to take longer than a '0'.

The Keccak example code has macro names that imply rotate, but on inspection they are buffer shift operations rather than register rotates. However, there could be a timing effect when the compiled target size (8/16/32 bit) does not match the underlying register size. For example if we compile for 16-bits, but the CPU registers are 8-bits then our shift may need to modify the least significant bit of the upper byte based on the bit value shifted out of the lower byte. In the case of native code implementation, developers would be expected to take the CPU size/shift/rotate into account. In the platform approach the mapping between application variables and underlying registers is unclear.

We have assumed that the chips have hardware countermeasures to prevent bit-level side-channel leakage, as software measures are inferior and significantly impact performance. For example, Hamming-weight equalisation is a technique that seeks to reduce leakage by ensuring that for each bit transition there is a complementary transition; so as a '1'changes to '0' there is also a '0' changing to '1'. In a practical implementation this could for example be a 16-bit processor where the lower 8-bits of a register handle the normal data and the upper 8-bits handle the complementary data. However, at the physical/electrical level, the register bits are unlikely to have equal contribution to the leakage and so Hamming-weight equalisation may not deliver a sufficient reduction. The impact on execution speed is also significant, as it is necessary to clear registers before and after use, and so a ten-fold rather two-fold reduction in performance should be anticipated.

As a final extension to the work, practical leakage experiments were carried out using power analysis to see if an attacker might learn anything useful from our implementation.

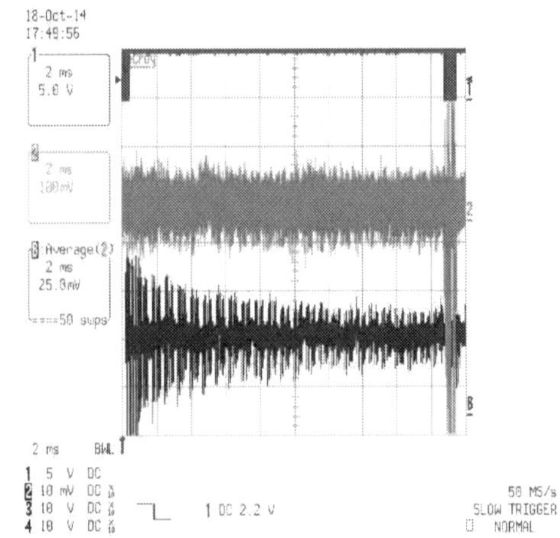

Figure 7. SLE77 8-bit Build Power Traces

C. Side-Channel Leakage Experiments

The main goal of the analysis was to try and accurately determine the keccak rounds from the leakage traces, as knowing this is often a prerequisite for attackers i.e., they may wish to target particular rounds for analysis and/or fault insertion. The first step to try and find the round structure was to crudely capture the entire run of the command/algorithm; from command to response. We know that keccak dominates the response time and that it has 24 rounds. We could have chosen any of the functions, however f5s() is convenient as it depends on just RAND and K; and has a constant output size regardless of the test data set selected. We initially focussed on the 8-bit build as this was expected to show most leakage.

Figure 7 shows the screen shot from SLE77 execution. The upper waveform is the I/O line used for triggering. The raw leakage information is the middle waveform and the lower trace is an average waveform computed over 50 traces. Examining the lower trace one can see a repeating pattern of pulse shapes. There are 24 in total, which matches the number of rounds in KECCAK. This characteristic pattern is in fact present for all the datasets - as would be expected. To check this in a little more detail we can refer to the start section of the algorithm shown in in Figure 8.

The repetitive structure is clearer in this waveform and there is a pattern that repeats twice every three time markers (1.5ms span). This gives an individual period of roughly 750us. If this is a KECCAK round then the algorithm would complete in 24x750us = 18ms. If we then refer back to Table 4 we

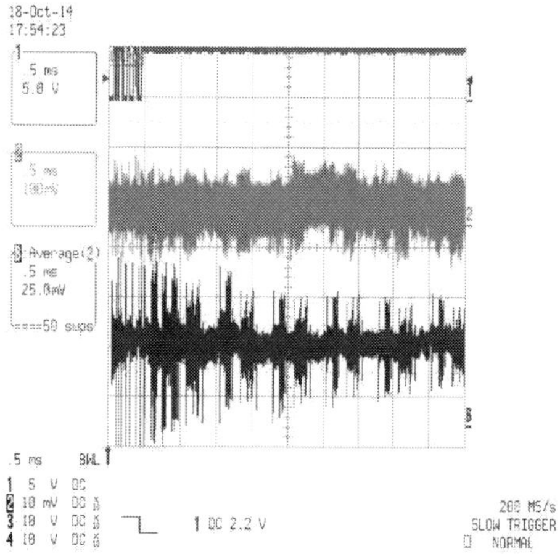

Figure 8. SLE77 8-bit Build Start of Power Trace

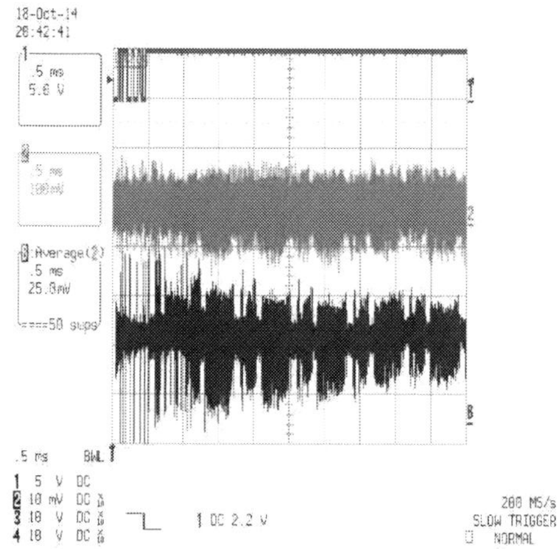

Figure 10. SLE77 32-bit Build Start of Power Trace

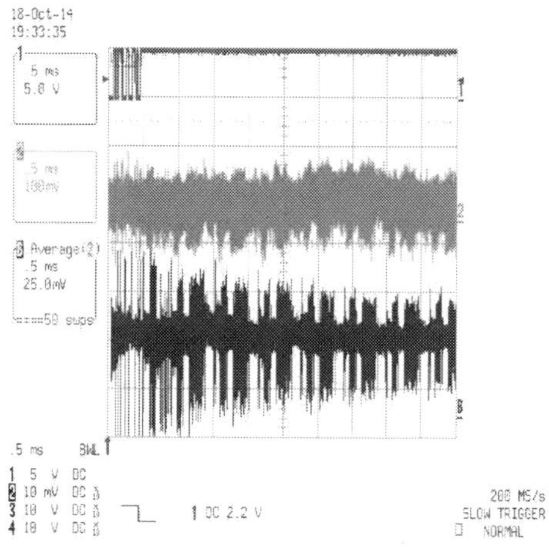

Figure 9. SLE77 16-bit Build Start of Power Trace

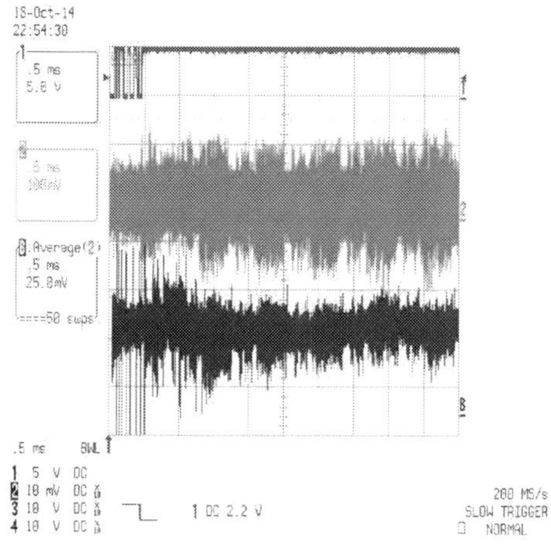

Figure 11. SLE78 32-bit Build Start of Power Trace

see that the command response time (which is dominated by the algorithm) takes 18.11ms, suggesting that we are indeed looking at the round cycle. The waveforms presented so far have been for the 8-bit build so the next step is to compare with the 16 and 32-bit builds.

Regarding Figures 8-10 , we see that although the timing of the waveforms differs a little due to performance aspects, the repetitive round structure is still clearly visible regardless of whether the build target is 8, 16 or 32 bits. As a final comparison we can use traces captured from the SLE78 chip, which might be expected to have more inherent leakage protection within the chip hardware.

Considering the SLE78 waveforms in Figure 11 we note that a single trace is noisier than the SLE77 equivalent shown in Figure 10. Furthermore, whilst there is some detectable structure within the averaged trace of the SLE78 it is far less obvious than for the SLE77, suggesting that the former is better at impeding statistical averaging of power leakage traces. An important point to note is that in all cases when using the SLE77, waveform averaging makes significant improvement to the SNR. This suggests that the chip is not automatically adding any randomisation (at least at the scale observed) to the processor timing.

VIII. Conclusions and Future Work

The main conclusion is that it is feasible to implement TUAK in software on typical smart card/SIM chips and meet the performance target for 3G/4G authentication algorithms, without the need for a cryptocoprocessor. Native mode implementation is required and so for a card platform (such as MULTOS) this should be supported via API calls. Processor and memory requirements are very modest suggesting that TUAK could meet performance targets even when implemented on simpler legacy CPUs. Although there is no high-level data dependent timing in TUAK, there is some potential for data dependent side-channel leakage due to shift operations, which will require countermeasures. Whilst high-end smart card chips (like the SLE78) may offer significant hardware-based resistance to side-channel analysis, other chips will require help from software countermeasures. Such measures may significantly impact performance; however the SLE77 results show that function execution time could be reduced by an order of magnitude and still satisfy the performance target. There is less of a margin to add defensive measures to the S3CC9E4/8 implementation, however the basic implementation is 3x faster than necessary to meet the 3GPP specification. When considering the impact on the AuC, TUAK is a little slower (x2.3) however this is not a large margin; and server performance tends to advance follow Moore's law, whereas smart cards have been restricted due to cost issues.

The primary impact of the work is that by showing TUAK to be a practical back-up or alterative to MILENAGE for typical SIM platforms, it will be adopted as a preferred public algorithm (initially in M2M systems); displacing proprietary solutions that are often the target and motivation for attack.

On-going work is considering side-channel leakage, and also whether TUAK could be re-used in other applications. Preliminary results indicate that TUAK is sufficiently fast for use on more limited chip platforms, and this suggests it might also be a candidate for Internet of Things protocols. In fact re-using a 3G algorithm is not a new idea as MILENAGE has already been reused outside of mobile communications.

ACKNOWLEDGMENT

The authors would like to thank members of ETSI SAGE for their expert advice.

REFERENCES

[1] K. Mayes, S. Babbage, and A. Maximov, "Performance Evaluation of the new TUAK Mobile Authentication Algorithm," in Proc. ICONS/EMBEDDED, pp. 38-44, 2016

[2] (2016, Dec.) The European Telecommunications Standards Institute website, [Online]. Available: http://www.etsi.org/

[3] (2016, Dec.) The Third Generation Partnership Project website, [Online]. Available: http://www.3gpp.org/

[4] M. Mouly and M. Pautet, The GSM System for Mobile Communications, Cell and Sys (1992)

[5] 3GPP TS 35.206: 3G Security; Specification of the MILENAGE algorithm set: An example algorithm set for the 3GPP authentication and key generation functions f1, f1*, f2, f3, f4, f5 and f5*; Document 2: Algorithm specification (2014)

[6] Federal Information processing Standards, Advanced Encryption Standard (AES), FIPS publication 197 (2001)

[7] 3GPP, TS 35.231: 3G Security; Specification of the TUAK algorithm set: A second example algorithm set for the 3GPP authentication and key generation functions f1, f1*, f2, f3, f4, f5 and f5*; Document 1: Algorithm specification (2014)

[8] G. Bertoni, J. Daemen, M. Peeters, and G. van Aasche, "The keccak Reference," version 3.0, 14 (2011)

[9] 3GPP TR 35.934: Specification of the TUAK algorithm set: A second example algorithm set for the 3GPP authentication and key generation functions f1, f1*, f2, f3, f4, f5 and f5*; Document 4: Report on the design and evaluation (2014)

[10] 3GPP TR 35.936: Specification of the TUAK algorithm set: A second example algorithm set for the 3GPP authentication and key generation functions f1, f1*, f2, f3, f4, f5 and f5*; Document 6: Security assessment (2015)

[11] G. Gong, K. Mandal, Y. Tan, and T.Wu, "Security Assessment of TUAK Algorithm Set," [Online]. Available: http://www.3gpp.org/ftp/Specs/archive/35_series/35.935/SAGE_report/Secassesment.zip (2014)

[12] (2016, Dec.) eBACS: ECRYPT Benchmarking of Cryptographic Systems, [Online]. Available: http://bench.cr.yp.to/results-sha3.html

[13] Y. Jararweh, L. Tawalbeh, H. Tawalbeh, and A. Mohd, "Hardware Performance Evaluation of SHA-3 Candidate Algorithms," Journal of Information Security, Vol. 3, No. 2, pp. 69-76, 2012

[14] NIST, Announcing Draft Federal Information Processing Standard (FIPS) 202, SHA-3 Standard: Permutation-Based Hash and Extendable-Output Functions, and Draft Revision of the Applicability Clause of FIPS 180-4, Secure Hash Standard, and Request for Comments, (2004)

[15] (2016, Dec.) MULTOS website, [Online]. Available: http://www.multos.com/

[16] Oracle, Java Card Platform Specifications V3.04, (2011)

[17] F. Hillebrand, GSM and UMTS - The Creation of Global Mobile Communication, Wiley, (2002)

[18] 3GPP, TS 33.102: 3G Security; Security Architecture (1999)

[19] 3GPP, TS 33.401: Telecommunications Specification Group Services and System Aspects; 3GPP System Architecture Evolution (SAE); Security architecture (2012)

[20] G. Bertoni, J. Daemen, M. Peeters, and G. van Aasche, "Cryptographic Sponge Functions," version 0.1, (2011)

[21] 3GPP, TS 35.232: 3G Security; Specification of the TUAK algorithm set: A second example algorithm set for the 3GPP authentication and key generation functions f1, f1*, f2, f3, f4, f5 and f5*; Document 2: Implementers' Test Data (2014)

[22] 3GPP TS 35.233: 3G Security; Specification of the TUAK algorithm set: A second example algorithm set for the 3GPP authentication and key generation functions f1, f1*, f2, f3, f4, f5 and f5*; Document 3: Design Conformance Test Data (2014)

[23] (2016, Dec.) Infineon, SLE77CLFX2400P(M) Short Product Overview v11.11, (2012) [Online]. Available: http://www.infineon.com/dgdl/SPO_SLE+77CLFX2400P(M)_2012-10.pdf?fileId=db3a30433fcce646013fe1b813c07ff1

[24] (2016, Dec.) Infineon, SLE78CAFX4000P(M) Description, [Online]. Available: http://www.infineon.com/cms/en/product/security-and-smart-card-solutions/security-controllers/sle78/SLE+78CAFX4000PM/productType.html?productType=db3a30433fa9412f013fbdeb221b7b6f#ispnTab1

[25] K. Mayes, and K. Markantonakis, Smart Cards, Tokens, Security and Applications, Springer (2008)

[26] (2016, Dec.) Infineon, Integrity Guard White Paper, [Online]. Available via: http://www.infineon.com/dgdl/Infineon-Integrity_Guard_The_newest_generation_of_digital_security_technology-WP-v04 _12-EN.pdf?fileId=5546d46255dd933d0155e31c46fa03fb

[27] MULTOS, Developer's Reference Manual MAO-DOC-TEC-006 v1.49, (2013)

[28] P. Kocher, "Timing Attacks on Implemenetationsof Diffie-Hellman, RSA, DSS, and other Systems," Advances in Cryptology (CRYPTO), Vol. 1109 LNCS, pp. 104-113, 1996

Cloud Cyber-Security: Empowering the Audit Trail

Bob Duncan
Computing Science
University of Aberdeen
Email: bobduncan@abdn.ac.uk

Mark Whittington
Accounting and Finance
University of Aberdeen
Email: mark.whittington@abdn.ac.uk

***Abstract*—Cyber-security presents a serious challenge. Cyber-security in the cloud presents a far more serious challenge, due to the multi-tenant nature of cloud relationships and the transitory nature of cloud instances. We have identified a fundamental weakness when undertaking cloud audit, namely the misconceptions surrounding the purpose of audit, what comprises a proper audit trail, what should be included, and how it should be achieved and maintained. A properly specified audit trail can provide a powerful tool in the armoury against cyber-crime, yet it is all too easy to throw away the benefits offered by this simple tool through lack of understanding, incompetence, mis-configuration or sheer laziness. A major weakness is the need to ensure the audit trail is properly preserved. We propose that some simple changes in approach are undertaken, which can considerably improve the status quo, while radically improving the ability to conduct forensic examination in the event of a breach, but of course, merely having an effective audit trail is not enough — we actually have to analyse it regularly to realise the potential benefits it offers.**

Keywords*—*cloud cyber-security; compliance; assurance; audit; audit trail.

I. Introduction

This article is based on an extended version of our 2016 paper [1], in which we examined the possible strengths and weaknesses of the proper use of the audit trail in cloud cyber security. Achieving information security is not a trivial process. When this involves a cloud setting, the problem intensifies exponentially. Let us first consider how we go about achieving security. Usually it is achieved by means of compliance with standards, assurance or audit. We provide some useful background on this in [2]. In a non-cloud setting, we have a range of established standards, which are well understood by industry. However, when we move to cloud, everything changes. There are an extensive range of cloud standard setting bodies, yet no comprehensive cloud security standard yet exists. We outline the status of cloud security standards in Section V.

Often, when a company moves its programmes to a cloud setting, there is an assumption that it is a straight transfer. Assurance in a non-cloud setting is well understood, but assurance in a cloud setting is much less well understood. There are a great many challenges to overcome and we addressed some of those in earlier work [3], with a colleague, developing a conceptual framework for cloud security assurance, where we addressed three key challenges, namely standards compliance, management method and complexity. There are a great many issues to consider, and many common mistakes are made in this process, and we discuss some of the most common of these in Section III.

One of the fundamental, long standing security concepts for internal business control is the concept of separation of duties, which is designed to remove both opportunity and temptation from staff employed in the business, and we look at this in more detail in Section IV.

A further primary tool that can be used to help ensure cloud security is the simple audit trail. There are, of course, many other challenges, and we revisit these in Section II, where we look at the definition of security goals, compliance with cloud security standards, audit issues, the impact of management approaches on security, how the technical complexity of cloud and the lack of responsibility and accountability affects cloud security. We look at the need for, and benefits derived from, proper measurement and monitoring. We also consider the impact of management attitude to security, the security culture in the company and the threat environment, both external and the possible impact of internal threats. In Section III, as noted above, we discuss some of the most common mistakes companies make when adopting cloud computing, and in Section IV, as already mentioned above, we review the separation of duties in more detail. In Section V, we review the current state of cloud security standards. The remainder of the paper is organized as follows: in Section VI we discuss how the literature approaches cloud auditing; in Section VII we consider the misconceptions prevalent across different disciplines of what exactly the audit trail is; in Section VIII we discuss how we might go about improving the audit trail in a cloud setting, suggesting the use of some simple measures that can easily be taken to improve the status quo. In Section IX, we provide a useful reminder of who should be responsible for carrying out mitigating steps for the problem areas, and in Section X we discuss our conclusions.

II. Cloud Security Challenges

There are a number of challenges that need to be addressed in order to achieve the goal of good security. The fundamental concepts of information security are confidentiality, integrity, and availability (CIA), a framework developed when it was common practice for corporate management to run a company under agency theory. We have all seen how agency theory has failed to curb the excesses of corporate greed. The same is true when applied to cloud security, which would suggest a different approach is needed.

Ten key security issues have been identified, namely:

- The definition of security goals [6];
- Compliance with standards[3] [2];
- Audit issues [2] [13];
- Management approach [3] [25];

- Technical complexity of cloud [3] [14];
- Lack of responsibility and accountability [6] [14];
- Measurement and monitoring [14];
- Management attitude to security [1];
- Security culture in the company [1];
- The threat environment [25].

These 10 key security issues are not the only issues that need to be tackled, but in our opinion, these represent the issues that present the greatest barriers to achieving a good level of cloud security. We discuss each of these in turn below.

In looking at the definition of security goals, we have recognised that the business environment is constantly changing, as are corporate governance rules and this would clearly imply changing security measures would be required to keep up to date. Many managers are unable, unwilling or unsure of how to define proper security goals [4] [5] [6]. More emphasis is now being placed on responsibility and accountability [7], social conscience [8], sustainability [9][10], resilience [11] and ethics [12]. Responsibility and accountability are, in effect, mechanisms we can use to help achieve all the other security goals. Since social conscience and ethics are very closely related, we can expand the traditional CIA triad to include sustainability, resilience and ethics (SRE). This expansion of security requirements can help address some of the shortcomings of agency theory, but also provides a perfect fit to stewardship theory. Stewardship carries a broader acceptance of responsibility than the self-interest embedded in agency. This breadth extends to acting in the interests of company owners and potentially society and the environment as a whole. Broadening the definition of security goals provides a more effective means of achieving a successful cloud audit, although the additional complexity cloud brings will potentially complicate the audit trail.

In earlier work [3], we developed a conceptual framework to address cloud security. In this work, we identified three key barriers to good cloud security, namely standards compliance, management method and complexity. We have already addressed compliance with standards [2]. The lack of coherent cloud standards undermines the effectiveness of cloud audit as well as introducing a fundamental weakness in that process [13] — the use of checklists. We also addressed complexity as part of [14]. Naturally, there are not just three barriers to good security to contend with, as we see from the above list.

On the matter of achieving compliance with cloud security standards in practice, we have identified the use of assurance to achieve security through compliance and audit. Turning first to compliance, there are a number of challenges to address. Since the evolution of cloud computing, a number of cloud security standards have evolved, but the problem is that there is still no standard that offers complete security — there is no "one size covers all", which is a limitation. Even compliance with all standards will not guarantee complete security, which presents another disadvantage [2]. The pace of evolution of new technology far outstrips the capacity of international standards organisations to keep up with the changes [15], adding to the problem and meaning it may not be resolved any time soon. We have argued that companies need to take account of these gaps in the standards when addressing issues of compliance. Reliance on compliance alone will undermine effective security. We believe that standards need to shift from a rule based approach to a risk based approach [16] [17] [18] [19] [5] [20].

In [21], we addressed the basic issues faced in cloud audit, namely the misunderstandings prevalent concerning the reasons for audit, where we identified the three main purposes of audit. We considered the impact of many factors on the audit process, including addressing the impact of these shortcomings on the successful outcome of the process. We expand on that work here. It is certainly the case that cloud audit is not a mature field, and much early work on cloud audit has focussed on addressing technical issues. We have long held the view that focussing on technical issues alone can never solve cloud security. The business architecture of a company comprises people, process and technology [22], not technology alone, thus focussing only on a technical solution is likely to undermine security. We suggest that management need to better understand the purpose, and importance, of audit [21] [23] [6] [14] [24]. It is also necessary to understand both the key importance and weaknesses offered by the audit trail [1].

We also considered the management approach [25], where we addressed the cloud security issue with management method, and argued that the historic reliance on agency theory to run companies can undermine effective security, and we outlined what the impact of this might be on security. There is no doubt that management approach is a key consideration to be aware of in addressing the complex relationships in the cloud ecosystem [25]. While all actors do not utilise the same approach, it is certainly helpful for management to recognise the management approach used by each of the actors involved within their own cloud ecosystem. This will better arm them to identify key risks they face and take appropriate mitigating action.

Having started to address complexity of cloud in [14], it is clear that there is a need for further research in this area. Too many cloud users take the view that cloud is a simple paradigm to use, but are unaware of the serious impact presented by the complexities of cloud. The increasing complexity that new technology brings, results in increased potential exposure to risk as a result of failure to grasp the significance of these risks [26]. Traditional distributed information systems present a multiplicity of technical layers, each of which must interact with one or more other layers, and this is already well understood. Cloud introduces further layers, each of which can be operated by different actors. Cloud brokers may also be involved, leading to yet more layers, more complexity, and more risk. This is an area that is less well understood. Cloud allows a user to quickly deploy, for example, a web server with a database back end, often relying on default settings, which can introduce a number of weaknesses [21]. These default settings usually pay far more attention to usability than to security.

Monahan and Yearworth [27] observe that Service Level Agreements (SLAs) should be meaningful, both for cloud users and providers, as defined by some objective criteria. Evidence from procurement failures for large IT systems suggests otherwise. This observation has inspired an investigation into the possibility of offering alternative security SLAs that would be meaningful to both customers and vendors. Duncan and Whittington [6] provide some useful background on these issues in SLAs. It is hard to allocate proper responsibility to the right actors [28], personal data [29] and privacy [30], far less persuade them to accept responsibility for it. Some [31] [30] [32], have long argued that responsibility and accountability should always be built in to the design of cloud systems.

While there has already been extensive research conducted into the security concepts of CIA, there is less research into our additional goals of SRE, We do see a good deal of research into measurement of Corporate Social Responsibility (CSR), [33] [34] [35] [36] [37] [38] [39] [40], resilience [41] [42] [43] [44] [45] [46] [47] [48] and sustainability [49] [50] [51], yet there is still some way to go before effective measures are properly developed and deployed. While measurement is extremely important, it can be very difficult to achieve. There is a clear need to use continuous monitoring when it comes to security management. Reports from global security companies, which cover both non-cloud and cloud data [22], [52], [53], suggest that over 85% of security breaches are achieved with a low level of technical competence, often facilitated by lack of understanding, lack of competence, or poor configuration of victims' systems. Duncan and Whittington [14] provide some useful background on this.

Our first key goal was to define proper security goals, and obviously proper measurement is essential to be able to understand whether these goals can be met. This obviously requires constant monitoring to ensure the goals are actually achieved, or to warn of possible failures before it becomes a more serious problem.

Management attitude to security has been a high priority [54] for a considerable time. In [55], 77% of security professionals have recognised the need to set security attitudes from the top. According to a report [22], management attitude is high, if you listen to the executives, yet low when you listen to IT practitioners. Thus management need to be fully aware that it is not simply a technical issue to be passed down the line, rather it is a fundamental business process that needs to be driven right from the top of the organisation. Information security presents one of the largest risks facing business today and needs to be given the proper attention and commitment it requires.

One of the most important aspects of creating good security in a company lies in the development and maintenance of a good security culture within the organisation. This has long been recognised [54] [55] [22], but its success is dependant on the attitude to security displayed by top management. This attitude must be coupled with proper staff training to ensure staff understand how to adequately deal with security threats. It is estimated [22], that in 2012, only 26% of companies with a security policy believed their staff understood how to use them.

It is necessary to recognise the magnitude of the threat environment. Attackers are constantly probing for weaknesses, which they will exploit without mercy. It is clear that the threat environment is developing just as quickly as the technological changes faced by industry [2] [25] [24]. We need to be aware of the threat this presents, be mindful of the fact that insider threats also pose a significant security risk, and try to minimise the possible impact. While we have absolutely no control over attackers, we can help reduce the impact by making life so difficult for them that they go away and attack an easier target instead. It is also necessary to understand that the threat environment is not restricted to outside actors. It is vital to understand that an equally dangerous threat may come from within the organisation. This can come in the form of employee laziness, incompetence, inexperience, lack of proper training, or worst of all, from malicious internal actors. This danger can be multiplied exponentially where they are acting in collusion with external malicious actors.

The above ten issues are of particular importance for management of a company, as they are the people responsible for determining the security position of the company, and enforcing the delivery of these goals. In the next sections, we consider a range of common mistakes made by management when adopting a cloud solution. Some of these mistakes are quite simple, some are more complex, but they all share a common thread, they all impact adversely on security.

III. Some Common Mistakes Companies Often Make When Transferring to Cloud

Companies should not believe the economic arguments of cloud service providers (CSPs) [56]. Instead, they should evaluate their needs properly for themselves, and where they are unsure, they should take neutral advice. It is necessary to prepare properly ahead of time, not to rush the decision to move to cloud, and to carry out their own due diligence on downtime history, data accessibility, pricing structure and CSP security and privacy record before signing any contract [57]. Companies should not assume it will be easy. Instead, they should think it through, understand the costs properly, and purchase the right service package rather than taking the first one that comes along [58].

Companies often wear cost blinkers when choosing cloud provisioning, but it is vital to factor in the risks and exposure too [59], not forgetting to just look at the short term, but to take the long view too. Before deciding, companies should check performance, making sure latency at end user nodes is acceptable. Remember, all clouds are not created equal. It is so important not to choose an inappropriate Cloud Service Provider (CSP).

Often, companies fail to prepare a proper disaster recovery plan [60]. Companies should always expect the unexpected, and plan for it. It is vital to be aware of what data must go to cloud, and who should be able to see it, and it is important not to forget access control. One key consideration is "location, location, location". Companies must understand where their data is stored [61], and how they can get their data back, if required. They need to understand who can gain access to their data. Cloud systems will not necessarily just be exposed to CSP personnel, but also other sub-contracted organisations [62], whose security and privacy approach may be nowhere near as good as that of the CSP. Companies often fail to account for data privacy risks. This presents a really good incentive for using encryption for their data.

When it comes to cloud security and privacy, there is no single solution [2]. In the first case, companies should not assume the CSP's security is good. CSPs have a heavy incentive not to release full details of previous security and privacy breaches so as not to adversely affect future sales. Companies should not use the wrong privacy approach, and should try to align security with its business goals [63]. Whatever approach is used, it must be cloud-friendly. For compliance, companies should always consider encryption [64], preferably with split encryption keys. Companies often sign up to cloud accepting the standard SLA. This can be a big mistake as many of these standard contracts are extremely vague about security and privacy, or do not even mention it. This lack of accountability on the part of the CSP will only help attackers breach company systems more easily.

When a company does switch to cloud, a common mistake is to try to do too much, too quickly. It is better to do small applications first, preferably those where failure will have minimal negative impact [65]. A company must not fail to understand the true threat against their employees, customers, suppliers and ultimately, their data. The company must have a cutting-edge comprehensive information security plan. The company needs to view security not just as an "IT problem", but rather as a "business problem" that also includes IT. Many who have implemented security as an IT problem have ended up with a strong IT implementation of data security controls but limited (if any) attention paid to the majority of available or required security controls such as physical security, security policies and procedures, training, and other administrative and environmental controls. People are generally the weakest link in the security chain, which is why special attention needs to be paid to their proper training in all security issues. This is also why security mirrors the business architecture of a company, people, process and technology [22], not technology alone.

It is also important for companies to "keep their eye on the ball", otherwise apathy soon follows, with consequent weakening of company security policies leading to disaster. Companies also need to keep up-to-date, by subscribing to threat intelligence feeds and collaborating with other leaders in the field [63]. New vulnerabilities and threats are discovered every day, and there is no room for complacency.

There have been a range of interesting approaches to try to alleviate some of the obvious issues in cloud security. One such area is the issue of how to ensure data integrity in the cloud. We see a number of interesting proposals, such as [66] [64] [67] [68] [69], which seek to provide assurance of data integrity to users through various forms of audit, which generally work quite well. There are those, such as [70] [71] [72] [73], who have suggested trust computing could be the way forward. Again, these can work well, but it is important to realise that despite establishing trust between providers and users, nevertheless, the fact remains that the work is being performed on someone else's systems, thus an element of risk will always remain. Others, such as [74] [75] [76] [77], believe provable data possession could help address this problem. Some believe that timeline entanglement, such as [78] [79] [80], is the way forward.

These systems, while generally proving capable of delivering what they promise, share a common flaw. They all provide an excellent means of achieving their objectives, but do not provide a means to deal with what happens after a serious security breach involving, usually brutal and indiscriminate, modification or deletion of multiple records. Where users do not understand the true purpose of an audit trail, it may be that they no longer have access to the necessary data with which to restore the modified or deleted data to its original state.

We can learn lessons from the accounting world, specifically in the area of the audit trail, as used with accounting systems for centuries. One of the key requirements in the accounting process is the separation of duties, and we discuss this more fully in the next section.

IV. The Importance of Separation of Duties

One of the core, long standing security concepts for internal business systems is that of "separation (or segregation) of duties." This concerns the advisability of separating and then parcelling out parts of a task to different people and places in order to reduce the opportunity for fraud or theft as multiple actors would need to take part. The fundamental nature of this concept is shown in the ground-breaking behavioural research of Ashton [81], who questioned auditors to seek an understanding of their consistency in applying judgement. He started with two questions in his questionnaire that embedded the concept of separation of duties

- Are the tasks of both timekeeping and payment of employees adequately separated from the task of payroll preparation?
- Are the tasks of both payroll preparation and payment of employees adequately separated from the task of payroll bank account?

The implications of judging that the answer to either of these two questions is "no" are obvious — an opportunity and a temptation arises for an individual to manipulate the payroll to their advantage. Clearly if it were possible to locate the payroll department away from the main work location and be confident that no one in payroll knew anyone in the rest of the company, then confidence would be increased yet further. Such separation not only makes fraud difficult, but also means unintentional errors are more likely to be spotted.

Gelinas et al. [82], pinpoint four basic transaction functions that should be separated: authorising transactions, executing transactions, recording transactions and safeguarding resources subsequent to the transactions being completed. Vaassen et al. [83], list five — "authorisation; custody; recording; checking and execution". Hall [84], takes the separation of duties logic and applies it specifically to computerised accounting, suggesting that the questions should now include "Is the logic of the computer program correct? Has anyone tampered with the application since it was last tested? Have changes been made to the programme that could have caused an undisclosed error?" (page 208). Whilst this may seem obvious and it might be assumed to be a problem that no longer causes grief, this is not the case. Ge and McVay [85], take advantage of the additional disclosures following the Sarbanes-Oxley Act [86], where executives were putting their lives on the line when signing off the integrity of their accounts, and examine companies that admit weaknesses. Looking at a two-year window (2002-2004) they find 261 firms with confessed internal control weaknesses and 45 of those admitted to a lack of segregation of duties. Computer firms were over-represented in the group of companies reporting problems.

The analogies to wider programming and software use are obvious and well known at least at a theoretical level. The more important question is whether the actual practice matches with the theory and then whether there is a record to demonstrate that such safety features were both in place and effective (i.e., the audit trail). As a real life example, one of the authors used to manage a large purchase ledger department and one of his staff got very confused with £2 million of invoices from a large supplier and had entered invoices, cancelled them, entered credit notes, cancelled them numerous times and had eventually come to him in tears. This was sorted, but the auditor some months later picked out these unusual transactions for investigation and an event log was able to show the mistakes, how they were rectified and who had performed each entry on the system.

We take a brief look at the current state of cloud security standards at the present time in order to demonstrate possible weaknesses in relying on compliance with these standards to provide cloud security assurance.

V. The Current State of Cloud Security Standards

There are a great many organisations who have worked on cloud security standards over the past decade. The following list, which is not exhaustive, gives a flavour of the variety of organisations working on the standards that are evolving today:

- AICPA [87];
  - AICPA Trust Service Criteria;
- ARTS [88];
- Basel 3 [89];
- BITS [90];
- CSA [32];
- CSCC [91];
- Control objectives for information and related technology (COBIT) [92];
- CSO [93];
- DPA [94];
- DMTF [95];
  - OVF;
  - OCSI;
  - CMWG;
  - CADFWG;
- ETSI [96];
  - TC Cloud;
  - CSC;
- FedRamp [97];
- Generally accepted privacy principles (GAPP) [98];
- GICTF [99];
- HIPAA [100];
- IATAC [101];
- ISACA [92];
  - COBIT;
- ISAE 3402 [102];
- ISO/IEC [103];
- Information technology infrastructure library (ITIL) [104];
- ITU [105];
- Jericho Forum [106];
- NIST [107];
- NERC [108];
  - CIP;
- OASIS [109];
  - OASIS Cloud-Specific or Extended TC;
    - OASIS CAMP TC;
    - OASIS ID Cloud TC;
    - OASIS SAF TC;
    - OASIS TOSCA TC;
    - OASIS CloudAuthZ TC;
    - OASIS PACR TC;
- OCC [110];
- OGF [111];
  - OCCI Working Group;
    - OCCI Core Specification;
    - OCCI Infrastructure Specification;
    - OCCI HTTP Rendering Specification;
    - Other OCCI-related Documents;
- OMG [112];
- PCIDSS [113];
- SNIA [114];
  - SNIA CDMI;
- The Open Group [115];
  - Cloud Work Group;
    - Cloud Computing Business Scenario;
    - Building Return on Investment from Cloud Computing;
- TM Forum [116];
  - Cloud Services Initiative;
    - TM Forum's Cloud Services Initiative Vision;
    - Barriers to Success;
    - ECLC Goals;
    - Future Collaborative Programs;
  - About the TM Forum;
    - TM Forum's Framework.

Most of these organisations have addressed specific cloud areas, particularly where they might relate to how their members might use cloud services with a better degree of safety. PCIDSS, for example, is specifically concerned with how cloud impacts on payment mechanisms. Larger organisations, such as CSA, ISACA, ISO/IEC, NIST tend to take a broader view to solving the problem. CSA and ISACA are cloud oriented organisations, while ISO/IEC and NIST have a much wider focus. Of the latter two, NIST were very quick to produce a cloud security standard, whereas the ISO/IEC standards approval process is very slow. On the plus side, once approved, an ISO/IEC standard will generally be adopted by large global corporates. To illustrate this process, NIST released their first cloud standard in 2009, followed in 2011 by a more comprehensive standard, which was well adopted by US corporates. Whereas, it took until 2014 before the ISO/IEC even mentioned cloud.

However, once they started moving, cloud standards started to flow, and ISO/IEC 27017:2015, which provides guidance for cloud specific security controls based on ISO/IEC 27002:2013, was finally approved in 2015. During the current decade, there has been a shift in the ISO 27000 series of standards from a compliance based approach to a risk based approach, and this is to be welcomed. ISO/IEC 27018:2014 was published in 2014, and covers use of personally identifiable information (PII) in public clouds. ISO/IEC 270364:2016 provides guidance on the security of cloud services. This standard does not address business continuity management or resiliency issues for cloud services. These are addressed in ISO/IEC 27031:2011, although this has been improved on in ISO 22301:2012.

There are three security studies currently being conducted by the ISO/IEC on: cloud security assessment and audit; cloud-adapted risk management framework; and cloud security components. Beyond that, the following four areas have been proposed: guidelines for cloud service customer data security; the architecture of trusted connection to cloud services; the architecture for virtual root of trust on cloud platforms; and emerging virtualization security.

Thus we will next take a brief look at cloud audit literature to see what lessons we can learn from this area.

VI. Cloud Audit Literature

Vouk [117], in an early description of the issues surrounding cloud computing, suggests there must be an ability to audit processes, data and processing results. By 2009, we see a little more concern being expressed in the area of cloud audit. Wang et al. [118] address how the cloud paradigm brings about many new security challenges, which have not been well understood. The authors study the problem of ensuring the integrity of data storage in cloud computing, in particular, the task of allowing a third party auditor (TPA), on behalf of the cloud client, to verify the integrity of the dynamic data stored in the cloud. The authors identify the difficulties and potential security problems and show how to construct an elegant verification scheme for seamless integration of these features into protocol design.

Leavitt [119] suggests CSPs will not be able to pass customer audits if they cannot demonstrate who has access to their data and how they prevent unauthorised personnel from retrieving information, a a line of enquiry they generally discourage. Some CSPs are addressing this by appointing TPAs to audit their systems in advance and by documenting procedures designed to address customers data security needs. Where the TPA is not an accounting firm, there may be some question as to auditor impartiality. Bernstein et al. [120] are excited by the prospect of a "cloud of clouds", but are worried about the security processes used to ensure connectivity to the correct server on the other clouds, and suggests some kind of audit-ability would be needed. The authors stress the need for cloud systems to provide strong and secure audit trails.

Pearson and Benameur [121] recognise that achieving proper audit trails in the cloud is an unresolved issue. Wang et al. [122] address privacy preserving public auditing for data storage security in cloud, and are keen to prevent TPA introduced weaknesses to the system. The authors present a mechanism to enable a more secure approach to public audit by TPAs. Zhou et al. [123] carry out a survey on security and privacy in cloud computing, and investigate several CSPs about their concerns on security and privacy issues, finding those concerns are inadequate. The authors suggest more should be added in terms of five aspects (i.e., availability, confidentiality, data integrity, control and audit) for security. Chen and Yoon [60] present a framework for secure cloud computing through IT auditing by establishing a general framework using checklists by following data flow and its life-cycle. The checklists are made based on the cloud deployment models and cloud services models.

Armbrust et al. [124] present a detailed description of what cloud computing is, and note that the possible lack of auditability presents the number three barrier to implementation. Ramgovind et al. [125] provide an overall security perspective of cloud computing with the aim of highlighting the security concerns that should properly be addressed and managed to realise the full potential of cloud computing. The authors note that possible unwillingness of CSPs to undergo audit presents a real barrier to take up. Grobauer et al. [126] note that discussions about cloud computing security often fail to distinguish general issues from cloud-specific issues. The authors express concern that many CSPs do not do enough to ensure good cloud audit practice can be provided to ensure proper security is achieved.

Doelitzscher et al. [127] present a prototype demonstration of Security Audit as a Service (SAaaS) architecture, a cloud audit system that aims to increase trust in cloud infrastructures by introducing more transparency to both user and cloud provider on what is happening in the cloud. This system aims to keep track of changes to the infrastructure as VMs are deployed, moved or shut down. Hale and Gamble [128] note that current SLAs focus on quality of service metrics and lack the semantics needed to express security constraints that could be used to measure risk. The authors present a framework, called SecAgreement (SecAg), that extends the current SLA negotiation standard to allow security metrics to be expressed on service description terms and service level objectives.

Pappas et al. [129] present CloudFence, a framework that allows users to independently audit the treatment of their private data by third-party online services, through the intervention of the cloud provider that hosts these services. The authors demonstrate that CloudFence requires just a few changes to existing application code, while it can detect and prevent a wide range of security breaches, ranging from data leakage attacks using SQL injection, to personal data disclosure due to missing or erroneously implemented access control checks. Xie and Gamble [30] outline a tiered approach to auditing information in the cloud. The approach provides perspectives on audit-able events that may include compositions of independently formed audit trails. Zhu et al. [77] propose the use of provable data possession (PDP), a cryptographic technique for verifying the integrity of data, without retrieving it, as part of a means of carrying out audit on the data.

Ruebsamen and Reich [130] propose the use of software agents to carry out continuous audit processing and reporting. The authors propose continuous audit to address the dynamically changing nature of cloud use, so as to ensure evidence concerning vital periods of use are not missed. Doelitzscher et al. [131] propose the use of neural networks to analyse and learn the normal usage behaviour of cloud customers, so that anomalies originating from a cloud security incident caused by a compromised virtual machine can be detected. While retrospective tests on collected data have proved very effective, the system has yet to reach a sufficient level of maturity to be deployed in a live environment.

Doelitzscher et al. [132] present a cloud audit policy language for their SAaaS architecture. The authors describe the design and implementation of the automated audit system of virtual machine images, which ensures legal and company policies are complied with. They also discuss how on-demand software audit agents that maintain and validate the security compliance of running cloud services are deployed. Thorpe et al. [133] present a framework for forensic based auditing of cloud logs. The authors explore the requirements of a cloud log forensics service oriented architecture (SOA) framework for performing effective digital investigation examinations in these abstract web services environments. Wang et al. [134] propose a secure cloud storage system supporting privacy-preserving public auditing. The authors further extend their proposal to enable the TPA to perform audits for multiple users simultaneously and efficiently.

Lopez et al. [135] propose privacy-friendly cloud audits by applying Somewhat Homomorphic Encryption (SHE) and Public-Key Searchable Encryption (PEKS) to the collection of digital evidence. The authors show that their solution can provide client privacy preserving audit data to cloud auditors. Shameli-Sendi and Cheriet [136] propose a framework for assessing the security risks associated with cloud computing platforms. Xiong and Chen [137] consider how to allocate sufficient computing resources but not to over-provision these resources to process and analyse audit logs for ensuring the guarantee of security of an SLA, referred to as the SLA-based resource allocation problem, for high-performance cloud auditing.

Now that we have looked at the cloud audit literature, will take a look at the audit trail in a bit more depth, to gain a better understanding of the detail we need to get to grips with to help us gain some benefit from it.

VII. The Audit Trail

Auditing in the accountancy world has enjoyed the benefit of over a century of practice and experience, yet there remain differences of opinion and a number of problems are yet to be resolved. Duncan and Whittington [2] provide some background on this issue. Cloud computing audit can not be considered a mature field, and there will be some way to go before it can catch up with the reflection and rigour of the accounting profession. An obvious area of weakness arises when taking audit professionals from the accounting world out of their comfort zone, and placing them in a more technical field. Equally, the use of people with a computing background can overcome some of these issues, but their lack of audit background presents an alternate weakness.

A fundamental element of the audit process is the audit trail, and having two disciplines involved in providing cloud audit services means we have two different professional mind-sets to contend with, namely accounting professionals and security professionals. An obvious concern is what is meant by the term "audit trail". It is easy to assume that everyone is talking about the same thing, but is that actually the case? To an accounting professional, the meaning of an audit trail is very clear.

The Oxford English Dictionary (OED) [138] has two useful definitions of an audit trail: "(a) Accounting: a means of verifying the detailed transactions underlying any item in an accounting record; (b) Computing: a record of the computing processes that have been applied to a particular set of source data, showing each stage of processing and allowing the original data to be reconstituted; a record of the transactions to which a database or a file has been subjected". As we can see, there is not a complete common understanding between the two disciplines of what an audit trail should be able to achieve.

In the accounting world, an understanding of exactly what is meant by an audit trail, and its importance, is a fundamental part of the training every accountant is subjected to. Some 20 years ago, the National Institute of Standards and Technology (NIST) [139] provided, in the context of computing security, a very detailed description of what an audit trail is, and this is wholly consistent with the OED definition. However, when we look at the definitions in use in some cloud audit research papers, we start to see a less rigorous understanding of what an audit trail is. For example, Bernstein [120] suggests the audit trail comprises: events, logs, and analysis thereof, Chaula [140] suggests: raw data, analysis notes, preliminary development and analysis information, processes notes, etc.

Pearson et al. [121] recognise that achieving proper audit trails in the cloud is an unresolved issue. Ko et al. [141] explicitly note that steps need to be taken to prevent audit trails disappearing after a cloud instance is shut down. Ko [142] recognises the need to collect a multiplicity of layers of log data, including transactional audit trails in order to ensure accountability in the cloud. The EU Article 29 Working Party [143] raises several cloud-specific security risks, such as loss of governance, insecure or incomplete data deletion, insufficient audit trails or isolation failures, which are not sufficiently addressed by the existing Safe Harbor principles on data security.

The audit trail can be a very powerful tool in the fight against attack. Just as the audit trail offers forensic accountants a means to track down fraudulent behaviour in a company, so the audit trail in a cloud setting, providing it can be properly protected against attack, offers forensic scientists an excellent basis to track intrusions and other wrongdoing. In the event of a catastrophic attack, it should be possible to reconstruct the system that has been attacked, in order to either prove the integrity of the system values, or in a worst case scenario, reconstruct the system from scratch. The redundancy offered by the simple audit trail, often seen by many IT people, as an unnecessary duplication, will prove invaluable in the event of compromise. One of the authors has spoken to countless IT people who have claimed they already have multiple backups of all their data, so do not see the need for a proper audit trail. This completely misses the point that after a breach occurs, the corrupted data will be duplicated over time into all the carefully maintained backup copies, resulting in multiple sets of corrupted data. This is particularly problematic where there is a considerable time between breach and discovery. Whereas, a simple, carefully protected audit trail would allow the corrupted system to be fully reconstructed.

Many cloud users are punctilious about setting up proper audit trails, but sometimes forget that when a virtual machine (VM) running in the cloud is shut down, everything, including the audit trail data they have so assiduously collected, disappears as soon as the VM shuts down [141], unless steps are taken to prevent their loss. In real world conditions, most database software ships with inadequate audit trail provision in the default settings. Anderson [144] states that the audit trail should only be capable of being read by users rather than being edited. While it is simple enough to restrict users to read-only access, this does not apply to the system administrators.

This presents an issue where an intruder gets into a system, escalates privileges until root access is obtained, and is then free to manipulate, or delete the audit trail entries in order to cover their tracks.

Cloud users often assume that the VMs they are running will be under their sole control. However, the VMs run on someone elses hardware — the CSPs. These CSPs also employ system administrators. CSPs also employ temporary staff from time to time, some of whom are also system administrators. While the CSP may vet their own staff to a high level, this may not the case with temporary employees [146]. Network connections too are often virtualized, opening up yet more avenues of attack.

A cloud user can take as many steps to secure their business as they wish, but a key ingredient in the equation is the fact that all cloud processes run on somebody elses hardware, and often software too — the CSPs. The cloud relationship needs to include the CSP as a key partner in the pursuit of achieving security [6]. Unless and until CSPs are willing to share this goal, technical solutions will be doomed to failure.

Thus in the next section, we will take a look at some of the practical approaches we can take to help us achieve the goal of a better level of security. Most of these recommendations will not be technically challenging, yet many companies fail to act on these simple actions, which could significantly improve security for their company.

VIII. How can we improve the audit trail?

There are three fundamental weaknesses here, which need to be addressed. First, inadequate default logging options can result in insufficient data being collected for the audit trail. Second, there is a lack of recognition that the audit trail data can be accessed by a malicious user gaining root privileges, which can lead to the removal of key data showing who compromised the system, and what they did once they had control of it. Third, failure to ensure log data is properly collected and moved to permanent storage can lead to loss of audit trail data, either when an instance is shut down, or when it is compromised.

To illustrate the first point, we discuss one of the most popular open source database programmes in general use today — MySQL. The vast majority of implementations will use either standard default settings on installation, or install the programme as part of a standard Linux, Apache, MySQL and PHP (LAMP) server. In the case of a LAMP server, all four of the constituent elements are set up using the default settings. This works very well for easy functionality "out of the box", which is the whole purpose of a LAMP server. Unfortunately this does not adequately address security in each of the four elements of the LAMP server.

MySQL offers the following audit trail options:

- Error log — Problems encountered starting, running, or stopping mysqld;
- General query log — Established client connections and statements received from clients;
- Binary log — Statements that change data (also used for replication);
- Relay log — Data changes received from a replication master server;
- Slow query log — Queries that took more than long_query_time seconds to execute;
- DDL log (metadata log) — Metadata operations performed by Data Definition Language (DDL) statements.

By default, no logs are enabled, except the error log on Windows. Some versions of Linux send the Error log to syslog.

Oracle offer an audit plugin for Enterprise (paid) Editions of MySQL. This allows a range of events to be logged, but again, by default, most are not enabled.

The MariaDB company, whose author originally wrote MySQL, have their own open source audit plug-in, and offer a version suitable for MySQL. It has the following functionality:

- CONNECTION — Logs connects, disconnects and failed connects (including the error code);
- QUERY — Queries issued and their results (in plain text), including failed queries due to syntax or permission errors;
- TABLE — Which tables were affected by query execution;
- QUERY_DDL — Works as the 'QUERY' value, but filters only DDL-type queries (CREATE, ALTER, etc);
- QUERY_DML — Works as the 'QUERY' value, but filters only Data Manipulation Language (DML) DML-type queries (INSERT, UPDATE, etc).

By default, logging is set to off. Thus, those users who rely on default settings for their systems are immediately putting themselves at a severe disadvantage.

Turning to the second point, as Anderson [144] states, the audit trail should only be capable of being read by users. This presents a problem in a cloud setting, where the software being used is running on someone else's hardware. There is a risk of compromise from an outside user with malicious intent. There is also a risk of compromise by someone working for the CSP. While the CSP may well take vetting of staff seriously, there may be situations that arise where a temporary contract worker is engaged at short notice who has been subject to lesser scrutiny.

Looking at the third point, where MySQL data logging is actually switched on, all data is logged to the running instance. This means the data remains accessible to any intruder who successfully breaches the system, allowing them to cover their own tracks by deleting any entries that relate to their intrusion of the system, or to simply delete the entire audit trail files. And, when the instance is shut down, all the data disappears anyway.

These three points are generally not much thought about, yet they present a serious weakness to the success of maintaining the audit trail. Equally, these are relatively trivial to address. Often management and IT staff will take the view "so what?".

Simply turn on data logging and send all log output to an independent secure server under the control of the cloud user. Adding an Intrusion Detection system (IDS) is also a useful additional precaution to take, and again, this should be run on an independent secure server under the control of the cloud user. The use of an audit plug-in in addition to all the basic logging capabilities, is also a useful thing to do. While there will be an element of double processing involved, it is better to have more data than none at all.

Where the MySQL instance forms part of a LAMP server, then it would also be prudent to make some elementary security changes to the setup of the Linux operating system, the Apache web server, and to harden the PHP installation.

It is rather worrying that as far back as 2012, Trustwave [145], report an average of 6 months between breach and discovery. It is also rather worrying to see that three years later [147], see Fig. 1, that 75% of breaches happen within days, yet only 25% of discoveries are actually made within the same time-frame. This still leaves a large gap where compromised systems may still be under the control of malicious users.

Fig. 1. The Lag Between Breach and Discovery © 2015 Verizon

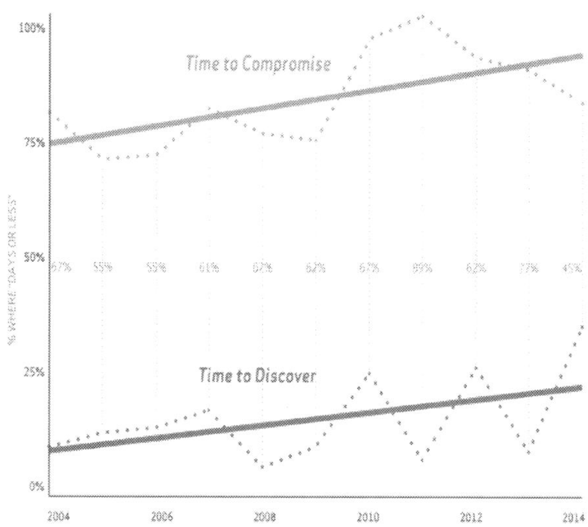

This presents a clear indication that very few firms are actually scrutinising their server logs. Back in 2012, Verizon [53] highlighted the fact that discovery of security breaches often took weeks, months or even years before discovery, with most discovery being advised by external bodies, such as customers, financial institutions or fraud agencies.

The Open Web Application Security Project (OWASP) carry out a survey every 3 years in which they collate the number of vulnerabilities with the greatest impact on companies. In TABLE I we can see the top ten list from 2013, 2010 and 2007:

Sitting at the top of the table for 2013, again for 2010, and in second place in 2007, we have injection attacks. It is very clear that companies are consistently failing to configure their database systems properly. Injection attacks rely on misconfigured databases used in dynamic web service applications, which allow SQL, OS, or LDAP injection to occur when untrusted data is sent to an interpreter as part of a command or query. The attackers hostile data can trick the interpreter into executing unintended commands or accessing data without proper authorization. This can lead to compromise, or deletion of data held in company databases.

TABLE I. OWASP TOP TEN WEB VULNERABILITIES — 2013 [148]

2013	2010	2007	Threat
1	1	2	Injection Attacks
2	3	7	Broken Authentication and Session Management
3	2	1	Cross Site Scripting (XSS)
4	4	4	Insecure Direct Object References
5	6	-	Security Misconfiguration
6	-	-	Sensitive Data Exposure
7	-	-	Missing Function Level Access Control
8	5	5	Cross Site Request Forgery (CSRF)
9	-	-	Using Components with Known Vulnerabilities
10	-	-	Unvalidated Redirects and Forwards

SQL injection attacks are relatively straightforward to defend against. OWASP provide an SQL injection prevention cheat sheet [149], in which they suggest a number of defences:

- Use of Prepared Statements (Parameterized Queries);
- Use of Stored Procedures;
- Escaping all User Supplied Input;

They also suggest that companies should enforce least privilege and perform white list input validation as useful additional precautions to take.

For operating system injection flaws, they also have a cheat sheet [150], which suggests that LDAP injection attacks are common due to two factors, namely the lack of safer, parameterized LDAP query interfaces, and the widespread use of LDAP to authenticate users to systems. Their recommendations for suitable defences are:

- Rule 1 Perform proper input validation;
- Rule 2 Use a safe API;
- Rule 3 Contextually escape user data.

And for LDAP system injection flaws, their cheat sheet [151], recommends the following injection prevention rules:

- Defence Option 1: Escape all variables using the right LDAP encoding function;
- Defence Option 2: Use Frameworks that Automatically Protect from LDAP Injection.

None of these preventative measures suggested by OWASP are particularly difficult to implement, yet judging by the recurring success of these simple attacks, companies are clearly failing to take even simple actions to protect against them.

When considering secure audit trail and system logging for a database, there are a number of simple configuration options open to the user. First, applying the above OWASP recommendations would considerably limit exposure. Looking at the database itself, the user access for posting records to the logging database can have the option to modify or delete records disabled. On the plus side, full database capabilities are retained. On the negative side, should an attacker be able to gain access to the database, and subsequently be able to escalate privileges, then these restrictions could be reversed, thus exposing the database.

Another simpler approach would be to configure the database as an archive database. This allows new records to be added, prevents modification of records in the database, and also prevents deletion of records. On the plus side, the attacker cannot change the database type, but on the negative side, the database cannot be indexed, thus making searching more difficult (time consuming).

Yet another possibility would be to configure the database such that full facilities are retained, but with the modify and delete commands completely removed. This would meet the goals for a proper audit trail, and would provide the ability to retain full search capabilities for rapid analysis and searching of the audit trail.

Thus, in addition to making the simple suggestions we propose above, cloud users should also make sure they actually review these audit trail logs. It is vital to be able to understand when a security breach has occurred, and exactly which records have been accessed, compromised or stolen. While recognising that this is not a foolproof method of achieving cloud security, it is likely to present a far higher level of affordable, achievable security than many companies currently achieve.

However, we must warn that even if a company implements these simple suggestions, that still will not guarantee security. While it will annoy the majority of attackers to such an extent that they will move on to easier pickings, it may well be that new vulnerabilities will arise. Therefore the company must remain vigilant at all times. It would be prudent to subscribe to security feeds, and follow leaders in the field to ensure they remain aware of all the latest security vulnerabilities and exploits. Of course, companies must also realise that the threat environment is not restricted to outside parties alone. Perhaps of greater concern is the threat posed by malicious internal actors, which can be even more serious where they act in concert with outside parties. This presents one of the most serious weaknesses to the security of a company. Equally, laziness on the part of staff or lack of knowledge, particularly where they have not been regularly trained to provide them with full awareness of all the latest threats, including social engineering attacks, and the consequence of falling victim to them, can also pose an extremely serious risk to company security.

In the event of a security breach, not if, but rather when it happens, it may be necessary to conduct a forensic examination to establish how the company defences were breached. With traditional distributed systems, there is usually something for the forensic computer scientists to find, somewhere in the system. They are completely accustomed to dealing with being able to find only partial traces of events, from which they can build a forensic picture of the breach. This becomes more problematic the longer the time between breach and discovery.

However, once a company adopts cloud use, this becomes far more problematic. While forensic computer scientists can work wonders with a range of partial discoveries, deleted or otherwise, once a cloud instance is shut down, there is virtually zero chance of regaining access to the shut down system. The disk space used by that system could be re-used, literally within seconds, and where the time interval between breach and discovery is considerably longer, as is generally the norm, then this opportunity becomes a physical impossibility. Thus, for forensic purposes, companies need to pay far more attention to what is actually going on in the cloud.

In the next Section, we provide a number of tables as a reminder of the issues we have discussed in this article and how to attempt to mitigate these issues.

IX. A Reminder on Who is Responsible to Mitigate the Problem Areas

In this Section, we provide some tables as a handy reminder of who is responsible for ensuring the mitigation of problem areas. We start, in TABLE II, by taking a look at the 10 key management risk areas we discussed in Section II.

TABLE II. 10 Key Management Risk Areas Weaknesses and Mitigating Responsibilities ©2016 Duncan and Whittington

Item	Weakness	Responsibility for Mitigation
1	Definition of Security Goals	Management
2	Standards Compliance	Management
3	Audit Issues	Management and Internal Audit
4	Management Approach	Management
5	Technical Complexity	Management and IT
6	Lack of Responsibility	Management
7	Measurement and Monitoring	Management and IT
8	Management Attitude to Security	Management
9	Security Culture	Management and All Employees
10	Threat Environment	Extreme Vigilance by Management and IT

Clearly, since these are key management risk areas, management must necessarily take a heavy responsibility for ensuring these areas are properly dealt with. First, the definition of clear security goals provides the fundamental basis for ensuring a good security posture can be achieved by the company. Note, there should be no delegation of this vital task to IT. Management must take full ownership of this task. On the matter of standards compliance, management must understand that since cloud security standards are not yet complete, they must recognise the risks involved in attempting to rely on this compliance for security. Management must also recognise the shortcomings pertaining to audit methodology, and should do so in conjunction with internal audit, and, if necessary, in consultation with the external auditors.

Management need to recognise the impact of the management approaches adopted by all cloud actors, and recognise how these differing approaches and risk appetites can increase risk to the company. Management, in conjunction with their IT department, must explicitly understand the potential impact due to the added complexity of cloud ecosystems, in order to ensure proper mitigation is achieved. Management must also recognise the potential impact brought about through a lack of responsibility and accountability from all the actors in the cloud ecosystem chain, including their own staff.

Management must recognise fully the need for establishing proper metrics in order to ensure proper measurement and monitoring can take place. In this way, there will at least be a recognition of when an attack has occurred, thus providing an opportunity to ensure mitigating steps are immediately taken. Management need to ensure they take a serious attitude towards security, preferably with a board member being appointed as the responsible security board member of the company. This will help to ensure a proper security culture can be developed, and maintained within the company.

Finally, there is a pressing need for management to take very seriously the potential danger posed by the threat environment. By ensuring that currently known vulnerabilities are quickly identified and mitigating action is taken promptly, this will help reduce the impact posed by the threat environment. Obviously, new vulnerabilities will become exposed all the time, and with the previous steps taken, and in particular extreme levels of vigilance, this should help to mitigate the overall danger posed.

In TABLE III, we consider the common mistakes companies often make when adopting cloud computing within their organisation, as we discussed in Section III.

TABLE III. COMMON MISTAKES WEAKNESSES AND MITIGATING STRATEGIES ©2016 DUNCAN AND WHITTINGTON

Item	Weakness	Action Required
1	CSP Sales Talk	Do not believe the hype. Do your own due diligence
2	Business Continuity	Prepare a proper disaster recovery plan
3	Cloud Security	Remember, there is no single solution
4	Rapid Deployment	Don't try to do it all at once
5	Ongoing Ennui	Do not relax. Be vigilant at all times
6	Other Approaches	Look out for the loopholes
7	After a Breach	Have a plan for what to do after a breach

Remember, the primary goal of the CSP is get your signature on the contract. Take nothing at face value, and scrutinise the small print very carefully. What will you do in the event of a security breach? You must have a proper and comprehensive disaster recovery plan in place before you start using cloud. Later will be too late. Do not forget that there is no single solution to cloud security. Identify the risks, take mitigating steps and above all remain vigilant at all times.

Do not try to implement your cloud installation too quickly. You need to thoroughly carry out security testing to ensure you eliminate as many issues as possible before you commit fully to the system. Once it is up and running, do not assume all will be well for evermore.

Do not assume new approaches will be a perfect solution to the problem. There will likely be one or more loopholes involved. Make sure that you are the one to find them. Above all else, have a plan in place for what to do the moment you have a breach. With cloud systems, you cannot afford to wait while you develop a plan. You have to take action right away, otherwise there might be very little for you to investigate where cloud systems are in use.

With regard to separation of duties, as discussed in Section IV, it is worth remembering that this advice can and should be applied to people, processes and technology. This will ensure proper internal control can be organised across the whole of the business architecture of the company.

When it comes to cloud security standards, as covered in Section V, remember there is no complete cloud security standard yet in existence, and often, the compliance mechanisms can be flawed, leading to a false sense of security evolving. Guard against this arising at all costs.

Finally, do not forget the benefits to be obtained from implementing a proper audit trail. In TABLE IV, we reiterate the main points addressed in Section VIII.

There is a great deal of work that can be carried out with databases to ensure a more robust environment is used to limit the damage from any security breach that might occur. It is vital to ensure that taking the easy option of using default settings is never to be allowed to happen. Default settings, while very easy to implement, are a vital security weakness which can be a great enabler for the attacker. A company should always take the trouble to take this treat away from potential attackers.

TABLE IV. POSSIBLE IMPROVEMENTS TO ENSURE A COMPLETE AUDIT TRAIL ©2016 DUNCAN AND WHITTINGTON

Item	Weakness	Action Required
1	Inadequate Default Logging	Make sure adequate logging is turned on
2	Insecure Audit Trail Data	Protect access to this data properly
3	Incomplete Audit Trail Data	Ensure full data collection
4	Secure Audit Trail	Use a separate secure server for this
5	Secure Server Setup	Setup a hardened server
6	Securing the Audit Trail Server	Add an Intrusion Detection system
7	Ensuring Security	Setup a live monitoring system
8	Ensuring Security	Update all security patches regularly
9	Ensuring Security	Setup immutable databases for the audit trail
10	Ensuring Security	Collect data from all running cloud instances

In the next section, we shall review our findings and discuss our conclusions.

X. CONCLUSION

We have looked at some of the challenges facing companies who seek to obtain good cloud security assurance. We have seen how weaknesses in standard CSP SLAs can impact on cloud security. We have identified issues with cloud security standards, and how that might impact on cloud security. We have considered how the lack of accountability can impact on security. We have discussed how a number of the above issues must additionally be addressed. It is clear that companies who use cloud need to understand the impact that the complexities of using cloud will have on their security will have to be very carefully considered in order to ensure they do not fall foul of the many opportunities that exist for security controls to "fall down the gaps" and thus become lost forever.

The practice of using default settings when installing software in a cloud environment is clearly asking for trouble. These simple steps we propose are relatively easy to implement, need not be particularly expensive to implement and maintain, and providing some on-going monitoring of the audit trail logs will certainly prove beneficial. Examination of the logs need not be challenging or costly — there are many software solutions available to address this task using programmatic means. Complicated solutions generally lead to complex problems, as the more complex the solution, the more the risk of ineffective configuration and maintenance can lead to compromise in security. Yet all. too often, the simple steps than can really help improve security are ignored.

We have touched on how these difficult areas of security might easily be approached as part of a comprehensive security solution using simple and inexpensive methods. Clearly, companies could benefit from further research in several of these areas. However, we would caution that action is needed now, not several years down the line when research reaches a more complete level of success in these areas. The threat environment is too dangerous. Companies have to act now to try to close the door, otherwise it may be too late.

REFERENCES

[1] B. Duncan and M. Whittington, "Enhancing Cloud Security and Privacy: The Power and the Weakness of the Audit Trail," in *Cloud Comput. 2016 Seventh Int. Conf. Cloud Comput. GRIDs, Virtualization*. Rome: IEEE, 2016, pp. 125–130.

[2] B. Duncan and M. Whittington, "Compliance with Standards, Assurance and Audit: Does this Equal Security?" in *Proc. 7th Int. Conf. Secur. Inf. Networks*. Glasgow: ACM, 2014, pp. 77–84.

[3] B. Duncan, D. J. Pym, and M. Whittington, "Developing a Conceptual Framework for Cloud Security Assurance," in *Cloud Comput. Technol. Sci. (CloudCom), 2013 IEEE 5th Int. Conf. (Volume 2)*. Bristol: IEEE, 2013, pp. 120–125.

[4] N. Papanikolaou, S. Pearson, M. C. Mont, and R. K. L. Ko, "Towards Greater Accountability in Cloud Computing through Natural-Language Analysis and Automated Policy Enforcement," *Engineering*, pp. 1–4, 2011.

[5] A. Baldwin, D. Pym, and S. Shiu, "Enterprise Information Risk Management: Dealing with Cloud Computing," *Abdn.Ac.Uk*, pp. 257—291, 2013.

[6] B. Duncan and M. Whittington, "Enhancing Cloud Security and Privacy: Broadening the Service Level Agreement," in *14th IEEE Int. Conf. Trust. Secur. Priv. Comput. Commun. (IEEE Trust.*, Helsinki, Finland, 2015, pp. 1088–1093.

[7] M. Huse, "Accountability and Creating Accountability: a Framework for Exploring Behavioural Perspectives of Corporate Governance," *Br. J. Manag.*, vol. 16, no. S1, pp. S65–S79, Mar 2005.

[8] A. Gill, "Corporate Governance as Social Responsibility: A Research Agenda," *Berkeley J. Int'l L.*, vol. 26, no. 2, pp. 452–478, 2008.

[9] C. Ioannidis, D. Pym, and J. Williams, "Sustainability in Information Stewardship: Time Preferences, Externalities and Social Co-Ordination," in *Weis 2013*, 2013, pp. 1–24.

[10] A. Kolk, "Sustainability, accountability and corporate governance: Exploring multinationals' reporting practices." *Bus. Strateg. Environ.*, vol. 17, no. 1, pp. 1–15, 2008.

[11] F. S. Chapin, G. P. Kofinas, and C. Folke, *Principles of Ecosystem Stewardship: Resilience-Based Natural Resource Management in a Changing World*. Springer, 2009.

[12] S. Arjoon, "Corporate Governance: An Ethical Perspective," *J. Bus. Ethics*, vol. 61, no. 4, pp. 343–352, nov 2012.

[13] B. Duncan and M. Whittington, "Reflecting on whether checklists can tick the box for cloud security," in *Proc. Int. Conf. Cloud Comput. Technol. Sci. CloudCom*, vol. 2015-Febru, no. February. Singapore: IEEE, 2015, pp. 805–810.

[14] B. Duncan and M. Whittington, "The Importance of Proper Measurement for a Cloud Security Assurance Model," in *2015 IEEE 7th Int. Conf. Cloud Comput. Technol. Sci.*, Vancouver, 2015, pp. 1–6.

[15] G. T. Willingmyre, "Standards at the Crossroads," *StandardView*, vol. 5, no. 4, pp. 190–194, 1997.

[16] E. Humphreys, "Information security management standards: Compliance, governance and risk management," *Inf. Secur. Tech. Rep.*, vol. 13, no. 4, pp. 247–255, Nov 2008.

[17] F. Albersmeier, H. Schulze, G. Jahn, and A. Spiller, "The reliability of third-party certification in the food chain: From checklists to risk-oriented auditing," *Food Control*, vol. 20, no. 10, pp. 927–935, 2009.

[18] K. Prislan and I. Bernik, "Risk Management with ISO 27000 standards in Information Security," *Inf. Secur.*, pp. 58–63, 2010.

[19] IsecT, "Information Security Frameworks from "Audit" to "Zachman"," Tech. Rep. March, 2011.

[20] Order, "Executive Order 13636: Improving Critical Infrastructure Cybersecurity," pp. 1–8, 2013.

[21] B. Duncan and M. Whittington, "Enhancing Cloud Security and Privacy: The Cloud Audit Problem," in *Cloud Comput. 2016 Seventh Int. Conf. Cloud Comput. GRIDs, Virtualization*. Rome: IEEE, 2016, pp. 119–124.

[22] PWC, "UK Information Security Breaches Survey - Technical Report 2012," London, Tech. Rep. April, 2012. [Online]. Available: www.pwc.comwww.bis.gov.uk [Last Accessed: 30 Nov 2016]

[23] T. Sang, "A Log-based Approach to Make Digital Forensics Easier on Cloud Computing," *Proc. 2013 3rd Int. Conf. Intell. Syst. Des. Eng. Appl. ISDEA 2013*, pp. 91–94, 2013.

[24] B. Duncan and M. Whittington, "Information Security in the Cloud: Should We be Using a Different Approach?" in *2015 IEEE 7th Int. Conf. Cloud Comput. Technol. Sci.*, Vancouver, 2015, pp. 1–6.

[25] B. Duncan and M. Whittington, "Company Management Approaches Stewardship or Agency: Which Promotes Better Security in Cloud Ecosystems?" in *Cloud Comput. 2015*. Nice: IEEE, 2015, pp. 154–159.

[26] E. Zio, "Reliability engineering: Old problems and new challenges," *Reliab. Eng. Syst. Saf.*, vol. 94, no. 2, pp. 125–141, Feb 2009.

[27] B. Monahan and M. Yearworth, "Meaningful Security SLAs," HP Labs, Bristol, Tech. Rep., 2008. [Online]. Available: http://www.hpl.hp.com/techreports/2005/HPL-2005-218R1.pdf [Last Accessed: 30 Nov 2016]

[28] M. Theoharidou, N. Papanikolaou, S. Pearson, and D. Gritzalis, "Privacy Risk , Security , Accountability in the Cloud," in *IEEE Int. Conf. Cloud Comput. Technol. Sci. Priv.*, 2013, pp. 177–184.

[29] C. Millard, I. Walden, and W. K. Hon, "Who is Responsible for 'Personal Data' in Cloud Computing? The Cloud of Unknowing, Part 2," *Leg. Stud.*, vol. 27, no. 77, pp. 1–31, 2012.

[30] S. Pearson, "Taking account of privacy when designing cloud computing services," *Proc. 2009 ICSE Work. Softw. Eng. Challenges Cloud Comput. CLOUD 2009*, pp. 44–52, 2009.

[31] S. Pearson and A. Charlesworth, "Accountability as a way forward for privacy protection in the cloud," *Lect. Notes Comput. Sci. (including Subser. Lect. Notes Artif. Intell. Lect. Notes Bioinformatics)*, vol. 5931 LNCS, no. December, pp. 131–144, 2009.

[32] C. C. V, "Security research alliance to promote network security," Cloud Security Alliance, Tech. Rep. 2, 1999. [Online]. Available: http://scholar.google.com/scholar?hl=en{\&}btnG=Search{\&}q=intitle:Security+Guidance+Critical+Areas+of+Focus+for{\#}0 [Last Accessed: 30 Nov 2016]

[33] T. Hahn, F. Figge, J. Pinkse, and L. Preuss, "Editorial Trade-Offs in Corporate Sustainability: You Can't Have Your Cake and Eat It," *Bus. Strateg. Environ.*, vol. 19, no. 4, pp. 217–229, 2010.

[34] A. Lindgreen and V. Swaen, "Corporate Social Responsibility," *Int. J. Manag. Rev.*, vol. 12, no. 1, pp. 1–7, 2010.

[35] D. J. Wood, "Measuring Corporate Social Performance: A Review," *Int. J. Manag. Rev.*, vol. 12, no. 1, pp. 50–84, 2010.

[36] T. Green and J. Peloza, "How does corporate social responsibility create value for consumers?" *J. Consum. Mark.*, vol. 28, no. 1, pp. 48–56, 2011.

[37] A. Christofi, P. Christofi, and S. Sisaye, "Corporate sustainability: historical development and reporting practices," *Manag. Res. Rev.*, vol. 35, no. 2, pp. 157–172, 2012.

[38] N. Rahman and C. Post, "Measurement Issues in Environmental Corporate Social Responsibility (ECSR): Toward a Transparent, Reliable, and Construct Valid Instrument," *J. Bus. Ethics*, vol. 105, no. 3, pp. 307–319, 2012.

[39] M. A. Delmas, D. Etzion, and N. Nairn-Birch, "Triangulating Environmental Performance: What Do Corporate Social Responsibility Ratings Really Capture?" *Acad. Manag. Perspect.*, vol. 27, no. 3, pp. 255–267, 2013.

[40] I. Montiel and J. Delgado-Ceballos, "Defining and Measuring Corporate Sustainability: Are We There Yet?" *Organ. Environ.*, vol. Advance on, pp. 1–27, 2014.

[41] D. Bodeau, R. Graubart, L. LaPadula, P. Kertzner, A. Rosenthal, and J. Brennan, "Cyber Resiliency Metrics ," *MITRE Rep. MP 120053 Rev 1.*, no. April, pp. 1–40, 2012.

[42] H. Carvalho, S. G. Azevedo, and V. Cruz-Machado, "Agile and resilient approaches to supply chain management: influence on performance and competitiveness," *Logist. Res.*, vol. 4, no. 1-2, pp. 49–62, 2012.

[43] M. Vieira, H. Madeira, K. Sachs, and S. Kounev, "Resilience Benchmarking," *Resil. Assess. Eval. Comput. Syst.*, pp. 283–301, 2012.

[44] A. V. Lee, J. Vargo, and E. Seville, "Developing a Tool to Measure and Compare Organizations' Resilience," *Nat. Hazards Rev.*, no. February, pp. 29–41, 2013.

[45] I. Linkov, D. A. Eisenberg, M. E. Bates, D. Chang, M. Convertino, J. H. Allen, S. E. Flynn, and T. P. Seager, "Measurable Resilience for Action-

able Policy," *Environ. Sci. Technol.*, vol. 47, no. ii, p. 130903081548008, 2013.

[46] I. Linkov, D. A. Eisenberg, K. Plourde, T. P. Seager, J. Allen, and A. Kott, "Resilience metrics for cyber systems," *Environ. Syst. Decis.*, vol. 33, no. 4, pp. 471–476, 2013.

[47] T. Prior and J. Hagmann, "Measuring resilience: methodological and political challenges of a trend security concept," *J. Risk Res.*, vol. 17, no. 3, pp. 281–298, 2014.

[48] C. Ioannidis, D. Pym, J. Williams, and I. Gheyas, "Resilience in Information Stewardship," in *Weis 2014*, vol. 2014, no. June, 2014, pp. 1–33.

[49] K. Gilman and J. Schulschenk, "Sustainability Accounting Standards Board," pp. 14–17, 2012. [Online]. Available: www.sasb.org [Last Accessed: 30 Nov 2016]

[50] R. Eccles, K. Perkins, and G. Serafeim, "How to Become a Sustainable Company," *MIT Sloan Manag. Rev.*, vol. 53, no. 4, pp. 43–50, 2012.

[51] R. G. Eccles, I. Ioannou, and G. Serafeim, "The Impact of Corporate Sustainability on Organizational Processes and Performance," *Manage. Sci.*, vol. 60, no. 11, pp. 2835–2857, 2014.

[52] Trend, "2012 Annual Security Roundup: Evolved Threats in a "Post-PC" World," Trend Micro, Tech. Rep., 2012.

[53] Verizon, N. High, T. Crime, I. Reporting, and I. S. Service, "2012 Data Breach Investigations Report," Verizon, Tech. Rep., 2012.

[54] ISACA, "An Introduction to the Business Model for Information Security," Tech. Rep., 2009.

[55] PWC, "Information Security Breaches Survey 2010 Technical Report," pp. 1–22, 2010.

[56] M. Armbrust, I. Stoica, M. Zaharia, A. Fox, R. Griffith, A. D. Joseph, R. Katz, A. Konwinski, G. Lee, D. Patterson, and A. Rabkin, "A View of Cloud Computing: Clearing the clouds away from the true potential and obstacles posed by this computing capability." *Commun. ACM*, vol. 53, no. 4, pp. 50–58, 2010.

[57] J. Opara-Martins, R. Sahandi, and F. Tian, "Critical review of vendor lock-in and its impact on adoption of cloud computing," *Int. Conf. Inf. Soc. i-Society 2014*, pp. 92–97, 2015.

[58] Q. Zhang, L. Cheng, and R. Boutaba, "Cloud computing: State-of-the-art and research challenges," *J. Internet Serv. Appl.*, vol. 1, no. 1, pp. 7–18, 2010.

[59] K. Dahbur, B. Mohammad, and A. B. Tarakji, "A Survey of Risks, Threats and Vulnerabilities in Cloud Computing," *Computing*, pp. 1–6, 2011.

[60] Z. Chen and J. Yoon, "IT Auditing to Assure a Secure Cloud Computing," in *Proc. - 2010 6th World Congr. Serv. Serv. 2010*, 2010, pp. 253–259.

[61] D. J. Abadi, "Data management in the cloud: limitations and opportunities," *IEEE Data Eng. Bull.*, vol. 32, no. 1, pp. 3–12, 2009.

[62] R. Chow, P. Golle, M. Jakobsson, E. Shi, J. Staddon, R. Masuoka, and J. Molina, "Controlling Data in the Cloud: Outsourcing Computation without Outsourcing Control," in *Proc. 2009 ACM Work. Cloud Comput. Secur.*, 2009, pp. 85–90.

[63] K. Popovic and Z. Hocenski, "Cloud computing security issues and challenges," *MIPRO, 2010 Proc. 33rd Int. Conv.*, pp. 344–349, 2010.

[64] S. Subashini and V. Kavitha, "A Survey on Security Issues in Service Delivery Models of Cloud Computing," *J. Netw. Comput. Appl.*, vol. 34, no. 1, pp. 1–11, 2011.

[65] C. Low, Y. Chen, and M. Wu, "Understanding the determinants of cloud computing adoption," *Ind. Manag. Data Syst.*, vol. 111, no. 7, pp. 1006–1023, 2011.

[66] Z. Hao, S. Zhong, and N. Yu, "A Privacy-Preserving Remote Data Integrity Checking Protocol with Data Dynamics and Public Verifiability," *IEEE Trans. Knowl. Data Eng.*, vol. 23, no. 9, pp. 1432–1437, 2011.

[67] D. Chen and H. Zhao, "Data Security and Privacy Protection Issues in Cloud Computing," *2012 Int. Conf. Comput. Sci. Electron. Eng.*, vol. 1, no. 973, pp. 647–651, 2012.

[68] K. Yang and X. Jia, "An Efficient and Secure Dynamic Auditing Protocol for Data Storage in Cloud Computing," *IEEE Trans. Parallel Distrib. Syst.*, vol. I, no. 9, pp. 2–5, 2014.

[69] L. Wei, H. Zhu, Z. Cao, X. Dong, W. Jia, Y. Chen, and A. V. Vasilakos, "Security and privacy for storage and computation in cloud computing," *Inf. Sci. (Ny).*, vol. 258, pp. 371–386, 2014.

[70] N. Santos, K. P. Gummadi, and R. Rodrigues, "Towards Trusted Cloud Computing," *Inf. Secur. Tech. Rep.*, vol. 10, no. 2, p. 5, 2005.

[71] Z. Shen, L. Li, F. Yan, and X. Wu, "Cloud Computing System Based on Trusted Computing Platform," *2010 Int. Conf. Intell. Comput. Technol. Autom.*, pp. 942–945, 2010.

[72] S. Sengupta, V. Kaulgud, and V. S. Sharma, "Cloud Computing Security - Trends and Research Directions," *2011 IEEE World Congr. Serv.*, no. October, pp. 524–531, 2011.

[73] Z. Xiao and Y. Xiao, "Security and Privacy in Cloud Computing," *Commun. Surv. Tutorials, IEEE*, vol. 15, no. 2, pp. 843–859, 2013.

[74] Y. Zhu, H. Wang, Z. Hu, G.-j. Ahn, H. Hu, S. S. Yau, H. I. Storage, and R. Information, "Efficient Provable Data Possession for Hybrid Clouds," in *Proc. 17th ACM Conf. Comput. Commun. Secur.*, 2010, pp. 756–758.

[75] G. Ateniese, R. Burns, R. Curtmola, J. Herring, O. Khan, L. Kissner, Z. Peterson, and D. Song, "Remote data checking using provable data possession," *ACM Trans. Inf. Syst. Secur.*, vol. 14, no. 1, pp. 1–34, 2011.

[76] Q. Wang, C. Wang, K. Ren, W. Lou, and J. Li, "Enabling Public Verifiability and Data Dynamics for Storage Security in Cloud Computing," in *IEEE Trans. Parallel Distrib. Syst.*, vol. 22, no. 5, 2011, pp. 847–859.

[77] Y. Zhu, H. Hu, G. J. Ahn, and M. Yu, "Cooperative provable data possession for integrity verification in multicloud storage," in *IEEE Trans. Parallel Distrib. Syst.*, vol. 23, no. 12, 2012, pp. 2231–2244.

[78] H. T. T. Truong, C.-L. Ignat, and P. Molli, "Authenticating Operation-based History in Collaborative Systems," *Proc. 17Th Acm Int. Conf. Support. Gr. Work*, pp. 131–140, 2012.

[79] M. Mizan, M. L. Rahman, R. Khan, M. Haque, and R. Hasan, "Accountable proof of ownership for data using timing element in cloud services," *Proc. 2013 Int. Conf. High Perform. Comput. Simulation, HPCS 2013*, pp. 57–64, 2013.

[80] S. L. Reed, "Bitcoin Cooperative Proof of Stake," pp. 1–16, 2014.

[81] R. H. Ashton, "An experimental study of internal control judgements," *J. Account. Res.*, pp. 143–157, 1974.

[82] S. S. G. Gelinas U.J. and A. E. Oram, *Accounting Information Systems (4th edition)*. South-Western College Publishing, Cincinnati, Ohio, US., 1999.

[83] E. Vaassen, R. Meuwissen, and C. Schelleman, *Accounting information systems and internal control*. Wiley Publishing, 2009.

[84] J. A. Hall, *Accounting Information Systems (3rd edition)*. South-Western College Publishing, Cincinnati, Ohio, US., 2001.

[85] W. Ge and S. McVay, "The disclosure of material weaknesses in internal control after the Sarbanes-Oxley Act," *Account. Horizons*, vol. 19, no. 3, pp. 137–158, 2005.

[86] Sox, "Sarbanes-Oxley Act of 2002," p. 66, 2002.

[87] AICPA, "AICPA SOC2 Standard," 2014. [Online]. Available: https://www.aicpa.org/InterestAreas/FRC/AssuranceAdvisoryServices/Pages/AICPASOC2Report.aspx [Last Accessed: 30 Nov 2016]

[88] ARTS, "Association for Retail Technology Standards," 2014. [Online]. Available: https://nrf.com/resources/retail-technology-standards-0 [Last Accessed: 30 Nov 2016]

[89] Basel3, "Basel 3 Impact," Basel, Tech. Rep. December 2010, 2011. [Online]. Available: http://www.bis.org/bcbs/basel3.htm?m=3\%257C14\%257C572 [Last Accessed: 30 Nov 2016]

[90] BITS, "Financial Services Roundtable Standards," Tech. Rep. [Online]. Available: http://www.bits.org/ [Last Accessed: 30 Nov 2016]

[91] CSCC, "Cloud Standards Customer Council," 2015. [Online]. Available: http://http://www.cloud-council.org/ [Last Accessed: 30 Nov 2016]

[92] ISACA, "Planning for and Implementing ISO 27001," *ISACA J.*, vol. 4, 2011. [Online]. Available: http://www.isaca.org/Journal/Past-Issues/2011/Volume-4/Documents/jpdf11v4-Planning-for-and.pdf [Last Accessed: 30 Nov 2016]

[93] CSO, "Cloud Standards," 2013. [Online]. Available: http://cloud-standards.org/ [Last Accessed: 30 Nov 2016]

[94] Crown, "Data Protection Act 1998," 1998. [Online]. Available: http://www.legislation.gov.uk/ukpga/1998/29/contents [Last Accessed: 30 Nov 2016]

[95] DMTF, "Distributed Management Task Force: Standards and Technology," 2014. [Online]. Available: http://www.dmtf.org/standards [Last Accessed: 30 Nov 2016]

[96] ETSI, "European Telecommunications Standards Institute," pp. 1–2, 2014. [Online]. Available: http://www.etsi.org/ [Last Accessed: 30 Nov 2016]

[97] FedRamp, "FedRamp," 2014. [Online]. Available: http://cloud.cio.gov/fedramp [Last Accessed: 30 Nov 2016]

[98] AICPA, "Generally Accepted Privacy Principles," 2014. [Online]. Available: https://www.aicpa.org/InterestAreas/InformationTechnology/Resources/Privacy/GenerallyAcceptedPrivacyPrinciples/Pages/default.aspx [Last Accessed: 30 Nov 2016]

[99] GICTF, "Global Inter-Cloud Technology Forum," 2012. [Online]. Available: http://www.gictf.jp/index_e.html [Last Accessed: 30 Nov 2016]

[100] P. Law, "Health Insurance Portability and Accountability Act of 1996," pp. 1936–2103, 1996. [Online]. Available: http://www.hhs.gov/ocr/privacy/ [Last Accessed: 30 Nov 2016]

[101] R. F. Mills, G. L. Peterson, and M. R. Grimaila, "Measuring Cyber Security and Information Assurance," Tech. Rep., apr 2009. [Online]. Available: http://www.scopus.com/inward/record.url?eid=2-s2.0-70350638023\&partnerID=tZOtx3y1 [Last Accessed: 30 Nov 2016]

[102] ISAE, "ISAE 3402," ISAE, Tech. Rep. [Online]. Available: http://www.ifac.org/sites/default/files/downloads/b014-2010-iaasb-handbook-isae-3402.pdf [Last Accessed: 30 Nov 2016]

[103] ISO, "ISO/IEC 27000:2009," 2014. [Online]. Available: www.iso.org [Last Accessed: 30 Nov 2016]

[104] ITIL, "Information Technology Infrastructure Library," Axelos, Tech. Rep., 2013. [Online]. Available: www.axelos.com/best-practice-solutions/itil [Last Accessed: 30 Nov 2016]

[105] R. Bank, "ITU - Telecommunication Standardization Sector," pp. 8 – 12, 2001. [Online]. Available: http://www.itu.int/en/ITU-T/publications/Pages/default.aspx [Last Accessed: 30 Nov 2016]

[106] Jericho Forum, "The Jericho Forum," Tech. Rep., 2011. [Online]. Available: http://www.opengroup.org/jericho/ [Last Accessed: 30 Nov 2016]

[107] NIST, "Security and Privacy Controls for Federal Information Systems and Organizations Security and Privacy Controls for Federal Information Systems and Organizations," Natioinal Institute of Standards and Technology, Gaithersburg, MD, Tech. Rep. February, 2014. [Online]. Available: http://nvlpubs.nist.gov/nistpubs/SpecialPublications/NIST.SP.800-53r4.pdf [Last Accessed: 30 Nov 2016]

[108] NERC, "NERC Reliability Standards," NERC, Tech. Rep. [Online]. Available: http://www.nerc.com/Pages/default.aspx [Last Accessed: 30 Nov 2016]

[109] OASIS, "Organization for the Advancement of Structured Information Standards," 2014. [Online]. Available: https://www.oasis-open.org/standards [Last Accessed: 30 Nov 2016]

[110] OCC, "OCC - Open Cloud Consortium," 2011. [Online]. Available: http://opencloudconsortium.org [Last Accessed: 30 Nov 2016]

[111] A. Sill, "Open Grid Forum," Tech. Rep., 2011. [Online]. Available: https://www.ogf.org/ogf/doku.php/standards/standards [Last Accessed: 30 Nov 2016]

[112] OMG, "Object Management Group," pp. 1–36, 2003. [Online]. Available: http://www.cloud-council.org/ [Last Accessed: 30 Nov 2016]

[113] PCI Security Standards Council LLC, "Data Security Standard: Requirements and Security Assessment Procedures," PCI Security Standards Council, Tech. Rep. November, 2013.

[114] SNIA, "Cloud data management interface," Tech. Rep., 2010.

[115] TOG, "The Open Group," Tech. Rep., 2014. [Online]. Available: http://www.opengroup.org/ [Last Accessed: 30 Nov 2016]

[116] TM Forum, "TM Forum Frameworx," The TM Forum, Tech. Rep., 2014. [Online]. Available: http://www.tmforum.org/Frameworx/1911/home.html [Last Accessed: 30 Nov 2016]

[117] M. Vouk, "Cloud Computing Issues, Research and Implementations," *ITI 2008 - 30th Int. Conf. Inf. Technol. Interfaces*, vol. 16, no. 4, pp. 235–246, 2008.

[118] L. Wang, J. Zhan, W. Shi, Y. Liang, and L. Yuan, "In Cloud, Do MTC or HTC Service Providers Benefit from the Economies of Scale?" *Proc. 2nd Work. Many-Task Comput. Grids Supercomput. - MTAGS '09*, pp. 1–10, 2009.

[119] N. Leavitt, "Is Cloud Computing Really Ready for Prime Time?" *Computer (Long. Beach. Calif).*, vol. 42, no. January, pp. 15–20, 2009.

[120] D. Bernstein, E. Ludvigson, K. Sankar, S. Diamond, and M. Morrow, "Blueprint for the intercloud - Protocols and formats for cloud computing interoperability," in *Proc. 2009 4th Int. Conf. Internet Web Appl. Serv. ICIW 2009*, 2009, pp. 328–336.

[121] S. Pearson and A. Benameur, "Privacy, Security and Trust Issues Arising from Cloud Computing," in *2010 IEEE Second Int. Conf. Cloud Comput. Technol. Sci.*, no. December. Ieee, nov 2010, pp. 693–702.

[122] C. Wang, Q. Wang, K. Ren, and W. Lou, "Privacy-Preserving Public Auditing for Data Storage Security in Cloud Computing," in *IEEE INFOCOM 2010*, vol. 62, no. 2, 2010, pp. 362–375.

[123] S. Srinivasamurthy, F. Wayne, and D. Q. Liu, "Security and Privacy in Cloud Computing : A Survey Security and Privacy in Cloud Computing :," in *2010 Sixth Int. Conf. Semant. Knowl. Grids*, vol. 2, 2013, pp. 126–149.

[124] M. Armbrust, A. Fox, R. Griffith, A. D. Joseph, R. Katz, A. Konwinski, G. Lee, D. Patterson, A. Rabkin, I. Stoica, and M. Zaharia, "A View of Cloud Computing," *Commun. ACM*, vol. 53, no. 4, pp. 50—58, 2010.

[125] S. Ramgovind, M. M. Eloff, and E. Smith, "The management of security in cloud computing," in *Proc. 2010 Inf. Secur. South Africa Conf. ISSA 2010*, 2010, pp. 1–7.

[126] B. Grobauer, T. Walloschek, and E. Stocker, "Understanding Cloud Computing Vulnerabilities," *IEEE Secur. Priv.*, vol. 9, no. 2, pp. 50–57, 2011.

[127] F. Doelitzscher, C. Fischer, D. Moskal, C. Reich, M. Knahl, and N. Clarke, "Validating Cloud Infrastructure Changes By Cloud Audits," in *Proc. - 2012 IEEE 8th World Congr. Serv. Serv. 2012*, 2012, pp. 377–384.

[128] M. L. Hale and R. Gamble, "SecAgreement: Advancing Security Risk Calculations in Cloud Services," in *Proc. - 2012 IEEE 8th World Congr. Serv. Serv. 2012*, 2012, pp. 133–140.

[129] V. Pappas, V. Kemerlis, A. Zavou, M. Polychronakis, and A. D. Keromytis, "CloudFence: Enabling Users to Audit the Use of their Cloud-Resident Data," 2012. [Online]. Available: http://hdl.handle.net/10022/AC:P:12821 [Last Accessed: 30 Nov 2016]

[130] T. Ruebsamen and C. Reich, "Supporting Cloud Accountability by Collecting Evidence Using Audit Agents," in *Proc. Int. Conf. Cloud Comput. Technol. Sci. CloudCom*, vol. 1, 2013, pp. 185–190.

[131] F. Doelitzscher, M. Knahl, C. Reich, and N. Clarke, "Anomaly Detection In IaaS Clouds," in *Proc. Int. Conf. Cloud Comput. Technol. Sci. CloudCom*, vol. 1, 2013, pp. 387–394.

[132] F. Doelitzscher, T. Ruebsamen, T. Karbe, M. Knahl, C. Reich, and N. Clarke, "Sun Behind Clouds - On Automatic Cloud Security Audits and a Cloud Audit Policy Language," ... *J. Adv. ...*, vol. 6, no. 1, pp. 1–16, 2013.

[133] S. Thorpe, T. Grandison, A. Campbell, J. Williams, K. Burrell, and I. Ray, "Towards a Forensic-based Service Oriented Architecture Framework for Auditing of Cloud Logs," in *Proc. - 2013 IEEE 9th World Congr. Serv. Serv. 2013*, 2013, pp. 75–83.

[134] C. Wang, S. S. M. Chow, Q. Wang, K. Ren, and W. Lou, "Privacy-Preserving Public Auditing for Secure Cloud Storage," *IEEE Trans. Comput.*, vol. 62, no. 2, pp. 362–375, 2013.

[135] J. M. Lopez, T. Ruebsamen, and D. Westhoff, "Privacy-Friendly Cloud Audits with Somewhat Homomorphic and Searchable Encryption," in *14th Int. Conf. Innov. Community Serv. "Technologies Everyone", I4CS 2014 - Conf. Proc.*, 2014, pp. 95–103.

[136] A. S. Sendi and M. Cheriet, "Cloud Computing: A Risk Assessment Model," *2014 IEEE Int. Conf. Cloud Eng.*, pp. 147–152, 2014.

[137] K. Xiong and X. Chen, "Ensuring Cloud Service Guarantees Via Service Level Agreement (SLA) -based Resource Allocation," in *Distrib. Comput. Syst. Work. (ICDCSW), 2015 IEEE 35th Int. Conf.* IEEE, 2015, pp. 35–41.

[138] OED, "Oxford English Dictionary," 1989. [Online]. Available: www.oed.com [Last Accessed: 30 Nov 2016]

[139] B. Guttman and E. A. Roback, "Computer Security," NIST, Tech.

Rep. 800, 2011. [Online]. Available: http://books.google.com/books?id=KTYxTfyjiOQC\&pgis=1 [Last Accessed: 30 Nov 2016]

[140] J. A. Chaula, "A Socio-Technical Analysis of Information Systems Security Assurance: A Case Study for Effective Assurance," Ph.D. dissertation, 2006. [Online]. Available: http://scholar.google.com/scholar?hl=en\&btnG=Search\&q=intitle:A+Socio-Technical+Analysis+of+Information+Systems+Security+Assurance+A+Case+Study+for+Effective+Assurance\#1 [Last Accessed: 30 Nov 2016]

[141] R. K. L. Ko, P. Jagadpramana, M. Mowbray, S. Pearson, M. Kirchberg, Q. Liang, and B. S. Lee, "TrustCloud: A framework for accountability and trust in cloud computing," *Proc. - 2011 IEEE World Congr. Serv. Serv. 2011*, pp. 584–588, 2011.

[142] L. F. B. Soares, D. a. B. Fernandes, J. V. Gomes, M. M. Freire, and P. R. M. Inácio, "Security, Privacy and Trust in Cloud Systems," in *Secur. Priv. Trust Cloud Syst.* Springer, 2014, ch. Data Accou, pp. 3–44.

[143] EU, "Unleashing the Potential of Cloud Computing in Europe," 2012. [Online]. Available: http://eur-lex.europa.eu/LexUriServ/LexUriServ.do?uri=SWD:2012:0271:FIN:EN:PDF [Last Accessed: 30 Nov 2016]

[144] R. J. Anderson, *Security Engineering: A Guide to Building Dependable Distributed Systems*, C. A. Long, Ed. Wiley, 2008, vol. 50, no. 5.

[145] Trustwave, "2012 Global Security Report," Tech. Rep., 2012.

[146] D. Catteddu and G. Hogben, Cloud Computing: Benefits, Risks and Recommendations for Information Security, Computing, Vol. 72, no. 1, pp. 20092013, 2009.

[147] Verizon, "Verizon 2015 Data Breach Investigation Report," Tech. Rep., 2015.

[148] OWASP, "OWASP Top Ten Vulnerabilities 2013," 2013. [Online]. Available: https://www.owasp.org/index.php/Category:OWASP_Top_Ten_Project [Last Accessed: 30 Nov 2016]

[149] OWASP, "OWASP SQL Injection Cheat Sheet," 2016. [Online]. Available: https://www.owasp.org/index.php/SQL_Injection_Prevention_Cheat_Sheet [Last Accessed: 30 Nov 2016]

[150] OWASP, "OWASP Injection Prevention Cheat Sheet," 2016. [Online]. Available: https://www.owasp.org/index.php/Injection_Prevention_Cheat_Sheet [Last Accessed: 30 Nov 2016]

[151] OWASP, "OWASP LDAP Injection Prevention Cheat Sheet," 2016. [Online]. Available: https://www.owasp.org/index.php/LDAP_Injection_Prevention_Cheat_Sheet [Last Accessed: 30 Nov 2016]

Collaborative and Secure Sharing of Healthcare Records Using Attribute-Based Authenticated Access

Mohamed Abomhara

Department of Information and Communication Technology
University of Agder
Grimsatd, Norway
Email: mohamed.abomhara@uia.no

Huihui Yang

NISlab and CCIS
Norwegian University of Science and Technology
Gjøvik, Norway
Email: huihui.yang@ccis.no

***Abstract*—The electronic health records are a widely utilized system in electronic health. It offers an efficient way to share patient health records among those in the medical industry, such as physicians and nurses. The barrier that currently overshadows the effective use of electronic health records is the lack of security control over information flow where sensitive health information is shared among a group of people within or across organizations. This study highlights authorization matters in cooperative engagements with complex scenarios in the collaborative healthcare domain. The focus is mainly on collaborative activities that are best accomplished by organized groups of healthcare practitioners within or among healthcare organizations with the objective of accomplishing a specific task (a case of patient treatment). In this study, we first investigate and gain a deep understanding of insider threat problems in the collaborative healthcare domain. Second, an authorization schema is proposed that is suitable for collaborative healthcare systems to address the issue of information sharing and information security. The proposed scheme is based on attribute-based authentication, which, is a way to authenticate users by attributes or their properties. Finally, we evaluate the security of the proposed scheme to ensure our proposed scheme is unforgeable, coalition resistant, and traceable as well as it providers confidentiality and anonymity.**

Keywords–Healthcare; Access control; Authorization; Collaboration environments; Attribute based authentication.

I. INTRODUCTION

The electronic health records (EHRs) [1], [2], [3] is a widely utilized application in healthcare sector. It offers an efficient way to share patient health records among those in the medical industry, such as physicians and nurses. Here, patient data is captured over time and electronically stored in databases to enable secure and reliable access. EHRs are highly beneficial to end users and health providers alike. Advances in EHRs systems will likely reduce the cost of care by facilitating easy collaborative support from multiple parties to fulfill the information requirements of daily clinical care [4], [3], [5]. Patient and healthcare providers can cooperate continuously with one another to attain health services at lower prices [6], [7]. In addition, enhancing the quality and delivery of health services by giving healthcare providers access to information they require to provide rapid patient care [1], [3]. Typically, rapid patient care requires the collaborative support of different parties including primary care physicians, specialists, medical laboratory technicians, radiology technicians and many other medical practitioners [1], [8], [9]. Moreover, collaboration among healthcare organizations is required for patients being transferred from one healthcare provider to another for specialized treatment [10], [11].

Although EHRs systems may improve the quality of healthcare, the digitalization of health records, the collection, evaluation and provisioning of patient data, and the transmission of health data over public networks (the Internet) pose new privacy and security threats [5], [12], [13] such as data breaches and healthcare data misuse, leaving patients and healthcare providers vulnerable to these threats. However, security control over information flow is a key aspect of such collaboration where sensitive information is shared among a group of people within or across organizations.

The patient health record is a sensitive collection of information that calls for appropriate security mechanisms to ensure confidentiality and protect integrity of data as well as filter out irrelevant information to reduce information overload [14], [15]. According to the Health Information Portability and Accountability Act (HIPAA) [16], [17], the keepers of health records are required to take the necessary steps needed to protect the confidentiality, integrity and privacy, among others, of the patient health records [18]. As a result, ensuring confidentiality and protect integrity of data in EHR systems with proper authorization control has always been viewed as a growing concern in the healthcare industry.

In this study, focus is mainly on authorization issues when EHRs are shared among healthcare providers in collaborative environments with the objective of accomplishing a specific task. The main concern with EHRs sharing during collaborative support is having an authorization mechanism with flexibility to allow access to a wide variety of authorized healthcare providers while preventing unauthorized access. Since healthcare services necessitate collaborative support from multiple parties and healthcare teamwork occurs within a dynamic group, dynamic authorization is required to allow team members to access classified EHRs.

A. Access Control Mechanism

Access control enables determining if the person or object, once identified, is permitted to access the resource. As shown in Figure 1, access control is a combination of authentication and authorization processes aimed at managing and securing access to system resources while also protecting resources' confidentiality and integrity, among others.

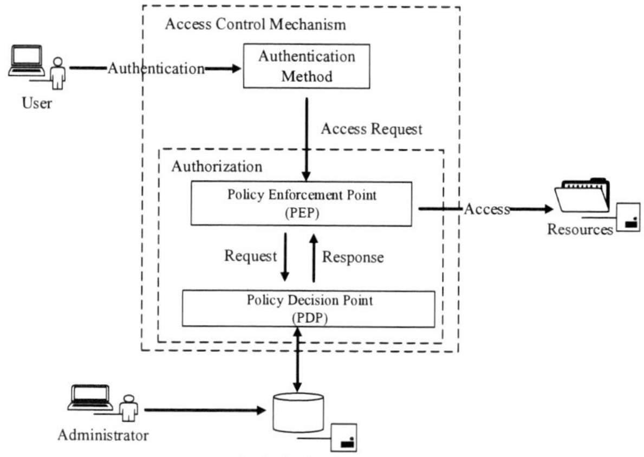

Figure 1. Authorization mechanism

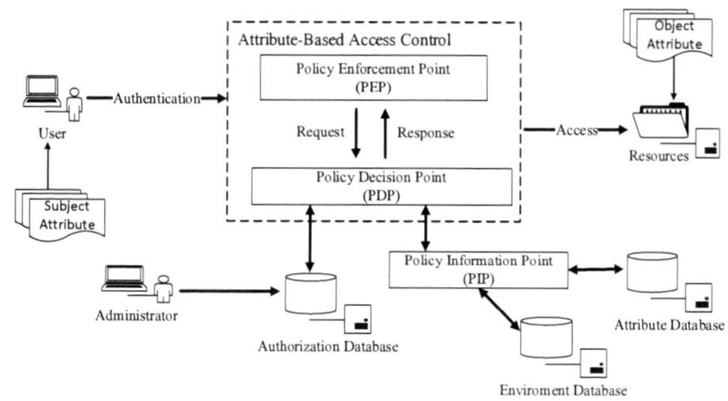

Figure 2. Access control mechanism for ABAC

Authentication entails validating the identity establishment between two communicating parties, showing what or who the user is? Authorization checks if the user can access the resources he/she has requested or not. When a user requests an access to resource on the system, first, the user has to authenticate himself/herself to the system, then the authorization process decides on the access request to be permitted or denied based on the authorization policies. The policy enforcement point (PEP) (Figure 1) intercepts a user's request to access a resource. The PEP forwards the request to the policy decision point (PDP) to obtain the access decision (permit or deny). PEP then acts on the received decision. The PDP is used to evaluate access requests against authorization policies and makes decisions according to the information contained in the request before issuing access decisions [19].

In the literature, two main access control models have been developed: role-based access control (RBAC) [20] and attribute-based access control (ABAC) [21]. RBAC allows organizations to enforce access policies based on user' roles (job functions) rather than users or groups [10]. RBAC promotes the management of related permissions instead of individual ones. The sets of permissions are compiled under a particular role. Consequently, all permissions are managed based on the role itself. Any changes in the permission within the role will impact the subjects who are assigned the corresponding role. In ABAC [21], permissions to access the objects are not directly given to the subject. It uses attributes of the subject (e.g., name, age or role in organization) and attributes of object (e.g., metadata properties) to provide authorizations as shown in Figure 2. The permissions in ABAC depend on a combination of a set of attributes and their relative values [22]. When a user wants to access an object, it sends an access request to the system with its attributes. PDP receives the request from PEP and combines the user's attributes, the object's attributes and environmental conditions (e.g., time and location), then check if they satisfy the authorization policies (Figure 2). If so, the subject's access request will be allowed and it will be enforced by the PEP [23]. During the process described above, PDP's decision making part can be considered as a part of authentication, while the authorization policy enforcing part by PEP be can considered as authorization.

To combine the strengths of both approaches without being hindered by their limitations, we proposed the work-based access control (WBAC) model [10], [24], [25], [26]. WBAC model is proposed by introducing the team role concept and modifying the user-role assignment model from RBAC and ABAC. The main goals of WBAC are flexibility, easy manageability, security, as well as suitability to support cooperative work of dynamic teams in healthcare environments [25]. In the proposed model, a secondary RBAC layer, with extra roles extracted from team work requirements, is added to RBAC and ABAC Layers to manage the complexity of cooperative engagements in the healthcare domain. Policies related to collaboration and team work are encapsulated within this coordinating layer to ensure that the attribute layer is not overly burdened. In this study, focus is mainly on authentication using attribute-based authentication (ABA) [27], [23], [28], [29]. We propose an authentication scheme using ABA to authenticate users by attributes or their properties.

ABA is part of ABAC and the authentication result of ABA is an important factor to decide whether a user's access request can be enforced or not. ABA is used as an approach to authenticate users by their attributes, so that users can get authenticated anonymously and their privacy can be protected [28]. Since there have already been lots of research on the cryptographic construction of attribute-based signatures (ABS) [30], [31] and attribute-based encryption (ABE) [32], it must be a good choice to utilize these results to construct ABA schemes for for collaborative healthcare systems.

B. *Study Contribution*

The main contribution of this work are as follows:

1) Investigate and gain a deep understanding of collaborative healthcare environment and insider security threats associated with it.
2) Design an attribute-based group authorization model that is suitable for collaborative healthcare systems to address the concern with information sharing and information access. The proposed model ensures that access rights are dynamically adapted to the actual needs of healthcare providers. Healthcare providers can access the resources associated with a work task, but only while the work task is active. Once the task is completed, access rights should be invalidated.
3) Evaluate and analysis the security of the proposed model.

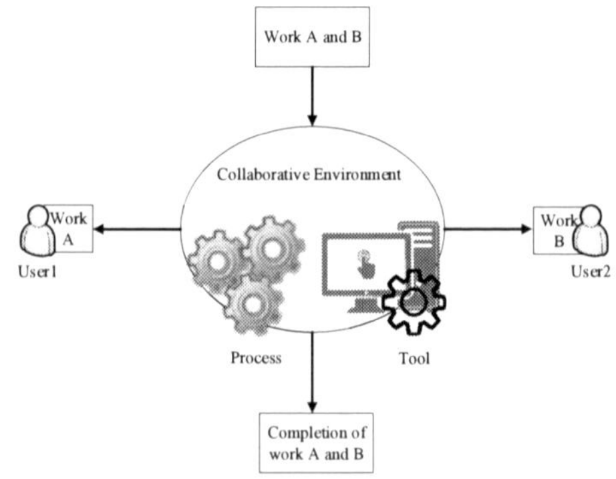

Figure 3. Collaborative environment and work sharing

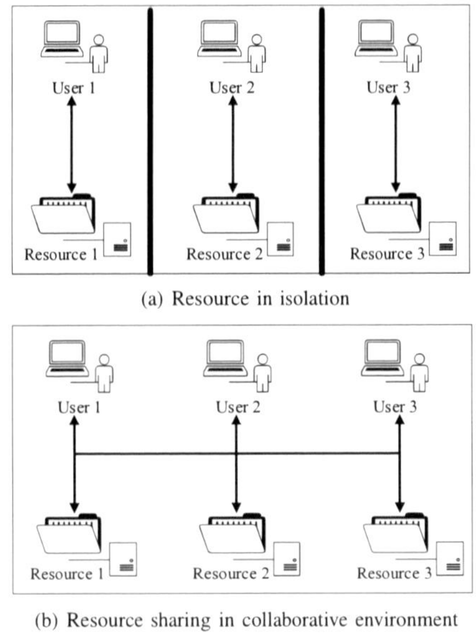

Figure 4. Resource in isolation and resource sharing

C. Structure of the Study

The remaining parts of this study are organized as follows. In Section II, a brief description of the collaboration environment and insider threats in healthcare is presented. An overview of the EHRs systems architecture and usage scenario are provided in Section III. Security assumption and requirements are given in Section IV. Section V presents the proposed scheme. Security analysis is provided in Section VI. Finally, conclusions and aspects for future work are given in Section VII.

II. Background Knowledge

In this section, relevant work related to the study is reviewed. An overview of healthcare collaboration environment is presented, followed by a brief summary of the insider threat problem in the healthcare domain is highlighted. The main aim of this section is to understand the security requirements and propose an attribute-based group authorization model that ensures sufficient security, which strikes a balance between collaboration and safeguarding sensitive patient information.

A. Collaborative Environment

A collaborative environment is a virtual infrastructure that allows individuals to cooperate with greater ease to perform their duties. It provides the necessary processes and tools to promote teamwork among individuals with similar goals [33]. For example, work can be divided amongst the team and performed separately (Figure 3). Afterwards, the outcome of each individual is assembled into a cohesive whole.

Collaboration at a medical facility is an integral part of the work process, whereby experts with different specializations and backgrounds must contribute together as a group in order to ensure treatment success. This necessity is further amplified with the increasing complexity of the medical domain. Healthcare services necessitate collaborative support from multiple parties to fulfill the information requirements of daily clinical care and provide rapid patient care. Collaborative support is required within healthcare organizations such as hospitals, where patient records must be moved among healthcare professionals, laboratories and wards, to name a few [10]. Collaboration among healthcare organizations is also essential for patients being transferred from one healthcare provider to another for specialized treatment. Such collaboration within or among healthcare organizations has been shown to provide cost-effective healthcare services [10]. EHRs improve how people work and enables more fluent cooperation between personnel at a medical facility. To cite an example, collaborative medical imaging [34] demonstrates the importance of sharing between medical practitioners. It utilizes cloud computing to provide a repository of medical imaging for physicians to discuss, diagnose and treat a particular disease effectively as a team.

One of the key aspects of a collaborative environment is the sharing of resources. To cooperate, each team member must be prepared to gather and share their findings with the rest of the team members. In Figure 4, initially each individual is accessing their own resource in isolation (Figure 4(a)). However, once collaboration is established, the process of sharing transpires (Figure 4(b)). Resource sharing is vital in collaboration. In order to analyze, decide and solve a certain problem collaboratively, team members must have similar knowledge of the defining situation. This way, cooperation can be achieved without the aggravating friction. However, balancing between collaboration and security of shared information is difficult. On the one hand, collaborative systems are targeted towards making all system elements (i.e., hardware, software, data, humans, processes) available to all who need it. On the other hand, security seeks to ensure the availability, confidentiality, and integrity of these elements while providing them only to those with proper authorization. Therefore, avoiding security and privacy violation are very important while sharing resources with others [10], [35].

B. Insider Threats

Although a collaborative environment can help enhance healthcare quality, it may also render the shared resources more vulnerable to insider threats [36], [37], [38]. This happens when someone within the collaborative team accesses shared resources for unethical reasons, for instance accessing a patient's private information for personal gain. In Figure 5,

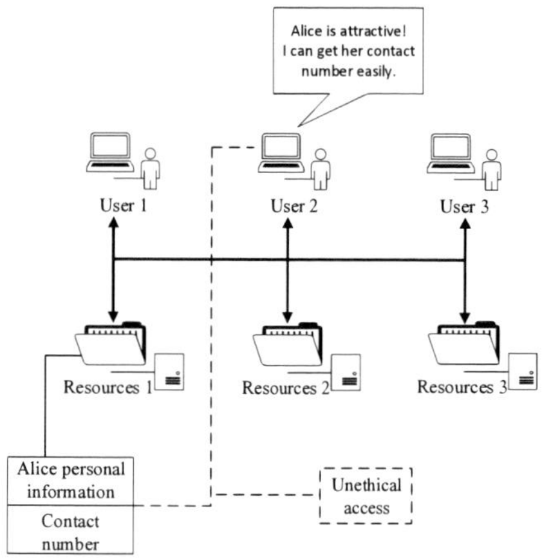

Figure 5. Insider Threat during collaboration

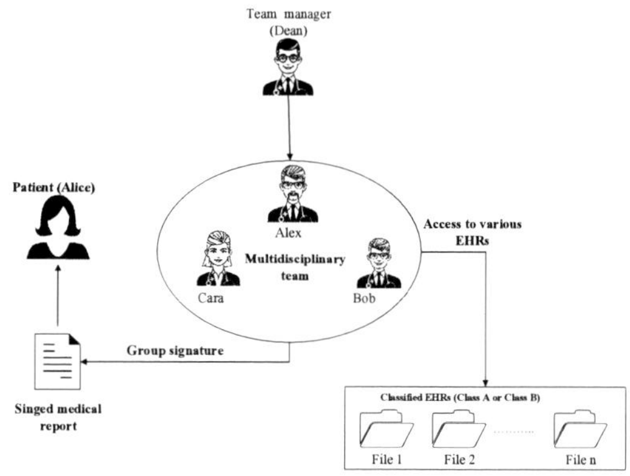

Figure 6. An example scenario of collaboration and sharing of healthcare data

it is assumed that three physicians are working collaboratively on a case at the hospital. They are discussing the possible treatment for a patient named *Alice*. To do so, they must analyze her medical file, but not her personal information. However, the 2nd physician is attracted to the patient. He exploits the collaborative environment to obtain her contact number without permission.

Insider threats pose a serious concern in the healthcare industry. In 2015, it was reported [39] that 35.5% of documented breaches involved medical counterparts. It is the second highest category in comparison. Breaches include stealing protected health information for later use to launch numerous fraud attacks on related medical parties. The danger with insider threats that occur due to the collaborative effort in healthcare is their low detectability. In other words, an incident could happen repeatedly over an extended period of time without being discovered by authorities. Actual attacks on victims can therefore be attempted at any time, which makes the threat harder to combat. Given the severity of insider threats within the healthcare sector, a number of countermeasures have been developed. These measures can be divided into two main categories: passive and active [36], [40], [41]. Passive measures are more geared toward detecting the perpetrators while active measures protect targeted assets from being compromised altogether.

To begin insider threat analysis, applying a framework can be quite useful [42], [43]. Insider threats are analyzed from four main aspects: the catalyst that can lead to an attack, the actor, the attack and the organization characteristic. These aspects can provide authorities with a method of formalizing the dominant patterns in an attack. Authorization and access control are the most popular approaches for developing an active form of mitigating insider threats [44], [10], [45], [46]. For instance, in order to secure a shared repository on epidemics, the group-based discretionary access control [47] is employed. It allows certain individuals to access the data and prohibits others based on their group membership.

III. Electronic Health Records

Healthcare providers deal with large number of sensitive healthcare records, which are shared and collaboratively used among different healthcare practitioners [8]. Collaboration occurs when a healthcare provider such as primary care doctor requests help from another healthcare provider to treat a case. To better understand collaborations in the healthcare domain, in this section, we present a usage scenarios provide examples of collaboration and healthcare data sharing, followed by the EHRs system architecture.

A. Usage Scenario: Multiple Healthcare Practitioners Cooperation Among Multiple Healthcare Organizations

As shown in Figure 6, a typical use case scenario adopted from [4] is presented. A patient named *Alice* is recently diagnosed with gastric cancer. Surgical removal of the stomach (gastrectomy) is the only curative treatment. For many patients, chemotherapy and radiation therapy are given after surgery to improve the chances of curing. *Alice* entered a cancer-treatment center at her chosen hospital (e.g., hospital A in Figure 8). *Alice* has a general practitioner (*Dean*) who she regularly visits. Upon entering the hospital, *Alice* also sees an attending doctor (*Bob*) from the hospital. *Alice*'s health condition has caused some complications, so her attending doctor would like to seek expert opinions and consultation regarding *Alice*'s treatment from different hospitals (e.g., hospital B in Figure 8), including *Alice*'s specific general practitioner who is fully informed about *Alice*'s medical history. Note that the invited practitioners are specialized in different areas, where some are specialists and others are general practitioners. In such group consultation, every participant needs to obtain the medical records they request based on the health insurance portability and accountability act (HIPAA) [16] minimal disclosure principle.

In such group consultation, also so-called multidisciplinary team consultation [48], [49], [50], it is noticeable that, several healthcare professionals are involved in various roles to provide patient care. That includes primary care doctors, general physicians and specialists. Every participant needs to obtain the medical records they request based on HIPAA [16] minimal disclosure principle [4], [8]. In this case, the act of managing the collaborative work must be clearly defined. By default, only the main practitioner should be aware of the patient's personal information. The other medical practitioners with supporting roles are given information based on their contributing roles (need-to-know principle) [51]. For instance, if the supporting party is included solely for consultation purposes concerning the disease, only information essential for diagnosis is provided. It is not necessary to allow perusal of personal information related to the patient.

Hospital personnel roles are often simplistically split into medical practitioners, nurses and administrators [52], [53]. However, in [10], we further categorized personnel roles into a total of nine roles per group, which are classified into main, action, thought and management roles, as shown in Figure 7.

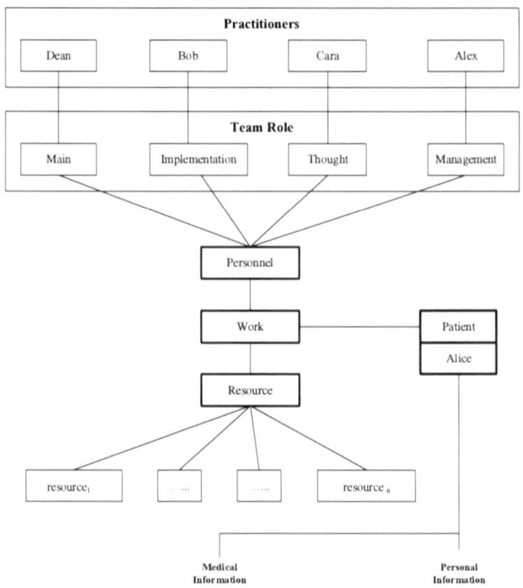

Figure 7. EHRs usage scenario

The workflow of every healthcare practitioner is as follows:

1) The general practitioner (*Dean*) could not solve *Alice*'s case. He invites multidisciplinary team including *Bob*, *Cara* and *Alex* to help. In this team consideration, *Dean* is the core physician of the collaborative work. He serves as the group manager. He is responsible for initiating the work (treatment of *Alice*'s case) and choosing the practitioners (group of doctors) who may be required to attend *Alice*'s consultation and treatment. This implies that his possesses the main team role (Figure 7). In other words, he owns the collaborative work initiated. Therefore, full access is given to *Dean* with regard to the information related to the patient. He can access the personal information of the patient as well as the medical records. Moreover, the general practitioner must revoke the team upon completion of the patient's diagnosis consultation.
2) *Bob* helps *Dean* with the operational part of the case. Operation refers to a series of responsibilities that entail interaction with the patient. *Bob* needs to see *Alice* on a face-to-face basis to perform various tasks that are related to her recovery. In this respect, there is a need for *Bob* to know personal and medical information about *Alice* to perform his duty effectively. It must be reminded however, that access to a collaborative resource can be tailored more specifically by harnessing the stipulated team roles. *Bob* is involved in the action part of the collaboration. Therefore, his team provider falls under the category of action.
3) *Cara* has more of a thought role. She is responsible for helping *Dean* solve the medical case. There is no need for *Cara* to meet *Alice* personally on a day-to-day basis. In fact, *Cara* is only required to analyze the medical situation and suggest a possible solution. *Cara*'s strategic role within the team implies a rather clear indication of the access that she needs. Since *Cara* is predominantly preoccupied with diagnosing the disease, there is no urgent need for her to know the patient's personal information. As such, she is only given access to the patient's medical information as per her strategic team role.
4) With the increasing number of physicians working on *Alice*'s case, their interaction can become more complex. For instance, if there exists a competition between conflicting diagnoses given by *Bob* and *Cara*, which would gain priority? This is where *Alex* comes in. He contributes to the team by coordinating the interaction of the other members by taking on the team management role. To work effectively, *Alex* does not really need to know the patient's personal information. However, he must be aware of the patient's medical information to enable coordination.

In addition, *Alice* may have some historical health information (e.g., mental illness or sexual issues, etc.), to which the group (or some of the team) of specialists and practitioners do not have to have access. In WBAC, we assume that each resource (EHR files) in the system are divided into two types, mainly *private* and *protected* during the collaborative work. The collaborative resources required for work are enumerated in Table form as proposed by Abomhara and Køien in [10]. Each resource is tied to the set of collaborative roles or team roles that can access it. In effect, the selected roles will determine the extent of collaborative access.

B. EHRs Systems Architecture

EHRs system is considered in this study. Multiple owners (referring to patients who have full control of their EHRs) and healthcare providers, such as physicians and nurses, among others, who require access to these EHRs to perform a task. In Figure 8, the architecture of the reference system is illustrated. The reference system includes the following main domains:

1) **EHRs**: The medical records are collected, stored and provisioned by the electronic health records system to achieve the features of low cost operation, collaborative support and ubiquitous services. The EHRs can reside in a centralized or distributed systems depending on the deployment needs [54]. Authorized healthcare providers, including hospitals and healthcare practitioners can access EHRs through different services such as web portals and health apps [55]. In WBAC, we assumed that all the medical records covered by WBAC are classified into two sets of objects (*private* and *protected*) listed in the permissions that are assigned to roles and team roles, which will be accessed by a users.

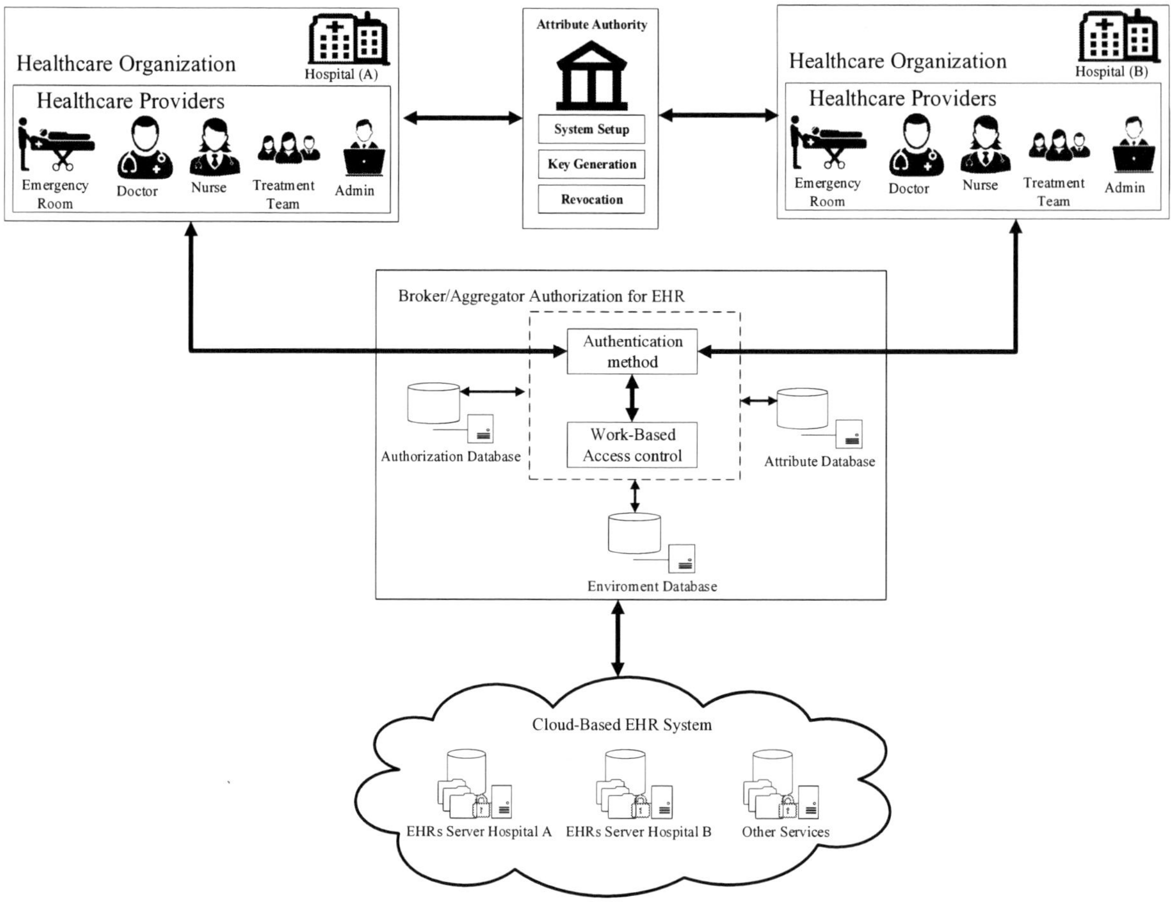

Figure 8. Reference system architecture overview

a) *Private* object contains medical records related to personal information such as names and addresses as well as resources that are not related to the current patient case such as family medical history and sexual health, among others.
b) *Protected* object contains resources related to current patient case. For example, consider *Alice*'s case (Section III-A), we could say that protected objects contains resources related to *Alice*'s current case such as past surgical history, data related to abdominal CT scan (computed tomography scan) and gastroscopy data, to name a few.

The access to medical records is controlled via the team roles and the requirements of attributes. For each medical records, the access policy is represented by a combination of attributes. When a user (healthcare providers who have already joined a team and assigned to team role) requires to access (read, write, etc) the file on EHRs, it should show an evidence that it satisfies the required attributes. Only if the evidence is valid, the user's access can be granted. This process will be implemented by an ABA scheme presented in Section V-A.

2) **Trusted authority**: A fully trusted authority such as the Ministry of Health is responsible for key generation, distribution and management of users' keys. The main responsibilities of the trusted authority include the following:
   a) Generate the main system public and private keys.
   b) Generate user keys for each user.
   c) Generate public and attribute keys for each attribute in the system.
   d) Generate attribute keys for attributes possessed by each user.

As for implementation, it is possible to have different authorities to perform these responsibilities separately, such that the compromise of one authority will not lead to the compromise of the whole system. More specifically, healthcare delivery organizations (e.g., hospitals) perform as a registration center with a certain qualification certified by the trusted authority. Healthcare delivery organizations are responsible for checking their healthcare practitioners' professional expertise and send their attributes to the trusted authority to issue the corresponding attribute-based credentials. As for implementation, it is possible to have different authorities to perform these responsibilities separately, such that the compromise of one authority will not lead to the compromise of the whole system. More specifically, healthcare delivery organizations (e.g., hospitals) perform as a registration center with a certain qualification certified by the trusted authority.

3) **Healthcare providers**: Healthcare providers from various domains, such as doctors, nurses, radiology technicians and pharmacists, among others, require access to patients' records to perform a task. Once a new healthcare practitioner joins a system, the healthcare delivery organization must send healthcare practitioner' attributes to the trusted authority to obtain attributes based credentials. Healthcare practitioners apply their authentication credentials obtained from the trusted authority to access classified EHRs through authorization mechanisms in the EHR aggregator. In case of group collaboration, multiple EHRs have to be shared with various healthcare providers and practitioners. A group manager is responsible for registering healthcare practitioners to form a group. The hospital's (registration center) responsibility is to verify the authenticity of each healthcare practitioners in the group based on the professional expertise and required access, and send it to the trusted authority to issue the corresponding group credentials for the group.

IV. Security Assumption and Requirements

In this study, we consider the healthcare providers are honest and trusted but curious. That means, they will try to find as much as confidential and private information just for curiosity. Therefore, healthcare providers will try to access files on EHRs, which are beyond their privileges (i.g, healthcare providers intend to access the medical records that needed to fulfill their tasks but sometimes they intentionally or unintentionally access patients' medical records that are irrelevant to their task [56]). For example, as shown in Figure 5, a healthcare provider may want to obtain information about the patient for his/her own interest. To do so, healthcare provider may impersonate other healthcare provider. Also, healthcare provider may collude with other healthcare providers to gain an access to information. Thus to achieve a secure sharing of EHRs, a core requirements of a well-designed ABA system were presented by Yang [28], [29]. According to our assumption and usage scenarioa, the system should fulfill the following requirements:

- **Confidentiality**: Unauthorized users who do not possess enough attributes satisfying the authorization policy should be prevented from reading EHR documents.
- **Minimum attributes leakage**: To be authenticated, a healthcare provider only need to provide required attributes rather than the whole package of attributes it possesses.
- **Signature**: The final medical report of *Alice*'s treatment should be signed by appropriate practitioners using digital signatures. *Alice* should be able to verify the authenticity of the consultation results through the practitioner's digital signature. Note that the practitioner's digital signature can be opened (reveal the practitioner's identity) depending on the requirements. In some cases, practitioners do not want to reveal their identities when participating in group treatment.
- **Unforgeability**: An adversary who does not belong to the group should not be able to impersonate a group member and forge a valid signature to get authenticated.
- **Coalition resistance**: Group members should not be able to pile up their attributes to forge a signature to help a member to get authenticated.

V. Proposed Scheme

In this section, the system setup and security analysis are presented.

A. System setup

System setup, including key generation, distribution and revocation are explained in this subsection. As mentioned before (Section III-B), the trusted authority is responsible for users' key and attribute key generation. For each user in the system, the trusted authority will generate a unique user key that represents the user's identity information and will be used to trace users' identities if necessary. The proposed scheme is based on bilinear mapping [57], [58].

Definition 1: **[Bilinear Mapping]** [59] Let G_1, G_2 and G_3 be cyclic groups of prime order p, with $g_1 \in G_1$ and $g_2 \in G_2$ as the generators. e is an efficient bilinear map if the following two properties hold.

1) Bi-linearity: equation $e(g_1^a, g_2^b) = e(g_1, g_2)^{ab}$ holds for any $a, b \in \mathbb{Z}_p^*$.
2) Non-degenerate: $e(g_1, g_2) \neq 1_{G_3}$, where 1_{G_3} is the unit of G_3.

Firstly, the proposed ABA scheme needs to set up the system, which is considered as a preparation for the phase of signature generation, verification and opening. During system setup, the system main parameters, such as main public and private key sets will be generated by the trusted authority. Based on the main private and public key sets, the trust authority will generate system attribute keys and users' keys. More importantly, the trusted authority will authorize *Dean* the power to generate attribute keys for group members. This is how *Dean* gains the control over the group.

Assume k_0 is the system security parameter. G_1, G_2 are two multiplicative groups of prime order p with $g_1 \in G_1$ and $g_2 \in G_2$ as their generators. Let $e : G_1 \times G_1 \rightarrow G_2$ be a bilinear mapping. Select $h \in G_1$, $\xi_1, \xi_2 \in \mathbb{Z}_p^*$, where $\mathbb{Z}_p^* = \{a \in \mathbb{Z}_p | gcd(a, p) = 1\}$ is a multiplicative group modulo a big prime number p. Set $u, v \in G_1$ such that $u^{\xi_1} = v^{\xi_2} = h$. Select $x_0, \beta_0 \in \mathbb{Z}_p^*$ as the top secret and compute $w_0 = g_1^{x_0}$, $f_0 = g_1^{1/\beta_0}$ and $h_0 = g_1^{\beta_0}$. The public key set of the trusted authority is denoted by $MPK =< G_1, G_2, g_1, g_2, h, u, v, f_0, h_0, w_0 >$ and the private key set is $MSK =< x_0, \beta_0, \xi_1, \xi_2 >$, where the pair $< \xi_1, \xi_2 >$ is handed to the opener as its tracing key tk.

Then the system setup proceeds as follows.

1) ***Dean*** **authorization**: *Dean* described in our usage scenario can be considered as an attribute domain authority in the scheme proposed in [60]. To authorize *Dean*, first, the trusted authority selects a secret $x_d \in \mathbb{Z}_p^*$ and computes $A_d = g_1^{(x_0+x_d)/\beta_0}$ and $w_d = g^{x_d}$. The pair $DSK =< A_d, x_d >$ is the *Dean*'s private key and A_d should be registered in the opener's database for identity tracing. $DPK =< w_d >$ as the *Dean*'s public key.
2) **User key generation**: All users in the system should register themselves and obtain their users' key from the trusted authority. Assume there are N users in the EHRs usage case. To generate the secret key of user U_i $(1 \leq i \leq N)$, the trusted authority randomly selects $x_i \in \mathbb{Z}_p^*$ and computes $A_i = g_1^{(x_0+x_i)/\beta_0}$. $bsk_i =< A_i, x_i >$ is U_i's secret key base and A_i should be handed to the opener.
3) **Attribute key generation**: Assume the attribute set owned by all members in the EHRs usage case is denoted by $\Psi = \{att_1, \cdots, att_{N_a}\}$ $(N_a = |\Psi|)$. To generate a pair of private and public attribute key for an attribute $att_j \in \Psi$ $(1 \leq j \leq N_a)$, the trusted randomly selects $t_j \in \mathbb{Z}_p^*$ as its private attribute key and computes $apk_j = {g_1}^{t_j}$ as its public attribute key.
4) **Attribute key authorization**: The trusted authority authorize attribute keys to *Dean*. For attribute att_j, the trusted authority selects $r_j \in \mathbb{Z}_p^*$ and computes $T_{d,j} = g_1^{(x_0+x_d)/\beta_0} H(att_j)^{t_j+r_j}$ and $apk_{dj} = g_1^{r_j}$ as *Dean*'s private and public attribute keys for attribute att_j respectively.
5) **User attribute key generation**: To be active in the EHRs usage case described above, each member should gain their attribute keys from *Dean*. Assume the attribute set possessed by user U_i is denoted by $\Psi_i = \{att_{i1}, \cdots, att_{iN_i}\}$ and attribute att_{ik} $(1 \leq k \leq N_i)$ corresponds to $att_j \in \Psi$. For simplicity, we will use att_j to represent att_{ik} instead. To generate a private attribute key of att_j $(1 \leq k \leq N_i)$ for U_i, *Dean* interacts with U_i and computes $T_{i,k} = f_0^{x_i} T_{d,j} = g_1^{(x_0+x_d+x_i)/\beta_0} H(att_j)^{t_j+r_j}$ as U_i's private attribute key for attribute att_j.

All these attribute keys are only active during the period of a specific workload. When this workload is finished, all attribute keys of users in this group should be revoked. This requirement can be realized by combining these attribute keys with a timing token. Thus, these attribute keys are only valid during this fixed time period.

B. Signature Generation, Verification and Opening

After the system setup, all entities in the group of the EHRs usage case have obtained their users' keys and attribute keys for authentication. As described before, each medical file is bound with access policies represented by a combination of attributes. More specially, this combination of attributes is represented by an attribute tree [28]. An attribute tree is a tree structure that represents the logical relations among required attributes, based on, which a user generates a signature as a proof of possessing the required attributes.

The user can only be authenticated when the signature is valid. However, it is also possible that the user's access request is reject even though the signature is valid because of other factors, such as system time, locations and so on.

Assume that U_i is a user to the authenticated, V is the verifier and f is the file that U_i wants to access. The verifier here can be the access system or another entity that is responsible for users' authentication. It depends on the specific enforcement of the system. The authentication phase proceeds as follows:

1) (U_i) **access request sending**: U_i sends a request to the verifier V wants to access file f.
2) (V) **attribute requirement embedding**: In this step, the verifier embeds a secret key K_s and the attribute requirements in an attribute tree and sends related parameters to U_i. The details are as follows:
Once V receives the access request, it retrieves the access policy related to the requested access and file f. Next, V will generate an attribute tree Γ with root value $\alpha_r \in \mathbb{Z}_p^*$ for root r to represent the access requirement as described in [28]. The same as in [60], we use $q_{Node}()$ to denote the polynomial bound to an interior node $Node$. For a leaf node y whose parent is interior node $Node$, $q_y(0)$ is computed by $q_{Node}(0)$. Thereafter, the verifier computes
$$K_s = (e(f_0, w_0)e(g_1, w_d))^{\alpha_r} = e(g_1, g_1)^{(x_0+x_d)\alpha_r/\beta_0}.$$
Let $L(\Gamma)$ be the leaf node set of the attribute tree Γ. V computes $\forall y \in L(\Gamma), C_y = g_1^{q_y(0)}$ and $C'_y = H(y)^{q_y(0)}$ and sends $\{\Gamma, g_1^{\alpha_r}, \forall y \in Leaf(\Gamma) : C_y, C'_y\}$ to U_i.
3) (U_i) **signature generation**: In this step, U_i recovers the embedded secret key K_s as K_v first if it owns all the required attributes. Next it generates a signature as a proof that it possesses the required attributes and to provide traceability, which means that an opener can trace the identity information of U_i given this signature.
The details are as follows. Assume U_i possesses all the required attributes represented by attribute tree Γ and att_{ik} owned by U_i is the attribute related to leaf node y in attribute tree Γ. After U_i receives the message from V, it computes
$$DecryptNode(T_{i,k}, C_y, C'_y, y) = \frac{e(T_{i,k}, C_y)}{e(apk_j apk_{dj}, C'_y)} = e(g_1, g_1)^{(x_0+x_d+u_k)q_y(0)/\beta_0}.$$
If x is an interior node, $DecryptNode(T_{k,j}, C_y, C'_y, y)$ proceeds as follows: for all x' children z, $DecryptNode(T_{k,j}, C_y, C'_y, y)$ is called and the output is stored as F_z. Assume S_x is the subset of all x's children z and $ind(x)$ is the index of node x. We define
$$\Delta_{S_x, ind(z)} = \prod_{l \in \{S_x - ind(x)\}} \frac{l}{ind(z) - l}.$$
Then we have

$$F_x = \prod_{z \in S_x} F_z^{q_z(0)\Delta_{S_x, ind(z)}}$$
$$= \prod_{z \in S_x} (e(g_1, g_1)^{(x_0+x_d+x_i)q_z(0)/\beta_0})^{\Delta_{S_x, ind(z)}}$$
$$= \prod_{z \in S_x} (e(g_1, g_1)^{(x_0+x_d+x_i)q_{par(z)}(ind(z))/\beta_0})^{\Delta_{S_x, ind(z)}}$$
$$= e(g_1, g_1)^{(x_0+x_d+x_i)q_x(0)/\beta_0}.$$

U_i calls $DecryptNode(T_{i,k}, C_y, C'_y, y)$ for the root and gets the result

$$F_r = e(g_1, g_1)^{(x_0+x_d+x_i)\alpha_r/\beta_0}.$$

Next U_i computes

$$K_s = F_r / e(g_1^{x_i}, g_1^{\alpha_r}) = e(g_1, g_1)^{(x_0+x_d)\alpha_r/\beta_0} = K_v.$$

Until here, U_i has successfully recovered the embedded secret key K_s as K_v. In the following, U_i generate a signature to provide traceability.
The signer randomly selects ζ, α, β, r_ζ, r_α, r_β, r_x, r_{δ_1}, $r_{\delta_2} \in \mathbb{Z}_p^*$ and calculates

$$C_1 = u^\zeta, C_2 = v^\beta, C_3 = A_i h^{\zeta+\beta},$$
$$\delta_1 = x_i\zeta, \delta_2 = x_i\beta,$$
$$R_1 = u^{r_\zeta}, R_2 = v^{r_\beta}, R_4 = C_1^{r_x} u^{-r_{\delta_1}}, R_5 = C_2^{r_x} v^{-r_{\delta_2}},$$
$$R_3 = e(C_3, g_1)^{r_x} e(h, w_d)^{-r_\zeta - r_\beta} e(h, g_1)^{-r_{\delta_1} - r_{\delta_2}},$$
$$c = H_{K_s}(M, C_1, C_2, C_3, R_1, R_2, R_3, R_4, R_5) \in \mathbb{Z}_p^*$$
$$s_\zeta = r_\zeta + c\zeta, s_\beta = r_\beta + c\beta, s_\alpha = r_\alpha + c\alpha,$$
$$s_x = r_x + cx_i, s_{\delta_1} = r_{\delta_1} + c\delta_1, s_{\delta_2} = r_{\delta_2} + c\delta_2.$$

Finally, the signer sends the signature $\sigma =< M, C_1, C_2, C_3, c, s_\zeta, s_\beta, s_\alpha, s_{\delta_1}, s_{\delta_2} >$ to the verifier.

4) (V) **signature verification**: V computes

$$R'_1 = u^{s_\zeta} C_1^{-c}, R'_2 = v^{s_\beta} C_2^{-c}, R'_4 = u^{-s_{\delta_1}} C_1^{s_x}, R'_5 = v^{-s_{\delta_2}} C_2^{s_x},$$
$$R'_3 = e(C_3, g_1)^{s_x} e(h, w_d)^{-s_\zeta - s_\beta} e(h, g_1)^{-s_{\delta_1} - s_{\delta_2}} \left(\frac{e(C_3, w_d)}{e(g_1, g_1)}\right)^c$$

and $c' = H_{K_v}(M, C_1, C_2, C_3, R'_1, R'_2, R'_3, R'_4, R'_5)$. If c' equals to c that V has received from U_i, V believes that U_i owns the required attributes and the authentication succeeds.

5) **(The opener) signature opening**: The opener computes $A_i = C_3/(C_1^{\varepsilon_1} C_2^{\varepsilon_2})$, where A_i was registered in the opener's database as U_i's identity information during system setup.

C. Group Operations

As described in Section III-A, *Bob* needs to read patients' personal and medical information, but *Cara* only needs to have access to patients' medical records. To achieve this goal, we first express these access policies based on attributes. When group members want to access the documents, they generate a signature based on the required attributes defined in the access policies. If their signatures are valid, we believe that they satisfy the access policies and will be granted with the required access.

In addition, *Dean* needs to revoke this temporary group and the privileges granted to group members after the workload is finished. There are two possible solutions. The first solution is to combine all keys generated for this temporary workload with a time token, but it requires a precise estimation about the time period how long this task will last. If the time period is too short, all keys will be revoked before the task is finished and the system has to be set up again. To the contrary, if the time period is too long, group members will still be able to access to patients' documents after the task is completed, which may cause security and privacy issues. The second solution is to add the temporary attribute public keys in a revocation list. Before signature verification, the verifier firsts check whether the related attribute public keys are valid. If not, the verifier will abort the signature verification, and group members will not gain additional access privileges when the temporary task finishes.

VI. Security Analysis

In this section, we analyze the security requirements of the proposed model based on the security analysis described in Section IV, including confidentiality, minimum attributes leakage, signature, unforgeability and coalition resistance.

Confidentiality: When a user U_i wants to read EHR documents, he should successfully be authenticated by the ABA scheme proposed in Subsection V-B. From [60], we know that our ABA scheme satisfies the security requirement traceability, which means that a user without the required attributes cannot generate a valid signature to successfully authenticated. As a result, as long as user U_i is required to pass the authentication described in Subsection V-B before he accesses EHR documents, the confidentiality can be satisfied.

Unforgeability: requires that a user outside the group (an outsider) cannot generate a valid signature in the ABA scheme proposed in Subsection V-B. We assume that an outsider does not possess any valid required attributes. From the analysis of confidentiality, we know that a valid user who does not possess all required attribute cannot generate a valid signature, so an outsider without any valid required attributes cannot generated a valid signature.

Coalition resistance: This security requirement is weaker than traceability, because it is one way to try to forge a valid signature that the opener cannot trace its identity. Assume that the ABA scheme proposed in Subsection V-B is not coalition resistant, it means that a couple of users can pile up their attributes and generate a valid signature. Since these attributes do not belong to the same user in the group and it is valid, the identity retrieved from the signature does not belong to any user in the group. It contracts with the security requirement traceability. Therefore, the ABA scheme proposed in Subsection V-B is coalition resistant.

Minimum attributes leakage: This security requirement is straight forward. To generate a valid signature, a user only needs to use the required attributes other than the whole package of attributes he possesses.

Signature: This property can be satisfied by requiring *Alice*'s practitioner to generate a signature using its attribute keys based on the ABA scheme proposed in Subsection V-B, where as the verifier, *Alice* can define the required attributes and therefore can check the validity of the signature. When necessary, the signature can also be identified by the opener in the system.

VII. Discussion and Conclusions

A. Discussion

The central trusted authority within the healthcare system sustains an EHRs data source of aggregated to ensure availability and to provide an easy access to the health professionals. However, accessing patient's health records raises patient concerns about the security of their data. This is because patients generally want to make sure that their sensitive information is accessed by authorized and trusted healthcare providers. As such, a health supplier needs to be sure that actual legal entity is the only party to grant access to the EHRs. Furthermore, patient permission must also be considered to create a EHRs accessibility role.

The goal of this study is to have attribute verification within a group of healthcare providers. The main purpose of our scheme is authenticating users by attributes or their properties to achieve security requirement (Section IV) including confidentiality, anonymity, traceability, unforgeability, coalition resistance and signature..

Confidentiality protects system resources and information from unauthorized disclosure. In our study, healthcare providers who join a team of treatment (e.g., *Cara* and *Alex*) should register themselves to obtain their authorization key from the trusted authority (Section V-A). Therefore, all the healthcare providers who join *Alice*'s treatment will be identified by the team manager (*Dean*) and authorized to access *Alice*'s EHRs once they obtain their authorization keys. An important concerns about user' identity are anonymity and traceability of healthcare provider's identity. In other words, the verifier cannot get any identifying information related to the user during the authentication process [23]. On the one hand, anonymity is important to keep a patient' privacy. For example, in our scenario (Figure 6), assume that *Alice* dose not need anyone to know that she was treated by a gastroenterologist (*Cara*). Therefore, keeping the identity of *Cara* anonymized is a very impotent aspect. On the other hand, tracing of healthcare providers' identities is of great importance. When disputes happen and the identify of the healthcare provider are treated as legitimate evidence, tracing of the identity is useful. The main purpose of our scheme is to achieve anonymity and allow tractability. Since our scheme is based on group signatures, it is traceable. In our ABA scheme the system tracing the signers' identity is done by the attribute authority (opener). The identity revealing can only be performed when a disputes happens and a legal authority should authorize it. There are two requirements for identity reveal [60], [23]. First, given a valid signature, the opener should be able to trace the signature and reveal the identity information. Second, the revealed identity should belong to real signer rather than a forged one.

Digital signature forgery is another concern when designing of ABA schemes. Forgeability is the ability to create a signature by illegitimate signer such as an adversary. Our proposed scheme ensures that, a user (healthcare provider or adversary) who does not possess all required attribute cannot generate a valid signature. It is said the scheme is strongly unforgeable if the signature is existentially unforgeable under chosen-message attack [61], [62] and, given signatures on some messages, the adversary cannot produce a new signature. In this study, we have not analyze our scheme against chosen-message attack. But we assume that it is unforgeable since the adversary need a number of required attributes to generate a valid signature.

Coalition attack is one of the most difficult tasks in developing a group signature, It occurs when a malicious collisions of group members that produce untraceable signatures [63]. Considering the coalition resistance, in our scheme the user can only generate the signature if he or she has all the required attributes. As we showed in security analysis (Section VI) it is not possible for different users to collude and generate a valid signature together if they as a whole have all the required attributes.

The security requirement "signature" is very important because it provides three properties. First of all, the signature should be able to be verified by *Alice* that it is generated by a legal practitioner according to *Alice*'s treatment requirements. This property can prevent the case that the signature was forged by an illegal practitioner or an adversary. Secondly, the practitioner can keep itself anonymous if he wants, and this property is provided by the security requirement anonymity of the ABA scheme proposed in Section V. Finally, the practitioner cannot deny that the signature was actually generated by him since there is an opener who can "open" the signature and retrieves the practitioner's identity, and this property is provided by the security requirement traceability of the proposed ABA scheme.

B. Conclusions and Further Work

In this work, an authorization scheme was proposed for collaborative healthcare system to address the problem of information sharing and information security. The proposed scheme provides an efficient solution to security challenges related to authorization. The security analysis has showed that our proposed scheme is unforgeable, coalition resistant, and traceable as well as it providers confidentiality and anonymity.

In the future, the plan is to develop and prototype the functionality to be implemented as well as evaluate the validity of the scheme based on its efficiency and practicality. Efficiency is the scheme's performance in terms of resource consumption, e.g., time and computational capability. Practicality denotes the possible difficulties in managing the model during actual implementation. The motivation behind studying the issue of efficiency and practicality is to simplify decentralized administrative tasks, and enhance the practicability of authorization in dynamic collaboration environments. It is very important to design a system to not only ensure shared information confidentiality but also to avoid administration and management complexity.

Furthermore, in recent years, cloud computing and information technology adaptation to healthcare has become increasingly important in many countries [7], [64]. EU countries are seeking new ways to modernize and transform their healthcare systems using information and communications technology in order to provide EU citizens (patients) with safe and high quality treatment in any European Union country [65], [66] (EU directive 2011/24/EU framework on cross-border health care collaboration in the EU [67], [68], [69]). Access to cross-border healthcare in the EU has undergone many developments in both academia and industries in order to meet EU healthcare domain needs. The eHealth Action Plan 2012-2020 [70] and the EU-funded project UNIversal solutions in TELemedicine deployment for European HEALTH care (United4health) [71] are among such developments. The aim of these projects is to provide solutions to improve healthcare quality, provide access to a high-quality healthcare system to all EU citizens around Europe, and support close cooperation between healthcare professionals and care providers from different organization.

Therefore, in future, the proposed scheme will be further investigated towards cross-border healthcare collaboration. The plan is to evaluate the validity of the scheme to provide solutions to improve healthcare quality, provide access to a high-quality healthcare system to all EU citizens around Europe, and support close cooperation between healthcare professionals and care providers from different organization.

Acknowledgment

The authors would like to thank Geir M. Køien for the support in investigating and typesetting this work.

References

[1] M. Abomhara and H. Yang, "Attribute-based authenticated access for secure sharing of healthcare records in collaborative environments," in the Eighth International Conference on eHealth, Telemedicine, and Social Medicine (eTELEMED 2016), 2016, pp. 138–144, ISBN:978-1-61208-470-1.

[2] C. Bain, "The implementation of the electronic medical records system in health care facilities," Procedia Manufacturing, vol. 3, 2015, pp. 4629–4634.

[3] S. Silow-Carroll, J. N. Edwards, and D. Rodin, "Using electronic health records to improve quality and efficiency: the experiences of leading hospitals," Issue Brief (Commonw Fund), vol. 17, 2012, pp. 1–40.

[4] R. Zhang and L. Liu, "Security models and requirements for healthcare application clouds," in Cloud Computing (CLOUD), 2010 IEEE 3rd International Conference on. IEEE, 2010, pp. 268–275.

[5] M. Abomhara, M. Gerdes, and G. M. Køien, "A stride-based threat model for telehealth systems," Norsk informasjonssikkerhetskonferanse (NISK), vol. 8, no. 1, 2015, pp. 82–96.

[6] U. D. of Health, H. Services et al., "Expanding the reach and impact of consumer e-health tools," Washington, DC: US Department of Health and Human Services. Office of Disease Prevention and Health Promotion, 2006.

[7] M.-H. Kuo, "Opportunities and challenges of cloud computing to improve health care services," Journal of medical Internet research, vol. 13, no. 3, 2011, p. e67.

[8] B. Fabian, T. Ermakova, and P. Junghanns, "Collaborative and secure sharing of healthcare data in multi-clouds," Information Systems, vol. 48, 2015, pp. 132–150.

[9] M. Li, S. Yu, Y. Zheng, K. Ren, and W. Lou, "Scalable and secure sharing of personal health records in cloud computing using attribute-based encryption," IEEE Transactions on Parallel and Distributed Systems, vol. 24, no. 1, 2013, pp. 131–143.

[10] M. Abomhara and G. M. Køien, "Towards an access control model for collaborative healthcare systems," in In Proceedings of the 9th International Joint Conference on Biomedical Engineering Systems and Technologies (BIOSTEC 2016), vol. 5, 2016, pp. 213–222.

[11] O. Moonian, S. Cheerkoot-Jalim, S. D. Nagowah, K. K. Khedo, R. Doomun, and Z. Cadersaib, "Hcrbac–an access control system for collaborative context-aware healthcare services in mauritius," Journal of Health Informatics in Developing Countries, vol. 2, no. 2, 2008.

[12] M. Meingast, T. Roosta, and S. Sastry, "Security and privacy issues with health care information technology," in 28th Annual International Conference of the IEEE Engineering in Medicine and Biology Society, 2006. EMBS'06. IEEE, 2006, pp. 5453–5458.

[13] A. Appari and M. E. Johnson, "Information security and privacy in healthcare: current state of research," International journal of Internet and enterprise management, vol. 6, no. 4, 2010, pp. 279–314.

[14] R. Gajanayake, R. Iannella, and T. Sahama, "Privacy oriented access control for electronic health records," electronic Journal of Health Informatics, vol. 8, no. 2, 2014, p. 15.

[15] B. Alhaqbani and C. Fidge, "Access control requirements for processing electronic health records," in Business Process Management Workshops. Springer, 2008, pp. 371–382.

[16] S. J. Dwyer III, A. C. Weaver, and K. K. Hughes, "Health insurance portability and accountability act," Security Issues in the Digital Medical Enterprise, vol. 72, no. 2, 2004, pp. 9–18.

[17] K. E. Artnak and M. Benson, "Evaluating hipaa compliance: A guide for researchers, privacy boards, and irbs," Nursing outlook, vol. 53, no. 2, 2005, pp. 79–87.

[18] H. Bidgoli, Handbook of Information Security, Information Warfare, Social, Legal, and International Issues and Security Foundations. John Wiley & Sons, 2006, vol. 2.

[19] N. Li, Q. Wang, W. Qardaji, E. Bertino, P. Rao, J. Lobo, and D. Lin, "Access control policy combining: theory meets practice," in the 14th ACM symposium on Access control models and technologies. ACM, 2009, pp. 135–144.

[20] D. F. Ferraiolo, R. Sandhu, S. Gavrila, D. R. Kuhn, and R. Chandramouli, "Proposed nist standard for role-based access control," ACM Transactions on Information and System Security (TISSEC), vol. 4, no. 3, 2001, pp. 224–274.

[21] V. C. Hu, D. Ferraiolo, R. Kuhn, A. Schnitzer, K. Sandlin, R. Miller, and K. Scarfone, "Guide to attribute based access control (abac) definition and considerations," NIST Special Publication, vol. 800, 2014, p. 162.

[22] A. Ubale Swapnaja, G. Modani Dattatray, and S. Apte Sulabha, "Analysis of dac mac rbac access control based models for security," International Journal of Computer Applications, vol. 104, no. 5, 2014.

[23] H. Yang, "Cryptographic enforcement of attribute-based authentication," doctoral Dissertations at the University of Agder, 2016, ISBN: 978-82-7117-826-0.

[24] M. Abomhara, H. Yang, and G. M. Køien, "Access control model for cooperative healthcare environments: Modeling and verification," in IEEE International Conference on Healthcare Informatics 2016 (ICHI 2016), 2016.

[25] M. Abomhara and M. Ben Lazrag, "Uml/ocl-based modeling of work-based access control policies for collaborative healthcare systems," in IEEE 18th International Conference on E-health, Networking, Applications, and Services (IEEE Healthcom 2016), 2016, doi: 978-1-5090-3370-6/16.

[26] M. Abomhara and H. Nergaard, "Modeling of work-based access control for cooperative healthcare systems with xacml," in the Fifth International Conference on Global Health Challenges (GLOBAL HEALTH 2016), 2016, pp. 14–21, ISBN: 978-1-61208-511-1.

[27] D. Khader, "Attribute based authentication schemes," Ph.D. dissertation, University of Bath, 2009.

[28] H. Yang and V. A. Oleshchuk, "A dynamic attribute-based authentication scheme," in Codes, Cryptology, and Information Security. Springer, 2015, pp. 106–118.

[29] ——, "An efficient traceable attribute-based authentication scheme with one-time attribute trees," in Secure IT Systems. Springer, 2015, pp. 123–135.

[30] H. K. Maji, M. Prabhakaran, and M. Rosulek, "Attribute-based signatures," in cryptographers Track at the RSA Conference. Springer, 2011, pp. 376–392.

[31] J. Li, M. H. Au, W. Susilo, D. Xie, and K. Ren, "Attribute-based signature and its applications," in Proceedings of the 5th ACM Symposium on Information, Computer and Communications Security. ACM, 2010, pp. 60–69.

[32] S. Yu, C. Wang, K. Ren, and W. Lou, "Attribute based data sharing with attribute revocation," in the 5th ACM Symposium on Information, Computer and Communications Security. ACM, 2010, pp. 261–270.

[33] C. Shah, "A framework for supporting user-centric collaborative information seeking," in PhD Thesis. University of North Carolina, 2010, pp. 1–268. [Online]. Available: http://comminfo.rutgers.edu/~chirags/papers/Shah_Dissertation.pdf

[34] I. H. Arka and K. Chellappan, "Collaborative compressed i-cloud medical image storage with decompress viewer," Procedia Computer Science, vol. 42, 2014, pp. 114–121.

[35] K. Asif, S. I. Ahamed, and N. Talukder, "Avoiding privacy violation for resource sharing in ad hoc networks of pervasive computing environment," in Proceedings of the 31st Annual International Computer

Software and Applications Conference-Volume 02. IEEE Computer Society, 2007, pp. 269–274.

[36] C. W. Probst, J. Hunker, D. Gollmann, and M. Bishop, Insider Threats in Cyber Security. Springer Science & Business Media, 2010, vol. 49.

[37] Y. Chen, S. Nyemba, and B. Malin, "Detecting anomalous insiders in collaborative information systems," Dependable and Secure Computing, IEEE Transactions on, vol. 9, no. 3, 2012, pp. 332–344.

[38] Y. Chen, S. Nyemba, W. Zhang, and B. Malin, "Leveraging social networks to detect anomalous insider actions in collaborative environments," in Intelligence and Security Informatics (ISI), 2011 IEEE International Conference on. IEEE, 2011, pp. 119–124.

[39] ITRC, "Identity theft rsesource centre (itrc) data breach reports," 2015. [Online]. Available: http://www.idtheftcenter.org/images/breach/DataBreachReports_2015.pdf

[40] N. T. Nguyen, P. L. Reiher, and G. H. Kuenning, "Detecting insider threats by monitoring system call activity." in IAW. Citeseer, 2003, pp. 45–52.

[41] M. Kandias, N. Virvilis, and D. Gritzalis, "The insider threat in cloud computing," in Critical Information Infrastructure Security. Springer, 2011, pp. 93–103.

[42] J. R. Nurse, O. Buckley, P. A. Legg, M. Goldsmith, S. Creese, G. R. Wright, and M. Whitty, "Understanding insider threat: A framework for characterising attacks," in Security and Privacy Workshops (SPW), 2014 IEEE. IEEE, 2014, pp. 214–228.

[43] M. B. Salem, S. Hershkop, and S. J. Stolfo, "A survey of insider attack detection research," in Insider Attack and Cyber Security. Springer, 2008, pp. 69–90.

[44] W. Tolone, G.-J. Ahn, T. Pai, and S.-P. Hong, "Access control in collaborative systems," ACM Computing Surveys (CSUR), vol. 37, no. 1, 2005, pp. 29–41.

[45] S. Alshehri, S. Mishra, and R. Raj, "Insider threat mitigation and access control in healthcare systems," 2013.

[46] C. E. Rubio-Medrano, C. D'Souza, and G.-J. Ahn, "Supporting secure collaborations with attribute-based access control," in Collaborative Computing: Networking, Applications and Worksharing (Collaboratecom), 2013 9th International Conference Conference on. IEEE, 2013, pp. 525–530.

[47] J. , D. Domingos, M. J. Silva, and C. Santos, "Group-based discretionary access control for epidemiological resources," Procedia Technology, vol. 9, 2013, pp. 1149–1158.

[48] C. Borrill, M. West, D. Shapiro, and A. Rees, "Team working and effectiveness in health care," British Journal of Healthcare Management, vol. 6, no. 8, 2000, pp. 364–371.

[49] C. Taylor, A. J. Munro, R. Glynne-Jones, C. Griffith, P. Trevatt, M. Richards, and A. J. Ramirez, "Multidisciplinary team working in cancer: what is the evidence?" BMJ, vol. 340, 2010, p. c951.

[50] P. Mitchell, M. Wynia, R. Golden, B. McNellis, S. Okun, C. E. Webb, V. Rohrbach, and I. Von Kohorn, "Core principles & values of effective team-based health care," Washington, DC: Institute of Medicine, 2012.

[51] R. S. Sandhu and P. Samarati, "Access control: principle and practice," IEEE communications magazine, vol. 32, no. 9, 1994, pp. 40–48.

[52] M. A. Valentine and A. C. Edmondson, "Team scaffolds: How mesolevel structures enable role-based coordination in temporary groups," Organization Science, vol. 26, no. 2, 2015, pp. 405–422.

[53] N. Meslec and P. L. Curşeu, "Are balanced groups better? belbin roles in collaborative learning groups," Learning and Individual Differences, vol. 39, 2015, pp. 81–88.

[54] D. Patra, S. Ray, J. Mukhopadhyay, B. Majumdar, and A. Majumdar, "Achieving e-health care in a distributed ehr system," in e-Health Networking, Applications and Services, 2009. Healthcom 2009. 11th International Conference on. IEEE, 2009, pp. 101–107.

[55] S. de Lusignan, F. Mold, A. Sheikh, A. Majeed, J. C. Wyatt, T. Quinn, M. Cavill, T. A. Gronlund, C. Franco, U. Chauhan et al., "Patients online access to their electronic health records and linked online services: a systematic interpretative review," BMJ open, vol. 4, no. 9, 2014, p. e006021.

[56] Q. Wang and H. Jin, "Quantified risk-adaptive access control for patient privacy protection in health information systems," in Proceedings of the 6th ACM Symposium on Information, Computer and Communications Security. ACM, 2011, pp. 406–410.

[57] T. Okamoto, "Cryptography based on bilinear maps," in Applied Algebra, Algebraic Algorithms and Error-Correcting Codes, ser. Lecture Notes in Computer Science. Springer Berlin Heidelberg, 2006, vol. 3857, pp. 35–50.

[58] R. Sahu and S. Padhye, "Efficient ID-based signature scheme from bilinear map," in Advances in Parallel Distributed Computing, ser. Communications in Computer and Information Science. Springer Berlin Heidelberg, 2011, vol. 203, pp. 301–306.

[59] Y. Qin, D. Feng, and X. Zhen, "An anonymous property-based attestation protocol from bilinear maps," in 2009 International Conference on Computational Science and Engineering (CSE '09), vol. 2, Aug 2009, pp. 732–738.

[60] H. Yang and V. A. Oleshchuk, "Traceable hierarchical attribute-based authentication for the cloud," in Communications and Network Security (CNS), 2015 IEEE Conference on. IEEE, 2015, pp. 685–689.

[61] D. Boneh, E. Shen, and B. Waters, "Strongly unforgeable signatures based on computational diffie-hellman," in International Workshop on Public Key Cryptography. Springer, 2006, pp. 229–240.

[62] S. Goldwasser, S. Micali, and R. L. Rivest, "A digital signature scheme secure against adaptive chosen-message attacks," SIAM Journal on Computing, vol. 17, no. 2, 1988, pp. 281–308.

[63] G. Ateniese, M. Joye, and G. Tsudik, On the difficulty of coalition-resistance in group signature schemes. IBM Thomas J. Watson Research Division, 1999.

[64] M. Dekker, "Critical cloud computing-a ciip perspective on cloud computing services," Report of the European Network and Information Security Agency, 2012.

[65] D. Byrne, Enabling Good Health for All : A Reflection Process for a New EU Health Strategy. Commission of the European Communities, 2004.

[66] M. Wismar, W. Palm, J. Figueras, K. Ernst, E. Van Ginneken et al., "Cross-border health care in the european union: mapping and analysing practices and policies." Cross-border health care in the European Union: mapping and analysing practices and policies, 2011.

[67] E. Commission, "Expert panel on effective ways of investing in health: Cross-border cooperation," 2015. [Online]. Available: http://ec.europa.eu/health/expert_panel/opinions/docs/009_crossborder_cooperation_en.pdf

[68] ——, "Overview of the national laws on electronic health records in the eu member states and their interaction with the provision of cross-border ehealth services," EU Health Programme (2008-2013), 2013. [Online]. Available: http://ec.europa.eu/health/ehealth/docs/laws_report_recommendations_en.pdf

[69] I. Passarani, "Patient access to electronic health records," Report of the eHealth Stakeholder Group, 2013. [Online]. Available: http://ec.europa.eu/health/expert_panel/opinions/docs/009_crossborder_cooperation_en.pdf

[70] E. Commission, "ehealth action plan 2012-2020 innovative healthcare for the 21st century," European Commission staff working document for informative purposes, 2012. [Online]. Available: http://eur-lex.europa.eu/LexUriServ/LexUriServ.do?uri=SWD:2012:0413:FIN:EN:PDF

[71] United4Health, "P7 eu project united4health 2013." [Online]. Available: Umbrellaproject:http://www.united4health.eu/;Norwegianproject:http://www.united4health.no/.

Detecting Obfuscated JavaScripts from Known and Unknown Obfuscators using Machine Learning

Bernhard Tellenbach
Zurich University of Applied Sciences
Switzerland
Email: tebe@zhaw.ch

Sergio Paganoni
SecureSafe / DSwiss AG
Zurich, Switzerland
Email: sergio.paganoni@dswiss.com

Marc Rennhard
Zurich University of Applied Sciences
Switzerland
Email: rema@zhaw.ch

***Abstract*—JavaScript is a common attack vector to probe for known vulnerabilities to select a fitting exploit or to manipulate the Document Object Model (DOM) of a web page in a harmful way. The JavaScripts used in such attacks are often obfuscated to make them hard to detect using signature-based approaches. On the other hand, since the only legitimate reason to obfuscate a script is to protect intellectual property, there are not many scripts that are both benign and obfuscated. A detector that can reliably detect obfuscated JavaScripts would therefore be a valuable tool in fighting JavaScript based attacks. In this paper, we compare the performance of nine different classifiers with respect to correctly classifying obfuscated and non-obfuscated scripts. For our experiments, we use a data set of regular, minified, and obfuscated samples from jsDeliver and the Alexa top 5000 websites and a set of malicious samples from MELANI. We find that the best of these classifiers, the boosted decision tree classifier, performs very well to correctly classify obfuscated and non-obfuscated scripts with precision and recall rates of around 99 percent. The boosted decision tree classifier is then used to assess how well this approach can cope with scripts obfuscated by an obfuscator not present in our training set. The results show that while it may work for some obfuscators, it is still critical to have as many different obfuscators in the training set as possible. Finally, we describe the results from experiments to classify malicious obfuscated scripts when no such scripts are included in the training set. Depending on the set of features used, it is possible to detect about half of those scripts, even though those samples do not seem to use any of the obfuscators used in our training set.**

***Index Terms*—Machine learning; Classification algorithms; JavaScript; Obfuscated; Malicious**

I. Introduction

JavaScript is omnipresent on the web. Almost all websites make use of it and there are a lot of other applications, such as Portable Document Format (PDF) forms or HyperText Markup Language (HTML) e-mails, where JavaScript plays an important role. This strong dependence creates attack opportunities for individuals by using malicious JavaScripts, which may provide them with an entry point into a victim's system. The main functionalities of a malicious JavaScript are reconnaissance, exploitation, and cross-site scripting (XSS) vulnerabilities in web applications.

The JavaScripts used in such attacks are often obfuscated to make them hard to detect using signature-based approaches. On the other hand, the only legitimate reason to obfuscate a script is to protect intellectual property. Our evaluation of the prevalence of such scripts on the Alexa top 5000 home pages suggests that this is fairly uncommon. One reason for this might be that a lot of JavaScript code on these pages is code from JavaScript libraries that are available to the public anyway. If it is indeed the case that there are not too many scripts that are both benign and obfuscated, it should be easy to capture these with a whitelist. A detector that can reliably detect obfuscated JavaScript code would then be a valuable tool in fighting malicious JavaScript based attacks. But even if there would be a lot of obfuscated benign JavaScript code, a detector could play an important role in that it helps to filtering such scripts and feed them to a component that performs a more in-depth analysis.

The most common method to address the problem of malicious JavaScripts is having malware analysts write rules for anti-malware or intrusion detection systems that identify common patterns in obfuscated (or non-obfuscated) malicious scripts. While signature-based detection is good at detecting known malware, it often fails to detect it when obfuscation is used to alter the features captured by the signature. Furthermore, keeping up with the attackers and their obfuscation techniques is a time consuming task. This is why a lot of research effort is put into alternative solutions to identify/classify malicious JavaScripts. See Section V for details.

In this paper, we analyze and extend our approach to automatically detect obfuscated JavaScripts using machine learning presented in [1]. Our paper makes the following three contributions. First, we make use of the cloud based Microsoft Azure Machine Learning Studio [2] to quickly create, train, evaluate and deploy predictive models of nine different classifiers and to do an analysis of what the most descriptive features are. The top performing one, the boosted decision tree classifier, was not among the three classifiers tested in [1]. Second, using the boosted decision tree classifier we perform a comprehensive analysis of how well this approach can cope with scripts obfuscated by an obfuscator not present in our training set. As pointed out in [1], such an analysis would be quite desirable since malicious JavaScripts are likely to make use of a custom obfuscation approaches. Finally, we describe the results from experiments to classify *malicious* obfuscated scripts when no such scripts are included in the training set.

For our experiments, we use the same data set as in [1] with two important modifications. First, we use the scripts from the Alexa top 5000 instead of the top 500 websites and second, we perform a rigorous preprocessing to get rid of scripts that are identical or almost the same as other scripts in the data set (see Section III). Not doing this could produce results that are better than they should be if there are scripts that appear on almost all of the pages (e.g., Google Analytics scripts).

The rest of the paper is organized as follows. Section II briefly explains the different JavaScript classes that we distinguish in this work. In Section III, we discuss our data set, the preprocessing steps performed, feature selection and the machine learning methodology and tools. Section IV presents our results, followed by a discussion of results IV. Section V discusses related works and Section VI concludes the paper.

II. Syntactic and functional varieties of JavaScript

Client-side JavaScript for JavaScript-enabled applications can be attributed to one of the following four classes: regular, minified, obfuscated, and malicious. Note that only regular, minified, and obfuscated are disjoint classes and that we distinguish only obfuscated, non-obfuscated, and malicious JavaScripts in the reminder of this paper.

A. Regular JavaScripts

The regular class contains the scripts as they have been written by their developers. These scripts are typically easy to read and understand by human beings.

B. Minified JavaScripts

Minified scripts are more compact versions of the regular scripts. To achieve this, minifiers such as the YUI Compressor [3] remove space and new line characters that only exist to make the code easier to read for humans. Some of the minifiers do also rename functions and variables to get rid of long function or variable names. While this makes the scripts harder to read and understand for a human, the program flow stays the same. Minification main purpose is to reduce bandwidth usage when loading JavaScripts.

C. Obfuscated JavaScripts

Obfuscation tools keep the original functionality of the code but modify the program flow with the goal to make it hard to understand. Many obfuscation techniques exist. For example, encoding obfuscation encodes strings using hexadecimal character encoding or Unicode encoding to make strings harder to read. Other obfuscation steps involve hiding code in data to execute it later using the eval JavaScript function (code unfolding). The following listing shows a simple example of the latter technique:

```
var a = "ale";
a += "rt(";
a += "'hello'";
a += ");";
eval(a);
```

Listing 1. A simple example of code unfolding

Note that the obfuscated files can also be considered minified. The obfuscators remove whitespaces and make the scripts more compact. Scripts that are first minified and then obfuscated look similar or are the same as when only obfuscation is applied. Applying obfuscation and then minification might lead to partial de-obfuscation (e.g., decoding of encoded strings) and is therefore unlikely to be used in practice.

D. Malicious JavaScripts

Whether or not a JavaScript is malicious is a question of its semantics and not of its syntax. Hence, a malicious JavaScript could be a regular, minified or obfuscated one. Previous work sometimes conflates obfuscation with maliciousness. In this work and in prior art (see [4]), it is explicitly stated that neither is all obfuscated code malicious nor is all malicious code obfuscated. However, in practice, it appears that at least for now, most malicious scripts are indeed obfuscated, as all of the recent malicious JavaScripts samples we collected in the wild were obfuscated.

III. Machine learning approach to JavaScript classification

In order to evaluate the feasibility and accuracy of distinguishing between different classes of JavaScript code, we adopted a classic machine learning approach. We collected a data set containing a number of JavaScripts representing each of the classes of interest, i.e., non-obfuscated, obfuscated and malicious. For each of the samples in the data set we extracted a set of discriminatory features, which we list in Table III below. The extracted features form fixed-length feature vectors, which in turn are used for training and evaluation of classifiers.

A. Data Set

Our data set consists of data from three different sources: (1) the complete list of JavaScripts available from the *jsDelivr* content delivery network, (2) the *Alexa Top 5000* websites and (3) a set of malicious JavaScript samples from the Swiss Reporting and Analysis Centre for Information Assurance *MELANI*.

jsDeliver: contains a large number of JavaScript libraries and files in both regular and minified form. We use the regular form of the files as a basis for our evaluation.

Alexa Top 5000: To have a more comprehensible representation of actual scripts found on websites [5], we downloaded the JavaScripts found on the Alexa Top 5000 home pages [6]. To extract the scripts from these websites, we parsed them with BeautifulSoup [7] and extracted all scripts that were either inlined (e.g., `<script>alert("foo");</script>`) or referenced via external files (e.g., `<script type="text/javascript" src="filename.js" ></script>`).

MELANI: The fileset from MELANI contains only malicious samples. Most of the malicious samples in the set are either JS droppers used in malspam campaigns or Exploit Kits (EK) resources for exploiting vulnerabilities in browser plugins. All samples are at least partially obfuscated and seem to make use of different obfuscation techniques and tools. The composition of the malicious data set is shown in Table I.

TABLE I. MALICIOUS DATA SET COMPOSITION

Name	Description	Count
CrimePack EK	Landing pages and iFrame injection code	2001
JS-Droppers	Malicious samples from different malspam campaigns	419
Angler EK	Landing pages	168
RIG EK	Landing pages	60
Misc	Different samples from other EKs (Nuclear Pack, Phoenix, BlackHole)	58

For our evaluation, we make the following three assumptions about the files from jsDelivr and the Alexa Top 5000 home pages: these files are non-malicious, non-minified and non-obfuscated.

Assuming that there are no malicious scripts in the files downloaded from the top 5000 home pages should be quite safe. The same is true for the files from jsDelivr since they are subject to manual review and approval. Nevertheless, we checked the scripts with Windows Defender and in contrast to the set of well-known malicious JavaScripts, Windows Defender did not raise any alarm.

The second assumption that these scripts are not minified, is very unlikely to hold since making use of minified scripts has become quite popular. In order to make this assumption hold, a preprocessing step is required to remove scripts that are not minified from the data set. Only then we have a clean starting point for the generation of the seven additional file sets (see III-B for details).

The last assumption about the absence of obfuscated scripts should hold for the jsDelivr data set since these scripts are subject to manual review and approval. It should also be true for the Alexa Top 5000 data set because there is little reason that home pages contain JavaScripts that need to be protected by obfuscating them. To check whether this is true, we inspected a random subset of about 150 scripts and found none that was obfuscated. Furthermore, we inspected those scripts that are later reported to be obfuscated by our classifier (supposedly false-positives) and found that from the 173 files only 15 were indeed obfuscated. However, when considering our results in relation to the presence or absence of a specific obfuscator in the data set, we cannot be sure that the Alexa Top 5000 data set does not contain scripts obfuscated by an obfuscator whose characteristics (as captured by our feature vector) are very different from the characteristics of the other obfuscators. Note that even if this were the case, it would not invalidate our results but confirm our findings concerning the presence or absence of a specific obfuscator.

In summary, after the preprocessing step, which removes minified scripts and does some additional sanitation of the dataset (see III-B for details), our data set should have the assumed properties and contain regular, non-obfuscated and non-malicious JavaScript files only.

Based on this set of files, we generated seven additional sets of files. For the first set, we processed the files with uglifyjs [8], the most popular JavaScript minifier, to obtain a minified version of them. Uglifyjs works by extracting an abstract syntax tree (AST) from the JavaScript source and then transforming it to an optimized (smaller) one. For the second to seventh set, we used six different JavaScript ofuscators:

- **javascriptobfuscator.com standard:** To use this commercial obfuscator [9], we wrote a C# application that queries its web API with the default settings plus the parameters MoveStrings, MoveMembers, ReplaceNames. The version used was the one online on the 28th of July 2016.
- **javascriptobfuscator.com advanced:** Since the two parameters DeepObfuscation and EncryptStrings change the way the resulting scripts look like significantly, we added them to the configuration from above to create another file set.
- **javascript-obfuscator:** This obfuscator is advertised as free offline alternative to [9]. We used version 0.6.1 in its default configuration.
- **jfogs:** This is a javascript obfuscator [10] developped by zswang. We used version 0.0.15 in its default configuration.
- **jsobfu:** This is the obfuscator [11] used by the Metasploit penetration testing software to obfuscate JavaScript payloads. We used its default configuration with one iteration.
- **closure:** The Closure Compiler [12] has not been developed to obfuscate JavaScripts but to make them download and run faster. Nevertheless, it makes most JavaScripts that contain more than a few lines of code hard to read and understand even when JavaScript beautifiers are applied to them. Scripts with a few lines of code are often left unchanged. That is why the set of scripts obfuscated with this tool is smaller than the others. We obfuscated only scripts that are at least 1500 characters long. We used version 20160822 with option *–compilation_level SIMPLE*.

The reason why we did not use the old but well-known Dean Edwards' Packer [13] from [1] is that it may create parsable but semantically incorrect JavaScripts. For example, in some cases, this obfuscator removed entire parts of the script because it uses regular expressions instead of a parser to identify multi-line comments correctly.

B. Preprocessing

The preprocessing of the files downloaded from jsDelivr and the Alexa Top 5000 home pages is divided into the following three steps:

1) Removal of duplicate and similar files
2) Removal of minified files
3) Removal of files that cannot be parsed

The preprocessing starts with a total of 42378 files downloaded from Alexa Top 5000 home pages and 4224 files from the jsDelivr data set used in [1].

The removal of duplicate and similar files in the first preprocessing step is performed using the tool ssdeep [14], a program for computing fuzzy hashes. ssdeep can match inputs that have homologies. It outputs a score about how similar two files are. We remove 13234 (Alexa) and 587 (jsDelivr) files that had a score of 90 or higher with 75 of them having a score equal or higher to 99. Not removing such files could produce results that are better than they should be if the same script appears in the training and the testing set. The impact is even worse if the same or a slightly modified script appears not just twice but multiple times in the training and testing data sets.

In the next step, we remove minified files downloaded from the Alexa Top 5000 home pages using the following heuristics:

- Remove files with fewer than 5 lines
- Remove files if less than 1% of all characters are spaces.
- Remove files where more than 10% of all lines are longer than 1000 characters).

14490, approximately half of the remaining files were minified and therefore removed. Note that in [1], this heuristic has also be applied to the jsDelivr files even though they should be non-minified. A manual inspection of a random subset of supposedly non-minified files showed that around 10% of them were minified.

It is important to point out that by doing this, we get rid of small scripts (fewer than 5 lines), which is likely to make classification of such scripts difficult. This limitation could be used to split an obfuscated script into multiple parts and (probably) circumvent detection. As a countermeasure, one would have to detect such behavior.

The third preprocessing step removes any of the remaining original jsDelivr and Alexa Top 5000 scripts, where the parsing of the script, or of one of its transformed versions (minified, obfuscated), failed. After this step, the data set contains the number of samples listed in Table II. Overall, there are 101974 samples. Note that since the closure compiler does not perform well on small files (no obfuscation), we are only obfuscating samples with more then 1500 chars. Therefore, the number of samples reported there is significantly smaller than for the other obfuscators.

TABLE II. DATA COLLECTIONS

Collection	Properties	#Samples
jsDelivr.com	regular	3403
jsDelivr.com	minified (uglifyjs)	3403
jsDelivr.com	obfuscated (closure)	2004
jsDelivr.com	obfuscated (javascript-obfuscator)	3403
jsDelivr.com	obfuscated (javascriptobfuscator.com standard)	3403
jsDelivr.com	obfuscated (javascriptobfuscator.com advanced)	3403
jsDelivr.com	obfuscated (jfogs)	3403
jsDelivr.com	obfuscated (jsobfu)	3403
Alexa Top 5000	unknown / potentially non-obfuscated	9519
Alexa Top 5000	minified (uglifyjs)	9512
Alexa Top 5000	obfuscated (closure)	6825
Alexa Top 5000	obfuscated (javascript-obfuscator)	9519
Alexa Top 5000	obfuscated (javascriptobfuscator.com standard)	9516
Alexa Top 5000	obfuscated (javascriptobfuscator.com advanced)	9516
Alexa Top 5000	obfuscated (jfogs)	9519
Alexa Top 5000	obfuscated (jsobfu)	9517
MELANI	malicious and obfuscated (see Table I)	2706

C. Feature Selection

For our experiments reported in this paper, we selected a set of 45 features derived from manual inspection, related work [15], [16], and analysis of the histograms of candidate features. For example, observations showed that obfuscated scripts often make use of encodings using hexadecimal, Base64 or Unicode characters (F17) and often remove white spaces (F8). Furthermore, some rely on splitting a job in a lot of functions (F14) and almost all use a lot of strings (F7) and are lacking comments (F9).

Table III lists the discriminatory features we used for training and evaluation of the classifiers in the reported experiments. These features are complemented with 25 features reflecting the frequency of 25 different JavaScript keywords: *break, case, catch, continue, do, else, false, finally, for, if, instanceof, new, null, return, switch, this, throw, true, try, typeof, var, while, toString, valueOf* and *undefined*. The rationale behind the selection of these keywords is that if control flow obfuscation [17] is used, the frequency of these keywords might differ significantly.

While the present set yielded promising results in our experiments, further investigations are required to determine an optimal set of classification features for the problem. The features labeled as 'new' in Table III are a novel contribution of the present paper. The special JavaScript elements used in feature F15 are elements often used and renamed (to conceal their use) in obfuscated or malicious scripts. This includes the following functions, objects and prototypes:

- **Functions**: eval, unescape, String.fromCharCode, String.charCodeAt
- **Objects**: window, document
- **Prototypes**: string, array, object

TABLE III. DISCRIMINATORY FEATURES

Feature	Description	Used in:
F1	total number of lines	[15]
F2	avg. # of chars per line	[15]
F3	# chars in script	[15]
F4	% of lines >1000 chars	new
F5	Shannon entropy of the file	[16]
F6	avg. string length	[15]
F7	share of chars belonging to a string	new
F8	share of space characters	[15]
F9	share of chars belonging to a comment	[15]
F10	# of `eval` calls divided by F3	new
F11	avg. # of chars per function body	new
F12	share of chars belonging to a function body	new
F13	avg. # of arguments per function	[15]
F14	# of function definitions divided by F3	new
F15	# of special JavaScript elements divided by F3	new
F16	# of renamed special JavaScript elements divided by F3	new
F17	share of encoded characters (e.g., `\u0123` or `\x61`)	[15]
F18	share of backslash characters	new
F19	share of pipe characters	new
F20	# of array accesses using dot or bracket syntax divided by F3	new
F21-F45	frequency of 25 common JavaScript keywords	new

D. Feature Extraction

To extract the above features, we implemented a Node.js application traversing the abstract syntax tree (AST) generated by Esprima [18], a JavaScript parser compatible with Mozilla's SpiderMonkey Parser API [19].

E. Machine Learning

To train and evaluate the machine learning algorithms, we decided to use Azure Machine Learning [2] (Azure ML) instead of a more traditional local approach. Azure ML is a cloud-based predictive analytics service that makes it possible to quickly create, train, evaluate, and deploy predictive models as analytics solutions. To design and run the experiments, we used Azure Machine Learning Studio, which provides an efficiently usable collaborative drag-and-drop tool.

Azure ML offers different classification algorithms [20]. Given the flexibility of the cloud-based service, we trained and evaluated several of them:

- Averaged Perceptron (AP)
- Bayes Point Machine (BPM)
- Boosted Decision Tree (BDT)
- Decision Forrest (DF)
- Decision Jungle (DJ)
- Locally-Deep Support Vector Machine (LDSVM)
- Logistic Regression (LR)
- Neural Network (NN)
- Support Vector Machine (SVM)

For a quick introduction into these classifiers and a comparison of their advantages and disadvantages, the Azure ML documentation [21] provides a concise overview. For more details about some of these algorithms, the reader is referred to [22].

For each experiment that we performed, the steps in the following list were carried out. These steps guarantee a sound machine learning approach with clear separation of testing data and training data.

1) Normalization of the data in the case of SVM-based classifiers using the Azure ML default normalizer (with the other classifiers, normalization is not required).
2) Partitioning of the the data into a *testing set*, a *training set*, and a *validation set*.
   a) First, the testing set is constructed. The samples to include in this set depends on the experiment (see Section IV).
   b) The remaining data is randomly partitioned into a training set and a validation set, using a split of 60%/40%.
   c) We always use stratified partitioning, which guarantees that the data in each set is representative for the entire data set.
3) Training of the classifier using the training set and optimizing it using the validation set.
4) Assessing the performance of the fully-trained classifier using the testing set.

For each script in the testing set, classification works as follows: The classifier computes a probability $p \in [0, 1]$ that states how likely the script is obfuscated. The probability is then mapped to the discrete labels *obfuscated* if $p \geq t$ and *non-obfuscated* if $p < t$, where t is the *threshold*. We set the threshold always to 0.5 to make the different experiments comparable. In practice, this threshold can be used to fine-tune the classification: Setting it to a higher value (e.g., 0.8) increases the probability that a script labeled as obfuscated is truly obfuscated (true positive), but also implies a higher rate of false negatives (obfuscated scripts falsely labeled as non-obfuscated). Conversely, setting it to a value below 0.5 increase true negatives at the cost of more false positives.

For each experiment, we report the *(p)recision*, *(r)ecall*, *(F1)-score* and *(s)upport* for each considered class and considered classifier. Precision is the number of true positives divided by the number of true positives and false positives. High precision (close to 1) means that most scripts labeled as obfuscated are indeed obfuscated. Recall is the number of true positives divided by the number of true positives and false negatives. High recall (close to 1) means that most of the obfuscated scripts are indeed labeled correctly as obfuscated without missing many of them. The F1 score conveys the balance between precision and recall, is computed as $2 * \frac{precision * recall}{precision + recall}$ and should ideally be close to 1. Finally, support is the total number of scripts tested for a specific label.

IV. RESULTS

In this section, we present the results of the three main experiments we performed. First, we show the performance of all nine different classifiers with respect to correctly classifying obfuscated and non-obfuscated scripts. The best of these classifiers is used in the further experiments. Next, we demonstrate how well this classifier is capable of correctly classifying scripts that were obfuscated with an unknown obfuscator, i.e., an obfuscator that was not used for any of the scripts in the training set. Finally, we describe the results from experiments to classify malicious obfuscated scripts when no such scripts are included in the training set.

A. Obfuscated vs. Non-Obfuscated

In the first series of experiments, we analyzed the performance of the classifiers with respect to correctly classifying obfuscated and non-obfuscated scripts. We used the entire data set (see Table II) and labeled the regular and minified files as non-obfuscated, the files processed with one of the obfuscator tools as obfuscated, and the malicious files also as obfuscated. 30% of all scripts are used in the training set and the other 70% are used for the training and validation sets, using a split of 60%/40%.

In the first experiment, all 45 features as described in Section III-C were used. All nine classifiers listed in Section III-E were trained and optimized using the training and validation sets and evaluated using the testing set. Table IV shows the results. The upper half shows the performance to classify non-obfuscated script correctly while the lower half shows the same for the obfuscated scripts. It can be seen that the best results can be achieved using a boosted decision tree classifier. With this classifier, only 80 of 7752 non-obfuscated scripts were classified as obfuscated (false positive rate of 1.03%) and only 73 of 22842 obfuscated scripts were classified as non-obfuscated (false negative rate of 0.32%). Overall, boosted decision tree was the only classifier that achieved F1-scores above 99% for both classifying obfuscated and non-obfuscated scripts.

At the bottom end with respect to classification performance, there are the averaged perceptron, logistic regression, and support vector machine classifiers. All three of them performed quite poorly. The explanation is that all of them are linear models (the support vector machine classifier in Azure ML only supports a linear kernel), which is apparently not well suited to classify obfuscated and non-obfuscated scripts.

Next, we performed the same experiment as above but instead of using all features, we only used the features that are most descriptive for correct classification. One advantage of using fewer features is that it reduces the time and memory requirements to train a classifier, but as we will see later, it has additional benefits when trying to classify scripts that are obfuscated with an unknown obfuscator. To determine the most descriptive features, we used Pearson's correlation. For each feature, Pearson's correlation returns a value that describes the strength of the correlation with the label of the scripts.

Table V lists the 20 most descriptive features based on Pearson's correlation, in descending order. The rightmost column shows the value of the Pearson's correlation and the column 'Feature' references the corresponding feature in Table III if the feature is also included in that table. The table contains several interesting findings. First of all, by comparing Table V with Table III, we can see that only five of the features that were described in previous works [15], [16] are among the 20 most descriptive features while 15 of them are new features that were introduced by us. Also, it appears that quite simple features such as the frequencies of some JavaScript keywords are well suited to distinguish between obfuscated and non-obfuscated scripts, as nine of them made it into the list.

Table VI shows the performance of all nine classifiers when using only the 20 most descriptive features listed in Table V instead of all features. It can be seen that in general, the performance is a little lower compared to Table IV, but the difference is small in most cases. For instance, in the case of the boosted decision tree classifier, the F1-scores were reduced by 1.12% and 0.42% resulting in 97.89% and 99.25%. This allows two conclusions: First, using only the 20 most descriptive features instead of all 45 features does not reduce classification performance significantly. Second, as 15 of the features in Table V are newly introduced features and only five of them have been used in previous works, the newly added features provide a significant improvement to classify the scripts.

To justify that using the 20 most descriptive features is a reasonable choice, we analyzed the performance when using the most descriptive 5, 10, 15,..., 40 features with the boosted decision tree classifier. Figure 1 shows the F1-scores depending on the number of used features. As expected, using fewer features results in lower performance while using more features increases the performance, getting closer and closer to the performance when using all features. In addition, Figure 1 shows that using 20 features is a good compromise between computational requirements during training and performance of the trained classifier because on the one hand, using 20 features provides a substantial improvement compared to using only 15 features and on the other hand, using more than 20 features only provides small further benefits.

As the number of malicious scripts in the data set is small compared to the others, it is important to have a more detailed look at the classification performance of these scripts. Table VII depicts the results when evaluating only the malicious scripts in the testing set. As all malicious scripts are labeled obfuscated, the figure only contains results to classify obfuscated scripts correctly. For the same reason, false positives cannot occur, which implies a precision of 100%. To assess the results, it is therefore best to use the recall value and comparing this value with the ones in Table IV and VI. Doing this, it can be seen that the recall value of malicious scripts is about 1% lower than of the other scripts. However, both recall values are still above 98%, which clearly shows that classifying malicious scripts still works well despite the relatively low fraction of malicious scripts in the data set.

TABLE IV. PERFORMANCE OF THE CLASSIFIERS TO CLASSIFY NON-OBFUSCATED AND OBFUSCATED SCRIPTS, USING ALL FEATURES

		AP	BPM	BDT	DF	DJ	LDSVM	LR	NN	SVM
Non Obfuscated	p	80.46%	92.44%	99.06%	98.50%	97.93%	93.53%	78.31%	95.64%	81.65%
	r	66.31%	78.03%	98.97%	98.14%	98.10%	88.40%	68.28%	90.02%	66.82%
	F1	72.70%	84.63%	99.01%	98.32%	98.02%	90.89%	72.95%	92.74%	73.50%
	s	7752	7752	7752	7752	7752	7752	7752	7752	7752
Obfuscated	p	89.21%	92.61%	99.65%	99.37%	99.36%	96.14%	89.68%	96.68%	89.39%
	r	94.54%	97.73%	99.68%	99.49%	99.30%	97.92%	93.58%	98.61%	94.90%
	F1	91.80%	95.10%	99.67%	99.43%	99.33%	97.02%	91.59%	97.63%	92.07%
	s	22842	22842	22842	22842	22842	22842	22842	22842	22842

TABLE V. 20 MOST PREDICTIVE DISCRIMINATORY FEATURES

Feature	Description	Used in	Corr.
F18	share of backslash characters	new	0.238
F9	share of chars belonging to a comment	[15]	0.236
	frequency of keyword if	new	0.233
F15	# of special JavaScript elements divided by F3	new	0.221
F4	% of lines >1000 chars	new	0.219
	frequency of keyword false	new	0.209
F17	share of encoded characters (e.g., `\u0123` or `\x61`)	[15]	0.208
F8	share of space characters	[15]	0.203
	frequency of keyword true	new	0.194
F20	# of array accesses using dot or bracket syntax divided by F3	new	0.160
F12	share of chars belonging to a function body	new	0.158
	frequency of keyword return	new	0.139
	frequency of keyword var	new	0.133
F7	share of chars belonging to a string	new	0.119
	frequency of keyword toString	new	0.112
F5	Shannon entropy of the file	[16]	0.106
F2	avg. # of chars per line	[15]	0.102
	frequency of keyword this	new	0.084
	frequency of keyword else	new	0.081
	frequency of keyword null	new	0.081

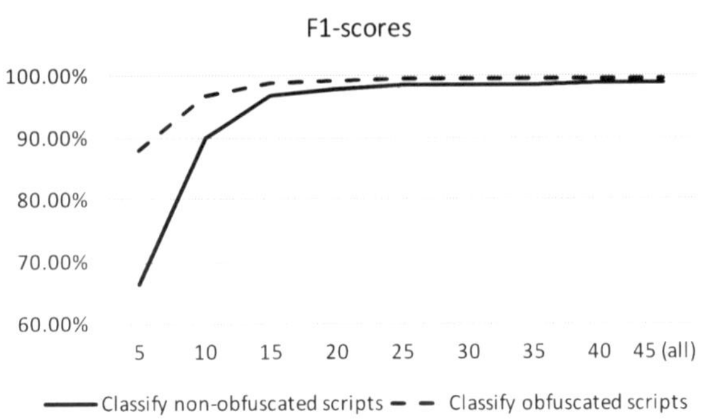

Figure 1. Performance of the Boosted Decision Tree classifier to classify non-obfuscated and obfuscated scripts, depending on the used number of most descriptive features.

To conclude this first series of experiments, we summarize the most relevant findings:

- Using our data set, classification between obfuscated and non-obfuscated scripts works well. The best classifier, boosted decision tree, yields F1-scores above 99% when using all 45 features.
- Using only the 20 most descriptive features, classification performance gets lower. However, the boosted decision tree classifier still achieves F1-scores close to and above 98% with the benefit of reduced time and memory requirements to train the classifier.
- Compared to the features used in previous works, the newly added features provide a significant improvement to classify the scripts.
- Even though the number of malicious scripts in the data set is relatively small, classifying them delivers only slightly lower performance as with the other scripts.

In the remainder of the paper, we will focus on the boosted decision tree classifier, as this has demonstrated to be the best classifier to classify obfuscated and non-obfuscated scripts.

B. Detecting Unknown Obfuscators

In the experiments performed above, all three sets (training set, validation set, and testing set) included scripts obfuscated with all different obfuscators that are used in our data set. This implies that the trained classifier 'knows' about all obfuscators and as a result, the evaluation using the testing set exhibited good classification performance. In reality, however, new obfuscators will be developed and used and ideally, the classifier should also perform well in classifying scripts that are obfuscated with such a new obfuscator.

To evaluate the performance to classify obfuscated scripts that were obfuscated using an unknown obfuscator, we first excluded the malicious scripts from the data set, which guarantees we are using a well-defined set of obfuscators. Then, we took the scripts that are obfuscated with a specific obfuscator (say obfuscator $Obf_{unknown}$) and put them into a testing set 1. From the remaining scripts, we put 30% into a testing set 2 and the rest was split into a training set and a validation set, using a split of 60%/40%. Note that this means that the scripts obfuscated with obfuscator $Obf_{unknown}$ are only present in testing set 1 and not included in any of the other sets. Training and validation sets were then used to train a boosted decision tree classifier and the trained classifier was evaluated

TABLE VI. PERFORMANCE OF THE CLASSIFIERS TO CLASSIFY NON-OBFUSCATED AND OBFUSCATED SCRIPTS, USING THE 20 MOST DESCRIPTIVE FEATURES

		AP	BPM	BDT	DF	DJ	LDSVM	LR	NN	SVM
Non Obfuscated	p	80.78%	74.43%	98.36%	97.35%	96.93%	94.51%	77.19%	95.65%	82.35%
	r	65.16%	63.97%	97.42%	95.18%	94.34%	85.13%	66.38%	89.33%	64.04%
	F1	72.13%	68.80%	97.89%	96.25%	95.61%	89.58%	71.38%	92.38%	72.05%
	s	7752	7752	7752	7752	7752	7752	7752	7752	7752
Obfuscated	p	88.90%	88.33%	99.13%	98.37%	98.10%	95.12%	89.11%	96.46%	88.65%
	r	94.74%	92.54%	99.45%	99.12%	98.98%	98.32%	93.34%	98.62%	95.34%
	F1	91.73%	90.39%	99.25%	98.75%	98.54%	96.69%	91.18%	97.53%	91.87%
	s	22842	22842	22842	22842	22842	22842	22842	22842	22842

TABLE VII. PERFORMANCE OF THE BDT CLASSIFIER TO CORRECTLY CLASSIFY MALICIOUS SCRIPTS AS OBFUSCATED

		BDT (all features)	BDT (20 features)
Obfuscated	p	100.00%	100.00%
	r	98.40%	98.52%
	F1	99.19%	99.25%
	s	811	811

using both testing sets. Classifying the scripts in testing set 2 should work well as it includes only obfuscators that are also included in the training set. Classifying the scripts in testing set 1 shows the performance of the classifier to classify scripts that were obfuscated with the unknown obfuscator $\text{Obf}_{\text{unknown}}$.

Table VIII shows the results. Each column contains the results when one specific obfuscator was excluded from the training and validation sets. The lower part with the results of evaluating training set 2 shows that classifying non-obfuscated scripts and scripts that were obfuscated with known obfuscators performs similar as in Table IV, which corresponds to the expected result. More interesting is the evaluation of training set 1 in the upper part of Table VIII, which shows the performance to detect scripts obfuscated with the excluded obfuscator. Just like in Table VII, false positives cannot occur, so the precision is always 100% and we use the recall value to assess the performance. The results vary greatly depending on the excluded obfuscator. Scripts obfuscated with closure or jfogs can hardly be detected (recall <1%) while those obfuscated with javascript-obfuscator and javascriptobfuscator.com advanced can be detected quite well (recall 76.93% and 99.80%). Scripts obfuscated with javascriptobfuscator.com standard and jsobfu are also hard to detect with recall values of 18.22% and 39.88%.

These results imply that some obfuscators are more similar than others. For example, scripts obfuscated with javascriptobfuscator.com advanced result in code that – with respect to the discriminatory features – is similar to the output of one or more of the other obfuscators. On the other hand, scripts obfuscated with jfogs must be very different from all other obfuscated scripts, as nearly none of them could be correctly classified as obfuscated. The results also imply that one should include many different obfuscators into the training and validation sets so the classifier can learn many different kinds of obfuscation techniques, which increases the probability that scripts obfuscated with unknown obfuscators can be detected.

In Table IX, the results of the same analysis while using only the 20 most descriptive features instead of all features is shown. Comparing the recall values of training set 1 in Tables VIII and IX, one can see that the performance is better when using only 20 features. While basically nothing changed for javascriptobfuscator.com advanced (it already had a very high recall value) and jfogs, the recall values for closure and javascriptobfuscator.com standard could be improved by about 2.5 %, for jsobfu by about 6% and for javascript-obfuscator by more than 16%.

Determining the exact reason of this increased performance requires more detailed analysis, but in general, using fewer features increases the fitting error of a trained classifier and at least with the obfuscators we used in the data set, this is beneficial for the recall value. Of course, this comes at a price: Reducing the number of features reduces the F1-scores when classifying scripts that are either non-obfuscated or obfuscated with a known obfuscator, as can be seen by comparing the evaluation results of training set 2 in Tables VIII and IX. This is not surprising and confirms what we already observed in Section IV-A.

To conclude this second series of experiments, we summarize the most relevant findings:

- It is possible to detect scripts obfuscated with an unknown obfuscator. Depending on the unknown obfuscator and the obfuscators in the training and validation sets, the recall value can range from close to 0% (closure and jfogs in our case) to more than 99% (javascriptobfuscator.com advanced in our case).
- One should include many different obfuscators into the training and validation sets so the classifier can learn many different kinds of obfuscation techniques, which increases the probability that scripts obfuscated with unknown obfuscators can be detected.
- Using only the 20 most descriptive instead of all features can increase the classification performance of scripts that are obfuscated with unknown obfuscators – at least with the obfuscators we used in our data set. On the downside, this has a slightly negative effect on classifying non-obfuscated scripts and scripts obfuscated with known obfuscators.

C. Detecting Malicious Scripts

With the results in Table VII, we demonstrated that correctly classifying malicious scripts as obfuscated if malicious scripts

TABLE VIII. Performance of the BDT Classifier to Detect Scripts Obfuscated With an Unknown Obfuscator, Using all Features.

		closure	javascript-obfuscator	javascript-obfuscator.com advanced	javascript-obfuscator.com standard	jfogs	jsobfu
Obfuscated (training set 1)	p	100.00%	100.00%	100.00%	100.00%	100.00	100.00
	r	0.05%	76.93%	99.80%	18.22%	0.24%	39.88%
	F1	0.09%	86.96%	99.90%	30.83%	0.48%	57.02%
	s	8829	12922	12919	12919	12922	12920
Non Obfuscated (training set 2)	p	99.53%	99.38%	99.34%	99.73%	99.55%	99.29%
	r	99.15%	99.03%	99.02%	99.45%	99.26%	98.99%
	F1	99.34%	99.21%	99.18%	99.59%	99.41%	99.14%
	s	7752	7752	7752	7752	7752	7752
Obfuscated (training set 2)	p	99.66%	99.59%	99.58%	99.76%	99.69%	99.57%
	r	99.81%	99.74%	99.72%	99.88%	99.81%	99.70%
	F1	99.74%	99.66%	99.65%	99.82%	99.75%	99.63%
	s	19382	18154	18155	18155	18154	18155

TABLE IX. Performance of the BDT Classifier to Detect Scripts Obfuscated With an Unknown Obfuscator, Using the 20 Most Descriptive Features

		closure	javascript-obfuscator	javascript-obfuscator.com advanced	javascript-obfuscator.com standard	jfogs	jsobfu
Obfuscated (training set 1)	p	100.00%	100.00%	100.00%	100.00%	100.00	100.00
	r	2.59%	93.48%	99.65%	20.76%	0.22%	45.89%
	F1	5.06%	96.63%	99.83%	34.38%	0.43%	62.91%
	s	8829	12922	12919	12919	12922	12920
Non Obfuscated (training set 2)	p	98.92%	98.21%	98.11%	98.81%	99.31%	98.89%
	r	98.09%	96.72%	97.30%	97.47%	98.93%	97.90%
	F1	98.50%	97.46%	97.71%	98.14%	99.12%	98.39%
	s	7752	7752	7752	7752	7752	7752
Obfuscated (training set 2)	p	99.24%	98.61%	98.85%	98.93%	99.54%	99.11%
	r	99.57%	99.25%	99.20%	99.50%	99.71%	99.53%
	F1	99.41%	98.93%	99.03%	99.21%	99.63%	99.32%
	s	19382	18154	18155	18155	18154	18155

using the same obfuscators are also included in the training set works well. In the final experiments, we analyzed how well this works if no malicious scripts are used in the training set. Basically, these experiments are similar to the ones done in Section IV-B as the malicious scripts use different obfuscators than the ones we used to create our own obfuscated scripts in the data set.

The setting is similar to the previous experiments, but this time, testing set 1 contains all malicious (and therefore also obfuscated) scripts from the data set. Table X illustrates the results. Just like above, the evaluation of training set 2 shows that classifying non-obfuscated scripts and scripts that were obfuscated with known obfuscators performs well. With respect to classifying the malicious scripts as obfuscated, the recall value is low (16.52%) when all features are used (left column). This indicates that the obfuscation techniques used for the malicious samples are not represented well by the obfuscators in the training set. However, using only the 20 most descriptive features (right column) increases the performance substantially: The recall value raises by more than 31% to 47.71%. This confirms the finding of Section IV-B that reducing the number of features can increase the performance to detect scripts that are obfuscated with an unknown obfuscator.

To conclude this third and final series of experiments, we summarize the most relevant findings:

TABLE X. Performance of the BDT Classifier to Detect Malicious Scripts, Using all Features or the 20 Most Descriptive Features.

		BDT (all features)	BDT (20 features)
Obfuscated (training set 1)	p	100.00%	100.00%
	r	16.52%	47.71%
	F1	28.35%	64.60%
	s	2706	2706
Non Obfuscated (training set 2)	p	99.38%	98.58%
	r	99.05%	97.67%
	F1	99.21%	98.12%
	s	7752	7752
Obfuscated (training set 2)	p	99.66%	99.18%
	r	98.78%	99.51%
	F1	99.72%	99.34%
	s	22031	22031

- It is possible to detect malicious obfuscated scripts that are obfuscated with an unknown obfuscator. Using all features and based on our data set, the recall value is low, though.
- Using only the 20 most descriptive substantially improves the recall value in our case. This confirms that reducing the number of features can increase the performance to detect scripts that are obfuscated with an unknown obfuscator.
- Ideally and for best possible recall value of malicious scripts, different malicious scripts should be included

into the training and validation sets as demonstrated in Table VII.

V. Related Work

In [23] Xu *et al.* study the effectivenes of traditional anti-virus/signature based approaches to detect malicious JavaScript code. They find that for their sample set, the average detection rate of 20 different anti-virus solutions is 86.4 percent. They also find that making use of additional data- and encoding-based obfuscation, the detection ratio can be lowered by around 40 and 100 percent respectively.

Likarish *et al.* [15] take an approach similar to ours. They apply machine learning algorithms to detect obfuscated malicious JavaScript samples. The authors use a set of 15 features like the number of strings in the script or the percentage of white-space that are largely independent from the language and JavaScript semantics. The results from their comparison of four machine learning classifiers (naive bays, ADTree, SVM and RIPPER) are very promising: the precision and recall of the SVM classifier is 92% and 74.2%. But since their study originates from 2009, it is unclear how recent trends like the minification of JavaScripts (see II-B) would impact on their results.

Wang *et al.* [24] propose another machine learning based solution to separate malicious and benign JavaScript. They compare the performance of ADTree, NaiveBayes and SVM machine learning classifiers using a set of 27 features. Some of them are similar to those of Likarish *et al.* [15]. Their results suggest a significant improvement over the work of Likarish *et al.*

Study from Kaplan *et al.* [4] addresses the problem of detecting obfuscated scripts using a Bayesian classifier. They refute the assumption made by previous publications that obfuscated scripts are mostly malicious and advertise their solution as filter for projects where users can submit applications to a software repository such as a browser extension gallery for browsers like Google Chrome or Firefox. Similarly, *ZOZZLE*, a malicious JavaScript detection solution from Curtsinger *et al.* [25] also uses a Bayesian classifier with hierarchical features but, instead of just performing pure static detection, it has a run-time component to address JavaScript obfuscation. The component passes the unfolded JavaScript to the static classifier just before being executed.

Other solutions toward dynamic analysis, like Wepawet [26] (now discontinued), use JavaScript instrumentation to extract features and apply anomaly detection techniques on them. JSDetox [27] on the other side is a tool that uses both static and dynamic analysis capabilities in order to help analysts understand and characterize malicious JavaScript.

AdSafe [28] uses a completely different approach, it defines a simpler subset of JavaScript, which is powerful enough to perform valuable interactions, while at the same time preventing malicious or accident damage. This allows to put safe guest code (e.g., third party advertising or widgets) on a web-page defeating the common malvertising scenario.

VI. Discussion and Conclusions

In this paper, we analyzed how well a machine learning approach is suited to distinguish between obfuscated and non-obfuscated JavaScripts. To perform the analysis, we used a data set with more than 100000 scripts consisting of non-obfuscated (regular and minified) scripts, obfuscated scripts that are generated with several different obfuscators, and malicious scripts that are all obfuscated. This large data set and the broad spectrum of obfuscators strengthen the general validity of our results. To train and evaluate the different classifiers, we used 45 discriminatory features from the samples.

The results in Section IV-A show that if the training set contains a representative set of all samples (i.e., it contains obfuscated samples of all obfuscators), very good classification performance can be achieved. Of the nine classifiers we compared, the boosted decision tree classifier provided the best performance, with F1-scores above 99% when using all 45 features. When using only the 20 most descriptive features, classification performance gets lower, but it is still possible to achieve F1-scores close to and above 98%, while having the benefit of reduced time and memory requirements to train the classifier. As these 20 most descriptive features have only a small overlap with the features used in previous works but still provide nearly as good classification performance as with 45 features, it can be concluded that the newly added features provide a significant improvement to classify the scripts.

We also evaluated the performance to classify obfuscated scripts that were obfuscated using an unknown obfuscator, i.e., one that is not used by the samples in the training set. The results in Section IV-B demonstrate that it is possible to detect such scripts, but the classification performance heavily depends on both the unknown obfuscator and the obfuscators in the training set and the recall value ranges from close to 0% to more than 99%. We also observed that using only the 20 most descriptive instead of all features increases the classification performance of scripts that are obfuscated with unknown obfuscators. While determining the exact reason of this increased performance requires more detailed analysis, the most plausible reason is that using fewer features increases the fitting error of a trained classifier, which is beneficial for the recall value of samples obfuscated with an unknown obfuscator. However, for best performance, it is important to include many different obfuscators into the training set so the classifier can learn many different kinds of obfuscation techniques, which increases the probability that scripts obfuscated with unknown obfuscators can be correctly classified. The best performing classifier trained with the full data set and using all of the 45 features can be tested under the following URL: http://jsclassify.azurewebsites.net.

Finally, we analyzed the classification performance of malicious obfuscated scripts if no malicious scripts are used in the training set. The results in Section IV-C show that it was possible to correctly classify such scripts with recall values of about 16% when all features are used and 47% when the 20 most descriptive features are used. This undermines two findings from above: Using fewer features increases the performance to detect scripts that use an unknown obfuscator and for best classification results, one should include many different malicious obfuscated scripts in the training set.

Besides showing that machine learning is a well-suited approach for classification of obfuscated and non-obfuscated JavaScripts, our work also created new questions that require more analysis. One of these questions is whether detection of JavaScripts that use unknown obfuscators can be improved by using additional or different features. This requires analyzing the obfuscated scripts that could only be classified poorly if the obfuscator was not used in the training set in more detail to understand their differences compared to scripts that are obfuscated with other obfuscators. In addition, while being able to distinguish between non-obfuscated and obfuscated scripts is already very helpful towards detecting malicious scripts because obfuscated scripts are likely candidates to be malicious, we envision to eventually being able to distinguish between malicious and benign scripts, independent of whether they are obfuscated or not. The main obstacle here is currently the data set: We have a good data set of non-obfuscated and obfuscated scripts, but the number of malicious samples is still relatively small. Getting more malicious samples is therefore the key to start a more detailed analysis about classifying malicious and benign scripts.

REFERENCES

[1] S. Aebersold, K. Kryszczuk, S. Paganoni, B. Tellenbach, and T. Trowbridge, "Detecting obfuscated javascripts using machine learning," in The 11th International Conference on Internet Monitoring and Protection (ICIMP). IARIA, May 2016.

[2] Microsoft, "Microsoft Azure Machine Learning Studio," last accessed on 2016-09-16. [Online]. Available: https://studio.azureml.net/

[3] J. Lecomte, "Introducing the YUI Compressor," last accessed on 2016-01-30. [Online]. Available: http://www.julienlecomte.net/blog/2007/08/13/introducing-the-yui-compressor/

[4] S. Kaplan, B. Livshits, B. Zorn, C. Siefert, and C. Curtsinger, ""nofus: Automatically detecting" + string.fromcharcode (32)+" obfuscated".tolowercase()+" javascript code," Microsoft Research, 2011.

[5] P. Likarish and E. Jung, "A targeted web crawling for building malicious javascript collection," in Proceedings of the ACM first international workshop on Data-intensive software management and mining. ACM, 2009, pp. 23–26.

[6] "Alexa Top One Million Global Sites," last accessed on 2016-01-30. [Online]. Available: http://s3.amazonaws.com/alexa-static/top-1m.csv.zip

[7] L. Richardson, "Beautiful Soup," last accessed on 2016-01-30. [Online]. Available: http://www.crummy.com/software/BeautifulSoup/

[8] M. Bazon, "UglifyJS," last accessed on 2016-01-30. [Online]. Available: http://lisperator.net/uglifyjs/

[9] CuteSoft, "JavaScriptObfuscator JavaScript obfuscator," last accessed on 2016-09-16. [Online]. Available: http://javascriptobfuscator.com/

[10] zswang (Wang Hu), "jfogs JavaScript obfuscator," last accessed on 2016-09-16. [Online]. Available: https://www.npmjs.com/package/jfogs

[11] rapid7, "jsobfu JavaScript obfuscator," last accessed on 2016-09-16. [Online]. Available: https://github.com/rapid7/jsobfu/

[12] Google, "Closure Compiler," last accessed on 2016-09-16. [Online]. Available: https://developers.google.com/closure/compiler/

[13] D. Edwards, "Dean Edwards Packer," last accessed on 2016-01-30. [Online]. Available: http://dean.edwards.name/packer/

[14] J. Kornblum, "ssdeep," last accessed on 2016-09-16. [Online]. Available: http://ssdeep.sourceforge.net/

[15] P. Likarish, E. Jung, and I. Jo, "Obfuscated malicious javascript detection using classification techniques," in Malicious and Unwanted Software (MALWARE), 2009 4th International Conference on, Oct 2009, pp. 47–54.

[16] B.-I. Kim, C.-T. Im, and H.-C. Jung, "Suspicious malicious web site detection with strength analysis of a javascript obfuscation," International Journal of Advanced Science and Technology, vol. 26, 2011, pp. 19–32.

[17] W. M. Wu and Z. Y. Wang, "Technique of javascript code obfuscation based on control flow tansformations," in Computer and Information Technology, ser. Applied Mechanics and Materials, vol. 519. Trans Tech Publications, 5 2014, pp. 391–394.

[18] A. Hidayat, "Esprima JavaScript Parser," last accessed on 2016-01-30. [Online]. Available: http://esprima.org/

[19] "SpiderMonkey Parser API," last accessed on 2016-01-30. [Online]. Available: https://developer.mozilla.org/en-US/docs/Mozilla/Projects/SpiderMonkey/Parser_API

[20] Microsoft, "Machine Learning / Initialize Model / Classification," last accessed on 2016-09-16. [Online]. Available: https://msdn.microsoft.com/en-us/library/azure/dn905808.aspx

[21] B. Rohrer, "How to choose algorithms for Microsoft Azure Machine Learning," last accessed on 2016-09-16. [Online]. Available: https://docs.microsoft.com/en-us/azure/machine-learning/machine-learning-algorithm-choice

[22] R. O. Duda, P. E. Hart, and D. G. Stork, Pattern Classification, 2nd Edition, 2001.

[23] W. Xu, F. Zhang, and S. Zhu, "The power of obfuscation techniques in malicious javascript code: A measurement study," in Malicious and Unwanted Software (MALWARE), 2012 7th International Conference on. IEEE, 2012, pp. 9–16.

[24] W.-H. Wang, Y.-J. LV, H.-B. Chen, and Z.-L. Fang, "A static malicious javascript detection using svm," in Proceedings of the International Conference on Computer Science and Electronics Engineering, vol. 40, 2013, pp. 21–30.

[25] C. Curtsinger, B. Livshits, B. Zorn, and C. Seifert, "Zozzle: Fast and precise in-browser javascript malware detection," in Proceedings of the 20th USENIX Conference on Security, ser. SEC'11. Berkeley, CA, USA: USENIX Association, 2011, pp. 3–3. [Online]. Available: http://dl.acm.org/citation.cfm?id=2028067.2028070

[26] "Wepawet," last accessed on 2016-01-30. [Online]. Available: http://wepawet.iseclab.org/

[27] sven_t, "JSDetox," last accessed on 2016-01-30. [Online]. Available: http://www.relentless-coding.com/projects/jsdetox

[28] J. G. Politz, S. A. Eliopoulos, A. Guha, and S. Krishnamurthi, "Adsafety: Type-based verification of javascript sandboxing," CoRR, vol. abs/1506.07813, 2015. [Online]. Available: http://arxiv.org/abs/1506.07813

International Academy, Research,
and Industry Association (IARIA)
412 Derby Way
Wilmington, DE 19810

ISBN 978-1-5108-5633-2

9 781510 856332

CURRAN ASSOCIATES INC.
proceedings
.com

Sixth International Conference on Intelligent Systems and Applications (INTELLI 2017)

Held at InfoWare 2017

Nice, France
23 - 27 July 2017

IARIA